COMPANION TO ROMAN BRITAIN

Guy de la Bédoyère

COMPANION TO ROMAN BRITAIN

Guy de la Bédoyère

TEMPUS

First published 1999

PUBLISHED IN THE UNITED KINGDOM BY:

Tempus Publishing Ltd
The Mill, Brimscombe Port
Stroud, Gloucestershire GL5 2QG

PUBLISHED IN THE UNITED STATES OF AMERICA BY:

Tempus Publishing Inc.
2A Cumberland Street
Charleston, SC 29401

Tempus books are available in France, Germany and Belgium
from the following addresses:

Tempus Publishing Group	Tempus Publishing Group	Tempus Publishing Group
21 Avenue de la République	Gustav-Adolf-Straße 3	Place de L'Alma 4/5
37300 Joué-lès-Tours	99084 Erfurt	1200 Brussels
FRANCE	GERMANY	BELGIUM

British Library Cataloguing in Publication Data.
A catalogue record for this book is available from the British Library.

ISBN 0 7524 1457 7

Typesetting and origination by Tempus Publishing.
PRINTED AND BOUND IN GREAT BRITAIN.

Contents

List of figures

Front cover: the restored west gate at the fort of South Shields (*Arbeia*). Many of the military and other official inscriptions listed in this book will once have been displayed on buildings like this.

Foreword

Despite the fact that the evidence for the history of Roman Britain is fairly limited, that evidence has been quite widely dispersed. Anyone new to the subject is faced with a plethora of references, often to very dated journals which are hard to come by. The inevitable consequence is a reliance on the many syntheses and summaries of the subject which are now available.

The only real problem here is that the reader or student is presented with material which rarely distinguishes between testified facts, and inferences which have become accepted as facts. There are many 'givens' in the history of Roman Britain which, strictly speaking, do not stand up to close scrutiny. This is partly the result of conflating history and archaeology, which do not always easily mix. Often, none of this is made plain to the reader who may be unaware that he or she has sometimes been presented with an individual, literally invented to reconcile a perceived discrepancy, or a chronology of legionary movements which has been substantially invented.

This book grew out of a private project to make an electronic record of the inscriptions of Roman Britain, during the course of which many of these problems became more and more obvious. This is an attempt to introduce the raw material. I have tried to be as rigorous as possible about what is reliable and what is not. On the whole no view is taken about how much of this should be interpreted other than to encourage the idea that commonsense and considered enquiry should lie behind everything.

I hope that this book will prove a useful companion. In the nature of things it is bound to be incomplete. Every effort has been made to ensure its accuracy but the sheer complexity of sources and material means that some errors and differences of interpretation and readings will have been unavoidable. A selection of the inscriptions has been illustrated, but I have tended to avoid including stones that are very well-known and widely available in other books on Roman Britain.

In the various treatments of topics it ought to be possible to see more clearly patterns of behaviour and observance which will help an understanding of what was Britain's first great historical phase. As ever I would like to thank Peter Kemmis Betty of Tempus for his unremitting support, and also, for their invaluable assistance with comments on the text, Richard Reece (especially for his acute and individual observations) and Neil Holbrook. Roger Tomlin kindly answered a number of detailed queries about certain stones and texts while Jürgen Malitz generously made his electronic version of *ILS* available for use. But the reader should be in no doubt that this book relies on decades of work by others and the credit for discovering, identifying, reading, and recording the thousands of sources belongs to them. For this reason full references are given for every item, to which the reader should turn for more detailed information. A special word of thanks is also due to

Anne Phipps of Tempus who had the arduous task of seeing this immensely complex text through the press.

Please note that throughout the text Latin words, phrases, and names of military units are normally italicised, but not in the case of names of gods, towns or provinces (except for British Roman towns and provinces), even where these contain integral Latin phrases or words, such as Genius loci. The sites at Vindolanda (Chesterholm) and Verulamium (St Albans) are commonly known today by their ancient names and these have been used throughout.

Guy de la Bédoyère

Eltham 1999

1 Introduction

HISTORY AND ARCHAEOLOGY

Antiquarian interest in Roman Britain took root in the fifteenth and sixteenth centuries. It is from then that the first useful records of remains and discoveries date. Private collections were amassed and, during the nineteenth and early twentieth centuries in particular, some of the most famous sites were exposed by antiquarian and early archaeological curiosity to public scrutiny (**1**).

Modern archaeologists may regret the shortcomings of their predecessors but their profession only exists because of the antiquarians. Many were competent in Latin and Greek and saw the remains of Roman Britain in a greater classical context, a culture in which they had been educated. By the early 1900s much of the historical and epigraphic record of Roman Britain had been uncovered. Not all of it made sense, largely because archaeological and analytical techniques were still so crude.

But Roman Britain is primarily an historical period. This is not the same as being a period from which a great deal of history has survived. In Roman Britain's case it has not, but its people were part of a culture which perceived and administered itself through the written word.

Archaeology is a vital ingredient in our understanding of Roman Britain's history. But archaeology cannot fill all the gaps. The great strides in archaeological technique over the last century have not altered the basic history of Roman Britain very much, though it has radically altered our appreciation of the breadth of Romano-British culture, its economy and society. But, along the way, facts have become merged with opinions, themselves awarded a gradually-enhanced aura of authority over time.

Archaeology and history tackle two different ways of studying the past. Dio Cassius and Tacitus tell us about aspects of the Roman conquest of Britain. They describe when this took place, how the campaign was prosecuted, and how the Romans built forts and then towns. Their descriptions are piecemeal, biased, incomplete, and form asides in texts much more concerned with the goings-on in Rome. But they provide us with the evidence for the randomness of human experience based on personalities, circumstances, and natural phenomena. An archaeologist might uncover the militarized expansion of Germany in the 1930s but he would never uncover the personality of Hitler.

No amount of digging could ever recover the occasion of the accession of Claudius in 41, and his need to consolidate himself as emperor. Instead, archaeology provides us with the remains of the physical manifestations of that series of events. We can see where and how forts were built, what artefacts were used within them and how the latter begin to appear beyond the Roman military structures and proliferate in civilian communities. The

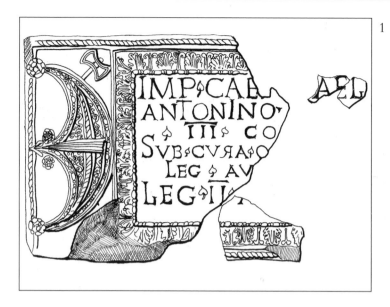

1 *Dedication by* II Augusta *from Corbridge to Antoninus Pius between 140-4,* sub cura, *'under the supervision', of a* leg(atus) Aug(usti) *whose name begins with* Q(uintus). *This can only be Quintus Lollius Urbicus (24). Found in 1907. Width 1.09m.* RIB 1148

excavated remains of both structures (**2**) and artefacts allow us to categorize, analyse, and ultimately visualize the history.

The history is fundamental because it is the creation of the chronology and the narrative which links us to the past. Our personal experience of life is based on the consequences of personality, circumstance and unexpected events. Events such as the death of a politician from a heart attack or the failure of the royal male line have acted as catalysts with far-reaching consequences. When an archaeologist recovers the skeleton of a man it is occasionally possible to identify a violent or sudden death. But even if the cause of death can be proved it would be impossible without documentary records to unravel what his demise meant to his community. It could have been extremely serious, with repercussions lasting for generations.

In contrast, an inscription can provide us with that kind of evidence. Without one, the short life and violent death of Flavius Romanus, *actarius*, killed by the enemy at Ambleside fort at the age of 35, would have been lost to the ages. A culture only defined in the form of artefacts, models and statistics is incomprehensible as a human experience. It conceals unpredictability, the factor which dictates all our existences. The study of Roman Britain, an historical period for which so much historical information is lacking, is dependent on both history and archaeology, but it is probably true that experts in one field do not perhaps always appreciate the qualities and limitations of the other.

The difference is easily illustrated. No artefact or site associated with Caesar's invasions of Britain in 55 and 54BC has ever been found. Yet there is no reasonable doubt that they occurred. Although archaeological evidence would be a desirable addition to the story, its absence does not affect our ability to form judgements about how and why the invasions took place and their implications for the future. Conversely, the Boudican Revolt is graphically described by Tacitus and can be associated with an exceptional amount of evidence for destructive fires in London, Colchester and Verulamium. However conspicuous the burnt layers are it would be impossible to reconstruct the cataclysmic

2   *Jewry Wall, Leicester. Part of the baths and one of the largest upstanding fragments of Roman masonry in Britain. Only archaeology has allowed attribution of the structure to the Hadrianic period*

sequence of events recorded by Tacitus from the archaeology. All we could say was that there was compelling evidence for destructive fires in several towns in early Roman Britain at approximately the same time.

The problem is that Romano-British historical data is relentlessly incomplete. Informative inscriptions are scarce and gaps in extant historical texts are unlikely to be filled. Nonetheless, they have created the framework of Romano-British history and it is not normally within the power of an archaeologist to make an irremediable alteration to the history, or to create history where conventional historical data is lacking. On the other hand, the discovery of an inscription can call into question all sorts of prior assumptions made from the archaeology.

The movements of the *XX* legion in the first century show this well. Until a building stone of the legion was found in Gloucester Cathedral, it had been thought impossible that *XX* had ever been stationed there. Indeed, a complicated series of movements amongst several fortresses in the Mendips, south Wales and the Welsh Marches before *XX* materialized at Chester had been devised to explain its activities. The stone found at the cathedral does not conclusively resolve the problem and at least one archaeologist has rejected it as a 'stray', a convenient device which leaves the earlier archaeological interpretation intact. This is too easy a way out. The perceived improbability of the legion's presence at Gloucester is a consequence only of the archaeological interpretation constructed before the stone was found. Once found, the stone means that we must examine all the evidence again. The stone is a fact, and so is its findspot. Everything else is interpretation.

Tacitus' description of the movements of the *XIV* legion between the years 68-70, unrepresented in the ground, shows how archaeology cannot provide substitute precision data. Tacitus was describing the civil war of 68-9, and occasionally provides news about legionary movements in a degree of detail, way in excess of the information we have for adjacent periods. This is typical of the incompleteness of the evidence. Rome herself had little sustained interest in bleak and remote provinces. Britain appeared intermittently in texts, and meanwhile her population indulged only sporadically in recording their lives and activities in inscriptions.

Much of the recovered evidence has been widely dispersed. Journals, fascicules, and monographs have been conscientiously prepared and published but it is sometimes difficult to trace associated information. Museums are extremely variable in allowing access to, or publicly displaying, their collections. Finds have often been appropriated to specialist fields, fragmenting the record. They appear in specialist reports within the bodies of site publications, often reliant on references to archaic works or unpublished private notes. There are many examples but perhaps samian pottery, that staple find of first- and second-century sites, is an area where much has to be taken for granted by non-specialists. The only one-volume guide to Roman coins which is comprehensive, authoritative and easily-available, is a collectors' handbook published by a dealer. The only textbooks covering brooches have been published by a private collector, now deceased.

Collingwood and Wright's great publication of inscriptions on stone (hereafter *RIB*) appeared in 1965, covering those found up to 1955. Revised or alternative readings and amendments appear in the second edition, published in 1995 (hereafter *RIB95*). New finds have been published in the *Journal of Roman Studies* and, from 1970, in *Britannia*. With other addenda and corrigenda confined to footnotes in *Britannia*, sometimes years after the items concerned were first published, the subject inevitably has become a minefield. Fortunately, new work is in hand to bring this remarkable and outstanding record up to date.

The reading (and television-viewing) public and students of the subject have sometimes only themselves to blame. Archaeology book dealers' catalogues carry a plethora of major reports that have been discounted for years and yet refuse to sell out. Printed in small numbers, most circulate amongst an even smaller audience and many are never read. Stockpiles of site reports for one of the great modern villa excavations are presently destined for the pulper.

In spite of this, a remarkable amount of excellent work has been done to create a workable understanding of Romano-British history and archaeology. The new *RIB* fascicules are the most valuable volumes produced for years. The clarity of editing and presentation in this series has brought together material which was dispersed in dozens of different journals and sources.

The end result has been books like Sheppard Frere's *Britannia* and, more recently, Peter Salway's *Roman Britain*. However, facts and inferences have often been conflated in such works. It is not always apparent which is which and what the basis for certain claims are. In this book I hope to provide some of that basis, and less of a point of view, though I make no apology for the opinions expressed in this Introduction.

THE TEXTS

We have no record by the Romano-British of their lives though accounts must have existed. Only the writings of men who lived on the continent survive. To them, remote frontier provinces were only of interest when something exciting or notorious happened. Tacitus was typical in being concerned with the military conquest of Britain because it was here, amongst other places, that the fortunes and reputations of great men were won and lost. Although he makes passing references to Romano-British civil affairs, such as describing Verulamium as a *municipium*, the information is so sparse that we are left little wiser.

During the second century and afterwards Britain receded from Roman consciousness, partly reflecting the absence of writers of Tacitus' stature. Hadrian's life, for instance, is only recorded in a fourth-century biography of varied quality and with minimal detail. The third-century emperors were also recorded in the same collection of biographies but in progressively more corrupt and degenerate form. This is scarcely inappropriate — most of the emperors concerned were corrupt and degenerate in a different way but they provide an historian with scanty information for the heart of government, let alone for news from the swirling fogs of Britain.

All these historians had their agendas, and this means that they need to be used with care. It is unusual to have more than one account of the same event, which makes a balanced judgement difficult. In time, copying errors have led to corrupt texts, and spectacular and tantalizing gaps.

Throughout, references to these texts are included where our knowledge of people, places, or events of note rely on the texts. The following notes are intended to give a little information about the problems individual authors provide.

Tacitus (*c*.55-117)

Publius Cornelius Tacitus is one of the few Roman historians worthy of the name. He is the primary source for the first century AD, divided between his two great works, the *Annals* (covering 14-68), and the *Histories* (68-96), and his biography of Agricola. Neither of the first two is complete and as a result the story of the invasion in 43 is lost, as is the entire period from 69 onwards. What remains is invaluable because he was contemporary with some of the events he describes. He was able to consult state records and speak to some of the participants. His story of the Boudican Revolt in 60 is, for example, a vivid account of a Roman province in crisis.

Some of the losses are made good in the *Agricola*. Tacitus produced an obsequious life of his father-in-law, Gnaeus Julius Agricola, governor of Britain between about 77 and 84, without which we would know very little about Britain during 69-84. When Agricola's career moved away from Britain so did Tacitus' attention. From then on there is no detailed historical account of Britain and we are dependent on scattered references.

It is a credit to Tacitus that we know so much about the years 47-84. However, Tacitus had never been to Britain. He described campaigns with topographical detail taken from other writings or eyewitness accounts, which he did not always understand. Also, he loathed Domitian (81-96) and used the reigns of Tiberius and Caligula as a vehicle for criticising him.

The latter is far less important to us here than the former. Archaeology of the period yields unnamed forts, marching camps and roads loosely dated by excavation, design or location. Assigning these to governorships and, in Agricola's case, the individual years of his campaigns, is essential for building up a complete picture. But Tacitus is rarely specific in locations and some of his topographical names cannot now be identified. This is not his fault, corrupt texts and time being amongst the causes, but it means that we are unlikely to establish an unequivocal association between forts and governorships.

Consequently, the progress of the military conquest of Britain is not as well-established as some historians believe. Surviving inscriptions of the period are extremely few, making the information given by Tacitus all the more important. Fortunately, the tombstones of the governor Quintus Veranius and the procurator Classicianus have survived and they provide us with the kind of verification which means we can afford generally to trust Tacitus.

Suetonius (*c*.69-145?)

Gaius Suetonius Tranquillus wrote at the beginning of the second century. Each 'life' in his celebrated *Twelve Caesars* is a mixture of serious history, family notes, personal descriptions, credulous and mischievous anecdotes, scandal and utter nonsense. They are delightful to read and wildly entertaining in the scurrilous pen portraits of villains like Tiberius, Caligula and Domitian. Writing in Rome when he did, gave Suetonius access to people who knew, or had known, these men and he revelled in the biographical bile that he uncovered.

History, as we would recognize it, took something of a back seat in this context though history was not strictly Suetonius' purpose. But there are occasional nuggets like the circumstances of Claudius' accession, and the information that Vespasian fought as a legionary commander during the invasion of Britain, captured 20 *oppida* (native strongholds in this context), two tribal areas and the Isle of Wight. As Tacitus tells us in the *Histories* that Vespasian commanded *II Augusta* in Britain we have here our only firm evidence for the activities of any of the legions in the conquest.

Dio Cassius (or Cassius Dio)

Dio Cassius came from Nicaea in Bithynia, which means that Britain was even remoter than it was for Tacitus. He also wrote in the late second and early third century, which distanced him in time from many of the events about which he wrote. The principal example is the invasion of Britain for which he is our only detailed source, thanks to the gaps in Tacitus.

Dio's description of the invasion is interesting because of how modern historians have elaborated the account. Dio says that Aulus Plautius led the invasion, confirmed by more contemporary sources such as Tacitus. Nothing is said about the army involved except to say that it sailed in three divisions and included auxiliaries ('Celts'). Shortly after landing it was involved in a river battle. Apart from a reference to crossing the Thames there is no information about where the landing or landings took place and where the river battle occurred. The legions involved have been inferred from later sources and evidence, while the landing places are still in dispute. The battle site is no more than likely to have been on the Medway. Archaeology has provided evidence for at least two Claudian military bases, at Richborough and Chichester harbour.

Dio's history is also corrupt and partly-lost. We do not even have his original work, relying instead on a later 'epitome' of what he wrote. But without it we would know little about the progress of the Claudian invading force between 43 and 47. The account provides an overview of the diplomatic preamble as well as a description of the military events.

Dio is equally useful for his references to Britain in the second century. References to the career of Sextus Julius Severus, governor of Britain about 130-4, and Ulpius Marcellus under Commodus, together with an account of the mutiny in Britain amongst the legions during Commodus' reign, provide invaluable embellishment of, and context for, the epigraphic record. His accounts of the civil war between Clodius Albinus and Septimius Severus and the latter's campaign in Britain are the most important descriptions of those events.

Herodian (third century)
Herodian, a Greek who wrote in Rome, produced a history of the years 180-238. For Romano-British history his principal value is the account of the civil war in which Clodius Albinus, then governor of Britain, challenged Severus for the Empire, and also the Severan campaigns in Scotland.

The *Scriptores*
The *Scriptores Historiae Augustae* is a cobbled-together series of imperial biographies running from Hadrian to Numerian. They were intended to follow Suetonius but omit biographies of Nerva and Trajan (96-117). They are almost the only narrative descriptions we have of many of these reigns but they are woefully inadequate. The best example is the reference to Hadrian's friendship and falling-out with Aulus Platorius Nepos. That Nepos was governor of Britain and presided over the construction of Hadrian's Wall goes entirely without mention. Were it not for the epigraphic evidence of inscriptions and diplomas we would never have known how pivotal a role he must have played in Britain during Hadrian's reign. Governors who had less opportunity to see their names displayed on new building work, and who go unmentioned by the *Scriptores* authors, are blanks in the record.

The reasons for such omissions are partly because most of the 'lives' were compiled in the fourth century by a number of different authors. The later ones are even less reliable. The better ones are those of the second-century emperors, which were probably based on reliable originals. Britain, like most provinces, was never of major interest to the writers. Hadrian's Wall and the Antonine Wall earn no more than a line mention each, reflecting their omission from contemporary coinage. The references help with the historical context but the emperors responsible for the walls are easily identifiable from inscriptions. The result has been a pedantic examination of single words, to extract precision from a line written by someone who wrote so long after the events described that the value of his precise choice of words is very dubious.

Other sources

For general background, and the rest of the third and fourth centuries and beyond we have a scattering of sources such as Ptolemy, Eutropius, Orosius, Zosimus, Procopius, the imperial panegyrics, Ammianus Marcellinus, and Gildas. Only Ammianus is an historian of stature but his text is incomplete and good only for the middle years of the fourth century. For this period he provides vital, but frequently-tantalizing, news of barbarian attacks and the defence of Britain. Grandiose titles of individuals and military units abound but there is practically no trace of them or their activities in the ground or on inscriptions.

Ptolemy produced his *Geography* around the time of Antoninus Pius (138-61). His record includes a description of Britain which provides invaluable details of place names and locations though it is subject to his own omissions and also the errors of copyists. Similar information also comes from the various route lists such as the Antonine Itinerary, probably compiled under Caracalla. The Ravenna Cosmography is much later, around 700, but used maps of classical date.

The remaining sources provide scattered anecdotes, details and statements of variable quality and usefulness. Eutropius, who wrote in the 360s, produced a history of Rome, which is our only worthwhile source for the Carausian revolt, supplemented by the works of his contemporary Aurelius Victor. Without these commentaries we would have only their coinage, one inscription, and the partisan imperial panegyrics composed in the names of members of the Tetrarchy.

Perhaps the most frustrating record of the late Empire is the *Notitia Dignitatum*. This catalogue of imperial offices, military dispositions and other administrative detail has also been recognized as a compilation of data gathered over decades. Some of the information was out-of-date when it was integrated and it is consequently difficult to use. The archaeology of the period, for example at Housesteads, suggests that part of its pompous parade of units and offices masks a reality in which some bands of ill-equipped troops eked out lives in derelict forts on the northern frontier.

This book is not concerned with providing the texts relevant to the history of Roman Britain. That job has already been done excellently in translation by Stanley Ireland. There is no other ready source of this information in the original Latin or Greek apart from the Loeb Classical Library, but many of the more obscure authors are not included in this series. The expense of individual volumes puts them out of the reach of many readers and, sadly, public libraries have usually disposed of their collections of these books. Major texts like those of Caesar, Tacitus and Suetonius are easily obtainable in paperback.

THE EPIGRAPHIC RECORD

Types and usage

Inscriptions, *tituli*, form one of the most important sources of information about the Roman Empire. The most significant survivors are the 'monumental' stone inscriptions. Examples of commemorations of emperors, buildings, events, gods, ownership, and deaths appear across the Empire. But inscriptions, however widespread, were not universal. They were favoured by different individuals or groups of people, and at different times. Many have not survived, or do so only as incoherent fragments. In Roman Britain, for example, the vast majority of known public buildings are not associated with any surviving inscriptions at all. Conversely, at the fort of Maryport altars to Jupiter were renewed regularly and the old ones buried nearby from where many have now been recovered.

Monumental inscriptions normally took the form of lettering carved (or painted) on stone or wood. Sometimes bronze letters were used, once attached to blocks of stone, but usually found as meaningless singletons. Other types include statue plinths of a god, an emperor, or an official, together with a host of different public and private religious dedications which often took the form of an inscribed altar, or a tombstone. More inscriptions marked official ownership such as tile-stamps, stamped ingots, or an impressed leaden seal from a sack of grain.

Personal inscriptions include marks of ownership on pottery, or documents on wooden writing tablets. Frequently barely-legible or even recognizable, these tablets occasionally carry enormously valuable information about daily life.

Inscriptions faced weathering, vandalism, stone-robbers, or official erasure. The importance of what remains to the study of Roman Britain is best illustrated by the floundering of historians and archaeologists dealing with the gaps. London's formal Roman rank will remain a mystery until a stone or document is unearthed which provides the information. J.C. Mann wryly observed recently that 'an inscription-detector would be a great help'.

The number of surviving Romano-British monumental inscriptions, which are explicit and complete is small. Of Collingwood and Wright's 2314 inscribed stones, some are practically illegible or are only single letters. A few were found centuries ago and have long since been lost, leaving an incoherent drawing made by someone who did not understand what he was illustrating. Eric Birley's review of *RIB* in 1966, and the 1995 edition, demonstrate how some of the barely-legible stones can be read quite differently. Some inscriptions from elsewhere in the Empire do refer to Britain, usually in the record of an individual's career. Most are available in the *ILS* and *CIL* catalogues but these are not easily available. Wherever possible these have been included in the present work.

Since 1955 the number of inscriptions known has increased but few add substantive information to our knowledge. Large stones left lying around or protruding from the soil were recovered mostly a long time ago. Others which were embedded into the ground or reused in later Roman levels are unlikely to be recovered except in large-scale excavations of parts of forts and towns. These have now, for the most part, ceased. In the last few years announcements of new inscriptions have steadily dwindled. In 1998 just two new inscribed stones were announced in *Britannia*. The recovery of a small, but partly restorable, slab in Greenwich Park in 1999 (from a site which yielded three in 1902) was an exceptional event.

The bias in the surviving record towards religious or sacred dedications in Roman Britain (of which most are military in association) has often been noted before. Why this should be remains a mystery. Such stones seem to have been no less susceptible to reuse

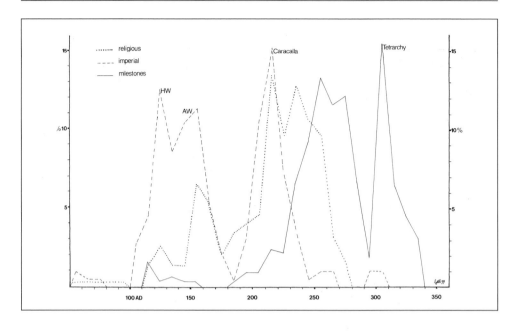

3 Inscriptions by date divided into: religious, imperial, and milestones. HW = Hadrian's Wall.
   AW = Antonine Wall

than any other. But it also reflects the fact that inscriptions recording personal or public munificence are very unusual in Britain. This may mean that in remote north-western provinces individual or civic gifts of public facilities were rare; but there was perhaps less inclination to record such gifts, or maybe inscriptions were more susceptible to destruction. Whatever the explanation, the consequences are that only a tiny number of inscriptions record urban development, while Hadrian's Wall and other northern forts have produced dozens, mainly unit or private religious dedications on altars as well as many records of building work, renewals, and governors.

When recorded in graph form, it is obvious that the main peak for dated religious and imperial dedications was during the early third century, with lesser peaks during the second century (**3**). Conversely, milestones peak later than any other class and is the only datable group reaching into the fourth century, apart from a very small number of dedications to the state using a formula (*Bono r(ei) p(ublicae)*, 'for the good of the state') datable to Constantine I's reign or later (such as *RIB* 412). However, none of these can be attributed to specific reigns. Demonstrably first-century inscriptions, apart from military tombstones, are very rare in Britain. But as the consolidation of military installations in stone, and the erection of many public buildings, did not take place until the second century perhaps this is not very surprising.

This contrasts with Suetonius' remark that Titus (79-81) had been so popular that statues and busts of him with accompanying inscriptions were 'multitudinous' (*multitudine, Titus* iv) in Britain. None has survived, unless the exceptional Verulamium forum-basilica inscription is one. This is a good example where the history conflicts with the archaeology. Either Suetonius was exaggerating, or perhaps older inscriptions had more opportunity to be destroyed, or reused in antiquity. Domitian (81-96) took no steps to favour his brother's memory, and was content to substitute his own name on earlier inscriptions. As his own was subjected to comprehensive erasure after his death (Suetonius, *Domitian* xxiii.1, Pliny, *Panegyricus*, lii.4), it becomes less difficult to explain the lack of known slabs with Titus' name.

Although such events must have affected the surviving record, it is also true that many extant later stones have been found reused in late- or post-Roman contexts, whereas first-century inscriptions (apart from military tombstones) rarely turn up in Roman Britain in any context. But the comprehensive absence of any inscriptions or statues of Titus in Britain cannot adequately be accounted for by simply rejecting Suetonius. It is equally inconceivable that no inscriptions were dedicated to Claudius (a bronze bust, found in a Suffolk river, has survived), though none is known. So the remaining record must, in some respects, have been distorted by events during the Roman period.

Perhaps literacy contributed to the pattern of distribution. Was the Roman army and its associated population more likely to favour inscriptions, in addition to an institutional stimulus to produce them? The military zone of northern and western Britain has always been the most fertile source of inscriptions. The assertion that this is thanks to the more widely-available stone is suspect because Cotswold stone in the south is much easier to carve. Yet the major Romano-British Cotswold towns of Gloucester and Cirencester have produced a tiny fraction of the number of inscribed stones found in the north. Paradoxically, the Cotswolds have produced one of the largest assemblages of Roman carved and architectural stonework in Britain, reflecting the easily-worked stone and also the evident numbers of masons who must have been operating there. By 1955 eighteen inscribed stones (two military) were recorded from Cirencester and six (two military) from Gloucester but sixty-seven were recorded from the Hadrian's Wall fort at Carvoran, and seventy-seven from the town and fort at Corbridge. The pattern is reflected elsewhere. A quarter of the inscriptions recorded at Bath in *RIB* were for, or by, soldiers or ex-soldiers. A third of those recorded at Wroxeter are the tombstones of soldiers, several of which are demonstrably first century in date. At Lincoln, half are military and many of these too are from before the end of the first century.

In Britain at least, it seems that producing inscriptions was more attractive both to soldiers as individuals and their units at certain times than it was to civilians. It was a way to exhibit unit pride, and provided another means of embellishing forts and their hinterlands, which reflected a military love of display. Soldiers also had a vested interest in declaring loyalty to regimes. A number of military dedications to Caracalla in Britain in 213 during the governorship of Gaius Julius Marcus are known. Caracalla had murdered a governor in Gaul; Marcus and his army perhaps thought it wise to advertise allegiance.

But inscriptions do not even survive at a consistent rate in military sites. *VI Victrix*, for instance, based at York, has left far more of a record of its building activities on the northern frontier than at York. Exeter, a probable early base of *II Augusta*, has produced no inscriptions at all. Amongst auxiliaries, circumstances of taste and habit, pay, and also the chances of excavation mean that some units are far better represented than others. The cache of *cohors I Hispanorum* altars at Maryport is a case in point.

4 *Town walls at Silchester, Calleva Atrebatum, south-east stretch. As with all other Romano-British urban defences there is no epigraphic evidence for a date*

Inscriptions of certain periods are also more common. Therefore many duplicate information. Typical is the group from the period *c*.205-8 under Septimius Severus. The implication is that they reflect central directives to units to build, and to record the fact. This tells us the governor Lucius Alfenus Senecio oversaw a good deal of building work. But it also means several stones tell us he was governor at that time, while governors and their activities from a few years either side may be unknown.

Whatever the reasons for the variable record, the blocks of repeated or similar texts and distribution mean we end up with a lot of evidence from a small number of places. The 2314 inscriptions published in 1965 include 791 from Hadrian's Wall alone, though this total includes many centurial stones marking stretches of curtain built, a type obviously not usually found elsewhere. But several hundred other inscriptions come from forts in its general vicinity.

Britain's medieval and post-medieval urban development, often on former Roman towns, must have led to reuse of stones or their burial. Conversely, towns which escaped such development like Silchester (**4**) and Verulamium, and which also have produced no more than the slightest evidence for military phases, have produced so few inscriptions that there cannot have been very many in the first place unless stone-robbers were prepared to remove them considerable distances. If so, we might expect to find them here and there in churches or castles. Verulamium was ransacked in the early middle ages to build the abbey but no inscribed stones have turned up in the church structure or anywhere else nearby. Urban Christianity, for which there is limited evidence, may have been responsible for the annihilation of some pagan religious dedications though there is no specific evidence for this in Britain.

Datable civic inscriptions are very scarce. Wroxeter and Verulamium are the only towns to have yielded restorable inscriptions associated with their forum-basilica complexes, yet almost every major Romano-British town had such buildings. Unrestorable fragments, which may be others, are known from Cirencester (*RIB* 114) and Winchester (*JRS* xlviii (1958), 150). Even the Verulamium and Wroxeter forum inscriptions had clearly been shattered by falling, perhaps from their original positions. Other public buildings are almost without exception unrepresented in the extant epigraphic record despite the many urban structures known like the amphitheatres at London, Silchester and Cirencester.

Major building activity in Romano-British towns had more or less ceased by the mid-third century and some public buildings gradually fell into disuse. Unlike the cyclical rebuilding in a fort therefore, where a new bath-house or granary might replace an old one and reuse inscribed stones which were preserved in the process, a town forum was unlikely to be rebuilt and thus reuse earlier dedications or feature fresh commemorations. The new fort structures were often recorded on new dedications, also susceptible to reuse at an even later date.

So it seems that the rate of inscription production and replacement was significantly higher in Roman Britain whenever and wherever the army was involved, either as an institution or as individual soldiers, at least until the middle of the third century. Although most civic public buildings were probably commemorated by at least one inscription the vicissitudes of time have meant that very few have come down to us. In the forts, where so many more inscriptions apparently existed, the chances of some surviving are simply higher.

Only in the fourth century did urban stonework start finding its way into new defensive works (for example **41, 65**). This was more common in Gaul, where urban defences were generally built under extreme pressure in the fourth century, and is often cited as the explanation for greater numbers of urban inscriptions surviving there than in Britain. But the mutilation involved in reuse often renders such stones useless for our purposes.

For a Romano-British town to produce serious numbers of inscriptions, a significant military phase, or military clientele, is an essential ingredient. That Wroxeter's and Lincoln's military stones both make up such a substantial proportion of their respective totals, and are mainly of early date, belies the theory that early stones are invariably likely to have been destroyed during later Roman phases. On balance it seems civilian inscriptions in Britain were neither numerous nor considered necessary, and that this extended even to tombstones. The result is that the military phases of towns and long-term military sites are disproportionately well-represented.

Style and composition

There were two significant epigraphic styles. *Monumentalis* (**33**), characterized by carefully-proportioned lettering, reached its zenith under Trajan but declined during the third century. *Actuaria* (**36, 39**) was modelled on official handwriting with its distinctively-vertical characters. There is some blurring between the two styles and, of course, there are numerous examples where the lettering lacks any style at all. Nonetheless, there is a discernible change in quality and style across the period (**5**).

a. IMPCAES

b. IMPCΛES

c. IMP CAES

d. I M P CΛES

e. IMP·CÆS

f. IMP·CÆS

g. IMP CÆS

h. IMPCÆS

5 Imp(erator) Caes(ar) *taken from a series of inscriptions dated between 100-337. a. RIB 310 (Caerleon), 100; b. RIB 1638 (Hadrian's Wall, mc 38), 122-6; c. RIB 2194 (Antonine Wall, nr Balmuildy), 139-61; d. RIB 757 (Brough-under-Stainmore), 197; e. RIB 1280 (High Rochester), 220; f. RIB 1091 (Lanchester), 238-44; g. RIB 334 (Caerleon), 255-60; h. RIB 2227 (Bitterne), 273-5; i. RIB 2233 (St Hilary), 307-37. Not to scale*

Some of the better military epigraphy was probably the work of a small number of talented individuals. Three inscriptions from Lanchester, all carved under Gordian III (238-44) and two dedicated to him, are surely the work of one man (**6, 37, 62**). A pair of slabs from Papcastle, across the Pennines, date to 241 and are so similar it is possible he carved them too (*RIB* 882, 883). Perhaps the prefect at Lanchester, Marcus Aurelius Quirinus, enjoyed the man's work and encouraged him, or perhaps he had a connection with Gordian III, dating back to the young emperor's grandfather's inferred time as governor of Britain. Gordian III is otherwise untestified on monumental inscriptions from Britain, apart from milestones. It seems too much to attribute the survival in the same fort of the only two dedications to him to chance. During World War II the celebrated 'nose-art' of the U.S. Eighth Air Force was often created by a skilled artist on any one base. At Great Ashfield, for example, the B-17s of the 385th Bomb Group were painted by an English Red Cross nurse.

An inscribed slab found at Caerleon was produced by a master craftsman. Carrying Trajan's titles for the year 99, it was amended to record them for the year 100. Yet the job of up-dating the text was handed to a lesser mason, perhaps because the original craftsman was unavailable, and the new work stands out today as a crude addition. The stone is so exceptional that one possible explanation is that it was not only quarried but also carved on the continent (the marble is Tuscan) and had to be updated on arrival at Caerleon by a local mason.

6 *Slab from Lanchester,
    naming Gordian III
    (238-44) and the
    building of a bath,*
    balneum, *with*
    basilica, *by* coh(ors)
    I L(ingonum)
    Gord(iana)
    *commanded by
    Marcus Aurelius
    Quirinus. See also
    the stylistically similar*
    37, 62. *Width
    0.79m.* RIB 1091

An experiment, conducted on-site at the excavation of a villa at Turkdean in 1998, demonstrated that a skilled mason could produce 20 finely-carved characters on a reproduction of a Roman altar in a couple of hours. The production of the altar itself from a block of Bath stone had taken only a few hours the day before. The present author also experimented, producing a very passable relief of three *genii cucullati* ('hooded geniuses') in under an hour. Considering the miserable standard of some Romano-British epigraphy the interesting possibility arises that some texts were carved by first-timers producing lettering on blanks purchased or carved for the purpose.

Primus, *custos armorum*, made his own altar to Hercules and Silvanus and states the fact, as does Titus Licinius Ascanius on his tombstone from London doubling as a statue base (*RIB* 796, and 14), but such texts are rare. The stone from Malton, recording a goldsmith's workshop, is surely a one-off by an amateur (**55**). No *tituli* carvers are testified in Britain but they are known elsewhere. An inscription from Palermo advertises that either religious or secular texts for buildings will be produced to order (Ireland 1983, 221-2), which usefully suggests that the dominance of religious texts in Britain might have been as much a matter of choice as circumstances of survival.

Restoring and reading inscriptions

To make efficient use of space, and for aesthetic reasons, Roman *tituli* carvers used abbreviations for stock titles and phrases. Thus IMP M AVR represents *Imperator Marcus Aurelius*, and D M represents *Dis Manibus* ('To the spirits of the departed'). Such phrases and sequences of letters appear over and over again, making it possible to restore damaged texts. However, some intact stones show that a mason might omit letters, misspell words, and jam in corrections (**14**). A slab from Corbridge (*RIB* 1147) shows that the mason had misspelled the emperor's name, supplying ANIONINO for *ANTONINO* and even introduced a stop mark in the governor's name, splitting it in half. Perhaps more curious is that it passed muster, though in our time the misuse of 'its' and 'it's' is ubiquitous even in official publications.

Restored texts from damaged stones are not infallible, an important aspect to remember when arguing finer historical points. The status of Togidubnus, 'king of the Regni', is perhaps the best-known example *(RIB* 91) (see Chapter 9). Part of the forum-basilica inscription at Verulamium has long been recognized to be the remains of what could be any one of three quite different texts (see Chapter 3). On a more mundane level, a small slab from Housesteads purportedly records a *d(ecreto) vica[norum]*, 'decree of the villagers' (**32**). But so little of the text remains that it is as easily restorable as a name.

An interesting case of a damaged inscription is the tombstone of the procurator Classicianus (see Chapter 9). A fragment naming him was recovered in 1852, and a second, confirming him as the man mentioned by Tacitus, was found in 1935. Before 1935 R.G. Collingwood refuted a suggestion that this was the post-Boudican procurator. It was 'obviously wrong' because there was, in theory, not enough room for the full name (1928, 171). Collingwood preferred to see the cognomen Classicianus as evidence for a former career with the fleet, *classis*.

This was understandable but it was also an uncompromising rejection of a then unprovable theory, which at least had some founding in historical fact. Collingwood preferred a theory that had no founding in any fact or precedent, including the interpretation of the name. This reflected the contemporary dogma that the Roman world was a series of reliable patterns, with a general preference for the military regardless of the context. In 1928 Collingwood would have been more prudent to have said that it was not possible to be certain either way. Apart from illustrating the fallibility of 'expert' opinion when evidence is lacking, it has increasingly emerged in recent years that the Roman world was less predictable than thought.

In some cases the actual stones show that some restorations, while plausible, rely on so many assumptions they should be discounted. The stone from Carrawburgh on Hadrian's Wall, supposedly recording building during the governorship of Sextus Julius Severus on the basis of a single surviving letter from his name, is a case in point *(RIB* 1550).

The decline of the epigraphic habit

By the mid-fourth century monumental inscriptions seem no longer to have been produced in Britain. Apart from milestones, only a very few are attributed to the fourth century, and then only on grounds of style (or lack of). Even so, no post-340 milestones are known. The Saxon Shore forts, amongst the very few new state building projects of the late-third and fourth centuries, have produced extremely few inscriptions, and those which are datable belong to earlier periods. Lympne, for example, has yielded a single altar dedicated by a man known to have been prefect of the *classis Britannica* some time in the first half of the second century (**72**). Its survival, and the lack of anything contemporary with the Saxon Shore fort period, only serves to illustrate the decline in the epigraphic habit.

Most other significant new Romano-British buildings in the fourth century were villas and pagan temples. As a rule, inscriptions are normally never found on these sites unless they have been reused, for example the third-century milestones found at Rockbourne, or the early-third-century procuratorial slab at Combe Down. The skills needed to produce inscriptions still existed. Many fourth-century villas and temples have yielded carved stone fixtures or statues. The mosaic couplets at Lullingstone and Frampton and the

7 *Tombstone found about 200m west of Lincoln town wall, naming G(aius) Juli(us) Calenus, veteran of* VI Victrix, *from* Lug(dunum) *(Lyons). Width 0.63m.* RIB *252*

general content of pavement designs show that literacy and familiarity with Latin were widespread amongst the upper classes. The wealthy Romano-British decorated their lives with allusions to, and images of, a Roman pagan bucolic past, reflected in a more widespread culture amply illustrated by the works of Ausonius and Claudian. But it seems to have been without public architecture and inscriptions to record the fact. Ultimately, it may simply have been a matter of taste.

Tombstones, tiles and seals

Military tombstones have turned up at most sites with a military period in their histories, sometimes (as noted above) in disproportionate numbers. By 1955 Lincoln had produced 27 inscriptions (and only a single one of significance since), nine of which were tombstones of serving soldiers in *II Adiutrix* or *IX Hispana*. Significantly, these legions are known to have left Britain early, in *II Adiutrix*'s case by the late 80s and in *IX Hispana*'s no later than *c.*120 (in any case testified at York by 107-8). They tell us that epigraphic skills were available in first-century Britain, and that soldiers seem to have been inclined to make more use of them per head than contemporary civilians, and also civilians of later centuries.

Elsewhere, military tombstones from towns are likely to have belonged to a military phase but do no more than approximately reflect the fact. They include those of veterans (**7**). Tombstones are usually undatable though are often attributable to periods on style. Sometimes, where the deceased or his ancestor had gained citizenship and adopted an imperial name in the process, a *terminus post quem* can be estimated. Marcus Aurelius Victor who died aged 50 at Chesters cannot have lived before the reign of Marcus Aurelius (161-80) (*RIB* 1481). Given his age at death, the tombstone probably does not predate the year 200.

Tombstones normally only confirm the burial of an individual. In the case of a soldier the naming of his unit is a useful piece of information but a single stone does not confirm that his unit was based near his place of burial. Only where a number of tombstones naming the same unit are known from a single area does it seem likely that this was their base.

Tiles produced for the procuratorial office in London, and those for the civic government of Gloucester, are the only cases of official civilian tile manufacture known in Britain (**25**). Most of the legions produced their own tiles and so did a few auxiliary units (**13**). More auxiliary units apparently issued lead sealings. But tiles, or the goods bagged and sealed, could be sold, transferred to other units, or even stolen. The presence of a stamped tile does not guarantee that unit's residence, though the procuratorial tiles in London reflect the procurator's testified presence.

In terms of historical evidence, tombstones, tiles and seals are often of little value for precise dates. Only where surviving texts record movements, or where the unit's title contains a reference to an imperial name can we be reasonably certain about a date.

Despite these problems, inscriptions provide crucial props for Romano-British history and for dating artefacts within structures. The stones which record buildings on Hadrian's Wall supply a chronological platform for the archaeology of the features. Inscriptions also provide us with more uncontaminated information than any other source about the administrators, soldiers, town councillors, priests, traders, workers, and women, of Roman Britain than anything else.

Diplomas

Military diplomas, inscribed on two plates of bronze (**8**), commemorate the honourable discharge of auxiliary veterans after 25 years' service. The formal record of this event was displayed on a bronze tablet 'behind the temple of Augustus near [the statue of] Minerva' in Rome (as stated in the texts). Certain legal privileges were granted to the veteran and this is probably the significance of the diplomas (the Roman name is unknown) which seem to be personal copies of the Rome texts. Whether they served as souvenirs or as a document needed for presentation at certain times is quite unknown. A wooden writing tablet from Egypt of the year 122 seems to be an exceptional instance of the actual document issued and used on the occasion of *honesta missio* ('honourable discharge').

The bronze diplomas, perhaps individually commissioned after discharge, seem to have been preserved by the veteran, though they are often found in perplexing contexts, such as Roman rubbish heaps or, in one case, the Wroxeter forum. The interesting possibility arises that they posthumously circulated as curios in antiquity, as military medals do today.

Diplomas bear the date of the discharge, the name of the governor of the province concerned, sometimes his predecessor, and the names of auxiliary units from which veterans were being discharged stationed in that province. One diploma has proved that the governor Ulpius Marcellus was in office for at least six years, which until its discovery was thought impossible (see Chapter 9). Each diploma is thus an unparalleled snapshot of provincial government and some of the auxiliary component of the garrison on that date. The numbers of units listed vary because only units discharging on that date are mentioned. Other problems are that the location of each unit is not included and they are sometimes so poorly preserved that the information is incomplete.

8   *Diploma found in the south gate at Chesters. The titles of Hadrian can be seen in the first four lines, providing the year December 145 to December 146. At the bottom right is the name of the governor Papirius Aeli[anus]. In between are the names of some of the units from which veterans had been discharged. (Copyright © The British Museum). RIB 2401.10*

A new diploma, which emerged onto the antiquities market in 1997, provides a good example of their use. Presented to a soldier called Itaxa, then in *cohors II Lingonum*, on 20 August 127 in Britain, it supplies the name of the hitherto-unknown successor to Aulus Platorius Nepos, one Trebius Germanus. As Trebius Germanus is untestified on Hadrian's Wall this suggests much of the primary construction on the Wall was confined to the governorship of Nepos. Two other diplomas firmly fix Nepos as governor in Britain in 122 and 124, much more precise dates than on Wall inscriptions naming him.

Diplomas are becoming one of the few sources of new historical information in Romano-British studies at a time when excavations are fewer and smaller-scale. It is unlikely that the epigraphic record will be augmented by significant quantities of new stone inscriptions for the forseeable future.

However assiduous the archaeology of the period has been, the material outlined above has provided the backbone of the chronology. Archaeology has supplied us with many of these inscriptions, diplomas, and coins, and also associated some sites with the events of the period. But archaeology cannot make good the gaps on its own. For example, if and when a datable inscription is recovered which records the building of urban defences at, say, Silchester (**4**), then we will have the first single fact around which decades of the archaeology of Roman urban defences can be hung.

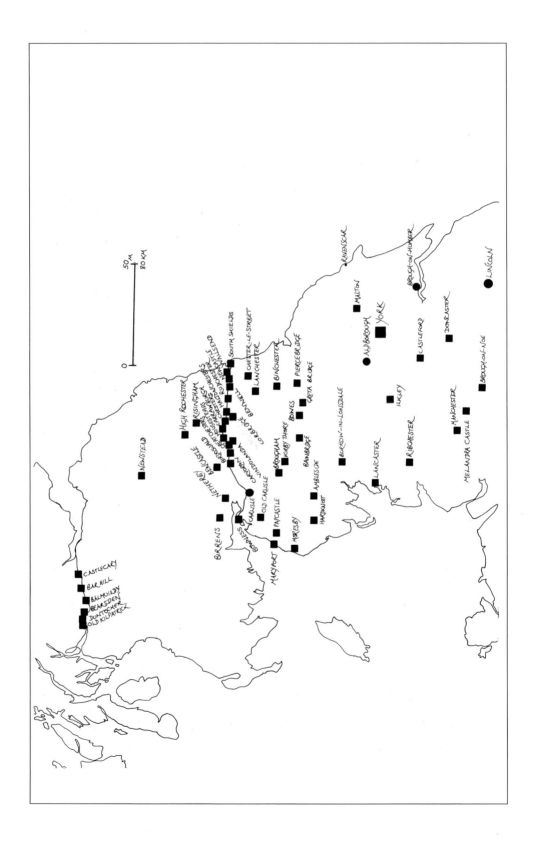

50 M
80 KM

RAVENSCAR

BROUGH-ON-HUMBER

LINCOLN

MALTON

ALDBOROUGH

YORK

CASTLEFORD

DONCASTER

BROUGH-ON-NOE

SOUTH SHIELDS

CHESTER-LE-STREET

LANCHESTER

BINCHESTER

PIERCEBRIDGE

GRETA BRIDGE

ILKLEY

MANCHESTER

HIGH ROCHESTER

RISINGHAM

CORBRIDGE/CORSTOPITUM

HALTWHISTLE

WALLSEND

CHESTERHOLM/VINDOLANDA

HOUSESTEADS

GREATCHESTERS

CARRAWBURGH

CHESTERS

BENWELL

KIRBY THORPE

BOWES

BURROW-IN-LONSDALE

MELANDRA CASTLE

NEWSTEAD

NETHERBY

BEWCASTLE

BROUGH

CARVORAN

STANWIX

BROUGHAM

BAINBRIDGE

LANCASTER

RIBCHESTER

CARLISLE

OLD CARLISLE

AMBLESIDE

HARDKNOTT

BARRENS

BOWNESS

PAPCASTLE

MORESBY

MARYPORT

CASTLECARY

BAR HILL

BALMUILDY

BEARSDEN

DUNTOCHER

OLD KILPATRICK

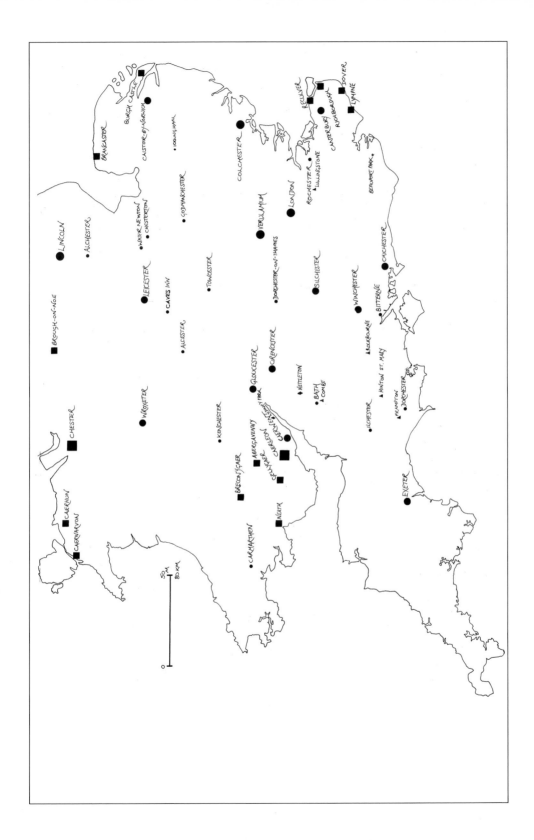

BURGH CASTLE
CAISTOR-BY-NORWICH
BRANCASTER
HOLME HALL
COLCHESTER
RECULVER
CANTERBURY
RICHBOROUGH
DOVER
LYMPNE
GODMANCHESTER
ROCHESTER
LULLINGSTONE
BEAUPORT PARK
WATER NEWTON
CHESTERTON
LONDON
VERULAMIUM
CHICHESTER
LINCOLN
ALCHESTER
DORCHESTER-ON-THAMES
SILCHESTER
WINCHESTER
BITTERNE
TOWCESTER
LEICESTER
CAVES INN
BROUGH-ON-NOE
ALCESTER
GLOUCESTER
CIRENCESTER
NETTLETON
BATH
COMBE
ILCHESTER
HINTON ST. MARY
FRAMPTON
DORCHESTER
WROXETER
KENCHESTER
ABERGAVENNY
BRECON/Y GAER
CHESTER
CAERLEON
CAERWENT
USK
EXETER
CAERHUN
CAERNARVON
CAERMARTHEN
NEATH

50 M
80 KM
0

2 The Roman army in Britain

Roman Britain was always one of the most heavily-garrisoned of all the provinces. The evidence is primarily epigraphic, though literary sources provide a backbone for the first century. Unfortunately, such texts tell us very little about the auxiliary units which formed half or more of Britain's garrison and which spent much of their time in the front line. Documents from Vindolanda of *c.*90-105 show that auxiliary units were often divided into vexillations, scattered amongst different forts. This has helped explain the contradictory evidence of more than one unit being testified on contemporary inscriptions from the same site.

An inscription therefore testifying a unit at a fort does not mean all the unit was there at the time, or that any of it was there a few months later. In describing the aftermath of the revolt by Clodius Albinus at the end of the second century, Sheppard Frere states that 'there are very few forts in northern Britain where the same garrison is certainly attested in the third century as was there in the late second' (1987, 155). He infers that therefore there must have been serious repercussions for the northern frontier when Clodius Albinus withdrew troops to support his cause.

The inference is certainly reasonable. But the evidence cannot be reliably used to support it. As it happens, very few units are testified at specific places before *and* after the period in question and most are not, something which is plain from the catalogue below. It is the diplomas (**8**) which tell us most about which units were in Britain before this date, but not *where* they were. Many of the datable inscriptions which record the presence of auxiliary units belong to the Severan period and afterwards.

During the early third century some of the auxiliary units seem to have favoured epigraphic display. But the habit died out in the middle years of the third century, no doubt due to the proliferating military chaos and haphazard reorganizations which followed. Only the *Notitia Dignitatum* provides a follow-up. It confirms some of the details from the third-century inscriptions but presents a host of its own problems.

THE LEGIONS

The Roman legion was made up of about 5500 infantry soldiers. Each was divided into ten cohorts, each of six centuries of 80 men except for the first cohort which had five double centuries. Each century had its own centurion and *optio* of which the most senior was the *primus pilus*, centurion of the first century of the first cohort. Each cohort had a *tesserarius*, *signifer*, and *cornicularius*. Although recruitment of legionaries had originally been in Italy, by the second century at the latest they were being recruited from other provinces.

35

9 *Tombstone from Lincoln of T(itus) Valerius Pudens of* II A(diutrix) P(ia) F(idelis)*, in the century (>) of Dossennius Proculus. Aged 30, Pudens' period of service* (aera) *could read* II, VI *or* XI. *The accepted period of* VI *(i.e. 6 years) depends on assuming that Pudens joined the legion when it was founded in 68-9, and whether his burial could only have occurred during* IX'*s absence on the Agricolan campaign and* II Adiutrix'*s move to Chester. Height 1.50m.* RIB 258

In addition the legion had its standard bearer, the *aquilifer*, 120 cavalry scouts, a *praefectus castrorum* ('prefect of the camp', normally an ex-*primus pilus*), six military tribunes, and a legate. The senior tribune, *tribunus laticlavius*, was of senatorial status and was being groomed as a leader. He would proceed to become a *quaestor* before being appointed perhaps to a legionary command. After a time as *praetor*, provincial governorships might follow. The other tribunes, *tribuni angusticlavii*, were equestrians. The rest of their military careers would normally involve commanding auxiliary units.

Soldiers of various ranks were sometimes detached for other duties, usually either to the legate's or governor's personal staff (see Chapter 7). As a result, individual soldiers may be testified in locations where their legions are not.

In the year 23 there were 25 legions in service (Tacitus, *Annals* iv.5), though requirements in the civil war of 68-9, together with other campaigns, elevated the total to around 30 between *c*.83-117. By the beginning of the third century Dio observed that the number had dropped to 19 (lv.23.2). Until the fourth century Britain had at least three and in the early days there were four. However, it was common practice to split the legions into vexillations and these were utilized as necessary. Britain thus sometimes had a garrison made up of members of more than three permanent legions. Individuals also moved between legions. T. Flavius Virilis served as centurion in the late-second and early-third centuries with *II Augusta*, *VI*, and *XX* (twice), before moving on to posts elsewhere in the Empire, taking with him his wife of British origin, Lollia Bodicca (*ILS* 2653).

The following legions were all stationed in whole or in part at some point during the Roman occupation of Britain, though in one or two cases this may only have amounted to an individual. The evidence for the activities of each legion is piecemeal, ranging from the detailed record by Tacitus of *XIV Gemina*'s movements during the years 68-70, to modern inferences based on undated tombstones. It is, for instance, remarkable that, apart from roof tiles, two of the legions based in Britain for very long periods of time, *VI* and *XX*, have produced no dated inscriptional evidence for their presence as units (as opposed to individual monuments like tombstones) at their respective fortresses of York and Chester.

I Italica

A vexillation may have helped build the Antonine Wall at Old Kilpatrick, evidenced by an altar of *cohors I Baetasiorum*, then under the charge of a centurion from *I Italica*. The arguments for and against the exact date of this altar are recounted by Frere (1987, 152-3, n. 34).

Inscription
Undated: Old Kilpatrick (AW), altar dedicated by *cohors I Baetasiorum* under the charge of Julius Candidus, *c(enturio)*, with *I Italica*. *Brit.* i (1970), 310, no. 20

II Adiutrix Pia Fidelis

Tacitus says that in 69 *II Adiutrix* had been 'recently raised' (*recens conscriptis*). It served alongside *XIV*, just withdrawn from Britain, in the campaign against Civilis under Petillius Cerialis. Tacitus does not identify it as *Adiutrix* ('Helper', a word applied to legions raised to strengthen an army), but just as *secunda*. It is distinguishable from *II Augusta* (see below) by virtue of its history.

It is normally stated that Petillius Cerealis brought *II Adiutrix* with him to Britain in 71. This is not a testified fact. However, a tombstone from Lincoln states the soldier's service life to have been six or eleven years. As the legion is known not have existed before the mid- to late-60s it can be assumed that *II Adiutrix* was at least in Britain, and probably at Lincoln, by any time from the early 70s on. This presupposes that he joined when the legion was founded. If he was recruited later, then the estimated date of his death would obviously be wrong.

That *II Adiutrix* left Lincoln in total for Chester by the 80s is not a certainty; it has become increasingly clear that units were not necessarily moved in their entirety. Transfers, vexillations, and other duties mean that soldiers from different legions can appear in the same place simultaneously.

Tombstones of *II Adiutrix* soldiers do turn up at Chester. One, giving seven or seventeen years' service, could therefore mean not before *c*.75. Others give eleven and thirteen years for not before the late 70s or early 80s. One other example records a deceased soldier of the legion at Bath, presumably there in a private capacity.

The legion's duties seem to have been to garrison Lincoln and/or Chester during the campaigns in the north of the 70s and 80s undertaken mainly by *IX* and probably *XX*.

*10 Slab from Corbridge,
recording the standard
belonging to a vexillation of
II Augusta. Height 533mm.
RIB 1154*

Following the withdrawal from Scotland *II Adiutrix* was withdrawn from Britain either in the piecemeal form of advance vexillations or all at once.

T. Cominius Severus of *II Adiutrix* was honoured for his part in a Dacian war. The date is not stated on his tombstone but is usually assumed to be the war of 89. Quintus Planius Sardus, perhaps the Sardus in the letters of Pliny the Younger (ix.31), is named as legate of *II Adiutrix in Pannonia* on his tombstone (*ILS* 9486). Evidently the legion had been removed, perhaps as early as the mid-80s. But it may not have been moved in toto immediately. The Chester tombstone of Q. Valerius Fronto (see below) requires explanation, assuming its reading is correct.

No epigraphic evidence for any building activity by *II Adiutrix* during its time in Britain survives.

Inscriptions
Undated: Lincoln, tombstone of T. Valerius Pudens, *mil(es)*, apparently 6 yrs service (though the figure has been restored). *RIB* 258 (**9**)

Undated: Chester, tombstone of G. Juventius Capito, *mil(es)*, 7 (or 17) yrs service. *RIB* 476
Undated: Chester, tombstone of Q. Valerius Fronto, *miles*, of 20 or more years' service. The long-
 service record, incompatible with a *c.*85 departure has been explained as including an earlier spell
 in another legion, interestingly overlooked as a possibility in the other cases. *RIB* 479
Undated: Chester, tombstone of [...]inus, *eque[s]*, of 11 yrs service. *RIB* 481
Undated: Chester, tombstone of [Voltim?]esis Pudens, *eques*, of 13 yrs service. *RIB* 482
By 89: Dacia, tombstone of T. Cominius Severus, decorated in a Dacian war. *ILS* 9193

Summary
69 — raised: Tacitus (*Histories*) iv.68, v.16
by *c.*75 — at Lincoln: *RIB* 258
by late 70s/early 80s all or part at Chester: *RIB* 476, 481, 482
by 89 — in Dacia: *ILS* 9193

Legates (in Britain): none known

II Augusta (10)

Claudian (43-54)
II Augusta took part in the invasion of Britain, and is the only legion testified in this role.
In 43 Vespasian, later emperor, commanded it during his campaign in south-western
Britain. A *praefectus castrorum* of *II Augusta*, P. Anicius Maximus, was decorated in a British
war which was probably the Claudian invasion.

In view of the area in which it was active, the assumption that *II Augusta* was the one
stationed in the legionary fortress at Exeter by *c.*55 is probably correct but not verified by
epigraphic evidence.

Sources: Tacitus (*Histories*) iii.44; Suetonius (*Vespasian*) iv.1

Inscriptions
Claudian: Antioch, dedication to P. Anicius Maximus, sometime *praef(ectus) castror(um) leg(ionis) II
 Aug(ustae) in Britannia*, and *hasta pura ob bellum Britannic(um)*, 'with iron-free spear [an honorific
 symbol] from the British war'. *ILS* 2696

Neronian (54-68)
Poenius Postumius, *praefectus castrorum secundae legionis*, ignored Suetonius Paullinus' orders
to help crush the Boudican revolt in 60. This deprived *II Augusta* of honours awarded to
XIV Gemina and *XX*. Postumius committed suicide. It is not clear why there was no legate
able to respond.

Source: Tacitus (*Annals*) xiv.37

Flavian-Trajanic (69-117)
In 69 a vexillation of the legion (along with vexillations of *IX* and *XX*) fought for Vespasian
at Cremona.

Caerleon is believed to have been established as a legionary base in 74-5, during the
governorship of S. Julius Frontinus on the basis of archaeological evidence. But not until

11 Building stone from Benwell, recording II Augusta *and depicting a legionary standard flanked by a capricorn and winged horse. Diameter 381mm. (Copyright © The British Museum).* RIB *1341*

the years 99-100 under Trajan is *II* testified there.

II Augusta was possibly also building at Gelligaer in 103-11 but the inscription is too fragmentary to be certain.

Sources: Tacitus (*Histories*) iii.22

Inscriptions
99-100: Caerleon, building stone with Trajan's titles. *RIB* 330
103-11: Gelligaer, building stone, legion's name missing. *RIB* 397

Hadrianic-Antonine (117-80)
During this period *II Augusta* was widely engaged in military affairs on the northern frontier, principally Hadrian's Wall (**11**, **12**). It is testified on several Wall inscriptions under the governor Platorius Nepos. These are mainly milecastle inscriptions; *II Augusta* is not yet testified at any Wall forts on datable stones or on the actual curtain.

II Augusta later helped build the Antonine Wall, recorded on several inscriptions from the frontier most of which only name Antoninus Pius for 139-61. A few add the name of the governor Lollius Urbicus (*c*.139-43). Here its role in building the curtain is specified on some stones. In 139 and 140 the legion was also building at Corbridge.

At Newcastle an inscription records reinforcements for *II*, *VI* and *XX* during the

12 Building stone of II Augusta from near milecastle 38 (Hotbank) on Hadrian's Wall. It supplies Hadrian's titles for 119-28, the name of the governor A(ulus) Platorius Nepos, known from diplomas to have served between 122-4+. Width 1.02m. RIB 1638

governorship of Julius Verus between *c*.155-9. It means either that reinforcements had arrived from the two German provinces for these legions, or had returned.

Inscriptions
c. 122-6: Hadrian's Wall under A. Platorius Nepos. *RIB* 1634 (mc 37), 1637-8 (mc 38) (**12**), 1666 (mc 42)
139-43: Antonine Wall under Q. Lollius Urbicus. *RIB* 2191 (Balmuildy) plus numerous others of Antoninus Pius' reign for 139-61 but lacking the governor's name. *RIB* 2186 from near Cadder records a length of wall (3666.5 paces) built by *II Augusta*. *RIB* 2180 from near Auchendavy shows that the legion was split into vexillations.
139: Corbridge, under Q. Lollius Urbicus. *RIB* 1147
140: Corbridge, under Q. Lollius Urbicus. *RIB* 1148 (**1**)
155-9: Newcastle, reinforcements arriving at, or leaving from. *RIB* 1322 (**14**)

Severan
Under the Severan reorganization Britain was divided into two provinces: *Inferior* (north) and *Superior* (south) according to Herodian. *II Augusta* is not mentioned but Dio, describing the dispositions of the legions around this date, states that its 'winter quarters' (i.e. Caerleon) were in *Britannia Superior*.

In 207 quarrying by the river Gelt in Cumbria, close to Hadrian's Wall was recorded on an inscription near another naming a vexillation of *II Augusta*. The date of *II Augusta*'s work is thus not certain but the work was probably linked with rebuilding work on the Wall under Severus. Restoration work by *II Augusta* at Caerleon between 198-209 may be recorded in a stone from Caerleon churchyard.

The prefect P. Sallienius Thalamus names the legion on a dedication made at Caerleon between 198-209.

Under Caracalla and possibly Elagabalus the legion was named *II Augusta Antoniniana*, as recorded on the tombstone from Chester of a legionary called Gabinius Felix. This stone also shows that individual tombstones are not necessarily reliable indicators of a legion's exclusive base as Chester was *XX Valeria Victrix*'s fortress.

A suspect inscription from Netherby (butchered and re-cut) may record a vexillation of *II Augusta* building here in 219 during the governorship of Modius Julius but the evidence is unreliable (see his biography, Chapter 9).

The legate T. Claudius Paulinus was elevated to the governorship in or around 220, recorded on a statue base from Caerwent, close to Caerleon. His command of the legion will have been some time during the preceding decade.

Sources: Herodian iii.8.2 (division of Britain); Dio lv.23.2-6 (dispositions of the legions)

Inscriptions
198-209: Caerleon, building(?), unit unnamed. *RIB* 333
198-209: Caerleon, dedication by P. Sallienius Thalamus, *praef(ectus)* of *II Augusta*. *RIB* 326
207: Gelt quarry, unit unnamed (see next example), work by Mercatius and with a consular date. *RIB* 1009
Undated: Gelt quarry, a vexillation of *II Augusta*. *RIB* 1008
213-22: Chester, tombstone of Gabinius Felix, *miles* of *II Augusta Antoniniana* (Caracalla or Elagabalus). *RIB* 488
213-22: Caerleon, tiles with the stamp LEG II AUG ANT/ANTO. *RIB* 2459.54-60
Undated (219?): Netherby, purportedly recording *II Augusta*, *XX Valeria Victrix* and *cohors I Hispanorum* during the governorship of Modius Julius. Butchered and re-cut. *RIB* 980
pre-220: Caerwent, statue base of T. Claudius Paulinus, legate. *RIB* 311 (**75**)

Third century (after 220)
Tiles were possibly manufactured at Caerleon by *II Augusta* during the reign of Severus Alexander (222-35). In 244 the birthday of Augustus, the legion's namesake, was celebrated by the senior centurion at Caerleon.

II Augusta was still at Caerleon and building between 255-60. Soldiers were still detached on other duties: G. Carinius Aurelianus, centurion of the legion, was in charge of an anonymous *numerus* in the Old Carlisle area between 255-9.

During the late second or early third century *II Augusta* may have supplied a vexillation for an expedition to Germany. Tadius Exupertus died on the German expedition but the memorial stone (his body was presumably not returned) supplies no rank or unit. It was erected by his sister and was found half a mile from Caerleon near a Roman building. His role on the expedition was perhaps in a civilian capacity. Strictly speaking then this is only evidence for an expedition to Germany, not *II Augusta*'s participation. Its style closely resembles stones of Caracalla's reign and thus may apply to the testified campaign there. A further, fragmentary, inscription appears to record Aurelian (270-5) but no further details survive.

Inscriptions
222-35?: Caerleon, tile bearing the stamp LEG II A(U)G S(everiana?), for Severus Alexander. *RIB*
2459.62
244: Caerleon, dedication by [....], *p(rimus) p(ilus)*, under the charge of Ursus, *actar(io)*, to Numina
Augustorum and Genius legionis *II Augustae*. *RIB* 327
255-60: Caerleon, seventh cohort *centurias*, 'barracks', rebuilt during the reigns of Gallienus and
Valerian, under the governor Desticius Juba, the legionary legate Vitulasius Laetinianus, and the
praef(ectus) leg(ionis) (a late form of *praefectus castorum*), Domitius Potentinus. *RIB* 334
255-9: Cardewlees (near Old Carlisle), altar dedicated by G. [.]arinius Aurelianus, *centurio*, to Jupiter
Optimus Maximus and Numina Dominorum Nostrorum for Valerian and Gallienus. *RIB* 913
268-70?: Caerleon, tiles possibly bearing the stamp [LEG II A]UG VI(ctoriniana?) for Victorinus.
The restoration is doubtful as there is no parallel, but the reading VI seems certain. *RIB* 2459.64
Undated: Caerleon, tombstone of Tadius Exuper(a)tus, no military connection cited, who died on
expeditione Germanica, 'the German expedition'. *RIB* 369

Carausian
The last dated reference to the legion is its appearance on some of the coins of Carausius
between 286-93. Either these celebrated the legion's loyalty or were issued to buy it.

Source: *RIC* 58 (Carausius), radiate coin bearing the legend LEG II AUG and the legionary
capricorn.

Fourth century
In *Notitia Dignitatum*, *II Augusta* is one of only two British legions to be mentioned by
name. By then it was controlled by a prefect at the Saxon Shore fort of Richborough in
Kent and formed part of the command of the *comes litoris Saxonici*, 'count of the Saxon
shore'. This can only be dated to some point in the fourth century. Archaeology at
Caerleon shows it was then in a state of advanced decay. Richborough was far smaller than
Caerleon (2ha compared to 20.5ha). Therefore the legion must have been vastly reduced
or dispersed amongst several forts.

Source: *ND* xxviii.19

Tile stamps of *II Augusta* (**13**)
Undated tiles of *II Augusta* are found almost exclusively in the south Wales area but outliers are
known from Carlisle and Devon. As with *VI* and *XX* only tiles from the period 213-35 can
usually be dated.
Undated: Carlisle. *RIB* 2459.1-2; South Wales: Brecon, Caerleon, Caerwent, Cowbridge, Risca,
Usk. *RIB* 2458.1, 2459.3-40, 42-53; Honeyditches (Devon): *RIB* 2459.41

Legates of *II Augusta*
T. Flavius Vespasianus, 42/3-49?. Tacitus (*Histories*) iii.44
[...]isus Claudius [Aem]ilius Quintus Julius Haterianus, second century. *RIB* 335
(Caerleon)
A. Claudius Charax, *c*.143. *AE* 1961.320
Fronto Aemilianus [...] Rufilianus (name uncertain), undated but belonging to a period of
joint emperors, perhaps 161-9. *RIB* 320 (Caerleon)
Q. Aurelius Polus Terentianus, *c*.180-5. *AE* 1965.240

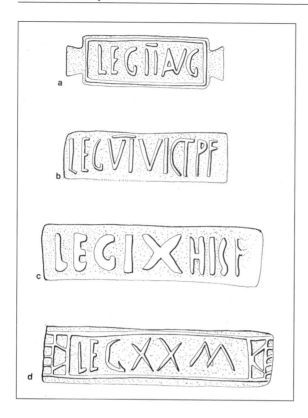

13 *Legionary tile-stamps, each a representative variant produced by four of the legions stationed in Britain:* II Augusta, VI Victrix, IX Hispana, *and* XX Valeria Victrix. *None is readily datable though* IX Hispana's *must belong to the late first century or early second.*

L. Julius Julianus, 198-212? *CIL* xi.4182; *RIB* 1138 (Corbridge)
T. Claudius Paulinus, *c.*200-220. *RIB* 311 (Caerwent)
T. Flavius Postumius Varus, mid-third century. *RIB* 316 (Caerleon)
Vitulasius Laetinianus, *c.*255-60. *RIB* 334 (Caerleon)

Prefects of *II Augusta*
P. Saliienus Thalamus, *c.*198-209. *RIB* 324, 326 (Caerleon)
Domitius Potentinus, *c.*255-60. *RIB* 334 (Caerleon)

Summary
43-7 — participated in invasion of Britain: Tacitus (*Histories*) iii.44
60 — denied participation in defeating Boudican Revolt: Tacitus (*Annals*) xiv.37
99-100 — at Caerleon: *RIB* 330
122-6 — building on Hadrian's Wall: (e.g.) *RIB* 1638 (milecastle 38)
139-43 — building on Antonine Wall: (e.g.) *RIB* 2191 (Balmuildy)
197 — after this date stated to be in *Britannia Superior*: Dio lv.23.2-6
286-93 — included in Carausian legionary coinage. *RIC* 58
300s — at Richborough: *ND* lxxviii.19

II Italica (Noricum)
See *RIB* 576 under **Vexillationes** below

14 Slab from the Tyne at Newcastle. It names Julius Verus, whose term is dated to c. 158 on a slab from Birrens (RIB 2110). The text refers to legionary movements in or out of Germany. An error in line four shows how the mason failed to leave room for 'LEG' and was forced to combine 'L' and 'E' and cram in a diminutive 'G'. Width 0.66m. RIB 1322

III Augusta
See T. Pontius Sabinus under *VIII Augusta* below (Hadrianic). Note also that a soldier who died at Colchester had served at some time as centurion with *III Augusta* (RIB 203).

III Italica (Raetia)
See *RIB* 576 under *Vexillationes* below

VI Victrix Pia Fidelis
Hadrianic

When *VI* arrived in Britain from Germania Inferior in *c.*122 it already had the full titles *Victrix Pia Fidelis*, awarded by Domitian for remaining loyal in 89 during the revolt of the legionary legate L. Antonius Saturninus on the Rhine.

VI Victrix first appears in Britain involved in the construction of Hadrian's Wall, recorded on a stone from Haltonchesters, erected during the governorship of Aulus Platorius Nepos in *c.*122-4+.

VI Victrix probably accompanied Nepos from Vetera in Germania Inferior where it had been based, and he had been governor, until 122. However, it could have arrived slightly earlier. The occasion of the transfer from Germany to Britain under Hadrian is confirmed on a career inscription on a statue base from Rome.

Other Wall work included building milecastles, for example stone milecastle 50, west of Birdoswald. This replaced the earlier Turf Wall in that sector in the latter part of Hadrian's reign or later in the second century.

Sources: Suetonius (*Domitian*) vi.2, vii.3

Inscriptions
Hadrianic: Rome, career inscription recording transfer of VI *Victrix*'s transfer *ex Germ in Brittan*. *ILS* 1100 (M. Pontius Laelianus, for his name see *ILS* 1094)
122-6: Haltonchesters (HW), naming A. Platorius Nepos and *VI Victrix*. *RIB* 1427
Undated: Hadrian's Wall (High House, mc 50), *RIB* 1934

Antonine
Vexillations from *VI Victrix* helped build the Antonine Wall, recorded for example at Old Kilpatrick but strictly datable only to the period 139-61. The references to vexillations, as with *II* and *XX*, show that not all the legion was involved.

At Newcastle an inscription records *II*, *VI* and *XX* during the governorship of Julius Verus between *c*.155-9 (see under *II Augusta* above).

In 158 *VI* was back repairing Hadrian's Wall, then being recommissioned, near Heddon. An undated stone from turret 33B (Coesike) names the legion as does another from milecastle 37, originally built by *II Augusta*.

During the governorship of S. Calpurnius Agricola, about 162-8, a vexillation of VI erected a monument to Sol Invictus at Corbridge.

That *VI* replaced *IX Hispana* at York is beyond doubt but no stone records it operating as a whole in the form of building work. Instead there are only tombstones and private dedications, none of which is dated. One records the soldier and pilot, Marcus Minucius Audens, providing useful evidence for the importance of water transport to Roman military units. Claudius Hieronymianus, legate of *VI Victrix*, dedicated a temple to Serapis in York. (**74**)

A late return to the Antonine Wall between 175-90 has been suggested on the basis of an undated dedication from Castlecary, recording a dedication by *VI* soldiers 'citizens of Italy and *Noricum*'. This combination is believed to be only possible where a legion has been raised in Italy and stationed in *Noricum*. As this was not where *VI* had been stationed it has been suggested that soldiers from *II Italica*, raised in Italy and stationed in *Noricum* around 165, had then been transferred to *VI*.

The argument relies on more assumptions than facts. Even if correct this may be just a small vexillation on a foray. There is no reason to believe that this is other than routine evidence for *VI* active on the Antonine Wall during the testified period of occupation.

Under Commodus *VI* may have participated in a British war, described by Dio and celebrated in victory coins of 184 (**84**). The only specific, but tenuous, link with *VI Victrix* is the Dalmatian tombstone of L. Artorius Justus where he is named as the legion's prefect. The fourth-century biography of Commodus states that during this war senatorial commanders of troops in Britain were replaced with equestrians. This would explain the anomalous rank of *VI*'s commander.

Sources: Dio lxxiii.8.1-2 (war of 184); *SHA* (Commodus) vi.1-2 (senators and equestrians)

Inscriptions

139-61: Old Kilpatrick, *VI Victrix* building the Antonine Wall. *RIB* 2205. *RIB* 2194 from near Balmuildy, for examples, names a vexillation of *VI Victrix*

155-9: Newcastle, reinforcements arriving at, or leaving from. *RIB* 1322 (**14**)

158: Hadrian's Wall (Heddon), *VI Victrix* rebuilding and, exceptionally, providing a consular date. *RIB* 1389

Undated: Hadrian's Wall (mc 37), *VI Victrix* building. *RIB* 1635

Undated: Hadrian's Wall (turret 33B), *VI Victrix* building. *Brit.* ii (1971), 291, no. 10

162-8. Corbridge, dedication by a vexillation of *VI Victrix* during the governorship of S. Calpurnius Agricola. *RIB* 1137

Undated: York, altar dedicated by M. Minucius Audens, *guber(nator)* and *mil(es)* of *VI Victrix*, to the Matres. *RIB* 653

Undated (late second/early third century): York, tablet dedicated by Cl. Hieronymianus, *leg(atus)* of *VI Victrix*. *RIB* 658 (**74**)

Undated: Castlecary (AW), altar dedicated to Mercury by *cives Italici et Norici* of *VI Victrix*. *RIB* 2148

Undated: Dalmatia, tombstone of L. Artorius Justus, *praef(ectus) leg(ionis) VI Victricis*, see Chapter 2. *ILS* 2770

Third century

Under the Severan reorganization after 197 (or possibly under Caracalla) Britain was divided into two provinces: *Inferior* (north) and *Superior* (south). *VI* is not mentioned but Dio, describing legionary dispositions after this date, says it was in *Britannia Inferior*, confirmed by the 237 dedication by Lunaris which states that York was in *Inferior* (**29**).

Building stones from South Shields name *VI* in a context associated with the Severan expansion of the fort into a supply base. The stones are undated and only confirm the presence of centuries detached from *VI* to do the work.

Tiles from Carpow name the legion and supply B for the title *Britannica*, corresponding with the title taken by Severus with Caracalla and Geta in 210 to celebrate the campaign. A fragmentary dedication from Carpow appears to name Caracalla between 212-17, suggesting a continuation of building work. The legionary name is uncertain. Other tiles belong to the reign of Severus Alexander (222-35).

These various duties may have stretched the legion. An undated statue base from Piercebridge records the presence of a vexillation of *VI Victrix* and the 'German army' (that is, legionaries drawn from those on the Rhine), commanded by M. Lollius Venator, centurion of *II Augusta*. The stone is not unreasonably associated with an altar dedicated by a centurion from Germania Superior in 217.

The governor of *Britannia Inferior* is believed to have been commander of *VI Victrix*. No inscription states this as a fact. A number of governors of *Britannia Inferior* in the early third century are known from inscriptions, many tightly dated, but none mentions *VI Victrix*. No specified legates of *VI Victrix* are known after 213. Tiberius Claudius Paulinus, governor of *Inferior* in 220, was 'attached to the *VI* legion'.

A stone from Stanwix may record *VI Victrix* building there during the reign of Gordian III (238-44). This depends on expanding G to read *Gordiana*. A centurion of *VI* seems to have been in charge of a Sarmatian cavalry unit bearing a similar epithet at Ribchester during Gordian III's reign.

Sources: Herodian iii.8.2 (division of Britain); Dio lv.23.2-6 (dispositions of the legions)

Inscriptions

*c.*210-11?: York, tiles bearing the stamp LEG VI VIC B(ritannica) P(ia) F(idelis). *RIB* 2460.75

210-11 or later: Carpow, tiles bearing the stamp LEG VI VIC B(ritannica) P(ia) F(idelis). *RIB* 2460.71-4

212-17: Carpow, inscription possibly naming Caracalla? Legion unnamed but the tiles (see previous) suggest it was *VI Victrix*. *JRS* lv (1965), 223, no. 10

213-22: York, tiles bearing the stamp [LEG VI] VIC ANT(oniniana) for Caracalla or Elagabalus. *RIB* 2460.70

217: Piercebridge, altar dedicated by Julius Valentinus, *ord(inatus)*, from Germania Superior. *RIB* 1022

Undated (c. 217): Piercebridge, statue base dedicated by M. Lollius Venator, *c(enturio)* of *II Augusta*, commanding a vexillation of *VI Victrix* and legionaries drawn from Germany. *JRS* lvii (1967), 205, no. 16

220: Vieux, identifying Ti. Claudius Paulinus as governor of Britain [Inferior] *ad legionum sex(tam)*, 'to the sixth legion'. *CIL* xvi.3162 (date fixed by *RIB* 1280 — see his biography, Chapter 9)

222-35: York, tiles bearing the stamp LEG VI SEV(eriana) for Severus Alexander. *RIB* 2460.41-42

238-44: York, tiles bearing the stamp LEG VI GOR(diana) for Gordian III. *RIB* 2460.44-7

238-44: Stanwix, building stone naming VI with the suffix G[O]R(diana), for Gordian III. *RIB* 2027

238-44: Ribchester, pedestal dedicated by Aelius Antoninus, centurion of *VI Victrix*, serving as *praep(ositus)* *n(umeri)* *et* *r(egionis)*, commanding *n(umerus)* *eq(uitum)* *Sar[m(atarum)]* *Bremetenn(acensium)* *[G]ordiani*. *RIB* 583

Undated: South Shields, building stones of *VI Victrix*. *RIB* 1061 (from the first headquarters, dated to *c.*163, see *Brit.* xviii (1987), 368, note 17); *JRS* lii (1962), 193, no.13; *Brit.* xviii (1987), 368, no. 8, and *Brit.* xxvi (1995), 379-80, no. 6

Carausian

VI Victrix was not included amongst the legionary coin types issued by Carausius. Either the legion's loyalty was guaranteed, or it spurned involvement in the revolt. However, the sole surviving inscription of Carausius' reign comes from *VI Victrix*'s command, *Britannia Inferior*, and implies the regime had power in the area.

Inscription

286-93: Gallows Hill, Carlisle, milestone of Carausius. *RIB* 2291

Fourth century

Notitia Dignitatum mentions *Praefectus legionis sextae*, 'Prefect of the legion *Sexta*', *under control of Dux Britanniarum*. This must be *VI Victrix* but no place is given which either means a scribal error and omission of York, or the legion was in transit or dispersed at the time. This is the last mention of the legion.

Source: *ND* xl.18

Tile stamps of *VI Victrix*

Numerous examples of *VI Victrix* tiles are known. Apart from some examples with highly-abbreviated imperial references none can be dated with any precision. The majority have been found in York but they are also found scattered throughout the northern frontier zone.

Undated: York, tiles with stamps of *VI Victrix*. *RIB* 2460

Undated: Wallsend, Chesters, Carrawburgh (HW), Aldborough, Corbridge, Vindolanda, Ebchester, Netherby. *RIB* 2460.48-52

Legates of *VI Victrix* to *c.*200

Q. Antonius Isauricus, between *c.*122-213. *RIB* 644 (York)

L. Minicius Natalis, 130-4? *ILS* 1061

Claudius Hieronymianus, late second, early third century. *RIB* 658 (York)

L. Junius Victorinus Flavius Caelianus, Antonine? *RIB* 2034 (Kirksteads)

Mummius Sisenna Rutilianus, before 146. *ILS* 1101; *RIB* 2401.8 (diploma)

[after the division of the provinces under Severus the governors of *Britannia Inferior* are regarded as legates of *VI Victrix*, see Chapter 3]

Prefects of *VI Victrix*

L. Artorius Justus (*c.*182-8?). *ILS* 2770

Summary

122-6 — building on Hadrian's Wall: *RIB* 1427

139-61 — building on Antonine Wall: *RIB* 2205

158 — repairing Hadrian's Wall: *RIB* 1389

162-8 — vexillation at Corbridge: *RIB* 1137

197+ — stated after about this date to be in *Britannia Inferior*: Dio lv.23.2-6

300s — at York: *ND* xl.18

VII Gemina

See T. Pontius Sabinus under *VIII Augusta* below.

VIII Augusta

There is some evidence that *VIII Augusta* participated in the invasion of 43. Although it undoubtedly did not stay, occasional vexillations were sent to Britain.

G. Gavius Silvanus, centurion of *VIII Augusta*, committed suicide in 65 despite having been acquitted of conspiring to kill Nero. A dedication to him survives and records his career which included a spell early on as *primus pilus* of *VIII Augusta*. It adds that he was decorated in the British war by Claudius. As *VIII Augusta* was the only legion he served with it seems reasonable to assume that the legion, or a vexillation, participated in the conquest of Britain. The career inscription of Lucius Coiedius Candidus also survives. He was a tribune in *VIII Augusta* and was also decorated by Claudius. However, this stone lacks any direct reference to a British war.

The tombstone of T. Pontius Sabinus from Ferentinum states that as *primus pilus* of *III Augusta* he commanded an expedition to Britain after 117 which included vexillations of 1000 men each from three legions: *VII Gemina*, *VIII Augusta*, and *XXII Primigenia*.

The shield-boss of Junius Dubitatus, found in the Tyne at Newcastle, names him as a soldier of *VIII Augusta*. Although undated it seems reasonable, given the location, to suggest that a vexillation arrived not before the reign of Hadrian.

VIII Augusta turns up on a stone of Antonine style found at Birrens bearing the name also of *XXII Primigenia*. A fragmentary slab from Hayling Island seems also to name the legion and a *tribunus militum*, name lost, of *VIII Augusta* appears on a dedication from Brougham. The latter may be a dedication by an auxiliary prefect appointed to the position with the legion, and did not necessarily serve in that capacity in Britain.

The inclusion of *VIII Augusta* on the coins of Carausius (286-93) raises the interesting question of whether he had any members of the legion at his disposal or was merely soliciting its support. As there is no inscriptional or other evidence to confirm or contradict either of these suggestions, it remains possible that part of the British garrison included a vexillation of the legion at that time.

Sources: Tacitus (*Annals*) xv.71 (death of Silvanus); see also Keppie 1971

Inscriptions
c.50: Suasa, dedication to L. Coiedius Candidus, former tribune of *VIII Augusta* and decorated by
   Claudius on return from military service. *CIL* xi.6163 (for text see Keppie 1971)
c. 64-5: Turin, dedication to G. Gavius Silvanus, former *primus pilus* of *VIII Augusta* and decorated by
   Claudius in *bello Britannico*, 'the British war'. *ILS* 2701, Keppie 1971
Hadrianic: Ferentinum (Italy), tombstone of T. Pontius Sabinus, *primus pilus* of *III Augusta*,
   vexillations of *VII Gemina*, *VIII Augusta* and *XXII Primigenia* on the British expedition. *ILS*
   2726B
Undated: Newcastle (river). Bronze shield boss of Junius Dubitatus of the century of Julius Magnus
   of *VIII Augusta*. *RIB* 2426.1
Undated (Antonine?): Birrens, building stone naming *VIII Augusta* and *XXII Primigenia*. *Brit.* xxiii
   (1992), 318, no. 20
Undated: Hayling Island, stone (tombstone?) naming *VIII (Augusta?)*. *Brit.* xii (1981), 369, no. 3
Undated: Brougham, dedication by a *[trib(unus)] mil(itum)* of the legion. But the stone is long lost
   and VIIII for *IX Hispana* is possible. *RIB* 782
286-93: included in the coinage sequence of Carausius. *RIC* 77

IX Hispana
Claudian-Neronian
IX Hispana is not testified in Britain by name until the campaign against Boudica in 60. Led by its commander, Petillius Cerialis, its cavalry raced to save Colchester but were routed and fled back to its unnamed fortress.

After 60, *IX* was reinforced with troops sent from Germany. Two thousand legionaries, eight auxiliary cohorts, and a thousand cavalry were required to make good the losses though how much went to *IX*, is not specified by Tacitus.

Source: Tacitus (*Annals*) xiv.32, 38

Flavian
In 69 a vexillation of *IX*, fought for Vespasian at Cremona. All or part of *IX*, was at Lincoln at some date between 60 and 107 but its presence is only confirmed by undated tombstones and stamped tiles. Further confirmation of its presence in Britain is an inscription recording the legate C.Caristanius Fronto.

Due to his earlier career with *IX Hispana* it has sometimes been assumed that the legion formed the backbone of Petillius Cerialis' (see Chapter 9) campaign into the north during his governorship. This is not testified and is merely an inference. The foundation of York as a fortress for *IX Hispana* is attributed to Cerealis exclusively through archaeology and is similarly treated as a fact, for example by Frere (1987, 83). But the reality is very far from certain (see for instance Birley 1973, 188, and note 45, and 190).

During this period *IX Hispana* participated in Agricola's campaign into Scotland, as testified by Tacitus. Once again it faced being routed, this time until Agricola arrived with reinforcements.

Following the Scottish campaign *IX* contributed a vexillation to Domitian's war against the Chatti in Germany, probably the campaign of 83.

Sources: Tacitus (*Histories*) iii.22 (at Cremona), (*Agricola*) xvii (Cerialis' campaign), xxvi (*IX* attacked)

Inscriptions
Late 70s: dedication naming C. Caristanius Fronto as *leg(atus) IX Hispana*e in *Britann(iam)* during the
   reign of Vespasian. *ILS* 9485
Undated, late 1st cent?: Dedication to L. Roscius Aelianus Maecius Celer, *trib(unus) mil(itum) leg(ionis)
   IX Hispan(ae)* who participated *in expeditione Germanica* with a vexillation of the legion. *ILS* 1025

Trajanic
IX Hispana is last testified in Britain at York on an inscription of 107-8. Its absence from the building work on Hadrian's Wall is crucial negative evidence for its removal from Britain between 108 and 122, and its replacement by *VI Victrix*. The absence of any building inscriptions from York naming *VI Victrix* suggests *IX Hispana* had built a substantial amount of the fortress before it left. Its subsequent history is a matter of some controversy but not relevant here.

Inscriptions
107-8: York, monumental inscription recording Trajan's titles for 107-8 and *IX Hispana*. Found by
   the SE gateway. *RIB* 665

Tile stamps of *IX Hispana* (**13**)
Undated: Scalesceugh, tile stamps in the form LEG VIIII H(ispana). *RIB* 2462.2, 4
Undated: Carlisle, tile stamps in the form LEG VI[III H?] (or VI VIC). *RIB* 2462.3, 2462.16
Undated: York, numerous tile stamps in the form LEG IX HIS/HISP. *RIB* 2462.5-9 (**15**)
Undated: Malton, tile stamp in the form [LEG I]X HISP. *RIB* 2462.14

Legates of *IX Hispana*
Petillius Cerialis, 60. Tacitus (*Annals*) xiv.32
C. Caristianius Fronto, late 70s. *ILS* 9485
Ferox? *c.*92-103. Unit/rank unnamed, see Bowman 1994, 22, 104-5, and *Tab. Vindol.* I.154

Summary
60 — cavalry nearly wiped out by Boudican rebels: Tacitus (*Annals*) xiv.32
60-1 — reinforced from Germany: ibid., xiv.38
69 — fighting with Vespasian at Cremona: Tacitus (*Histories*) iii.22
77/8-83/4 — participated in Agricola's Scottish campaign: Tacitus (*Agricola*) xxvi
c. 89 — vexillation serves in Germany: *ILS* 1025
107-8 — building at York: *RIB* 665

15 Tile-stamp of IX Hispana *from York. Diameter 134mm.* RIB *2462.9*

X Fretensis

Represented by M. Censorius Cornelianus, centurion of, apparently, *X Fretensis*, serving at Maryport as *praepositus* in charge of *cohors I Hispanorum* from Nemausus. He was almost certainly on individual attachment but may have accompanied a vexillation. However, there is no further evidence for members of *X Fretensis* in Britain.

Inscription: altar dedicated by M. Censorius Cornelianus, *c(enturio) leg(ionis)* [X Fr]etensis. *RIB* 814

XIV Gemina Martia Victrix

Claudian-Neronian

Like *IX* and *XX*, *XIV* is not testified in the invasion of 43. The earliest dated evidence for *XIV Gemina's* presence is during the Boudican Revolt of 60. It was serving as the backbone of Suetonius Paullinus' march against Anglesey. Tacitus describes how the governor had all of *XIV* and a vexillation of *XX* with him at the battle which defeated Boudica.

The choice of *XIV* for the Anglesey campaign may have been its location in north Wales, indicated by a pair of undated tombstones from Wroxeter. It may only be said that the lack of the title *Martia Victrix*, awarded after 60-1, makes it possible the stones precede that date but this is a demonstrably fallacious 'rule' (see below).

Apart from a single other tombstone, of a veteran of *XIV*, at Lincoln there is no other epigraphic evidence for the legion's presence in Britain.

Sources: Tacitus (*Annals*) xiv.34 (against Anglesey and Boudica)

Inscriptions
Undated: Wroxeter, tombstone of [Titus F]laminius, *mil(es)*, of *XIV Gemina*, 22 years' service. *RIB* 292
Undated: Wroxeter, tombstone of Marcus Petronius, *mil(es)* and *sign(ifer)* of *XIV Gemina*, 18 years' service. *RIB* 294
222-35: dedication to Cn. Petronius Probatus gives *XIIII Gemina*, but not *Martia Victrix*. *ILS* 1179 (also *ILS* 9200 under the Flavians; 5013 under Septimius Severus or Severus Alexander; *CIL* xiii contains many examples of the legion with and without *Martia Victrix*)

Post 60-1

As a result of its success in Britain *XIV* enjoyed an empire-wide reputation. Its later name of *XIV Gemina Martia Victrix* is probably attributable to the victory. Tacitus says Nero regarded *XIV* as his best troops. An inscription of 66, of a veteran called M. Vettius Valens, records a period with the legion as tribune, giving the title *XIV Gem(ina) Mart(ia) Victr(ix)* shows that it had been given the names by that date.

By 68-9 *XIV* had been moved to Dalmatia and Pannonia. Nero had been succeeded by Galba who was in turn succeeded by Otho, a friend of Nero's. Thanks to their honours under Nero *XIV* was loyal to his memory and joined Otho.

Otho was defeated by Vitellius in early 69. Vitellius transferred *XIV* back to Britain in 69. They were garrisoned with Batavian auxiliaries, their sworn enemies, and the journey back to Britain was marred by the burning of towns and threats to Vienna.

Once in Britain the legion was invited to side with Vespasian, now marching against Vitellius. By 70 the civil war was largely over and Vespasian was emperor. However, he faced the revolt of the Batavian chieftain Civilis on the Rhine border which had begun in 69. Civilis exploited the chaos of civil war and mixed loyalties amongst the Rhine border troops. *XIV* was ordered back to the continent from Britain to help quell the revolt. In the ensuing hostilities the legionaries were celebrated by Petillius Cerialis as *domitores Britanniae*, 'conquerors of Britain'.

Here *XIV Gemina* leaves Romano-British history. Its activities between 60-70 form an interesting example of short-term movements in and out of Britain which would be virtually impossible to detect archaeologically. Only the texts supply the information and is a sobering reminder of how erratic and unpredictable troop movements could be and how inadequate archaeology is as a tool to measure such activities.

Sources: Tacitus (*Annals*) xiv.37 (exploits of *XIV*), (*Histories*) ii.11 (*XIV*'s reputation), ii.66 (dispute with Batavians and returned to Britain), ii.86 (civil war affiliation), iv.68 (summoned from Britain), v.16 (Cerialis celebrates)

Inscriptions
66: dedication from Rimini of M. Vettius Valens, sometime *trib(unus) leg(ionis) XIIII Gem(ina) Mart(ia) Victr(ix)*. Decorated in a British war, but no date given, and nor is the unit he was in at the time specified. *ILS 2648*

Legates of *XIV* in Britain
None known (but see unattributed legates below)

Summary
60 — backbone of campaign into Anglesey and defeat of Boudica: Tacitus (*Annals*) xiv.34, 37
68 — fights on Otho's side in civil war (*Histories* ii.11)
69 — returned to Britain (*Histories* ii.66)
69 — help solicited from *XIV* in Britain for Vespasian (*Histories* ii.86)
70 — withdrawn to confront Civilis (*Histories* iv.68)

16 Slab found near the east gate at High Rochester, recording a vexillation of XX Valeria Victrix,
*flanked by figures of Mars and Hercules and, at the bottom, the boar emblem of the legion.
Undated. Width 1.35m.* RIB *1284*

XX *Valeria Victrix* (16)
Claudian-Flavian

XX, like *IX*, and *XIV*, is not testified in Britain until the description of the Boudican
Revolt. Suetonius Paullinus used a vexillation of *XX* in his campaign against Boudica
along with all of *XIV*, as they had probably already been combined for the assault on
Anglesey. Its role in the defeat of Boudica may have earned *XX* the title *Valeria Victrix* ('the
victorious eagle').

Tacitus states that by about 49 problems with the Silures (in southern Wales) required
the installation of a *castris legionum*, 'legionary camp' in order to crush them. This was made
possible by withdrawing a legion from *Camulodonum* (Colchester) and establishing a
colony of veterans. The well-known tombstone of M. Favonius Facilis, centurion with
XX, from Colchester, and which lacks the titles *Valeria Victrix*, makes it probable that all or
part of *XX* had been stationed at Colchester from 43-9 and was the legion despatched
against the Silures under Ostorius Scapula.

Facilis' tombstone is not unequivocal evidence for a pre-Boudican date. The use of
post-Boudican titles was apparently not universal after 60. For example, a tombstone from
Chester (a site archaeologically associated with a Flavian and later date), names G. Valerius
Justus, *actarius* of *XX* (no titles). Similarly, a tombstone of a veteran from Gloucester is
confidently dated on stylistic grounds by *RIB* to the late second or third century but it too
lacks post-Boudican titles. Normally, the lack of titles would otherwise date the stones to
before 60. Neither case fits the archaeology. Clearly either the practice of dating stones by

the lack of dated titles, or the archaeology, is unreliable. Much later, a building stone from Maryport of 238-44 also lacks them (see below).

The movements of *XX* after 49 until it appeared at Chester towards the end of the first century therefore rely on a series of inferences drawn from archaeology and very limited epigraphic evidence. Frere, in particular, draws a complex series of movements from Colchester to Chester via Kingsholm (near Gloucester), Usk, and Wroxeter, ruling out a time in the legionary fortress at Gloucester attributed to the mid-60s. This is difficult to reconcile with the epigraphic evidence, some of which has only turned up in recent years.

The evidence for *XX* at Kingsholm, where the legion is usually stated to have been by 49, is a tombstone of an unnamed soldier of *XX* found nearby in 1824 and long since lost. No drawing even exists. That the legion's post-60 titles are not recorded cannot be relied on in this instance for a date. Conversely, a centurial stone of a cohort of *XX*, found in Gloucester cathedral and thus either surely from Kingsholm or Gloucester, suggests that all or part of the legion was there at some time after 60. It bears V V for *Valeria Victrix*.

A tombstone from Wroxeter of G. Mannius Secundus, soldier of *XX*, and recorded without the victory titles of 60, is possible proof that *XX* was there as well as *XIV*. But he was serving as a *beneficiarius* and thus had presumably been detached from his legion.

The movements of *XX* until its presumed appearance at Chester by the end of the first century are therefore all guesswork. As Tacitus described a vexillation only of *XX* serving with Suetonius Paullinus, the legion must have been divided amongst two or more bases for all or part of this period. He also refers to a body of soldiers at Colchester at the time of the Boudican Revolt. If this had been *XX*'s former base then it is possible one of its vexillations was stationed here as late as 60. This general picture is supported by archaeology which has identified contemporary legionary-style fortresses in various parts of Britain, most of which are too small to have held a whole legion. In the area relevant to *XX*, Clifford and Clyro are two examples (see Frere and St. Joseph 1983, 38).

The most likely scenario is that *XX* was resident at all or most of these places on and off in the period but often in the form of vexillations or individuals, and perhaps sharing fortresses with vexillations of other legions, such as *XIV*. There is no need or justification to go through contortions to create a sequence of movements involving the whole legion.

During the civil wars of 68-9, *XX* supported Vitellius, egged on by their legate Roscius Coelius who used the conflict to promote his own personal hatred for the governor Trebellius Maximus. In 69 members of the legion fought for Vespasian at Cremona.

Vespasian gave Agricola command of *XX* in about 69 and was charged with winning the legion's loyalty to the new regime. Although it is always stated as a fact that *XX* subsequently formed the main part of Agricola's campaign, when governor, into Scotland this is never said by Tacitus. Similarly, the assumption that *XX* formed the garrison of the short-lived legionary fortress at Inchtuthil is no more than just that. Nothing from the site names the legion.

By the late first century *XX* was probably based at Chester. A number of undated tombstones indicate the legion's long-term presence as do stamped tiles. Lead pipes

17 *Slab from Moresby recording building work by* XX Valeria Victrix *under Hadrian, between 129-38. Width 0.99m.* RIB 801

bearing the name of Agricola and Vespasian's titles for the year 79 show that the fortress was certainly under construction by that date. But the pipes carry no legionary titles.

Sources: Tacitus (*Annals*) xii.32 (colony at Colchester and transfer of a legion to Silurian territory), xiv.32 (troops stationed at Colchester), xiv.34 (vexillation of *XX* with Suetonius Paullinus); Tacitus (*Histories*) i.60 (*XX* and Roscius Coelius), iii.22 (Cremona); Tacitus (*Agricola*) vii.3 (Agricola's command of *XX*)

Inscriptions
Before 56: career inscription of P. Palpellius Clodius Quirinalis, *p(rimus) p(ilus) leg(ionis) XX. ILS* 2702, Tacitus (*Annals*) xiii.30
79: Chester, lead pipes bearing imperial titles for 79 and Agricola's name as *leg(atus) Aug(usti) pr(o) pr(aetore)*. No military unit or civilian body named. *RIB* 2434.1-3
Undated (pre-60?): Colchester, tombstone of M. Favonius Facilis, *c(enturio)* of *XX. RIB* 200
Undated: Gloucester, tombstone (name lost) of a soldier(?) of *XX* (no titles), 13 years' service. *RIB* 122
Undated: Wroxeter, tombstone of G. Mannius Secundus, *miles* of *XX* (no titles), and *ben(eficiarius) leg(ati) pr(o praetore)*, 31 years' service. *RIB* 293
Undated: Gloucester, tombstone of L. Valerius Aurelius, *vet(eranus)* of *XX* (no titles). *Brit.* xv (1984), 333, no. 1 (where dated to late second or even third century)
Undated: Gloucester, centurial stone of the centurion Cornelius Crescens of *XX V(aleria) V(ictrix)*. *Brit.* xvii (1986), 429, no. 3
Undated: Chester, tombstone of the wife of G. Valerius Justus, *actarius*, of *XX* (no titles). The reference to marriage is suggested as evidence for a third-century date. *RIB* 507

Hadrianic
XX helped build Hadrian's Wall. Unlike *II Augusta* in particular its presence is poorly recorded. The only surviving dedication slab recording the legion here under Hadrian is from near milecastle 47. No governor's name was included. However, stylistic similarities

18 Slab from Ferrydyke, near Old Kilpatrick, probably once displayed at the west end of the Antonine Wall. The text gives Antoninus Pius' titles for 139-61 and records that a vexillation of XX Valeria Victrix had built 4411 feet-worth of rampart. Width 0.74m. RIB 2208

with other milecastles make it improbable that this was its only contribution though only a single other undated building stone from west of Stanwix is known. The legion was also working further west at Moresby at some point between 128-38.

Inscriptions
117-38: Hadrian's Wall (near mc 47), building stone of *XX Valeria Victrix. RIB* 1852 (N.B. *RIB* 2035 may be another Hadrianic building stone of this legion, perhaps originating from mc 70, but found in the river Eden to the north)
128-38: Moresby, building stone of *XX Valeria Victrix. RIB* 801 (**17**)
Undated: Hadrian's Wall (north of mc 70, 4 miles west of Stanwix), building stone of the fifth cohort of *XX Valeria Victrix. RIB* 2035

Antonine
XX subsequently served in the building of the Antonine Wall, recorded on many more inscriptions, for example at Ferrydyke near Old Kilpatrick (**18**). However, it is only datable to the period 139-61 on the basis of its text. None of the Antonine Wall *XX* stones record a governor's name.

At Newcastle an inscription found in the Tyne records *II*, *VI* and *XX* during the governorship of Julius Verus between 155-9 (see under *II Augusta* above) (**14**).

At Corbridge a vexillation of *XX* was building during the governorship of Calpurnius Agricola, a time when building work was certainly also going on at Chester.

An undated series of stones from Newstead name a centurion, G. Arrius Domitianus, of *XX*. This is confidently stated in *RIB* to be evidence of a vexillation of *XX* under his command during 'the early Antonine occupation of Newstead'. None of Domitianus' inscriptions name a vexillation and none bears any evidence which could date his presence so precisely. It is no less probable that he had been personally detached, at some unspecified date, to command *ala Augusta Vocontiorum* which was there at some time.

Inscriptions

139-61: Ferrydyke, Old Kilpatrick (AW), building stone of a vexillation of *XX Valeria Victrix* recording 4,411 feet erected. *RIB* 2208 (**18**) (see also, for example, *Brit.* i (1970), 310, no. 19 and pl. xviii)

155-9: Newcastle, reinforcements arriving at, or leaving from. *RIB* 1322 (**14**)

161-9: Corbridge, building stone of *XX Valeria Victrix* during the governorship of S. Calpurnius Agricola. *RIB* restores the date to 163, relying on over-optimistic restoration of the fragmentary slab. *RIB* 1149 (see also *RIB* 1137 for a dedication to Sol Invictus by a vexillation of *XX* at Corbridge under the same governor)

167: Chester, tile exceptionally stamped with a legion's name (presumably *XX*, but damaged), the name of the maker Aulus Vidu(cius?) and a note of the third consulship of Lucius Verus, thus providing the date. *RIB* 2463.59

Undated: Newstead, altars dedicated by G. Arrius Domitianus, centurion of *XX*. *RIB* 2122-4 (and *RIB* 2121 for *ala Vocontiorum*)

Third century

Under the Severan reorganization after 197 Britain was divided into two provinces: *Inferior* (north) and *Superior* (south) according to Herodian. *XX* is not mentioned but Dio says it was in *Britannia Superior*. Tile stamps from Chester of this date confirm its presence.

A Thracian tribune, M. Aurelius Syrio, of *XX* was at Carlisle some time between 213 and 222 when he dedicated an altar to Jupiter Optimus Maximus, Juno, Mars, Minerva, and Victory. He may have been in command of a vexillation of the legion, perhaps even a unit made up of vexillations from more than one legion. Another, undated, stone from Carlisle even refers to a unit made up of vexillations from *II Augusta* and *XX*.

A suspect inscription from Netherby (butchered and re-cut) may record a vexillation of the *XX* building here in 219 but the text is unreliable.

XX was probably building at Maryport under Gordian III (238-44), recorded on a fragmentary stone. The only visible letters are ORD for [G]ord(iana) (?), along with the boar, known from other *XX* inscriptions to have been its symbol.

A fragmentary dedication from Chester to a Genius can be expanded to read *XX V(aleria) V(ictrix)* D(eciana). If correct this records a name for the legion which must belong to the reign of Trajan Decius (249-51). An alternative for this and tile stamps of the legion marked DE is that they represent *Devensis*, 'of *Deva* (Chester)'. This use of a fortress name is testified elsewhere but not in Britain.

XX was featured on a series of gold coins issued by the Gallic emperor Victorinus (268-70) (see Chapter 10), the only British legion to be so.

Soldiers from *XX* were passing by or building in the vicinity of milecastle 52 on Hadrian's Wall between 262-6. Other, undated, altars naming legions on garrison duty suggests that they might also have been allocated to frontier patrols on the Wall (for example *RIB* 1583). This is an activity not normally attributed to legionary vexillations.

Source: Dio lv.23.2-6 (disposition of legions)

19 *Damaged and reused altar from
  Carlisle, dedicated to Jupiter Optimus
  Maximus, Juno, Minerva, Mars and
  Victory by M(arcus) .... Syrio from
  Trh[ac(ia)]* (sic = Thracia, Thrace)
  *with the remains of his town name,
  restored by Tomlin as* Ulpia
  Nicopolis. *Syrio adds that he is a
  military tribune with* XX Valeria
  Victrix Antoniniana, *which dates the
  altar to 212-22. Height 0.98m.*
  Britannia *xx (1989), 331-3, no. 5*

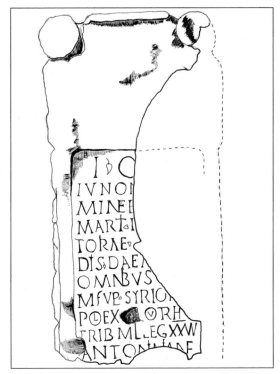

Inscriptions

213-22: Chester, tiles bearing the stamp LEG XX ANTO(niniana) for Caracalla or Elagabalus. *RIB*
2463.51-3

Undated (219?): Netherby, purportedly recording *II Augusta, XX Valeria Victrix* and *cohors I
Hispanorum* during the governorship of Modius Julius. Butchered and re-cut. *RIB* 980

Undated: Carlisle, relief dedicated to the Concord of *II Augusta* and *XX Valeria Victrix. Brit.* xx (1989),
331, no. 4

213-22: Carlisle, altar dedicated by M. Aurelius Syrio, *trib(unus) mil(itum)* of *XX V(aleria) V(ictrix)
Antoniniana. Brit.* xx (1989), 331-3, no. 5 (**19**)

238-44: Maryport, building stone of *[XX G]ord(iana)* with *XX*'s boar emblem. *RIB* 854

249-51?: Chester, door jam dedicated by Titus Vet[...] to a Genius, apparently with the titles *V(aleria)
V(ictrix) D(eciana)*. But the expansion is not certain and may be *D(evensis)* for the fortress name
(see *RIB* II, fasc 4, 191, l. column). *RIB* 449

249-51?: Chester, tiles stamped LEG XX V V DE(ciniana?) or DE(vensis) (see previous). *RIB*
2463.54-5

262-6: Hadrian's Wall (milecastle 52), altar dedicated by soldiers of *XX* to Cocidius. *RIB* 1956

268-70: Chester, tiles stamped LEG XX V V V(ictoriniana?), for Victorinus, but highly dubious. *RIB*
2463.56-7 (but note that *RIB* gives dates of 265-7 without reference to the fact that Victorinus
is normally attributed to 268-70)

Carausian

The last reference to *XX* is on the legionary coins of Carausius between 286-93. The
legion is omitted from *Notitia Dignitatum*, perhaps because it had been disbanded at some
point in the fourth century and absorbed into other units.

Source: *RIC* 275

Tile stamps of *XX Valeria Victrix*
Tiles stamped with *XX*'s name are known from mainly the north Wales area and around Carlisle.
   The legion's tile-manufacturing works at Holt near Chester have been excavated (Grimes 1930).
Undated: Carlisle area (Old Penrith, Scalesceugh, Stanwix. *RIB* 2463.1-3
Undated: Chester and north Wales area (Caernarvon, Caersws, Ffrith, Holt, Oakenholt,
   Wilderspool). *RIB* 2458.2-8 (**20**), 2463.4-50, 57-58, 60
Undated: Whittlesbury. *RIB* 2463.29 (xiii)
Undated: Wroxeter, one example only of dubious provenance. *RIB* 2463.29 (xv)

Legates of *XX Valeria Victrix*
M. Roscius Coelius, -69. Tacitus (*Agricola*) vii.3, (*Histories*) i.60
Gn. Julius Agricola, *c.*69-74. Tacitus (*Agricola*) vii.3
T. Pomponius Mamilianus, *c.*95-120? *RIB* 445 (Chester, legion not stated; see *RIB* for a
discussion of his date)

Summary
60 — participates in Anglesey campaign and defeat of Boudica. Tacitus (*Annals*) xiv.34
69 — commanded by Agricola. Tacitus (*Agricola*) vii.3
119-28 — building on Hadrian's Wall. *RIB* 1852
128-38 — building at Moresby. *RIB* 801
139-61 — building on Antonine Wall *RIB* 2208
163 — building at Corbridge. *RIB* 1149
213-22 — vexillation at Carlisle? *Brit.* xx (1989), 331-3, nos. 4, 5
238-44 — building at Maryport. *RIB* 854
249-51 — possibly testified at Chester. *RIB* 449

XXII Primigenia
The tombstone of T. Pontius Sabinus from Ferentinum says he commanded an expedition
to Britain some time after the year 117 which included vexillations of 1000 men each from
three legions: *VII Gemina*, *VIII Augusta*, and *XXII Primigenia*.

   XXII reappears a generation later on a stone, probably from Falkirk and the Antonine
Wall (thus approximately dating it to 139-61), recording building work. Another from
Birrens, possibly of the same general date, mentions it once more in company with *VIII
Augusta*.

   An undated tombstone from Piercebridge also records the death of a centurion of *XXII*,
though there is no reliable means of associating him with either of the testified
vexillations. This is sometimes associated with an altar erected by a centurion from
Germania Superior in 217 (*RIB* 1022). See Chapter 8, Piercebridge under Jupiter
Optimus Maximus Dolichenus for dedications which may be contemporary.

   The inclusion of *XXII Primigenia* on the coins of Carausius (286-93) raises the
interesting question of whether he had any members of the legion at his disposal or was
merely soliciting its support. It remains possible that part of the British garrison included
a vexillation of the legion at that time. Considering past history that would be hardly
surprising.

Sources: Herodian iii.14.3 (Severan campaign); Stephens 1987

20 Tile antefix *(a decorative terminal)*
with the stamp and symbol of XX
Valeria Victrix. *Made at the*
legionary tile works at Holt. Height
218mm. RIB 2458.4

Inscriptions
Hadrianic: Ferentinum (Italy), tombstone of T. Pontius Sabinus, *primus pilus* of *III Augusta*,
    commanding vexillations of *VII Gemina, VIII Augusta* and *XXII Primigenia* on the British
    expedition. *ILS* 2726B
139-61?: Falkirk (AW)? (location uncertain), building stone of *vexi[llatio] XXI[I] Primig[en(iae)]. RIB*
    2216
Undated: Birrens, building stone naming *VIII Aug(usta)* and *XXII Pr(imigenia). Brit.* xxiii (1992), 318,
    no. 20
Undated: Piercebridge, tombstone of [.... G]racilis, from Germania Superior, *[ord]inato* of *XXII. RIB*
    1026
286-93: represented on coins of Carausius. *RIC* 80-1

XXX Ulpia Victrix
Unknown in Britain, this legion's possible passing presence is indicated on a dedication
from Xanten to the *Matres Brittiae* by L. Valerius Simplex, *miles*, with the legion. Either he
came from Britain himself, or had retained a veneration for her Mother Goddesses. *ILS*
4789. The legion was featured on the coins of Carausius (see below).

OTHER LEGIONS AND LEGIONARY COMMANDERS

Unattributed legates of legions in Britain
Gnaeus Hosidius Geta, implied legionary command in 43. Dio lx.20
Manlius Valens, 60. That he suffered a defeat in the Silurian territory of south Wales
    suggests his command was *II* or *XX*. Tacitus *Annals* xii.40
Priscus, *c*.184. Dio lxxii.9

Carausian legions

Carausius issued a series of bronze radiates with legionary reverses (auxiliary forces were not represented). Of the British legions *II Augusta* and *XX Valeria Victrix* feature in the series, but *VI Victrix* does not. In addition to the coins issued for *VIII Augusta* and *XXII Primigenia* mentioned under the respective legions above, Carausius also issued radiates for five other legions not based in Britain:

> *I Minervia*. RIC 55-6
> *II Parthica*. RIC 60-5
> *IV Flavia*. RIC 69-72
> *VII Claudia*. RIC 74-6
> *XXX Ulpia Victrix*. RIC 84-6 (see above also)

THE PRAETORIAN GUARD

Some of the Praetorian Guard accompanied Claudius to Britain. One tribune of *cohors XII*, G. Gavius Silvanus, was decorated by Claudius for his part.

The Praetorians may have participated in the Severan campaigns of 208-11. G. Cesennius Senecio, a centurion of the second cohort, died in Britain and his body returned to Rome for burial. The Praetorian title, *pia vindex*, given on the tombstone, did not predate Severus. However, the stone is otherwise undated and it makes no mention of participation in fighting or campaigning.

Inscriptions

*c.*45-55: Turin, dedication to G. Gavius Silvanus, *[tr]ibunus* of the twelfth cohort of Praetorians, decorated by Claudius in the British war. *ILS* 2701

Severan or later: Rome, tombstone of G. Cesennius Senecio, *c(enturio)* and *p(ia) v(index)* (a Severan title), of the second cohort of Praetorians, 'his body brought from Britain'. *ILS* 2089

THE AUXILIA

Introduction

Auxilia ('assistants') were all non-legionary parts of the Roman army. Much of Britain's garrison, perhaps half or more, was made up of *auxilia*. Most forts were garrisoned by auxiliaries throughout the period. Their epigraphic record varies from the stylish to the illegible and has supplied much of the evidence for military, and also civilian, life in Roman Britain.

Auxiliary careers for ordinary soldiers led to the reward of citizenship after 25 years which legitimized them and their children. These legal privileges altered over time but Caracalla's edict of universal citizenship eventually wiped out the formal distinction. The record of retirement on the diplomas has provided us with some of the most important evidence for the auxiliary forces in Britain (**8**).

The basic auxiliary unit was the *ala* (cavalry) and the *cohors* (infantry) in various configurations (see Appendices). The *ala* was invariably commanded by a prefect; the *cohortes* were commanded by prefects or in the case of the milliary ('1000-strong') units usually by tribunes (but not, for instance, at Housesteads where *cohors I Tungrorum* was commanded by a prefect). However, there are instances of legionary centurions appointed to command of auxiliary units.

The structure of auxiliary units resembled that of legionary cohorts. However, some names are uncertain thanks usually to the highly-abbreviated form given on inscriptions and diplomas, made worse by damage. During the period more irregular units appeared, such as the *numerus*, about which we know even less.

Auxiliary units were normally raised in provinces and maintained in ethnically-distinct units which retained homeland names and fighting skills. But many units spent centuries stationed in Britain, even though the proliferation of usurpers in the third and fourth centuries may have drawn away soldiers by compulsion or opportunists who preferred the prospect of a continental war than a lifetime of frontier garrison work.

Over time the ethnic identities may have been maintained but in practice they probably became rapidly less distinctive. Marriage to local women as well as to women from elsewhere in the Empire, and the recruitment of soldiers' sons, will have created a homogeneity diminishing the differences from the indigenous community around a fort. Sometimes recruits came from further afield, but still within Britain, such as [Satu?]rninus of *cohors I fida Vardullorum* who came from Gloucester and is recorded on a diploma.

However, evidence for the origins of soldiers and women is limited to a very few from inscriptions and it would be unwise to draw firm conclusions. But there is scarcely a single instance in Britain where a soldier and his wife demonstrably both came from the same nominal homeland. Verecunda Rufilia, by contrast, was a British Dobunnian but married to a man of unknown origin serving with, probably, *cohors IIII Gallorum* (*RIB* 621). Further details of this woman and others are given in Chapter 11.

Within a generation or two of settling into a more or less permanent base few auxiliaries will have even known what being a Dacian or Pannonian meant. As Anthony Birley has pointed out, 'the presumption' must be that where individuals have Celtic or conventional Latin names, those individuals were probably British by birth. Even the survival of a personal name from elsewhere in the Empire need only refer to personal lineage from, say, a Dacian forbear and is no guarantee that its current holder had not been born in Britain. The instance of Nectovelius of *cohors II Thracum* at Mumrills (*RIB* 2142), and a Brigantian by birth (not necessarily a British Brigantian — see Chapter 3), shows how we cannot make assumptions about any individual's origins unless he or she specifically states it.

Auxiliary units were rarely referred to by historians. Diplomas provide no information about locations. Inscriptions normally supply the latter but often lack dates. Our dependence on these sources, and the paucity of alternatives, is well illustrated by the recovery of a writing tablet from Carlisle recording *ala Gallorum Sebosiana* in Britain during the governorship of Agricola (*c*.78-84). No other auxiliary unit is so firmly fixed in Britain this early. Another example is *cohors III Batavorum*, testified in Britain only on tablets from Vindolanda. Apart from the undated evidence of a few tombstones, and an occasional reference in Tacitus or Dio, we know little else about auxiliary units in Britain in the first century.

Undated stones have been omitted unless the unit is otherwise untestified at a given place or where the stone provides the name of a commanding officer. Individual religious dedications are otherwise generally ignored except in unusual instances, for example *cohors I Nerviorum*, where such stones are the only extant epigraphic evidence for the unit. However, tombstones or dedications by individuals, even if they name the unit, do not necessarily mean that the unit itself was present. The altar dedicated by Aurelius Campester, tribune of *cohors I Ulpia Traiana Cugernorum*, to Coventina at Carrawburgh is a case in point. He may merely have been passing or, alternatively he and his cohort may have been stationed there for a few weeks or months, too short a time to be otherwise testified in the archaeological record. Similarly, a unit was liable to be temporarily detached for other duties. Thus we find *cohors I Thracum equitata*, otherwise testified at Bowes, at Birdoswald between 205-8 building a granary with the resident garrison, *cohors I Aelia Dacorum* (*RIB* 1909).

Units are listed according to geographic origin and names are given in their fullest form. It is not always entirely clear from fragmentary sources which unit is being referred to as only the number distinguishes those with similar names. It is possible that in or two cases units with similar names have been unintentionally conflated.

A number of auxiliary units were raised in Britain for service overseas. Sixteen such units, all raised during the first and early second centuries, are listed by A. Birley (1979, 188-9; see also Dobson and Mann 1973). Where their members provide evidence for Romano-British tribal names (by far the minority) they are listed in Chapter 3.

classis Britannica

The British fleet during the Roman occupation was a seaborne arm of the Roman army in Britain. Command was of a procuratorial rank senior to prefects of auxiliary units. It thus lay somewhere between the legions and the auxiliaries. Members of the fleet were obliged to serve an additional year (making 26; from 209 it rose to 28 years) before earning citizenship at the end of service.

The inscriptions which record the commanders of the fleet in the early second century make it clear that the post, *praefectus*, was a senior procuratorship which represented a promotion from similar commands of conventional auxiliary cavalry or infantry units.

83-84: at *Trucculensis portus* (unlocated). Tacitus (*Agricola*) xxxviii.4
122-4: at Benwell building a granary during the governorship of A. Platorius Nepos. *RIB* 1340 (**21**)
130-4?: under the prefect M. Maenius Agrippa (formerly tribune commanding *cohors I Hispanorum* at Maryport, *RIB* 823-6). His son was consul in 161/2, which helps limit the date possibilities. *ILS* 2735
130-5?: at Lympne, altar dedicated by the prefect L. Aufidius Pantera to Neptune. *RIB* 66
140s?: under Q. Baienus Blassianus. *AE* 1974.123
150s?: under S. Flavius Quietus. *AE* 1960.28
244-9: *CIL* xii.686 (see Salway 1981, 529)
Undated: tile stamps at Beauport Park, Dover, Folkestone, Lympne, Cranbrook, Bardown, Beauport Park, London and Southwark. *RIB* 2481 (various) (**22**)
Undated: building on Hadrian's Wall (vicinity of Birdoswald). *RIB* 1944-5
N.B. also the *legatus iuridicus* (Chapter 3) and a case involving a fleet member.

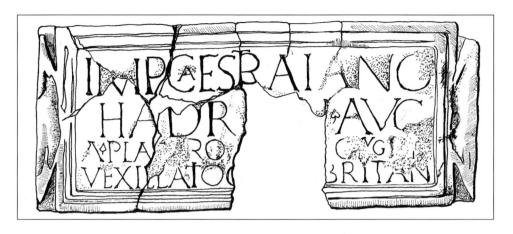

21 Slab from the granaries at Benwell. The text refers to Aulus Platorius Nepos' governorship under Hadrian (c. 122-4+). The c[lassis] Britan(nica) *is the most plausible restoration for the unit. This is the only datable inscription naming the fleet. Width 1.50m. RIB 1340*

Alae (cavalry wings) (order as RIB 2401, Table I, with additions)

ala Augusta Gallorum Petriana milliaria civium Romanorum
98: diploma (restored as *[Gallorum Petria]na cR. CIL* xvi.43
122 (Jul 17): diploma. *CIL* xvi.69
124 (Sep 16): diploma. *CIL* xvi.70 (*RIB* 2401.6)
127 (Aug 20): diploma. Nollé (forthcoming)
135 (Apr 14): diploma. *CIL* xvi.82 (*RIB* 2401.8)
300s: Stanwix. *ND* xl.45
Undated: Carlisle. *RIB* 957
Undated: Corbridge?, tombstone of Flavinus, *eq(ues)* and *signifer*, 7 years' service (now in Hexham Abbey). Traditionally dated to pre-98 on the absence from the text of *c(ivium) R(omanorum)*, present on *CIL* xvi.43. But this is no guarantee of date. *RIB* 1172
Undated: Stanwix, lead sealing. *RIB* 2411.84

ala Agrippiana Miniata
122 (Jul 17): diploma. *CIL* xvi.69

ala I Hispanorum Asturum
98: diploma (restored as *[I Hispanorum Ast]urum*). *CIL* xvi.43
122 (Jul 17): diploma. *CIL* xvi.69
124 (Sep 16): diploma. *CIL* xvi.70 (*RIB* 2401.6)
127 (Aug 20): diploma. Nollé (forthcoming)
145-146 (Dec 10-Dec 9): diploma. *CIL* xvi.93 (*RIB* 2401.10)
158 (Feb 27): diploma. *Brit.* xxiii (1992), 463-4, no. 28
205-8: Benwell. *RIB* 1337
238 (Mar-Jun): Benwell under prefect T(erentius?) Agrippa. *RIB* 1334 (see notes in *RIB* for the dating)
300s: Benwell. *ND* xl.35
Undated: Benwell, dedication. *RIB* 1348
Undated: South Shields, tombstone of Victor, *libertus* of Numerianus, *eques*. *RIB* 1064
Undated: *in Britannia* under the prefecture of an unknown man, and stated on his tombstone to be from Ilipia (Baetica, Spain). *ILS* 2712
Undated: Benwell, tile-stamps, e.g. *RIB* 2464
Undated: London, lead sealing. *RIB* 2504.23

22 *Stamped tile of the classis Britannica from Beauport Park. The tile also bears the impression of a wooden tile-comb (used for producing parallel grooves to enhance adherence to mortar) with the fleet's name.* RIB 2481.7 *(tile stamp),* 2444.2 *(tile-comb)*

ala II Asturum
122 (Jul 17): diploma. *CIL* xvi.69
127 (Aug 20): diploma. Nollé (forthcoming)
176-84: Chesters. *RIB* 1463, 1464
205-8: Chesters. Unit name entirely lost but restored in *RIB*. *RIB* 1462
221 (30 Oct): building at Chesters. *RIB* 1465
221-2: Chesters. *RIB* 1466
300s: Chesters. *ND* xl.38
Undated: Chesters (probably fallen from the adjacent bridge), Aelius Longinus, *praef(ecto) eq(uitum)*, 'prefect of cavalry', probably of this unit. *RIB* 1470
Undated: Lincoln, tombstone of a former *[d]ec(urio)* of II *Asturum*, aged 70. *RIB* 266
Undated: Ribchester, altar dedicated by M. Ingenuius Asiaticus, *dec(urio)*, to the Matres (dependent on Camden's reading in 1580). *RIB* 586
Undated: Corbridge, lead sealing. *RIB* 2411.82
Undated: Carlisle, lead sealing. *RIB* 2411.83
Undated: Chesters, lead sealing. *Brit.* xxvi (1995), 382, no. 15

ala Augusta ob virtutem appellata
(although testified on numerous inscriptions this unit is absent from all the known diplomas and may be identical with another known under a different name)
122-38: Chesters. *Brit.* x (1979), 346, no. 7
180-92?: Carlisle under the prefect P. Sextianus [...] (in this case the unit's name is absent from the slab and is restored from the partial epithet *ob virtu(tem)*, which appears elsewhere). *RIB* 946
185: Old Carlisle, unit name lost but probably this one on the pattern of the next five), under the prefect P. Aelius Septimenus/Septimianus Rusticus. *RIB* 903
188: Old Carlisle under the prefect T. Claudius Justinus. *RIB* 893
191: Old Carlisle under the prefect P. Aelius Magnus. *RIB* 894
197: Old Carlisle under the prefect Egnatius Verecundus. *RIB* 895
213: Old Carlisle under the prefect [........]. *RIB* 905
242: Old Carlisle under the prefect Aemilius Crispinus. *RIB* 897
Undated: Old Carlisle under the prefect Rufinus. *RIB* 890
Undated: Chesters, lead sealing. *RIB* 2411.81

ala Gallorum Indiana
pre-135: Cirencester, tombstone of Dannicus, *eq(u)es*, 16 years' service. Usually attributed to the first century on grounds of location but this is only probable rather than certain. The unit's full name comes from a diploma (*CIL* xiii.6495) which states it to have been in Germania Superior by 135. *RIB* 108

ala Gallorum Picentiana
122 (Jul 17): diploma. *CIL* xvi.69
124 (Sep 16): diploma. *CIL* xvi.70 (*RIB* 2401.6)
Undated: Malton under the prefect J[...] Can[didus?]. *Brit.* ii (1971), 291, no. 9

ala Augusta Gallorum Proculeiana
114-30 (but not 122, 124, or 127): diploma. *CIL* xvi.88 (*RIB* 2401.7), under the prefect [... Pro]pinquos
135 (Apr 14): diploma. *CIL* xvi.82 (*RIB* 2401.8)
145-146 (Dec 10-Dec 9): diploma. *CIL* xvi.93 (*RIB* 2401.10)
158 (Feb 27): diploma. *Brit.* xxiii (1992), 463-4, no. 28

ala Gallorum Sebosiana
78-84: wooden writing tablet from Carlisle sent by a member, detached as *sing(ularis consularis)* to Agricola. *Brit.* xxix (1998), 74, no. 44
103 (Jan 19): diploma. *CIL* xvi.48 (*RIB* 2401.1)
122 (Jul 17): diploma. *CIL* xvi.69
127 (Aug 20): diploma. Nollé (forthcoming)
158 (Feb 27): diploma. *Brit.* xxiii (1992), 463-4, no. 28
178 (Mar 23): diploma. *RMD* 184
262-6 (Aug 22): Lancaster under the prefect Flavius Ammausius. *RIB* 605 (giving *ala Sebussiana [Po]s[t]u[mi]anae*)
Undated: Bollihope Common (i.e. Bowes?), under the prefect G. Tetius Veturius Micianus (boar hunt). *RIB* 1041 (secondary text)
Undated: Lancaster, lead sealing. *RIB* 2411.88
Undated: Brough-under-Stainmore, lead sealing. *RIB* 2411.89
Undated tiles: Quernmore. *RIB* 2465.1
Undated tiles: Lancaster. *RIB* 2465.2

ala Gallorum et Thracum Classiana civium Romanorum
105 (May-Jul): diplomas, *CIL* xvi.51 (*RIB* 2401.2), and *RMD* 8 (*RIB* 2401.3)
122 (Jul 17): diploma. *CIL* xvi.69
178 (Mar 23): diploma. *RMD* 184

ala I Herculea
300s: Elslack or Ilkley? (*Olenacum*). *ND* xl.55. N.B. this unit's name may be a late honorific version, replacing an older name, represented amongst the others of this list. Maximian (286-305, 307-8), for example, favoured Hercules and posed as him on some coin portraits.

ala I Pannoniorum Sabiniana
122 (Jul 17): diploma. *CIL* xvi.69
127 (Aug 20): diploma. Nollé (forthcoming)
145-146 (Dec 10-Dec 9): diploma. *CIL* xvi.93 (*RIB* 2401.10) naming *[Pannoniorum Sab](iniana)?*
178 (Mar 23): diploma. *RMD* 184
300s: Haltonchesters. *ND* xl.37
Undated: Haltonchesters, tombstone of a man, erected by his brother Messorius Magnus, *dupl(icarius)*. *RIB* 1433 (lettering style resembles dated examples of early third century, e.g. *RIB* 1091/2)
Undated: Pittington Farm, lead sealing. *RIB* 2411.85
Undated: South Shields, lead sealing. *RIB* 2411.86
Undated: Corbridge, lead sealing. *RIB* 2411.87

ala I Pannoniorum Tampiana
103 (Jan 19): diploma. *CIL* xvi.48 (*RIB* 2401.1), under the prefect C.Valerius Celsus
122 (Jul 17): diploma. *CIL* xvi.69, under the prefect Fabius Sabinus

ala Sarmatarum
Undated: Ribchester, tombstone of the wife and child of Julius Maximus, *s(ingularis) c(onsularis) alae Sar(matarum)*. *RIB* 594
Undated: Ribchester, tombstone (name lost) of a *[de]c(urio)*. *RIB* 595
N.B. also Dio lxxi.16.2 stating the despatch of 5500 Sarmatian cavalry to Britain in the latter part of the reign of Marcus Aurelius. The unit is not specified and may have been temporary.

ala I Thracum
103 (Jan 19): diploma. *CIL* xvi.48 (*RIB* 2401.1)
124 (Sep 16): diploma. *CIL* xvi.70 (*RIB* 2401.6) ([I Thr]ac)
Undated: Cirencester, tombstone of S. Valerius Genialis, *eq(u)es*, 20 years' service. *RIB* 109
Undated: Colchester, tombstone of Longinus, *duplicarius*, 15 years' service. *RIB* 201
Undated: Caerleon, bronze skillet stamped *ala I Thr(acum)*. *RIB* 2415.39

ala I Tungrorum
98: diploma. *CIL* xvi.43
105 (May-Jul): diploma. *CIL* xvi.51 (*RIB* 2401.2)
122 (Jul 17): diploma. *CIL* xvi.69
135 (Apr 14): diploma (but the damaged reference is possibly to *cohors I Tungrorum*). *CIL* xvi.82 (*RIB* 2401.8)
139-61: Mumrills, altar erected by the *dupli(carius)* Valerius Nigrinus. *RIB* 2140
158 (Feb 27): diploma. *Brit.* xxiii (1992), 463-4, no. 28

ala Hispanorum Vettonum civium Romanorum
103 (Jan 19): diploma. *CIL* xvi.48 (*RIB* 2401.1)
122 (Jul 17): diploma. *CIL* xvi.69
158 (Feb 27): diploma. *Brit.* xxiii (1992), 463-4, no. 28
178 (Mar 23): diploma. *RMD* 184
197-202: building at Bowes, but probably while based at Binchester, for *cohors I Thracum* under the prefect Valerius Fronto. *RIB* 730
Undated: Bath, tombstone of L. Vitellius Tancinus, *eq(ues)*, 26 years' service. *RIB* 159
Undated: Y Gaer, tombstone of Cand[idus], of 3 years' service. *RIB* 403
Undated: Y Gaer, tombstone of Valerius Primus, *[e]q(ues)* (dependent on corrected reading of misread stone, now lost). *RIB* 405
Undated: dedication by M. Aurelius [...]ocomas, *medicus*, for the unit, at Binchester. *RIB* 1028
Undated: Binchester, altar dedicated to the Suleviae. *RIB* 1035
Undated: Binchester under the prefect [....]onius Rufus. *Brit.* xxiii (1992), 314, no, 10

ala Augusta Vocontiorum civium Romanorum
122 (Jul 17): diploma. *CIL* xvi.69
127 (Aug 20): diploma. Nollé (forthcoming)
178 (Mar 23): diploma. *RMD* 184
Undated: dedication by Aelius Marcus, *dec(urio)*, at Newstead. *RIB* 2121 (see Antonine under *XX Valeria Victrix* above)

Cohortes (cohorts, infantry or mixed infantry and cavalry)

cohors I Aelia Dacorum milliaria

Undated, but probably 122-30?: Hadrian's Wall (digging Vallum between t 7b — mc 8) west of Benwell. *RIB* 1365

127 (Aug 20): diploma. Nollé (forthcoming)

145-146 (Dec 10-Dec 9): diploma. *CIL* xvi.93 (*RIB* 2401.10)

158 (Feb 27): diploma. *Brit.* xxiii (1992), 463-4, no. 28

205-8: Birdoswald under the tribune Aurelius Julianus. *RIB* 1909

235-8: Birdoswald under the tribune Flavius Maximian. *RIB* 1896, and *JRS* xlvii (1957), 229, no. 17

237: Birdoswald under the tribune [A]urelius Fa(u)s[t]us. *RIB* 1875

238-44: Birdoswald. *RIB* 1893

259-68: Birdoswald under the tribune Marc(ius) Gallicus. *RIB* 1882, 1883

259-68: Birdoswald under the tribune Probius Augendus. *RIB* 1886

270-3: Birdoswald under the tribune Pomponius Desideratus [....]. *RIB* 1885

276-82: Birdoswald under the tribune Aurelius Verinus. *JRS* li (1961), 194, no. 12

300s: probably at Birdoswald. *ND* xl.44 (*ND* appears to have conflated two entries here; see *PNRB* p.221, note 44)

Undated: Bewcastle. *RIB* 991 (lacking *Aelia* from the title and thus possibly pre-Hadrianic but the only record of the stone is an eighteenth century drawing)

Undated: Birdoswald under the tribune [Tere]ntius Valerianus. *RIB* 1872

Undated: Birdoswald under the tribune Ammonius Victorinus. *RIB* 1874, 1906

Undated: Birdoswald under Aurelius Sa[t]urn[inus]. *RIB* 1876

Undated: Birdoswald, unit styled *Augusta* (unrepeated), under Aurelius [....]. *RIB* 1877

Undated: Birdoswald under F[l(avius?) ....] (reading unreliable). *RIB* 1878

Undated: Birdoswald under the tribune Funisul[an]us Vetto[ni]anus. *RIB* 1879

Undated: Birdoswald under Julius Marcellinus, centurion of *II Augusta*. *RIB* 1880

Undated: Birdoswald (probably) under the tribune Julius Saturninus. *RIB* 1881

Undated: Birdoswald under the tribune Do[mitius H]onor[atus]. *RIB* 1884 (see *Brit.* xxii (1992), 309, (e))

Undated: Birdoswald under the tribune Statius Longinus. *RIB* 1887

Undated: Birdoswald under the tribune M. Claudius Menander (during the governorship of Modius Julius, said to be *c*.219, see his biography). *RIB* 1914

Undated: Birdoswald under the tribune Reginius Justinus (unit not named). *Brit.* v (1974), 462-3, no. 9

cohors I Augusta Nervia/Nervana Germanorum milliaria equitata

122 (Jul 17): diploma. *CIL* xvi.69

127 (Aug 20): diploma. Nollé (forthcoming)

158 (Feb 27): diploma. *Brit.* xxiii (1992), 463-4, no. 28

178 (Mar 23): diploma. *RMD* 184

Undated: Bewcastle? (but recorded at Netherby), dedication to Cocidius by Paternius Maternus, tribune of *cohors I Nervana*. *RIB* 966

Undated: Burgh-by-Sands under the tribune Arrius Ursinianus/Q. Pius Asinianus (reading uncertain)? *RIB* 2041

Undated: Birrens, altar dedicated to Fortuna by the unit. *RIB* 2093

Undated: Birrens, under the tribune L. Faenius Felix. *RIB* 2097

cohors I Tungrorum milliaria

90-100: Vindolanda under the prefect Julius Verecundus (*Tab. Vindol.* II.154)

103 (Jan 19): diploma. *CIL* xvi.48 (*RIB* 2401.1)

122 (Jul 17): diploma. *CIL* xvi.69

122-38: Carrawburgh. *JRS* lvi (1966), 218, no. 5

124 (Sep 16): diploma. *CIL* xvi.70 (*RIB* 2401.6)

127 (Aug 20): diploma. Nollé (forthcoming)

135 (Apr 14): diploma (damaged reference may correctly be to *ala I Tungrorum*). *CIL* xvi.82 (*RIB* 2401.8)

139-61: Castlecary. *RIB* 2155

146 (Jan-Mar): diploma. *RMD* 97 (*RIB* 2401.9)

300s: Housesteads. *ND* xl.40

Undated: Vindolanda, tombstone of the (legionary?) centurion T. Ann[...], possibly serving as commander of *[coh I] Tungr[orum]*. Location and style suggest a date at the beginning of the second century. *Brit.* xxix (1998), 299-305

Undated: Housesteads under the prefect Q. Florius Maternus. *RIB* 1578, 1591

Undated: Housesteads under the prefect P. Aelius Modestus. *RIB* 1580

Undated: Housesteads under the prefect Q. Julius Maximus. *RIB* 1584

Undated: Housesteads under the prefect Q. Julius [Cur?]sus. *RIB* 1585

Undated: Housesteads under the prefect Q. Verius Superstis. *RIB* 1586

Undated tiles: Hare Hill. *RIB* 2477

cohors II Tungrorum milliaria equitata civium Latinorum

139-61?: Cramond. *RIB* 2135 (revised reading)

157-8: Birrens. *RIB* 2110

241: Castlesteads under the prefect T. Claudius Claudianus, and the *princ(eps)* P. Aelius Martinus. *RIB* 1983

Undated: Castlesteads under the prefect Albius Severus. *RIB* 1981

Undated: Castlesteads under the prefect Aurelius Optatus and the *princ(eps)* Messius Obse[quens]. *RIB* 1982

Undated: Birrens for the prefect P. Campanius Italicus. *RIB* 2094

Undated: Birrens under the prefect G. Silvius Auspex. *RIB* 2100, 2104, 2108

Undated: Birrens. *RIB* 2092

cohors I Vangionum milliaria equitata

c. 92-103: Vindolanda? *equites Vardulli* (detached from this unit?). *Tab. Vindol.* II.181

103 (Jan 19): diploma. *CIL* xvi.48 (*RIB* 2401.1)

122 (Jul 17): diploma. *CIL* xvi.69

124 (Sep 16): diploma. *CIL* xvi.70 (*RIB* 2401.6)

135 (Apr 14): diploma. *CIL* xvi.82 (*RIB* 2401.8)

158 (Feb 27): diploma. *Brit.* xxiii (1992), 463-4, no. 28

178 (Mar 23): diploma. *RMD* 184

205-8: Risingham under the tribune L. Aemilius Salvianus. *RIB* 1239 (and undated, *RIB* 1215)

211-17? (or Marcus Aurelius for 169-77): Risingham (unit not named but see the numerous examples below) by the tribune M. Messorius Diligens. *RIB* 1237

213: Risingham. *RIB* 1235

Undated: Colchester, tombstone, name lost, unit uncertain (possibly *I Vardullorum*). Probably a veteran, rather than an indication of a garrison. *RIB* 205

Undated: Risingham under the tribune Aemilius Aemilianus. *RIB* 1216

Undated: Risingham under the tribune Julius Victor. *RIB* 1217

Undated: Risingham under the tribune M. Peregrinius Super. *RIB* 1231

Undated: Risingham under the tribune Julius Paullus. *RIB* 1241

Undated: Risingham under the [tribune] M. Aurelius Castus. *RIB* 1242

Undated: Risingham under the tribune G. Valerius Longinus (unit not named but location makes it highly probable it is this one). *RIB* 1210 (**61**)

Undated: Risingham under the tribune G. Julius Publilius Pius (unit not named but see previous). *RIB* 1220, 1221

Undated: Risingham under the tribune Julius Severinus (unit not named but as previous). *RIB* 1212

Undated: Benwell under the prefect [....] Cassi[anus?]. *RIB* 1328

Undated: Chesters, tombstone of Fabia Honorata, daughter of the tribune Fabius Honoratus. *RIB* 1482

cohors I fida Vardullorum milliaria equitata civium Romanorum

98: diploma. *CIL* xvi.43 ([I] fida Vardullorum)

105 (May-Jul): diploma. *CIL* xvi.51 (*RIB* 2401.2)

122 (Jul 17): diploma. *CIL* xvi.69

124 (Sep 16): diploma. *CIL* xvi.70 (*RIB* 2401.6)

135 (Apr 14): diploma. *CIL* xvi.82 (*RIB* 2401.8)

138-61: Castlecary under the tribune Trebius Verus. *RIB* 2149 (this man may be mentioned on the diploma of 159 (see below).145-146 (Dec 10-Dec 9): diploma. *CIL* xvi.93 (*RIB* 2401.10)

158 (Feb 27): diploma. *Brit.* xxiii (1992), 463-4, no. 28

159? (this date is only estimated): diploma, recording [...] Verus (Trebius Verus?, see above), commanding the unit and [Satu]rninus, a veteran, who came from Gloucester. *CIL* xvi.130 (*RIB* 2401.12)

c. 175-8: Lanchester under the tribune Flavius Titianus. *RIB* 1083

178 (Mar 23): diploma. *RMD* 184

216: High Rochester. *RIB* 1279 (35)

218-22?: High Rochester under the tribune L. Caecilius Optatus. *RIB* 1272

220: High Rochester under the tribune P. Aelius Erasinus. *RIB* 1280 (name restored from *RIB* 1286)

225-35: High Rochester under the tribune Aurelius Quintus. *RIB* 1281

238-41: High Rochester under the tribune Cassius Sabinianus. *RIB* 1262

Undated (but 161-9 or later): Corbridge under the tribune [Calpur]nius Vic[tor]. *RIB* 1128

Undated: on Hadrian's Wall (mc 19), recording the building of a temple to the Matres, directed by Publius D(...) V(...) (rank not stated). *RIB* 1421

Undated: High Rochester under the tribune T. Licinius Valerianus. *RIB* 1263

Undated: Cappuck under the tribune G. Quintius Severus. *RIB* 2118

cohors I Afrorum equitata civium Romanorum
122 (Jul 17): diploma. *CIL* xvi.69

cohors I Alpinorum
103 (Jan 19): diploma. *CIL* xvi.48 (*RIB* 2401.1)

cohors I Aquitanorum
122 (Jul 17): diploma. *CIL* xvi.69

124 (Sep 16): diploma. *CIL* xvi.70 (*RIB* 2401.6)

127 (Aug 20): diploma. Nollé (forthcoming)

114-30 (but not 122, 124, or 127): diploma (identification not certain). *CIL* xvi.88 (*RIB* 2401.7)

*c.*158: Brough-on-Noe under the prefect Capitonius [...]scus. *RIB* 283

Undated: Bakewell under the prefect Q. Sittius Caecilianus. *RIB* 278

Undated: Carrawburgh under the prefect [...]ius Nepos. *RIB* 1550 (usually dated to 130-3 on the grounds that the governor S. Julius Severus is mentioned; his name is in fact not visible but note above that by *c.*158 the unit was at Brough-on-Noe)

Undated: Leicester, lead sealings. *RIB* 2411.95-6

Undated tiles: Brancaster. *RIB* 2466 (*RIB* II states these are third century; only the date of the fort indicates they could not be earlier, the tiles are themselves undated)

cohors I Asturum equitata
ND xl.42: Chesters — probably an error, see *cohors II Asturum* below

cohors II Asturum equitata
105 (May-Jul): diploma. *CIL* xvi.51 (*RIB* 2401.2)

122 (Jul 17): diploma. *CIL* xvi.69

124 (Sep 16): diploma. *CIL* xvi.70 (*RIB* 2401.6)

127 (Aug 20): diploma. Nollé (forthcoming)

225: Greatchesters under the legionary centurion Valerius Martialis. *RIB* 1738

300s: Greatchesters. *ND* xl.42 (*ND* records *I Asturum* — presumably an error)

Undated: Llanio. *RIB* 407, 408

Undated: Bainbridge, lead sealing. *RIB* 2411.97

Undated tiles: Greatchesters. *RIB* 2467.1-2

cohors I Baetasiorum civium Romanorum
103 (Jan 19): diploma. *CIL* xvi.48 (*RIB* 2401.1)

122 (Jul 17): diploma. *CIL* xvi.69 (*I Betasiouru*)

124 (Sep 16): diploma. *CIL* xvi.70 (*RIB* 2401.6)

139-61: Bar Hill. *RIB* 2170 (unit name restored from *RIB* 2169)

139-61: Old Kilpatrick under the prefect Publicius Maternus, work carried out by Julius Candidus, centurion with *I Italica*. *Brit.* i (1970), 310, no. 20. The arguments about this unit and a later occupation of the Antonine Wall (see Frere 1987, 152-3, n. 34, and above under *VI Victrix* — Antonine) are too arcane to be recounted here and of dubious merit.

300s: Reculver. Under command of *comes litoris Saxonici*. *ND* xxviii.18

Undated: Maryport under the prefect T. Attius Tutor. *RIB* 830, 837, 842

Undated: Maryport under the prefect Ulpius Titianus. *RIB* 838, 843

Undated tiles: Reculver. *RIB* 2468

cohors I Batavorum equitata

122 (Jul 17): diploma. *CIL* xvi.69

124 (Sep 16): diploma. *CIL* xvi.70 (*RIB* 2401.6)

135 (Apr 14): diploma. *CIL* xvi.82 (*RIB* 2401.8)

178 (Mar 23): diploma. *RMD* 184

post 198-211: Carrawburgh under the prefect A. Cluentius Habitus. *RIB* 1545

213-22: Carrawburgh (HW) under the prefect L. Antonius Proculus. *RIB* 1544

237: Carrawburgh under the prefect Burrius [....].stus. *RIB* 1553

300s: Carrawburgh. *ND* xl.39

Undated: Carrawburgh under the prefect Titus D[...] Cosconianus. *RIB* 1534 (**58**)

Undated: Carrawburgh under the prefect M. Flaccinius Marcellus. *RIB* 1536

Undated: Carrawburgh under the prefect M. Simplicius Simplex(?) (unit not named). *RIB* 1546

Undated: Carvoran. *RIB* 1823, 1824

Undated: Carrawburgh under the prefect M. Hispanius Modestinus. *JRS* li (1961), 193, no. 9

Undated: Hadrian's Wall (near mc 59), by the centurion Martius. *RIB* 2015

cohors III Batavorum

c. 92-103: Vindolanda? *Tab. Vindol.* II.263

cohors IX Batavorum

c. 92-103: Vindolanda under the prefect Flavius Cerealis. *Tab. Vindol.* II.159, 225-90

cohors I Bracaraugustanorum equitata?

Undated: York, possibly an altar dedicated by P. Aelius Marcianus prefect of possibly *cohors I Bracaraugustanorum*. *RIB* 649 (see note citing Birley)

cohors III Bracaraugustanorum equitata

103 (Jan 19): diploma. *CIL* xvi.48 (*RIB* 2401.1)

122 (Jul 17): diploma. *CIL* xvi.69

124 (Sep 16): diploma. *CIL* xvi.70 (*RIB* 2401.6)

127 (Aug 20): diploma. Nollé (forthcoming)

145-146 (Dec 10-Dec 9): diploma. *CIL* xvi.93 (*RIB* 2401.10)

158 (Feb 27): diploma. *Brit.* xxiii (1992), 463-4, no. 28

Undated tiles: Manchester. *RIB* 2469.i-iii

Undated tiles: Melandra Castle. *RIB* 2469.iv

cohors IIII Breucorum

122 (Jul 17): diploma. *CIL* xvi.69

130-3: Bowes (or possibly IIII Delmatarum). *RIB* 739

213-22: altar dedicated by Julius Gr[....]nus, *actar[ius]*, at Ebchester. *RIB* 1101

Undated: 'Lincolnshire', bronze skillet with punched-dot inscription *coh(ors) IIII Bre(ucorum)*. *RIB* 2415.41 (re-examined: *Brit.* xxvi (1995), 390, (h))

Undated tiles: Aldborough, Castleford, Castlehaw, Ebchester, Grimescar, Manchester, Slack. *RIB* 2470

[cohors?] Brittonum (type of unit unknown)

Undated altar: Castlecary. *RIB* 2152

cohors I Celtiberorum
105 (May-Jul): diploma. *CIL* xvi.51 (*RIB* 2401.2)
122 (Jul 17): diploma. *CIL* xvi.69
127 (Aug 20): diploma. Nollé (forthcoming)
145-146 (Dec 10-Dec 9): diploma. *CIL* xvi.93 (*RIB* 2401.10)
158 (Feb 27): diploma. *Brit.* xxiii (1992), 463-4, no. 28

cohors I Aelia Classica
145-146 (Dec 10-Dec 9): diploma. *CIL* xvi.93 (*RIB* 2401.10)
158 (Feb 27): diploma. *Brit.* xxiii (1992), 463-4, no. 28, under the prefect [.] Caecidius Severus
300s: *Tunnocelo* (unknown) *ND* xl.51
Undated: Hadrian's Wall (nr t25a), centurial stone recording a cohort probably from this unit. *Brit.*
    xvii (1986), 368, no. 9
Undated: Ravenglass, lead sealing. *RIB* 2411.94. N.B. another diploma of 158, identical to that cited
    above but very fragmentary, belonging to a veteran of *cohors I Aelia Classica* was found close to the
    fort at Ravenglass (*Brit.* xxvi (1995), 389-90 (f)).

cohors I Cornoviorum
300s: Newcastle. *ND* xl.34

cohors I Cubernorum, see *cohors I Ulpia Traiana Cugernorum*

cohors I Ulpia Traiana Cugernorum civium Romanorum
103 (Jan 19): diploma. *CIL* xvi.48 (*RIB* 2401.1)
122 (Jul 17): diploma. *CIL* xvi.69
124 (Sep 16): diploma. *CIL* xvi.70 (*RIB* 2401.6)
140-4: milestone near Cramond. *RIB* 2313
213: Newcastle. *Brit.* xi (1980), 405, no. 6. Reading uncertain.
Undated: Carrawburgh, altar dedicated by Aurelius Campester to Coventina. *RIB* 1524

cohors I Dalmatarum/Delmatarum
122 (Jul 17): diploma. *CIL* xvi.69
124 (Sep 16): diploma. *CIL* xvi.70 (*RIB* 2401.6)
135 (Apr 14): diploma. *CIL* xvi.82 (*RIB* 2401.8)
138-61: Maryport under the prefect P. Postumius Acilianus. *RIB* 832 (and also 810, 847, 850)
158 (Feb 27): diploma. *Brit.* xxiii (1992), 463-4, no. 28
Undated: Maryport under the prefect L. Caecilius Vegetus. *RIB* 831
Undated: Chesters. *JRS* xlvii (1957), 229, no. 14 (**23**)

cohors II Dalmatarum/Delmatarum
105 (May-Jul): diploma. *CIL* xvi.51 (*RIB* 2401.2) (reading *[II Del]mata[rum]*)
122 (Jul 17): diploma. *CIL* xvi.69
127 (Aug 20): diploma. Nollé (forthcoming)
135 (Apr 14): diploma. *CIL* xvi.82 (*RIB* 2401.8), under the prefect Julius Maximus
300s: Carvoran. *ND* xl.43
Undated: Carvoran, altar dedicated by Julius Pastor, *imag(inifer)*. *RIB* 1795

cohors IIII Delmatarum
103 (Jan 19): diploma. *CIL* xvi.48 (*RIB* 2401.1)
118-38: Hardknot. *JRS* lv (1965), 222, no. 7
122 (Jul 17): diploma. *CIL* xvi.69

cohors I Frisiavonum/Frixagorum?
105 (May-Jul): diploma. *CIL* xvi.51 (*RIB* 2401.2)
122 (Jul 17): diploma. *CIL* xvi.69
124 (Sep 16): diploma. *CIL* xvi.70 (*RIB* 2401.6)
158 (Feb 27): diploma. *Brit.* xxiii (1992), 463-4, no. 28

23 Slab from Chesters, reused as a step down to the headquarters' strongroom, naming cohors I
Dalmat(arum). *It provides an instance of an infantry cohort at a cavalry fort where the other
testified units are all cavalry (see* **82**), *reflecting growing evidence of much more fluid military
situation. Undated, but the style is mid to late second century. Width 1.2m.* JRS *xlvii (1957),
229, no. 14*

178 (Mar 23): diploma. *RMD* 184
300s: Rudchester. *ND* xl.36 (giving '*Frixagorum*')
Undated: Melandra Castle. *RIB* 279
Undated: Manchester. *RIB* 577-9
Undated: Carrawburgh, altar dedicated by Mausaeus, *optio*, giving '*Frixiav(onum)*'. *RIB* 1523
Undated: Rudchester, the prefect Pub. Aelius Titullus (unit not named), perhaps commanding this
  unit on the basis of *ND*. *RIB* 1395
Undated: Rudchester, the prefect T. Claudius Decimus Cornelius Antonius (unit not named), as
  previous. *RIB* 1396

cohors II Gallorum equitata
122 (Jul 17): diploma. *CIL* xvi.69
127 (Aug 20): diploma. Nollé (forthcoming)
145-146 (Dec 10-Dec 9): diploma. *CIL* xvi.93 (*RIB* 2401.10)
158 (Feb 27): diploma. *Brit.* xxiii (1992), 463-4, no. 28
178 (Mar 23): diploma. *RMD* 184
c. 178: Old Penrith under the prefect T. Domitius Hieron. *RIB* 917 (dated and name confirmed by
  the unpublished diploma of 23 March 178, found Rhodope; see *Brit.* xxvi (1995), 390, (g))
225-38: Old Penrith under Aurelius [...] (rank lost), assuming the restoration of Severus Alexander's
  name to the unit title is correct. *RIB* 929
244-9: Old Penrith (naming *coh [II] Gallo[rum]*). *RIB* 915
Undated: Old Penrith under the prefect Aurelius Attianus (naming *[c]oh II [Gall(orum)]*). *RIB* 916
Undated: Old Penrith (unit not named), Julius Augustalis, *actor* of the prefect Julius Lupus. *RIB* 918
Undated: Piacenza (Italy), prefect of this unit L. Naevius Verus Roscianus, fulfilling a vow brought
  from Britain. *ILS* 2603

cohors IIII Gallorum equitata
127 (Aug 20): diploma. Nollé (forthcoming)
138-61(?): Castlehill under the prefect Q. Pisentius Justus. *RIB* 2195
145-146 (Dec 10-Dec 9): diploma. *CIL* xvi.93 (*RIB* 2401.10)
158 (Feb 27): diploma. *Brit.* xxiii (1992), 463-4, no. 28
178 (Mar 23): diploma. *RMD* 184
212-3: Vindolanda. *RIB* 1705
213-35: Vindolanda under the prefect Q. Petronius Urbicus. *RIB* 1686
223: Vindolanda, probably (unit number lost), during the governorship of Claudius Xenophon
    (here given as Xenephon; his dates fixed by *RIB* 2299, 2306). *RIB* 1706
276-82: Vindolanda commanded by Muc(ius) [.....]. *RIB* 1710
300s: Vindolanda. *ND* xl.41
Undated: Templeborough, tombstone of Cintusmus, *m(iles)*. *RIB* 619
Undated: Templeborough, tombstone of Crotus, *emerito*, aged 40. *RIB* 620
Undated: Risingham. *RIB* 1227
Undated: Risingham, tombstone, name lost, of a *m(iles)*, 14 years' service. *RIB* 1249
Undated: Vindolanda under the prefect Pituanius Secundus. *RIB* 1685
Undated: Vindolanda under the prefect L. [...]gius Pudens. *RIB* 1688
Undated: Castlesteads under the prefect Ca[.]s[...] Ir[...]. *RIB* 1979
Undated: Castlesteads under the prefect Volcacius Hospes. *RIB* 1980
Undated: Hadrian's Wall area (probably Vindolanda) under the prefect Naevius Hilarus. *RIB* 2062
Undated building stone: High Rochester, *vex(illatio) coh(ortis) IIII Gall(orum)*. *Brit.* xiv (1983), 337,
    no. 12
Undated tiles: Templeborough. *RIB* 2472.1-2

cohors V Gallorum equitata
122 (Jul 17): diploma. *CIL* xvi.69
127 (Aug 20): diploma. Nollé (forthcoming)
138-61(?): Cramond under the prefect L. Minthonius Tertullus. *RIB* 2134
158 (Feb 27): diploma. *Brit.* xxiii (1992), 463-4, no. 28
213?: South Shields. *Brit.* xvi (1985), 325-6, no. 11
222: South Shields. *RIB* 1060
Undated: South Shields. *RIB* 1059
Undated: South Shields, lead sealings. *RIB* 2411.100-105
Undated tiles: South Shields. *RIB* 2473.1-9

cohors I Hamiorum sagittaria
122 (Jul 17): diploma. *CIL* xvi.69
124 (Sep 16): diploma. *CIL* xvi.70 (*RIB* 2401.6)
127 (Aug 20): diploma. Nollé (forthcoming)
135 (Apr 14): diploma. *CIL* xvi.82 (*RIB* 2401.8)
136-8: Carvoran under the prefect T. Flavius Secundus. *RIB* 1778
139-61: Bar Hill under the prefect [C]aristian[ius J]ustinianus. *RIB* 2167
139-61: Bar Hill, tombstone of the prefect G. Julius Marcellinus. *RIB* 2172
158 (Feb 27): diploma. *Brit.* xxiii (1992), 463-4, no. 28
163-6: Carvoran under the prefect Licinius Clemens. *RIB* 1809

cohors I Hispanorum equitata/cohors I Aelia Hispanorum milliaria equitata
(These seem to be the same unit, doubled in size at some point in the early second century)
98: diploma. *CIL* xvi.43
103 (Jan 19): diploma. *CIL* xvi.48 (*RIB* 2401.1)
105 (May-Jul): diploma. *CIL* xvi.51 (*RIB* 2401.2)
122 (Jul 17): diploma. *CIL* xvi.69
124 (Sep 16): diploma. *CIL* xvi.70 (*RIB* 2401.6) ([I] Hisp)
127 (Aug 20): diploma. Nollé (forthcoming)
123-38?: Maryport under the tribune M. Maenius Agrippa (afterwards commander of *classis
    Britannica*). *ILS* 2735 with *RIB* 823 (see his biography, Chapter 9)

145-146 (Dec 10-Dec 9): diploma. *CIL* xvi.93 (*RIB* 2401.10)

178 (Mar 23): diploma. *RMD* 184

213-16?: Netherby, but most of the unit name is missing from the manuscript record of this slab, only *Ael(ia)* surviving. *RIB* 976

213-22 (or 213-16): Netherby under the tribune [...] Maximus, but the unit name is entirely missing and its attribution to this unit is exclusively by restoration. *RIB* 977

222: Netherby under the tribune M. Aurelius Salvius. *RIB* 978

222: Netherby, but once more the unit name is entirely missing. *RIB* 979

300s: possibly at Bowness. *ND* xl.49 (giving Stanwix in probable error; see *PNRB* p.221, note 49)

Undated: Maryport under the prefect M. Censorius [C]ornelianus, *c(enturio)* of *[X Fr]etensis*. *RIB* 814

Undated: Maryport under the prefect L. Antistius Lupus Verianus. *RIB* 816

Undated: Maryport under the tribune G. Caballius Priscus. *RIB* 817 (also, but with no unit name, *RIB* 818-20)

Undated: Maryport under the prefect P. Cornelius Ur[.....]. but unit name entirely restored. *RIB* 821

Undated: Maryport under the prefect Helstrius Novellus. *RIB* 822 (and 846, no unit name)

Undated: Maryport under the prefect L. Cammius Maximus (probably being transferred to *cohors XVIII Voluntariorum* in Pannonia Superior). *RIB* 827-9

Undated: Ardoch, tombstone of Ammonius, *c(enturio)*, 27 years' service. *RIB* 2213 (possibly 139-61 in date)

Undated tiles: Maryport. *RIB* 2474

cohors II Hispanorum

178 (Mar 23): diploma. *RMD* 184

cohors I Lingonum equitata

105 (May-Jul): diploma. *CIL* xvi.51 (*RIB* 2401.2)

122 (Jul 17): diploma. *CIL* xvi.69

139-43: High Rochester. *RIB* 1276 (**24**)

238-44: Lanchester under the prefect M. Aurelius Quirinus. *RIB* 1091, 1092 (**6, 37**)

Undated: Lanchester, unit number missing (possibly II, III or IIII), under the prefect [F]ulvius [Fel]ix. *Brit.* xix (1988), 492, no. 10

Undated: Corbridge, unit number missing (possibly II, III or IIII), naming Iliomarus, possibly *c(enturio)*. *RIB* 1186

cohors II Lingonum equitata

98: diploma. *CIL* xvi.43

122 (Jul 17): diploma. *CIL* xvi.69

124 (Sep 16): diploma. *CIL* xvi.70 (*RIB* 2401.6)

127 (Aug 20): diploma. Nollé (forthcoming), under the prefect C. Hedius Verus

158 (Feb 27): diploma. *Brit.* xxiii (1992), 463-4, no. 28

178 (Mar 23): diploma. *RMD* 184

300s: Drumburgh. *ND* xl.48

Undated: Ilkley under the prefect Clodius Fronto. *RIB* 635

Undated: Moresby under G. Pompeius Saturninus. *RIB* 798

Undated: Moresby under the prefect Valerius Lupercus. *RIB* 800

Undated: Brough-under-Stainmore, lead sealings. *RIB* 2411.106, 108

Undated: Ilkley, stamped tiles. *RIB* 2475

cohors III Lingonum equitata

103 (Jan 19)?: diploma (the text has III on one face, IIII on the other). *CIL* xvi.48 (*RIB* 2401.1)

122 (Jul 17): diploma. *CIL* xvi.69

178 (Mar 23): diploma. *RMD* 184

cohors IIII Lingonum equitata

103 (Jan 19)?: diploma (the text has III on one face, IIII on the other). *CIL* xvi.48 (*RIB* 2401.1)

24 Slab from High Rochester, reused in a water-tank by the headquarters. The clumsy text names the governor Quintus Lollius Urbicus (c. 139-43) and cohors I Lingonum. H(A)D has been jammed in before ANTONINO. The two leaf-stops in line one caused Antoninus Pius' name to be crammed in. In the last line E Q F, purportedly for eq(uitata) f(ecit), seems strangely widely-spaced. It may stand for e(quitata) q(uingenaria) f(ecit). Width 1.19m. RIB 1276

145-146 (Dec 10-Dec 9): diploma. *CIL* xvi.93 (*RIB* 2401.10)
158 (Feb 27): diploma. *Brit.* xxiii (1992), 463-4, no. 28
300s: Wallsend. *ND* xl.33
Undated: Wallsend under Julius Honoratus, *c(enturio)* of *II Augusta*. *RIB* 1299
Undated: Wallsend under the prefect Aelius Rufus. *RIB* 1300
Undated: Wallsend under the prefect [Cor]nelius Celer. *RIB* 1301
Undated: Wallsend (unit illegible), the prefect [Di]dius Severus. *RIB* 1302
Undated: Hadrian's Wall (E of mc 59). *RIB* 2014
Undated: Wallsend, lead sealing. *RIB* 2411.109
Undated: Wallsend, stamped tiles. *RIB* 2476.1-2

cohors I Menapiorum
122 (Jul 17): diploma. *CIL* xvi.69
124 (Sep 16): diploma. *CIL* xvi.70 (*RIB* 2401.6)

cohors I Morinorum et Cersiacorum
103 (Jan 19): diploma. *CIL* xvi.48 (*RIB* 2401.1)
122 (Jul 17): diploma. *CIL* xvi.69
114-30 (but not 122, 124, or 127): diploma. *CIL* xvi.88 (*RIB* 2401.7)
178 (Mar 23): diploma. *RMD* 184
300s: Ravenglass. *ND* xl.52
Undated: in Britain under the prefect Q. Servilius Pacuvianus. *CIL* iii.2049

cohors I Nerviorum
105 (May-Jul): diploma. *CIL* xvi.51 (*RIB* 2401.2)
Undated: Caer Gai (near Bala), statue of Hercules erected by Julius, *mil(es)*. *RIB* 418

cohors II Nerviorum civium Romanorum
98: diploma. *CIL* xvi.43
122 (Jul 17): diploma. *CIL* xvi.69
124 (Sep 16): diploma. *CIL* xvi.70 (*RIB* 2401.6)
127 (Aug 20): diploma. Nollé (forthcoming)
114-30 (but not 122, 124, or 127): diploma. *CIL* xvi.88 (*RIB* 2401.7)
213: Whitley Castle. *RIB* 1202
214-17: Whitley Castle, unit name entirely missing. *RIB* 1203
Undated: Whitley Castle, unit number missing. *RIB* 1198
Undated: Wallsend. *RIB* 1303
Undated: Carrawburgh, a vexillation of Texandri and Suevae from this unit. *RIB* 1538
Undated: Vindolanda, dedication to Cocidius by the prefect Decimus Caerellius Victor. *RIB* 1683
   (probably a private dedication at a nearby shrine)
Undated: High Rochester. *Brit.* xiv (1983), 337, no. 12 (a vexillation of a Nervian cohort, numeral
   lost, is known from Risingham. *RIB* 1240)
Undated: Brough-under-Stainmore, lead sealings. *RIB* 2411.111-40

cohors III Nerviorum
124 (Sep 16): diploma. *CIL* xvi.70 (*RIB* 2401.6)
127 (Aug 20): diploma. Nollé (forthcoming)
114-30 (but not 122, 124, or 127): diploma. *CIL* xvi.88 (*RIB* 2401.7)
135 (Apr 14): diploma. *CIL* xvi.82 (*RIB* 2401.8)
300s: Maryport. *ND* xl.53
Undated: Vindolanda under the prefect [..] Caninius [...]. *RIB* 1691
Undated: Maryport, tombstone, name lost, erected by Julius Senecianus. *JRS* lvii (1967), 204-5, no.
   14
Undated: Newstead, lead sealing. *RIB* 2411.142

cohors IIII Nerviorum
114-30 (but not 122, 124, or 127)?: diploma. *CIL* xvi.88 (*RIB* 2401.7)
135 (Apr 14): diploma. *CIL* xvi.82 (*RIB* 2401.8)

cohors VI Nerviorum
122 (Jul 17): diploma. *CIL* xvi.69
124 (Sep 16): diploma. *CIL* xvi.70 (*RIB* 2401.6)
127 (Aug 20): diploma. Nollé (forthcoming)
114-30 (but not 122, 124, or 127)?: diploma. *CIL* xvi.88 (*RIB* 2401.7)
135 (Apr 14): diploma. *CIL* xvi.82 (*RIB* 2401.8)
139-61?: Rough Castle, under the command of Flavius Betto, *c(enturio)* of *XX Valeria Victrix*. *RIB*
   2144.
139-61: Rough Castle. *RIB* 2145
145-146 (Dec 10-Dec 9): diploma. *CIL* xvi.93 (*RIB* 2401.10)
205: Bainbridge under the prefect L. Vinicius Pius. *JRS* li (1961), 192-3; amended in *JRS* lix (1969),
   246, Addenda and Corrigenda (b)
206: Bainbridge under the prefect L. Vi[nic]ius Pius. *RIB* 722
300s: Bainbridge. *ND* xl.56
Undated: Greatchesters under the prefect G. Julius Barbarus on a statue base. *RIB* 1731

cohors I Pannoniorum equitata?
Undated: Cawfields (HW mc 42). *RIB* 1667 (or more likely *II Pannoniorum*)

cohors II Pannoniorum
105 (May-Jul): diploma (number of unit lost). *CIL* xvi.51 (*RIB* 2401.2)
124 (Sep 16): diploma. *CIL* xvi.70 (*RIB* 2401.6)
Undated: Beckfoot under the prefect [....]lia. *RIB* 880
Undated: Cawfields (HW mc 42). *RIB* 1667 (or *I Pannoniorum* o/w untestified in Britain)
Undated: Vindolanda, lead sealing. *RIB* 2411.143

cohors V Pannoniorum?
Undated: Brough-under-Stainmore, lead sealing but the unit is otherwise unknown. *RIB* 2411.144

cohors V Raetorum equitata
122 (Jul 17): diploma. *CIL* xvi.69
Undated: Carrawburgh (HW), altar dedicated by P[...]anus, *m(i)l(es)*. *RIB* 1529

cohors VI Raetorum
Trajanic: in Britain under the prefect C. Rufius Moderatus. diploma. *CIL* iii.5202
166-9: Greatchesters (unit number dubious; may be VII or VIII, but neither of these is otherwise
    testified). *RIB* 1737
Undated: Brough-under-Stainmore, lead sealing. *RIB* 2411.147-51

cohors I Sunicorum/Sunucorum
122 (Jul 17): diploma. *CIL* xvi.69
124 (Sep 16): diploma. *CIL* xvi.70 (*RIB* 2401.6), under the prefect M. Junius Claudianus
127 (Aug 20): diploma. Nollé (forthcoming)
198-209: Caernarfon, restoration of an aqueduct. *RIB* 430

cohors I Thracum equitata civium Romanorum
122 (Jul 17): diploma. *CIL* xvi.69
127 (Aug 20): diploma. Nollé (forthcoming)
158 (Feb 27): diploma. *Brit.* xxiii (1992), 463-4, no. 28
178 (Mar 23): diploma. *RMD* 184
197-202: Bowes (building work supervised by Valerius Fronto, prefect of *ala Vettonum*). *RIB* 730
205-8: Bowes. *RIB* 740
205-8: Birdoswald, building with *cohors I Aelia Dacorum milliaria* under the tribune Aurelius Julianus.
    RIB 1909
Undated: Bowes under the prefect L. Caesius Frontinus. *RIB* 733, 734
Undated: Bowes under the prefect [...] Aem[ilian]us. *RIB* 741
Undated: Scargill Moor, near Bowes, under the prefect T. [O]rbius Pri[mia]nus (unit not named).
    Brit. xix (1988), 491, no. 7
Undated: Hadrian's Wall (near milecastle 4). *RIB* 1323

cohors II Thracum equitata
103 (Jan 19): diploma. *CIL* xvi.48 (*RIB* 2401.1)
122 (Jul 17): diploma. *CIL* xvi.69
139-61: Mumrills, tombstone of Nectovelius, 9 years' service (rank not stated but presumably *miles*).
    Unusually, this man states his origin and tells us he was from the *nationis Brigans*, 'the Brigantian
    tribe' of northern Britain, demonstrating that we need never automatically assume that
    members of auxiliary units had any connection with the nominal homelands. *RIB* 2142
178 (Mar 23): diploma. *RMD* 184
300s: Moresby. *ND* xl.50
Undated: Moresby under the prefect Mamius (or Manilius) Nepos. *RIB* 797
Undated: Moresby, tombstone of Smert[ri]us, *m(iles)*, 10 years' service. *RIB* 804

cohors VI Thracum
Undated: Gloucester, tombstone of Rufus Sita, *eques*, 22 years' service. *RIB* 121
Undated: Brough-under-Stainmore, lead sealing. *RIB* 2411.152-60

cohors VII Thracum
122 (Jul 17): diploma. *CIL* xvi.69
127 (Aug 20): diploma. Nollé (forthcoming)
135 (Apr 14): diploma. *CIL* xvi.82 (*RIB* 2401.8)
158 (Feb 27): diploma. *Brit.* xxiii (1992), 463-4, no. 28
178 (Mar 23): diploma. *RMD* 184, under the prefect Ulpius Marcianus
Undated: Brough-under-Stainmore, lead sealing. *RIB* 2411.161-92, 194-240

cohors ?? Thracum
Undated: Wroxeter, tombstone of T. Claudius Tirintius, *eq(ues)* in a *cohors Thracum* (unit number lost). With no parallels from Wroxeter or the area it cannot be allocated though *cohors VI Thracum* is a possibility. *RIB* 291

cohors Usiporum
83: transferred to Britain and participated in Agricolan campaign prior to mutinying and circumnavigating Britain. Tacitus (*Agricola*) xxviii.1, and Dio lxvi.20

cohors II Vasconum equitata civium Romanorum
105 (May-Jul): diploma. *CIL* xvi.51 (*RIB* 2401.2)
122 (Jul 17): diploma. *CIL* xvi.69
Undated: *in Britannia* under the prefecture of an unknown man who also served as tribune with *II Augusta*, stated on his tombstone from Ilipia (Baetica, Spain). *ILS* 2712

Vexillationes (vexillations of units otherwise not testified)
vexillatio M[a]r[sacorum?].
The name is restored from *ILS* 2508, naming a citizen of this tribe, and Tacitus (*Histories*) iv.56 also naming the tribe, though the actual unit is not otherwise testified.
222-35: Old Penrith. *RIB* 919 (drawing of a stone, long lost)

vexillatio G(aesatorum) R(aetorum)
Undated: Cappuck, as *ve[x]il(l)atio R(a)etorum Gaesat(orum)*, commanded by the tribune Julius Severinus. *RIB* 2117
Undated: Greatchesters, commanded by Tabellius Victor, *c(enturio)*, giving *G(aesatorum) R(a)eto(rum)*. *RIB* 1724
Undated: Risingham, under Aemilius Aemilianus, tribune of *cohors I Vangionum*. *RIB* 1216
Undated: Risingham, under Julius Victor, tribune of *cohors I Vangionum*. *RIB* 1217

vexillatio Germa[no]r(um) V[o]r[e]d(ensium)
Undated: Old Penrith. *RIB* 920 (from a seventeenth-century transcript)

vexil(latio) Raetor(um) et Noricor(um)
Undated: Manchester, commanded by a *[prae]posi[tus]*, name lost. These may be legionaries from *legio III Italica* and *legio II Italica* but there is no means of verification. *RIB* 576

vexillatio Sueborum Lon(govicianorum) Gor(dianae)
238-44: Lanchester. *RIB* 1074

Cunei
c[u]neus Frisionum Aballavensium Philipp(ianorum)
241: Papcastle. *RIB* 883 (and probably also 882)

cuneus Frisiorum Ver(covicianorum) Se(ve)r(iani) Alexandriani
222-35: Housesteads. *RIB* 1594

c(uneus) Fris(iorum) Vinovie(nsium)
Undated: Binchester. *RIB* 1036

cuneus Sarmatarum, Bremetenraco
(see also *n(umerus) eq(uitum) Sar[m(atarum)] Bremmetenn(acensium)* below)
300s: Ribchester *ND* xl.54
N.B. also Dio lxxi.16.2 stating the despatch of 5500 Sarmatian cavalry to Britain in the latter part of the reign of Marcus Aurelius. The unit is not specified and may have been temporary.

Equites

equites Catafractariorum
300s: *Morbio* (unknown). Under command of *dux Britanniarum*. *ND* xl.21

equites Crispianorum
317-26+: Doncaster? or Jarrow? Under command of *dux Britanniarum*. *ND* xl.20

equites Delmatarum
300s: *Praesidio* (unknown; *PNRB* suggests York). Under command of *dux Britanniarum*. *ND* xl.19

equites Dalmatarum Branodunensium
300s: Brancaster. Under command of *comes litoris Saxonici*. *ND* xxviii.16

equites stablesianorum Garrionnensium
300s: Burgh Castle. Under command of *comes litoris Saxonici*. *ND* xxviii.17

eq(uites) [St]ratonicianorum
Undated: Brougham, altar dedicated by Januarius to Mars. *RIB* 780

Milites

milites Tungrecanorum
300s: Dover (Kent). Under command of *comes litoris Saxonici*. *ND* xxviii.14

Numeri (and other unspecified units)

numerus Abulcorum, Anderidos
300s: Pevensey. Under command of *comes litoris Saxonici*. *ND* xxviii.20

numerus Alamannorum
372: in Britain under command of the tribune Fraomarius. Ammianus xxix.4.7

numerus Barc(ariorum)
Undated: Lancaster under the *p(rae)p(ositus)* Sabinus. *RIB* 601

numerus Barcariorum Tigrisiensium, Arbeia
300s: South Shields. Under command of *dux Britanniarum*. *ND* xl.22

numerus Batavorum
367: brought to Britain by Theodosius. Ammianus xxvii.8.7

numerus Concangensium
Undated tiles: Binchester (though the unit name refers to the fort name of Chester-le-Street, *Concangis*). *RIB* 2480.1-2

numerus Defensorum, Braboniaco
300s: Kirkby Thore. Under command of *dux Britanniarum*. *ND* xl.27

numerus Directorum, Verteris
300s: Brough. Under command of *dux Britanniarum*. *ND* xl.26

numerus Explorator(um) Brem(eniensium) Gor(diani)
238-44: High Rochester, under the tribune Cassius Sabinianus, commanding *cohors I Vardullorum*. *RIB* 1262
Undated: High Rochester, altar erected by the *dupl(icarii)* of the unit under the tribune Caepio Charitinus. *RIB* 1270

(numerus?) Expl[oratores Habitancenses?]
213: Risingham. *RIB* 1235

numerus Exploratorum, Lavatrae
300s: Bowes. Under command of *dux Britanniarum. ND* xl.25

numerus Exploratorum, Portum Adurni
300s: Portchester. Under command of *comes litoris Saxonici. ND* xxviii.21

numerus Fortensium, Othonae
300s: Bradwell-on-Sea. Under command of *comes litoris Saxonici. ND* xxviii.13

numerus Herulorum
367: brought to Britain by Theodosius. Ammianus xxvii.8.7

numerus Hnaudifridi
Undated: Housesteads. *RIB* 1576

numerus Joviorum
367: brought to Britain by Theodosius. Ammianus xxvii.8.7

numerus Longovicanorum, Longovicio
300s: Lanchester. Under command of *dux Britanniarum. ND* xl.30

numerus Magne<c>e(n)s(ium)
Undated: Carvoran. *RIB* 1825

n(umerus) Maur[o]rum Aur(elianorum) Valeriani Gallieniq(ue), Aballaba
253-8: Burgh-by-Sands under the tribune Caelius Vibianus. *RIB* 2042
300s: Burgh-by-Sands. Under command of *dux Britanniarum. ND* xl.47

numeri Moesiacorum
360: two *numeri* sent to Britain with Lupicinus. Ammianus xx.1.2

numerus Nerviorum Dictensium, Dicti
300s: Wearmouth? Under command of *dux Britanniarum. ND* xl.23

numerus Pacensium, Magis
300s: Burrow Walls? Under command of *dux Britanniarum. ND* xl.29

numerus Raetorum Gae[sa]torum
213: Risingham. *RIB* 1235

n(umerus) eq(uitum) Sar[m(atarum)]] Bremmetenn(acensium)
238-44: Ribchester, pedestal dedicated to Apollo Maponus. *RIB* 583
Undated tiles?: Bainesse, near Catterick, giving BSAR. *RIB* 2479

numerus Solensium, Maglone
300s: Old Carlisle? Under command of *dux Britanniarum. ND* xl.28

numerus Supervenientium Peturiensium, Derventione
300s: Malton. Under command of *dux Britanniarum. ND* xl.31

numerus S(yrorum) s(agittariorum)?
Undated: Kirkby Thore. *RIB* 764

numerus Turnacensium, Lemannis
300s: Lympne (Kent). Under command of *comes litoris Saxonici. ND* xxviii.15

numerus Victorum
367: brought to Britain by Theodosius. Ammianus xxvii.8.7

numerus vigilum, Concangios
300s: Chester-le-Street. Under command of *dux Britanniarum*. *ND* xl.24

Areani or *Arcani*
368-9: military border patrols or spies in Britain. They were in existence under Constans but Ammianus says they had been *a veteribus institutum*, 'established in early times'. By 369 they had become susceptible to bribes from barbarians. They are otherwise untestified. Ammianus xxviii.3.8

Venatores
venatores Banniesses
Undated: Birdoswald (HW), altar dedicated to Silvanus. Not necessarily a discrete unit, these hunters probably served in the resident garrison of *cohors I Aelia Dacorum* and styled themselves accordingly as a matter of pride. *RIB* 1905

Unspecified
Aeruli
360: sent to Britain with Lupicinus. Ammianus xx.1.2

Batavii
360: sent to Britain with Lupicinus. Ammianus xx.1.2

The following units are listed in the *Notitia Dignitatum* under the command of the *comes provinciarum Britanniarum* (nothing else is known about them though the *equites Honoriani seniores* suggest a date in the reign of Honorius or later (393-423)):
equites catafractarii juniores. *ND* vii.200
equites scutarii juniores. *ND* vii.201
equites Honoriani seniores. *ND* vii.202
equites Stablesiani. *ND* vii.203
equites Syri. *ND* vii.204
equites Taifali. *ND* vii.205

The *comes provinciarum Britanniarum* is also attributed with command of the following:
Victores juniores Britannici. *ND* vii.154
Primani juniores. *ND* vii.155
Secundani juniores. *ND* vii.156

3 Civil administration and organizations

THE PROVINCES OF BRITANNIA

Britannia consisted of England and Wales, together with such parts of southern and eastern Scotland as were under control at any given time. But the Empire will have regarded the whole island as technically her possession.

From 43 until some time during or just after the reign of Septimius Severus Britain was governed as a single province. From at least 216 until approximately 296 (when she was recovered after the Carausian and Allectan Revolt) Britain was divided into *Britannia Superior* (the south, Midlands and Wales), and *Britannia Inferior* (the north). This division was a consequence of the civil wars of 193-6 and was intended to prevent a governor of Britain ever again being able to exploit the province's substantial garrison in an attempt to become emperor.

From about 296 until the end Britain was further divided into *Maxima Caesariensis*, *Flavia Caesariensis*, *Britannia Prima* and *Britannia Secunda*. A fifth provincial name, *Valentia*, is known but whether this was a new province or a renamed one is uncertain. The exact boundaries of none of these provinces are known.

The hierarchy is also unknown. For example, *Britannia Inferior*'s governorship seems to have been synonomous with command of *VI Victrix*. Tiberius Claudius Paulinus is interesting in this respect. He is known from an inscription in Britain to have been governor without stating where, clarified on another from Vieux in Gaul to have been *in Britannia ad legionem sex(tam)*, 'in Britain, with the sixth legion' (see Chapter 9). The governorship of *Inferior* was thus in some senses nominally equal to that of *Superior* while in practice implicitly subordinate. Evidently Paulinus felt no need to be more specific.

London is believed to have been the official premier town of Britain from the years following the Boudican Revolt until the end. The presence of a procuratorial tombstone and other items associated with the office, a dedication perhaps by the *legatus iuridicus*, and textual references make it more than likely. In reality, apart from the various versions of the *acta* of the council of Arles in 314, London's rank is never stated in any source and the absence of any inscription which refers to London's status compounds the problem. Ptolemy said that London was a city of the *Cantii* (meaning the *Cantiaci*) which raises an interesting question about whether it ever actually achieved formal high status (see Mann (ii), 1998).

The following list details the evidence for the individual provinces. The numerous references to Britain as a whole in Tacitus, Suetonius, and other literary sources are not given here and likewise the references simply to the name *Britannia*, for example on the Togidubnian stone from Chichester (*RIB* 91).

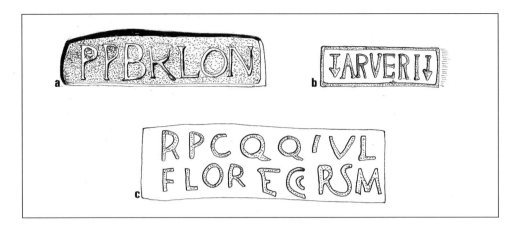

25 Tile-stamps. These three stamps were produced by the state, city, and private firms.

    a. stamp of the Procurator Provinciae BRitanniae LONdinii, *'procurator of the province of Britannia at London.'*

    b. stamp of the firm of Arverus. From Cirencester

    c. stamp of Rei Publicae Glevensium, *'the city government of Gloucester', from the civic tile-making site at St Oswald's Priory. This example also bears the names of the* duoviri QuinQuennales *for an unknown year: J(ulius) Flor(us), and another whose name is uncertain.*

43-196/216

Britannia

Post 61: tombstone from London naming G. Julius Alpinus Classicianus (see his biography, chapter 9) as *proc(urator) provinc(iae) Brit[anniae]*. Its provenance implies that London was now the capital of *Britannia*. The stone is the earliest from Britain bearing the name of the province of *Britannia*. Classicianus is testified in London as procurator following the Boudican Revolt. His date of death is unknown but it presumably occurred while he was in office. See also below under *Procurator Augusti provinciae Britanniae. RIB* 12

102/106?: a stone from London purportedly commemorating Trajan's victory in Dacia of 102 or 106 can be restored to read that it was made by the *[le]g(atus) [Augusti iuridi]cus [provinciae Bri]tanniae*. The restored text referring to Dacia is highly dubious and calls the date into question. However, that the dedication had been made by an unnamed imperial juridical legate is slightly more convincing. *RIB* 8

Undated: tiles from London recording the procuratorial office of the province of *Britannia* at London (see under *procurator Augusti* below). *RIB* 2485 (**25**)

Undated: a slab (now lost) dedicated to *Num(en) C[aes)ari Aug(usti)]* from Nicholas Lane, London, names *prov[incia] Brita[nnia]*. It cannot be dated but the dedication was presumably made by the provincial council. *RIB* 5

196/216-296

Britannia Superior

Post 196: Herodian states that control of Britain was divided into two separate commands by Severus. Herodian iii.8.2.

Post 196: *Britannia Superior* is named by Dio Cassius as containing *II Augusta* and *XX Valeria Victrix*. Dio lv.23.2-6

255-60: *Britannia Superior* was governed by a man of senatorial rank, in this case Desticius Juba recorded at Caerleon (*RIB* 334). Two undated examples of a *beneficiarius consularis* of *Britannia Superior* in northern locations (Greta Bridge, *RIB* 745, and Vindolanda, *RIB* 1696) suggest that

Britannia Inferior was subordinate to *Superior*.

Undated: *Britannia Superior* is recorded on a dedication slab by Postumius Urbanus, rank or post lost, from Greta Bridge. *RIB* 747

Undated: a lead sealing from Combe Down bears P B R S, in theory for *p(rovinciae) Br(itanniae) S(uperioris)*, and an image of a stag (*RIB* 2411.37). But another, from the Roman wharf at London, also bears the stag but with the legend BRITA SANC, for *Brita(nnia) Sanc(ta)*, 'holy Britannia' (*RIB* 2411.33). Clearly the Combe Down example's S might stand for *sancta* too but see the *B(ritannia) I(nferior)* examples below.

Britannia Inferior

Post 196: *Britannia Inferior* is named by Dio Cassius as containing *VI Victrix*. Dio lv.23.2-6

223: Claudius Xenophon/Xenephon is supposedly named as *[l]eg(ato) [Aug(usti)] n(ostri) pr(o) [pr(aetore) Br(itanniae) Inf(erioris)]*, 'our imperial propraetorian legate of Britannia Inferior', on a dedication at Vindolanda by *cohors IIII Gallorum* in the reign of Severus Alexander (222-35). However, the relevant part of the inscription is entirely restored and there is no precedent for the restoration (but see next example). His tenure is known to have covered December 222 to December 223. *RIB* 1706

237: named on an altar at Bordeaux dedicated by M. Aurelius Lunaris, *sevir Aug(ustalis)* at the colonies of York and Lincoln in *prov(inciae) Brit(anniae) Inf(erioris)*, with the consul names for the year 237 in the reign of Maximinus I. *JRS* xi (1922), 102

Undated: lead seals with the legend P B I for *p(rovinciae) B(ritanniae) I(nferioris)* and a picture of a bull, presumably the symbol of *Britannia Inferior*. *RIB* 2411.34 (Felixstowe, Suff, probably from the Saxon Shore fort at Walton Castle now destroyed by coastal erosion); 2411.35 (York); 2411.36 (Binchester, Durham); possibly an example from Aldborough, depending on the restored text [P]B[I] (*Brit.* xix (1988), 504, no. 97).

Provinciae Britanniae

An inscription referring to 'the provinces of Britannia' could date to any point after the division of Britain by Severus. A marble slab from Rome bears the text *devotissimae votorum ... provinciae Britanniae*. The slab and its possible significance are discussed and illustrated by Beard (1980).

296-410

Maxima Caesariensis (SE England and East Anglia)

312-4: Verona List vii (*PNRB*, 76-7)

300s: *ND* xxiii.10, governed by a consular governor

315+: lead sealing from Silchester, restored as *[p(rovincia)] M(axima) C(aesariensis)*. The inclusion of the Christian Chi-Rho symbol means it should post-date the Edict of Milan in 315. *Brit.* xx (1989), 345, *addenda* (c) and Boon 1974, 183, and fig. 24.7

Britannia Prima (Wales, south-west, west Midlands)

Post 296: column base from Cirencester naming *B[ritannia]* on one line, and *Primae Provinciae* on another. Dedicated to Jupiter by the governor (*pr[aeses]* and *rector*) Lucius Septimius [...]. *RIB* 103 (**26**)

312-4: Verona List vii (*PNRB*, 76-7)

300s: *ND* xxiii.13, governed by a *praeses*

Flavia Caesariensis (NE Midlands and Lincolnshire)

312-4: Verona List vii (*PNRB*, 76-7)

300s: *ND* xxiii.15, governed by a *praeses*

Britannia Secunda (northern Britain)

312-4: Verona List vii (*PNRB* 76-7)

300s: *ND* xxiii. 14, governed by a *praeses*

Valentia (unknown = *Maxima Caesariensis*?)

300s: *ND* xxiii.11, governed by a consular governor

368: Ammianus xxx.3.7 (see note below)

26 One face of the Jupiter column base from Cirencester. This component names Septimius, governor of (Britannia) Prima, primae provinciae rector. The other faces describe the restoration of the column according to the 'old' religion. It must date after 296 and probably before the Edict of Milan in 313. However, a later date, perhaps under the pagan Julian II (360-3), is possible. Width 430mm. RIB 103

After 367

Ammianus Marcellinus describes the restoration by Theodosius of a British province, now named *'Valentia'* to commemorate the event occurring under Valentinian I (364-75). Either this means one of the existing four provinces had been renamed or subdivided, or there was a new province which was a territorial accretion to Roman Britain.

Ammianus says the province was 'recovered' (*recuperatam*), 'restored' (*reddiderat*), and, 'thereafter' (*deinde*) named *Valentia*. This clearly implies that a province, previously named something else, was now called *Valentia*. However, the *Notitia* appears to list five provinces of Britain. *Valentia* is the second named, following *Maxima Caesariensis* and was also governed by a senator, *consularis*, whereas all the others were governed by an equestrian *praeses*.

One of the most convincing explanations which has been proposed is that, because the Notitia was compiled at different times, a mistake crept in and *nunc* was omitted. Restored, the text reads *Maxima Caesariensis nunc Valentia* ('Maxima Caesariensis, now [named] *Valentia*'). On the assumption that *Maxima* was the south-east with London as its capital, this fits the description of events by Ammianus, in particular the lack of any reference to fighting outside the London area. This also explains why it is listed as being under a senatorial command.

In reality the position will remain unresolved until, or if, an inscription is found. This is most unlikely to occur but illustrates the futility of the present debate, which does not have the resources to provide an unequivocal solution.

Source: Ammianus xxviii.3.7

CIVIL AND MILITARY GOVERNMENT *c.*43-296

legatus Augusti pro praetore — imperial propraetorian legate

The Roman world maintained for as long as possible the fiction that the Republic was intact. The Empire was theoretically governed by a hierarchy of magistrates drawn from the uppermost tiers of Roman society, the senators and the equestrians. Augustus had, however, created a situation in which one man occupied a unique collection of those magistracies. He and his successors thus held supreme power in practice but professed themselves to be guardians and restorers of the constitution, *senatus consulto*, 'by order of the senate'. Augustus' personal prestige allowed him to bequeath this eligibility to an exceptional portfolio to his nominated successor. The title *imperator*, 'general', was included in the portfolio and came to be synonomous with supreme power.

The Roman Empire was made up of two classes of provinces: senatorial provinces, and imperatorial provinces. Senatorial provinces, as their name suggests, were controlled by the Senate though obviously in practice only because the emperor allowed it. Their governors were selected from the proconsuls, senators who already served as consuls in Rome.

Imperatorial provinces were usually those where the army was stationed and which had been acquired through military conquest. The army was controlled by the emperor, as *imperator*, himself of proconsular rank. As the spoils of war such provinces were the property of the emperor. Their government was therefore his immediate concern. In practice he could not administer such vast tracts of territory so control was delegated to his personal representatives, the *legati*.

The *legati* normally had to be senators of propraetorian status, those who had already been praetors. Usually they served as governors for about three to four years, but this was liable to extension where military requirements made continuity essential, or curtailment when incompetence, illness, or a change of regime occurred. There were, at different times, exceptions to the centralized powers of the governor. Day-to-day legal administration might be the preserve of a *legatus iuridicus*, and finance was the responsibility of an equestrian *procurator Augusti*.

Britain, like other heavily-garrisoned frontier provinces, had senior governors who had already served as consuls, and were therefore of proconsular rank. But being a grade higher than propraetorian governors of imperial provinces created an anomaly in which the proconsular governor was equivalent in nominal personal rank to the emperor. To avoid this, the post of governor of Britain was always officially graded as propraetorian, and described as such on inscriptions (**12**).

Military diplomas, recording the honourable discharge of auxiliary veterans, name the governor but not his position. They merely state imperial titles and a consular date before proceeding to list the military units which *sunt in Britannia sub* ('are in Britain under [...]'). A name follows which is obviously that of the governor, sometimes confirmed explicitly on stone inscriptions. Not all inscriptions are unequivocal, however. A slab from Bainbridge refers to Gaius Valerius Pudens as merely being of distinguished consular rank (*amplissimi co(n)sularis*).

For the period after about 197 we know the names of very few governors of *Britannia Superior*. More governors of *Inferior* are known but are mostly such obscure individuals it was probably a minor post handed to men who had little or no future in more elevated circles. Many are known only from their appearance on inscriptions in Britain.

During the fourth century the governing structure of Britain was completely altered, largely as a result of the new system created by Diocletian. Not only was she divided into four provinces but a whole range of new positions were introduced: *vicarius*, *praeses*, *dux*, and *comes* (see below).

Known legates of Britain (all dates are approximate). For details of individuals see the biographies in Chapter 9:

A. Plautius 43-7
P. Ostorius Scapula 47-51/2
A. Didius Gallus 51/2-7
Q. Veranius 57/8
G. Suetonius Paullinus 57/8-61
P. Petronius Turpilianus 61-63
M. Trebellius Maximus 63-69
M. Vettius Bolanus 69-71
Q. Petillius Cerialis 71-73/4
S. Julius Frontinus 73/4-77/78
G. Julius Agricola 77/78-83/84
....
Sallustius Lucullus (under Domitian) c.84-94
....
P. Metilius/Maecilius Nepos -98
T. Avidius Quietus 98-102?
L. Neratius Marcellus 102?-6?
....
M. Atilius Metilius Bradua Trajan/Hadrian. Perhaps 114-18
Q. Pompeius Falco 118?-22
A. Platorius Nepos 122-6
(L.?) Trebius Germanus 126-30
S. Julius Severus 130-3/4
P. Mummius Sisenna 133/4-8
Q. Lollius Urbicus 138-42?
G. Papirius Aelianus 142?-6
....
Gn. Julius Verus 158
[..]anus L[.....] 154 or 159
M. Statius Priscus 161-2
S. Calpurnius Agricola 163
Q. Antistius Adventus -177?
Ulpius Marcellus c.177-84

P. Helvius Pertinax c.185
Clodius Albinus c.192-7
Virius Lupus c.197-202
C. Valerius Pudens 205
L. Alfenus Senecio 205-8
    (or possibly A. Triarius Rufinus c.211)
C. Julius Marcus 213
....
after c.213/16:
Britannia Inferior
Se[m]p[ronius?] 213-16
[M. Antonius Gor?]dianus 216
Modius Julius early 200s (c. 219?)
T. Claudius Paulinus 220
Marius Valerianus 221/2
Claudius Xenophon/Xenephon 222-3
..... Maximus 225
Calvisius Rusonus c.225-35
V. Crescens Fulvianus c.225-35
Claudius Apellinus c.225-35
[T?]uccianus 237
Maecilius Fuscus 238-44
Egnatius Lucilianus 238-44
Nonius Philippus 242
....
Britannia Superior
200s? M. Martianius Pulcher
c. 225-35? Q. Aradius Rufinus
....
262-6 Octavius Sabinus under Postumus

legatus Augusti legionis — imperial legionary legate

Legionary commanders in Britain are far less well-known than the governors even though they were drawn from the same ranks but earlier in their careers. The post was reserved for those of senatorial rank prior to holding a consulship except for a short period during the reign of Commodus when equestrians were appointed. This is stated by Dio and apparently confirmed by the tombstone of L. Artorius Justus, prefect of *VI Victrix* (see Chapters 2, and 9). In many cases governors of Britain are quite often likely to have served earlier as legionary legates in Britain but this is only known for certain to have occurred in a small number of cases, for example Agricola or T. Claudius Paulinus.

Sources: see the lists of testified legionary legates in Britain under the legions in Chapter 2 and their individual biographies in Chapter 9.

legatus Augusti iuridicus — imperial judicial legate

The judicial delegate of the emperor seems to have been a Flavian creation. Unknown before this date, it was probably a necessary device in Britain and other heavily-garrisoned frontier provinces to liberate a governor preoccupied with campaigning. It was an intermediate rank between a legionary command and becoming a governor. Two early incumbents both commanded legions before becoming *legati iuridici* and after their time in Britain went on to provincial governorships elsewhere.

There is little evidence for their activities in Britain. A single case heard by one of them, L. Javolenus Priscus, regarding the estate of a helmsman in the *classis Britannica*, remained enshrined in legal records. An inscription from London (*RIB* 5 and see under *Britannia* above) may record a dedication in the name of the office while a scattering of legal documents, also from London, certainly suggest that this was where their headquarters lay (for example *RIB* 2504.29, amending *RIB* 2443.19, dated to 14 March 118 and relating to woodland in Kent).

By the late second century it was possible for a *legatus iuridicus* to serve as acting governor, recorded on a stone detailing the career of M. Antius Crescens Calpurnius.

Known judicial legates of Britain (see the individual biographies in Chapter 9):

C. Salvius Liberalis. *c.*75–85
L. Javolenus Priscus. *c.*85+? (but before 91)
M. Vettius Valens. 130s
C. Sabucius Major Caecilianus. 170s
M. Antius Crescens Calpurnius. 180s/190s

procurator Augusti provinciae Britanniae — imperial procurator of the province of Britain

Provincial financial affairs were allocated to an imperial procurator. Procurators in general were drawn from the ranks of the equestrians. Their various posts were graduated according to pay. The imperial procurator alleviated his governor from excessive responsibilities and also lessened the chances that the latter might exploit the system to line his own pockets or finance a rebellion. A procurator had no axe to grind because the governorships of almost all provinces, as senatorial posts, were beyond his reach. Instead he could hope for elevation to the great equestrian positions as prefect of the grain supply, of Egypt or, ultimately, of the Praetorian Guard.

In Britain an imperial procurator, Decianus Catus, is first testified by the year 60-1. Few others are known. A wooden writing tablet, marked with the official stamp of the imperial procuratorial office, is further evidence that the procurator was based in London. However, this tablet gives the office in plural suggesting that there may have been more than one incumbent at any given time, *Proc(uratores) Aug(usti) dederunt Brit(anniae) Prov(inciae)*, 'the imperial procurators of the province of Britain issued (this)'.

The post of procurator was also used for a host of minor administrative postings, for example at Combe Down (*RIB* 179), which should not be confused with provincial procuratorships.

Undated: some tiles from London are stamped P P BR LON, taken to stand for *Procurator Provinciae Britanniae Londinio*, 'Procurator of the Province of Britain at London' (but see Wright 1985, for a discussion of the possibilities). The stamp indicates provincial government control of stamps manufactured for the province, presumably for use in government establishments in London and its vicinity. Others have been found at Barking (Essex), Brockley Hill (Herts), and Saunderton (Bucks). Their use and distribution is covered by Betts (1995), but this predates the discovery of another example in Greenwich Park (south-east London) in July 1999 during an excavation initiated by a television programme. The site is not yet properly identified but finds, including inscriptions, suggest a monumental temple complex of official status. *RIB* 2485 (various)

Undated: wooden writing tablet from London stamped PROC AUG DEDERUNT BRIT PROV for *Procuratores Augusti dederunt provinciae Britanniae*, 'The imperial procurators of the province of Britain issued this'. The plural (from the verb and not from the usual convention PROCC) may be explained by the fact that the procuratorial office in London oversaw all procuratorial positions. *RIB* 2443.2

Known procurators of Britain (see the individual biographies in Chapter 9)

Decianus Catus. -61
Gaius Julius Alpinus Classicianus. 61-
Ti. Claudius Augustanus. *c.*78-84
Cn. Pompeius Homullus. *c.*85+
Q. Lusius Sabinianus. 2nd cent
M. Maenius Agrippa. Antonine
M. Cocceius Nigrinus, *c.*212-17
Oclatinius Adventus. *c.*205-8
C. Valerius Pansa
Sex. Varius Marcellus

rex magnus
See Chapter 7

CIVIL AND MILITARY GOVERNMENT POST-296

comes

The *comes*, literally 'companion', had its origins in the friends of the emperor serving as his military aides. They formed part of his personal retinue and accompanied him on campaign. These men were often appointed to prestigious posts like provincial governorships. Aulus Platorius Nepos was one of Hadrian's circle and this led him to the governorship of Britain in around 122, even though they later fell out.

By the early fourth century *comes* had become an official position in its own right and is now normally translated as 'count'. The *comes* was theoretically placed in charge of a unit of the mobile field army, regarded as the emperor's personal guard. Its purpose was to provide a rapid response in the form of mounted crack troops.

However, the *Notitia Dignitatum* records the *comes litoris Saxonici per Britanniam*, 'count of the Saxon shore in Britain', a force which was by definition anything but a crack mobile unit. This post was also described as being held by a *vir spectabilis*, a rank meaning 'man of the highest regard'. As a frontier (*limitaneus*) command this was an anomaly but requires no further explanation beyond observing that rigorous attention to precise terminology was by then a thing of the past. Other versions of the title are testified in Britain. Nectaridus, for example, called *comes maritimi tractus*, 'count of the maritime area', by Ammianus in 367 may very well have commanded the forts of the Saxon shore.

Another military command, *comes Britanniarum*, 'count of the Britons', or even 'count of the Britannias (i.e. the provinces of *Britannia*)', is also listed in the *Notitia*. He controlled a small number of mounted units, just the sort of soldiers a *comes* should have been in command of. But why they were in Britain is unknown.

The *comes sacrarum largitionum* was in charge of provincial finances and treasuries. The post means literally 'count in charge of state hand-outs', a kind of Orwellian 'Ministry of Grants' operating a punitive taxation system. He oversaw the *rationalis*, 'treasurer', and the *praepositus*, 'supervisor', of the treasury — stated by the *Notitia* to have been based in Britain and London respectively. We have no idea of any incumbents or their day-to-day duties.

Sources: SHA (Hadrian) iv.2 (for A. Platorius Nepos); ND xxviii.1, 12 (Saxon shore); Ammianus xxvii.8.1 (Nectaridus), and xxx.7.2-3 (Gratianus); ND xi.3 (*comes sacrarum largitionum*)

dux

Before the fourth century a provincial governor was responsible for military and some civil affairs. Under the fourth-century reorganization these responsibilities were split between a *dux* and a *praeses*. The *dux* oversaw the provincial army, sometimes stretching over more than one province, while the *praeses* maintained civilian administration.

Although *dux* is normally translated as 'duke', the word comes from *duco*, 'I lead', and so simply means 'leader'. A Roman *dux* had none of the hereditary territorial aristocratic associations we link with the term thanks to its medieval meaning.

The *Notitia Dignitatum* provides the only detailed record of what units the *dux* commanded. The entire army in all the four provinces of Britain, except those at the

Saxon Shore forts, fell under his control. They ranged from *VI Victrix* at York to a *numerus* of scouts at Bowes. However, some forts, such as Piercebridge and Binchester, have produced late-fourth-century pottery but are omitted from the *Notitia*. The explanation is likely to be either that occupation at omitted sites was civil rather than military or that sources used for compiling the *Notitia* were based on various differently-dated lists of dispositions. Another possibility is that garrisons based at these forts were not on official pay-rolls. The operation of private armies, funded by provincials, is testified in Gaul in the writings of Sidonius.

Sources: *ND* xl (units commanded by the *Dux*); Ammianus xxvii.8.10; see also the individual biographies in Chapter 9; Sidonius (*Letters*) III.iii.7 (the private army of Ecdicius)

praeses **and** *rector*

Praeses, the late-Roman governor, was technically an equestrian rank though the distinction was less relevant in the fourth century. The *Notitia* says that the provinces of *Britannia Prima, Secunda*, and *Flavia Caesariensis*, were each governed by a *praeses*, while *Maxima Caesariensis* was governed by a man of consular rank, *consularis*, by the time the *Notitia* was compiled. They were responsible to the *vicarius Britanniarum* who oversaw the diocese of Britain, made up of the respective British provinces. Its first appearance in Britain is at Lancaster on an inscription of 262-6 during the reign of Postumus.

Theoretically, the post was civil but Aurelius Arpagius, named on an inscription from Birdoswald of *c.*297-305, evidently had control of the frontier garrison in *Britannia Secunda*. The explanation may be that this was so early in Diocletian's reorganization that transfer of military responsibilities to a *dux* had not yet occurred. Nevertheless, it would be ridiculous to imply that we possess any detailed knowledge of how these offices operated.

The other appearance of the title is on the undated Jupiter column base from Cirencester. Lucius Septimius calls himself *pr(aeses)* of *Britannia Prima* and *rector*. The terms are essentially synonomous and illustrate the lack of precision and order in the late-Roman world.

Sources: *ND* xxiii.12-15; *RIB* 605 (Lancaster); *RIB* 1912 (Birdoswald); *RIB* 103 (Cirencester) (**26**)

vicarius

Regionalization of authority was a principle of Diocletian's new order. This began with the division of imperial responsibilties between two, then four, emperors. Provinces were also assembled into administrative blocks called dioceses. A diocese, made up of several provinces each with its own governor, *praeses*, and general, *dux*, was subject to overall control by a *vicarius.*

Britain, being made up of four provinces in the fourth century, had its own vicar, the *vicarius Britanniarum*.

Sources: Verona List vii (the diocese of Britain); *ND* xxiii (responsibilities of the *vicarius Britanniarum*)

Known vicars of Britain (see the individual biographies in Chapter 9):

L. Papius Pacatianus. 319   Civilis (called *pro praefectis*). *c.*367–
Martinus. -353   Chrysanthus. *c.*380-400
Alypius. 353-   Victorinus. *c.*380-400

REGIONAL GOVERNMENT

Britannia was divided into zones of local government, based on pre-Roman tribal groupings. Some of the tribal kingdoms at the edge of the conquered area were initially utilized as buffer zones. This well-established Roman principle of conquest provided frontier security without committing large numbers of troops. In Britain the *Regni*, *Iceni* and *Brigantes* (see Boudica, and Cartimandua, in Chapter 9) seem to have been allowed this privilege. The rulers left with this conditional power are known now as 'client kings'.

Eventual absorption into the Empire was almost inevitable, fossilizing what had once been a rather fluid situation. Until the Roman occupation tribal boundaries fluctuated according to the ambitions and fortunes of their respective leaders.

In the Roman order there was a fairly clear hierarchy. At the top the provincial council in the provincial capital enjoyed primacy, though in London's case we have no idea what its official status really was. The *coloniae* enjoyed independent status, each with its own territory and the prestige of its veteran origins, Roman citizen status and imperial foundations. After these came the *civitates*, the tribal areas adapted into Roman administrative zones, each with its own capital. Below came a multitude of lesser towns and villages with forms of civic government based on those in the more formal towns. The evidence for all these is sketchy in Britain.

Government in official towns, *coloniae, municipia*, and civitas capitals, was similar. The differences were the civitas capitals' lack of financial magistrates, *quaestores*, and special officers of the imperial cult, *seviri Augustales*. In other respects they were effectively identical, being governed by a council of 100 decurions supervised by the two annually-elected magistrates, normally *duoviri iure dicundo* and their aides, *aediles*. The *aediles* dealt with the installation and maintenance of public facilities. Only a few of each are testified in Britain (see Chapter 5). An exception is the case of the official tiles produced for the authorities at Gloucester, some of which name the *duoviri*.

Every fifth year the annually-elected pair of magistrates were of higher rank, known as *duoviri quinquennales*. These men were responsible for reviewing the composition of the council, as well as supervising a census and revaluation of property.

Coloniae

The *colonia*, normally founded in conquered territory, was a social, military, and political device used to pay off troops. The *colonia* was a cheap means of providing property for veterans. It created an armed reserve and, where necessary, acted as an example of romanized law-abiding urban life. At the same time, veterans were given a way to earn a living other than roaming provinces as bands of landless outlaws.

Colonies were not exclusively designated for veteran troops. Land grants were also made to civilian Roman citizens, and in this respect they served as a conduit of opportunity, much as north America did in the seventeenth and eighteenth century until the War of Independence.

In the provinces the colonies were distinguished by having a population of Roman citizens which, until the edict of universal citizenship under Caracalla, remained the highest rank of citizenship in the Empire. Each colony also had its *territorium*, land around the settlement, which was controlled by the inhabitants. Of course, the introduction of a colony was not necessarily straightforward. It was the manner of appropriation and abuse of privilege by the colonists at Colchester which helped occasion the Boudican Revolt.

Britain had at least four colonies: Colchester, Gloucester, Lincoln, and York. London is also described as one in a version of the *acta* of the Council of Arles in 314 but this is unverified, and contradicted in another version. The others each began life as a legionary fortress though in Colchester's case this period lasted little more than four or five years. Archaeology has vividly revealed the piecemeal adaptation of military structures and lay-out in the new colony's early years. However, nothing found on the site has provided factual evidence of its status, which has instead come from literary sources and epigraphic evidence found elsewhere.

Colchester is, incidentally, the only Romano-British colony for which we have an exact date of foundation, thanks to Tacitus. All the others are individually testified as colonies but the date of foundation of each remains a matter for debate. Most histories of Roman Britain state Lincoln's colonial foundation during the Flavian period to be a fact, without elaborating on the evidence. The basis is a single inscription from Mainz which records the name of Marcus Minicius Mar[cellinus?] of Lincoln, and a member of the voting tribe *Quirina* 'in which the Flavian foundations were enrolled' (Salway, 1981, 152 note). The origins of this statement and similar observations by Frere and others lie in a 1946 paper by I.A. Richmond. However, Richmond himself was merely repeating an opinion expressed by Mommsen in 1877.

Quirina is less specific than it seems. Although the name of an Italian tribe, it came to be used as a general synonym for citizens but was not, however, exclusively used by Flavian emperors. Interestingly, the only testified instance of a member of the *Quirina* in Britain is Lucius Antistius Lupus Verianus from *Sicca Veneria*, a colony in north Africa established by Augustus (*RIB* 816).

Obviously Lincoln was not an Augustan foundation but the example shows that the epigraphic 'evidence' for Lincoln's Flavian origins is a good deal less precise than the impression generally created. A Flavian origin is more soundly argued on the basis that *II Adiutrix* had been withdrawn and *IX Hispana* was at York by the end of the first century. It is therefore *probable* that Lincoln was made a colony under Domitian or shortly afterwards. The military requirements of Agricola's campaigns were over by *c*.87 by when it was realistic to allow retirements.

More convincing is the argument that Gloucester's foundation belongs to the reign of Nerva (96-8). Marcus Ulpius Quintus came from Gloucester and belonged to the Nervian tribe. But it is also possible that Nerva subsumed foundations made by Domitian and renamed them. As with Lincoln it is in any case likely that the foundation occurred in

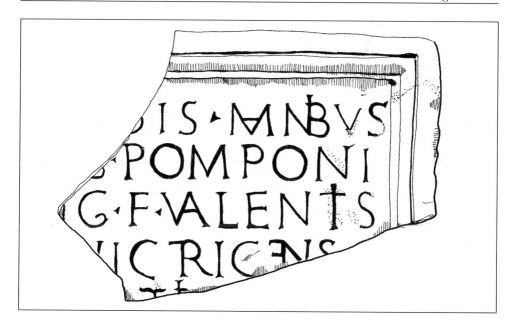

27 *Tombstone from High Holborn, London. It names Gaius Pomponius Valens and, unusually, part of the full ceremonial name of Colchester,* (colonia Claudia) Victricens(is), *presumably his place of birth. His rank is unknown but the appearance of* TRI[B?] *at the very bottom makes it possible he was a* beneficiarius tribuni. *Width 0.56m.* JRS *lii (1962), 191, no. 1*

the late first century, reflecting the movement of the legions into their permanent bases at Caerleon, Chester, and York.

Colchester (*Camulodunum*)
49 and 60: Colchester is testified by name as a *colonia* by Tacitus, founded as a means of controlling the area and imposing romanization. Tacitus is specific about the institution of the *colonia*; he was not using a term which referred to a later date. It is named again in the account of the Boudican Revolt in 60-1. By this date Colchester had a senate house, theatre, and statue of Victory. Tacitus (*Annals*) xii.32, xiv.32, (*Agricola* xiv.1 repeats the fact without identifying the place).
Undated: inscription from *Nomentum* naming Gnaeus Munatius Aurelius Bassus, onetime *censitor civium Romanorum coloniae Victricensis Camulodunum quae est in Brittannia Camaloduni*, 'Censor of Roman citizens of the Victricensian colony at *Camulodunum* which is in *Britannia*'. ILS 2740
Undated: tombstone from London of G. Pomponius Valens of Colchester, providing part of the town's full ceremonial name. *JRS* lii (1962), 191, no. 1 (**27**)

Gloucester (*Glevum*)
Undated: tombstone, recording an anonymous *dec(urio) coloniae Glev[ensis]* who had died (presumably) at Bath. *RIB* 161
Undated: tombstone from Rome naming Marcus Ulpius Quintus, a soldier of *VI Victrix*, then serving as a *fr(umentarius)*, as a member of the Nervian tribe from Gloucester. This is taken to suggest that Gloucester was instituted as a colony during the brief reign of Nerva (96-8), or perhaps under Domitian and afterwards renamed. *ILS* 2365 (**28**)
Undated: numerous tile stamps from the colony and environs are stamped RPG (*R(ei) P(ublicae)*

D · M
M·VLPIO·NER
QVINTO·GLEVI
MIL·FR·LEG·VI·V
CALIDIVS
QVIETVS·COLLEGA
FRATRIOBSERVATO
PIISSIMO B·M·F·C

28 *Tombstone from Rome of M(arcus) Ulpius Quintus, detached from VI Victrix* to serve as a fru(mentarius). *He was of the Nervian voting tribe Glevi, 'of Gloucester', perhaps suggesting the colony here was founded no later than the reign of Nerva (96-8).* ILS *2365*

G(levensium)). They show that tile production, presumably for civic works was an organized operation. The stamps, some of which give abbreviated names for the annual *duoviri iure dicundo*, will have allowed batch and production controls as well as discouraging theft. *RIB* 2486-8 (**25**)

Undated: lead sealing from Cirencester with the legend R P G (as the tiles above). However, there are at least two further letters, Q(?) and A, which might completely alter the meaning. *RIB* 2411.40

Lincoln (*Lindum*)

237: the existence of a colony at Lincoln is also stated on the altar erected at Bordeaux by M. Aurelius Lunaris in 237 (see York below). *JRS* xi (1921), 102

253-9: *R(es) P(ublica) L(indensis)* is named on a milestone of Valerian found originally in Lincoln High Street. *RIB* 2240

Undated: a dedication from Mainz to Fortuna by M. Minicius Marcellinus of Lincoln, for the eagle of *XXII Primigenia*, is said to be evidence of Lincoln's conversion to a colony by 90. See the discussion above. *CIL* xiii.6679

London (*Londinium*)

314: described variously as *civitas Londiniensium* and *colonia Londiniensium* in different versions of the *acta* of the council of Arles of this year, when naming the bishop Adelphius. *PNRB* 49ff

York (*Eboracum*)

237: York is named as a *colonia* on an altar erected at Bordeaux by M. Aurelius Lunaris (see Chapter 9) in 237. The date of York's foundation as a colony is known, though suggestions have included the aftermath of the victories of Antoninus Pius in 154, and also the Severan campaigns of 208-11. Unlike other colonies York remained a legionary fortress; the military and civilian sites lay side by side. *JRS* xi (1921), 102 (**29**)

29 *Altar from Bordeaux dedicated to the goddess Boudiga. In the second line is the name of* M(arcus) Aur(elius) Lunaris *who gives his post of* sev(ir) Aug(ustalis) *in the colonies of* Ebor(acum) *(York) and* Lind(um) *(Lincoln) in the province of* Brit(annia) Inf(erior) . *The last line names the consuls for the year,* Perpetuus and Cornel(ianus), *who served in 237. JRS* xi *(1921), 102*

Undated: York is stated, or probably stated, to be a colony on various undatable tombstones or sarcophagi. *RIB* 648, 678; *Brit.* xviii (1987), 367, no. 5

Municipia

The *municipium* was a category of privileged urban status superior to civitas capitals but inferior to colonies. The normal practice under Roman government was to apply it to significant towns that were already in existence at the time of Roman rule. Its inhabitants were awarded Roman citizenship or the lesser status of Latin citizenship. Only one example is testified in Britain, as not surprisingly there were unlikely to have been many (if any) settlements which the Romans would normally have regarded as towns:

Verulamium (St Albans)
60-1: the only recorded instance of a *municipium* in Britain is that of Verulamium during the Boudican revolt of 60-1. The status may have been that at the time, or when Tacitus was writing about thirty years later; nevertheless he does state quite specifically that the *municipio Verulamio* fell to the rebels. The Agricolan forum inscription may or may not have named the *municipium* (see *Catuvellauni* below). Tacitus (*Annals*) xiv.33; *JRS* xlvi (1956), 146-7

Civitates peregrinae 'communities of aliens'

The *civitas peregrina* was a device for the government of provincials, based on a tribal region. It was controlled from a civitas capital not politically distinguished from the region. The names of the civitas capitals illustrate this, for example *Corinium Dobunnorum*, '*Corinium* of the *Dobunni*' (Cirencester).

In Britain it was necessary for the Roman government physically to install a formal town, usually by developing a nascent romanized settlement outside a fort, itself often close to an earlier tribal centre. In such cases it is normally possible to demonstrate archaeologically that a Roman civitas capital represented a continuity of traditional gatherings and markets.

As observed elsewhere, the epigraphic evidence from Britain is so overwhelmingly in favour of the religious and military that it is unsurprising so few of the *civitates* are explicitly testified. As Rivet and Smith have pointed out it would scarcely be necessary to name towns within the actual settlement (*PNRB*, 228); likewise, names of forts scarcely ever appear on inscriptions unless they had been absorbed into the name of the military unit. For the *coloniae* (see above), evidence for the town name and its status is usually in the form of a personal record of rank, often not even found in Britain. In the civitas capitals such positions were perhaps less significant, or at any rate less eagerly brandished.

For the actual towns and their names we are far more reliant on the various ancient geographers such as Ptolemy and various Roman itineraries, and other scattered pieces of evidence. But these are subject to all sorts of errors of copying and sometimes a new piece of epigraphic evidence can produce a correction.

Silchester is named on inscriptions from the site, reinforcing pre-Roman evidence of Celtic tribal coinage (**30**). But this is relatively unusual. Leicester, for instance, called *Ratis* or *Ratae*, is known from Ptolemy and the Ravenna list. Otherwise it occurs only on a diploma of 106 from Dacia, naming a soldier whose home it was (*CIL* xvi.160), and on a milestone of 119-20 from the Leicester area (*RIB* 2244). But the true name of the cantonal tribe, *Corieltauvi*, has only materialized in recent years on a tile.

The following summarizes what epigraphic evidence there is for the *civitates*, either in references to the civic body or to individuals who held office in, or who are stated to be citizens of, those cantons. References from route itineraries or to the tribal name only (for example *RIB* 76, or 1065) are not included except in particularly interesting cases. Geographical areas are only approximate and it can be seen in some cases that tribal names sometimes occur outside their nominal areas.

Belgae (central southern England)
110: diploma naming M. Ulpius Longinus, *Belgus*, of *cohors I Brittonum*. *CIL* xvi.163
238-44: milestone/honorific pillar of Gordian III from Bitterne (Hants), naming the *R(es) P(ublica) BI(= Bel(garum)?)*. *RIB* 2222
238-44?: milestone/honorific pillar of Gordian III? from Wonston, Worthy Down (Hants), naming the *R(es) P(ublica) B(elgarum)*. *Brit.* xvi (1985), 324, no. 3
Undated: tombstone of Julius Vitalis, *fabriciensis* of *XX Valeria Victrix*, and a member of *natione Belga*, 'the Belgic nation' — this is not certainly the British *Belgae*. *RIB* 156

30 *Dedication from Silchester
providing the town's name*
Calleva. *The rest of the text is
believed to refer to a gift to an
unknown recipient by a*
con[legio
pere]gr[i]norum, *'guild of
peregrini'. Height 380mm.*
RIB *70*

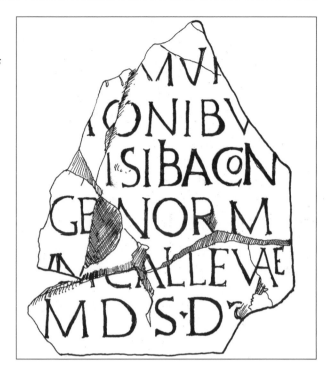

Brigantes (northern England, except extreme north-west)
Undated: centurial stone from Hadrian's Wall, found between Castlesteads and Stanwix, recorded
as naming the *civitat(is) Bricic*, probably for *Brig(antum)* or *Brig(ant)ic(ae)*. *RIB* 2022
Undated: Nectovelius, *nationis Brigans*, but a soldier in *cohors II Thracum* on a tombstone from
Mumrills. This is an exceptional instance of an auxiliary origin giving a place of origin as well as
his unit. Whether the fact that they differ was also exceptional, or common, is unknown for this
reason. But the tribal name *Brigantes* is known outside Britain (*PNRB*, 279) so perhaps
Nectovelius was not a British Brigantian at all. *RIB* 2142

Cantiaci/Cantii (Kent)
118: *in civitate Cantiacorum*, 'in the canton of the *Cantiaci*', appears on a wooden writing tablet from
London referring to a wood called *Verlucionium* in the canton, and said to be owned by Lucius
Julius Bellicus. This find is interesting given Ptolemy's assertion (see above) that London was a
city of the *Cantii* (sic), though the location of the property is unknown. *RIB* 2443.19, revised at
2504.29
Undated: recorded on a sandstone base dedication at Colchester by Similis, *ci(vis) Cant(iacus)*,
'citizen of the *Cantiaci*'. It may be assumed he was visiting or had moved. *RIB* 192 (and see *Brit.*
xxv (1994), 302, no. 34)

Carvetii (north-western England, Carlisle area)
259-68: milestone/honorific pillar of Postumus (259-68) found by the Roman road at Brougham
dedicated by the *R(es) P(ublica) C(ivitas) Car(vetiorum)*. *JRS* lv (1965), 224, no. 11
Undated: possibly recorded on the tombstone of Flavius Martius, named as a *sen(ator)* of C
CARVETIOR which can be expanded as *c(ivitas)* or *c(ohors) Carvetior(um)*. *RIB* 933 (Old Penrith)

Catuvellauni (Herts, Berks, Middlesex, and Cambs)
79/81: forum dedicatory inscription from Verulamium. The stone is very fragmentary but enough may

be read to attribute it to the governorship of Agricola (named) during the reign of Titus in 79 or 81. At least two restorations of the last line, which names the organization responsible, are possible:
[civitas Catu]ve[llaunorum], or
[municipium] Ve[rulamium]

Thus, either the *Catuvellauni* are named, or the town of Verulamium. *JRS* xlvi (1956), 146-7

Undated: building stone naming Tossodio, of the *civitate Catuvellaunorum* on Hadrian's Wall from near milecastle 55. *RIB* 1962

Undated: tombstone from South Shields of Regina, *liberta et coniuge*, 'freedwoman and wife', of Barates the Palmyrene (Syria). Aged 30 she was *natione Cat(u)vallauna*, 'a Catuvellaunian by tribe'. *RIB* 1065 (**87**)

Corieltauvi (East Midlands)

Undated: tile from Cave's Inn names *[ci]vitatis Corieltauvorom* (sic), altering the formerly-accepted *Coritanorum* for *Coritani*. *RIB* 2491.50

Undated: lead seal from Thorpe in the Glebe (Notts) bearing *C(ivitas) Cor(i)el(tauvorum)*. *Brit.* xxiv (1993), 318, no. 18

Corionototae

Undated: recorded by Q. Calpurnius Concessinius, prefect of an unnamed unit of cavalry, on an altar. The stone celebrated his victory over and slaughter of this otherwise-unknown tribal group. As the altar was found at Corbridge, *Coria*, it seems likely their territory was close to the northern frontier. The stone is now only known from an eighteenth-century drawing so there is little opportunity to date it on style. *RIB* 1142

Cornovii (West Midlands, Welsh Marches)

129-31: forum dedicatory inscription from Wroxeter, recording *civitas Cornov[iorum]*. The stone is damaged but the date can be restored as between 129-31 in the reign of Hadrian, depending on whether the 13th or 14th year of tribunician power is meant. *RIB* 288 (**34**)

300s: *cohors I Cornoviorum* at Newcastle (unusually, a unit apparently stationed in the province in which it was raised). *ND* xl.34

Undated: tombstone from Ilkley names Ved[.]ic[...], of *c(ivis) Cornovia*. *RIB* 639

Dobunni (Gloucestershire Cotswolds, Hereford and Worcs, Oxon)

105: diploma from *Pannonia* recording *Lucconi Treni F(ilio) Dobunn*, 'Lucco the Dobunnian, son of Trenus, then serving with *cohors I Britannica*. *CIL* xvi.49

283-4: milestone from Kenchester with an abbreviation restorable as *R(es) P(ublica) C(ivitatis) D(obunnorum)*, erected during the reign of Numerian (283-4). *RIB* 2250

Undated: tombstone from Templeborough of Verecunda Rufilia, *coniugi karissima[e]*, 'beloved wife', of Excingus. Aged 35 she was a *cives Dobunna*, 'citizen of the Dobunni'. The unit testified at the fort is *cohors IIII Gallorum* (see Chapter 2). *RIB* 621

Dumnonii (Devon and Cornwall)

Undated: Aemilius, *civis Dumnonius*, recorded on his tombstone at Cologne as having served with *classis Germanica*. *AE* 1956.249

Undated: centurial stones from Hadrian's Wall between Carvoran and Birdoswald, naming *civitas Dum(no)ni(orum)*. *RIB* 1843-4

Undated: tombstone of [....] Carinus, *civi [D]om(nonio)*, 'citizen of the *Dumnonii*' from Dorchester (Dorset). The former restoration as a citizen of Rome is now rejected. *RIB* 188 (see *RIB 95*, note to *RIB* 188, p.760)

Durotriges (Dorset and Somerset)

Undated: centurial stones from Hadrian's Wall (near Cawfields mc 42), naming *c(ivitas) Dur(o)tr(i)g(um) [L]endin(i)e(nsis)*, 'the civitas of the Durotriges at *Lindiniae* (Ilchester)'. *RIB* 1672-3 (**31**)

31 Centurial stone from near Cawfields milecastle (Hadrian's Wall) naming C(ivitas) Dur(o)tr(i)g(um) [L]endin(i)e(n)sis, *'the Durotrigan canton of* Lendiniae *(Ilchester)'. Date unknown, but believed to be fourth century. Width 343mm. RIB 1672*

Parisi (East Yorks) — now rejected
The postulated reference to this canton on the dedication slab from Brough-on-Humber recording the dedication of a new theatre stage was originally believed also to record the *c(ivitas) [P](arisiorum)*. This was assumed solely from the presumed survival of a single letter C on a side panel. It is now recognized to be a decorative motif and is rejected as evidence for the tribal name. See under **Vicus** below. *RIB* 707 (**40**)

Silures (south-east Wales)
Pre-220: explictly named at Caerwent as *civit(atis) Silurum* dedicating a statue to T. Claudius Paulinus, then commander of *II Augusta* at nearby Caerleon. By 220 Claudius Paulinus was governor of *Britannia Inferior* (*RIB* 1280), which means that this dedication must precede 220. *RIB* 311

32 *Slab from the* vicus *at Housesteads naming* Jul(ius) S[...] *and supposedly a* d(ecreto) vica(norum), *'decree of the villagers'. The fragmentary text allows other expansions, for example* D(omitia) *or* D(ecimiana) Vica[na] *(RIB 111 records a* P(ublia) Vicana*) and is perhaps the remains of a tombstone of a husband and wife. Width 254mm. RIB 1616*

The *vicus* and other small-town government organizations

Vicus was a semi-formal rank awarded to towns that were considered worthy of self-government. In reality this extended from significant, even walled, towns like Water Newton to the villages which straggled along the roads outside forts. Nowadays the term is frequently applied to any settlement outside a fort though in reality only a small number are officially testified to have been of this status. The practice of self-government ranges from the high end at Brough, where the sole aedile from Roman Britain is testified, to simple bodies of *vicani*, 'villagers'.

vicus Durobrivae (Caister/Water Newton)
Undated: mortarium stamps reading *Cunoarda vico Durobr(ivis)*, 'Cunoarda [made this] at the *vicus* of *Durobrivae*'. Said to be of third/fourth century date. Tyers p.128

vicus Petuariensis (Brough-on-Humber or North Ferriby)
140-61: named as *vici Petu[ar(iensis)]* on a slab found at Brough-on-Humber commemorating the gift of a new stage to the *vicus* of *Petuaria* by the aedile Marcus Ulpius Januarius during the reign of Antoninus Pius. The findspot is difficult to reconcile with the military archaeology. North Ferriby, 4km (2.5 miles) to the east has been suggested as the slab's original home. *RIB 707* (**40**)

curia Textoverdi
Undated: on an altar to the goddess Sattada from, or from near, Vindolanda, named as *curia Textoverdorum*, 'assembly of the Textoverdi'. *RIB 1695*

vicani castello Veluniate
Undated: named on an altar to Jupiter Optimus Maximus at Carriden as *vikani castello Veluniate*, 'The vicus dwellers at the fort of *Velunia*'. *JRS xlvii* (1957), 229-30, no. 18.

vicani Vindolandesses
Undated: altar from Vindolanda is a dedication to Vulcanus and the Numina Augustorum by *vicani Vindolandesses*, 'villagers of Vindolanda'. *RIB* 1700

vicani ('villagers') of unnamed *vici*
Undated: named on a dedication from Old Carlisle to Jupiter Optimus Maximus and Vulkanus (sic) for the welfare of Gordian III by *vik(anorum) mag(istri)*, 'masters of the villagers'. *RIB* 899
Undated: dedication from Housesteads reputedly records the *d(ecreto) vica(norum)*, 'decree of the villagers'. The very incomplete and unparalleled nature of the text means that the restoration of *decreto* is dubious. A name is as likely. *RIB* 1616 (**32**)

4 Imperial dedications

These inscriptions all contain dedications to or in the name of the incumbent regime, other than milestones (see Chapter 6) and dedications to a god for the benefit of such and such an emperor (Chapter 8). Their importance comes from the fact that they can be dated from an imperial name or titles. Slabs which are too fragmentary to associate with a reign have been excluded, for example a tantalising inscription from Winchester (illustrated in Wacher 1974, 282).

The information is revealing. Most surviving dedications are of second- and early-third-century date. Those of the reigns of Hadrian and Antonius Pius belong largely to their respective frontiers. The numbers from the Antonine Wall are elevated by the practice of installing elaborate inscriptions recording stretches of wall building and the emperor's name. The equivalent stones on Hadrian's Wall normally name just the *centuria* responsible and are undatable.

Other inscriptions can be dated on stylistic grounds but the process is subjective and as yet no structured analysis based on dated stones has been made; they have therefore have been omitted. Obviously this creates a self-selecting and perhaps misleading sample in the sense that any period in which inscriptions were less likely to bear dating information will therefore be poorly represented. Equally, the sample partly depends on when and where excavations have taken place. Of the seven Trajanic slabs, three come from Gelligaer alone.

Dates are the *maximum* possible on the basis of the surviving texts (see Appendix 1). *RIB* often provides more optimistically precise dates but usually from substantial restorations of damaged texts. Where dates have been allocated on what seem to be dubious grounds, for example *RIB* 1550 from Carrawburgh which bears no unequivocal dating information at all, those inscriptions have been excluded.

Where specific buildings are referred to the Latin name used is given here. More details of these will be found in Chapter 5 which details all specific-building stones. But such texts are rare. Most building stones either imply building work or state that one had been 'restored' or 'built'. Where possible the context or association has been mentioned briefly. Sometimes this makes it likely which structure was being referred to.

Neronian-Flavian
Nero (54-68)
58-60: Chichester. *RIB* 92

Vespasian (69-79), see also Titus, 81
76: Bath (cornice stone). *RIB* 172

Titus, with Domitian (79-81)
79: Chester ('in remains of a large Roman building'), but heavily restored. *RIB* 463
81 (or 79): Verulamium (forum-basilica by context). *JRS* xlvi (1956), 146-7

IMP·CAES·DIVI·NERVAE·F·
NERVAE·TRAIANO·AVG·
GER·PONTIF·MAXIMO·TRIB·
POTEST · P · P ·
COS III
LEG II AVG

33 Marble (of probable Italian origin) slab from Caerleon by II Augusta *with Trajan's titles for the year 99 (COS II),* amended to COS III *for the year 100. The slab may not have been produced in Britain. Width 1.47m. RIB 330*

Trajanic-Hadrianic
Trajan (98-117)
99/100: Caerleon (building, but not specified). *RIB* 330 (**33**)
102-17 (or Hadrianic): Chester (E gate by proximity). *RIB* 464
102-17: Lancaster. *RIB* 604
103-12: Gelligaer (SE gate by proximity). *RIB* 397
103-12: Gelligaer (SE gate by proximity). *RIB* 398
103-12: Gelligaer (NW gate by context). *RIB* 399
107-8: York (SE gate by context). *RIB* 665

Hadrian (117-38)
117-38 (or 98-117): Melandra Castle. *RIB* 280
117-38: Maryport. *RIB* 851
117-38: Netherby (building, but not specified). *RIB* 974
117-38: Vindolanda (building, but not specified). *RIB* 1702 (in reality this is probably 122-6 and,
    possibly, from a Wall location as *RIB* 1637, 1638 below)
117-38: Carvoran (building, but not specified; N gate?). *RIB* 1808
117-38: Gelligaer (SE gate by context). *JRS* xlviii (1958), 151, no. 6 and *JRS* lii (1962), 193, no. 10
119-38: Hardknott (SE gate by context). *JRS* lv (1965), 222, no. 7
119-38: Jarrow (monument?). *RIB* 1051
122-6: Benwell (granary by context). *RIB* 1340 (**21**)
122-6: Haltonchesters (W gate by context). *RIB* 1427
122-6: Hadrian's Wall (mc 38 by proximity). *RIB* 1637
122-6: Hadrian's Wall (mc 38 by tradition). *RIB* 1638 (**12**)
122-6: Hadrian's Wall (mc 42). *RIB* 1666
122-6: Hadrian's Wall (TW mc 50). *RIB* 1935
122-8: Hadrian's Wall (mc 47 by proximity). *RIB* 1852
122-38: Housesteads (bath-house by proximity?). *JRS* lii (1962), 193-4, no. 15
[122-38?]: Carrawburgh (building probably, but not specified). *JRS* lvi (1966), 218, no. 5
122-38: Bewcastle (building, but not specified). *RIB* 995
128-38: York (gate by context). *RIB* 666

34 *Forum-basilica dedication from Wroxeter, found by its east entrance, bearing Hadrian's titles for*
December 129 to December 130 (TR POT XIIII); only XIII is visible but the superscript bar,
used to group numerals, makes it clear that XIIII is meant. The last line mentions the civitas
Cornov(iorum), 'canton of the Cornovii'. For clarity details of the innumerable fragments have
been omitted. Diameter 3.7m. RIB *288*

128-38: Moresby (E gate by proximity). *RIB* 801
128-38: Greatchesters (E gate by proximity). *RIB* 1736
129-30: Wroxeter (forum-basilica by context). *RIB* 288 (**34**)
130-3: Bowes. *RIB* 739

Antonine
Antoninus Pius (138-61)
139: Corbridge (building, but not specified). *RIB* 1147
138-9: Chesters (headquarters by context). *RIB* 1460
139-43: High Rochester (building, but not specified; headquarters by context?). *RIB* 1276 (**24**)
139-43: Balmuildy (building, but not specified). *RIB* 2191
139-43: Balmuildy (N gate by context). *RIB* 2192
139-61: Balmuildy (building AW, 0.25 mile NW). *RIB* 2193
139-61: Balmuildy (building AW, 0.5 mile NW). *RIB* 2194
139-61: Maryport. *RIB* 850
139-61: Chesters (building, but not specified). *RIB* 1461
139-61: Bridgeness (building AW, E end of AW). *RIB* 2139
139-61: Rough Castle (headquarters by context). *RIB* 2145
139-61: Castlecary (building, but not specified). *RIB* 2155
139-61: Bar Hill (headquarters by context). *RIB* 2170
139-61: Bar Hill (building AW, provenance uncertain). *RIB* 2173
139-61: Kirkintilloch (building AW, 1 mile NE). *RIB* 2185
139-61: Kirkintilloch (building AW, provenance uncertain). *RIB* 2186
139-61: Castlehill (building AW, provenance uncertain). *RIB* 2196
139-61: Castlehill (building AW, 100m SW). *RIB* 2197
139-61: near Castlehill (building AW, 0.6 mile W). *RIB* 2198
139-61: Antonine Wall (building not specified, provenance uncertain). *RIB* 2199
139-61: Antonine Wall (building *vallum* of AW, 1100m SW Duntocher). *RIB* 2200
139-61: Antonine Wall (building AW, 1 mile W Duntocher). *RIB* 2204
139-61: Antonine Wall (building AW, 0.75 mile E Old Kilpatrick). *RIB* 2205
139-61: Antonine Wall (building AW, 0.75 mile E Old Kilpatrick). *RIB* 2206
139-61: Antonine Wall (building AW, W end of AW). *RIB* 2208 (**12**)

140-4: Corbridge (E granary by context). *RIB* 1148
140-4: Castlesteads. *RIB* 1997
140-61: Brough-on-Humber (*proscaenium*). *RIB* 707 (**40**)
155-9: Newcastle (from bridge by context). *RIB* 1322 (**14**)
157-8: Birrens (headquarters by context). *RIB* 2110
158: Brough-on-Noe (headquarters by context). *RIB* 283

Marcus Aurelius, with Lucius Verus (161-9)
161-9: Ilkley. *RIB* 636
161-9: Corbridge (building, but not specified). *RIB* 1149
161-9 or 176-80: Corbridge. *RIB* 1153
163-9: Ribchester. *RIB* 589
163-6: Vindolanda (imperial dedication assumed). *RIB* 1703
166-9: Greatchesters. *RIB* 1737

Marcus Aurelius, with Commodus (177-80)
177: Netherby (building, but not specified). *RIB* 975
177-85: Chesters (adjacent to cistern by repute). *RIB* 1464
177-80: Caerleon (*aedes*). *Brit.* i (1970), 305, no. 3

Commodus (180-92)
of doubtful authenticity:
180-92: Caerleon (extra-mural baths by context). *RIB* 332
and, as above:
[177-85: Chesters (adjacent to cistern by repute). *RIB* 1464]

Severan
Septimius Severus (193-211), with Caracalla as Caesar (197-8), then Augustus (198-211) and Geta
    as Caesar (198-209), then Augustus (209-12)
c. 196: Chester (with Albinus too?). *RIB* 465
197: Brough-under-Stainmore. *RIB* 757
197-202: Ilkley (building, but not specified). *RIB* 637
198-209: Caerleon. *RIB* 326
198-209: Caerleon (from a frieze). *RIB* 333
198-209: Caernarvon (*[aq]uaeductium*). *RIB* 430
198-209: Ribchester (headquarters by context). *RIB* 591
198-209: Housesteads (possibly headquarters). *RIB* 1612
198-209: Birdoswald. *RIB* 1910
198-235: York. *RIB* 667 (or possibly Marcus Aurelius)
205: Bainbridge (*centuriam/s*). *JRS* li (1961), 192, no. 4 (revised in *JRS* lix (1969), 246)
205-8: Ribchester (headquarters by context). *RIB* 591 (see Stephens 1987, 239-40)
205-8: Bainbridge (*[vallo cum] bracchio caementicium*). *RIB* 722
205-8: Bainbridge. *RIB* 723
205-8: Bowes. *RIB* 740
205-8: Greta Bridge (N gate by proximity). *RIB* 746
205-8: Corbridge (*horre[u]m*). *RIB* 1151
205-8: Risingham (S gate by context). *RIB* 1234 (**39**)
205-8: Birdoswald (*horreum*). *RIB* 1909
205-8: Housesteads (commandant's house by context). *JRS* lvii (1967), 205-6, no. 17 (very tentative
    restoration of a very fragmentary text)

Caracalla (211-17), with Geta (211-12)
211-12?: Manchester. *RIB* 581
212-13: Vindolanda. *RIB* 1705
212-17: Charterhouse on Mendip. *RIB* 185 (or possibly Severus)
212-17: Caerleon (building, but not specified). *RIB* 331
212-17: Ribchester. *RIB* 590

35 Slab from High Rochester. Bearing the titles of Caracalla for 216 it states that coh(ors) I fida Vardul(orum) fecit, *built (this), during the governorship of, probably, M. Antonius Gordianus, afterwards the emperor Gordian I (see Chapter 9). Width 0.94m. RIB 1279*

212-17: 'Cumberland area'. *RIB* 1018
212-17: Risingham (bath-house by context). *RIB* 1236
212-17?: Carpow (E gate by context). *JRS* lv (1965), 223, no. 10 (very tentative restoration)
212-22: Combe Down (*principia*). *RIB* 179 (Caracalla or Elagabalus)
213: Old Carlisle. *RIB* 905
213: Netherby (3 miles S). *RIB* 976
213: Whitley Castle. *RIB* 1202
213: Risingham (headquarters by context). *RIB* 1235
213: High Rochester. *RIB* 1278
213: Carrawburgh. *RIB* 1551
213: Newcastle. *Brit.* xi (1980), 405, no. 6
213: South Shields. *Brit.* xvi (1985), 325-6, no. 11
213-17: Whitley Castle. *RIB* 1203
216: High Rochester (building, but not specified). *RIB* 1279 (**35**)
N.B. *RIB* 68 from Silchester was possibly a civilian equivalent of the 213 inscriptions but this is uncertain. It may alternatively date to the reign of Elagabalus.

Elagabalus (218-22)
see Combe Down (*principia*). *RIB* 179, under Caracalla
218-22: High Rochester (building, but not specified). *RIB* 1272
218-22: High Rochester (*ballistarium*). *RIB* 1280

Severus Alexander (222-35)
222: Netherby (*baselicam equestrem exercitatoriam*). *RIB* 978
222: South Shields (*aquam*). *RIB* 1060
222-3: Chesters (bath-house by context). *RIB* 1467
222-35: Old Carlisle. *RIB* 901
222-35: High Rochester. *RIB* 1282
223: Ebchester (*por[tam cum tu]rribus*). *RIB* 1706
225: Greatchesters (*horreum*). *RIB* 1738
225-35: Old Penrith. *RIB* 929

The later third century
Maximinus I (235-8)
236: Birdoswald (building, but not specified). *RIB* 1922
237: Carrawburgh (building, but not specified). *RIB* 1553

Gordian III (238-44)
238-44: Lanchester (*balneum cum basilica*). *RIB* 1091 (**6**)
238-44: Lanchester (*principia et armamentaria*). *RIB* 1092 (**37**)

Gallienus and Valerian (253-60), with Valerian II, as Caesar (235-5)
255-60: Caerleon (*centurias*). *RIB* 334

Postumus (259-68)
262-6: Lancaster (*balineum [et] basilicam*). *RIB* 605

Aurelian (270-5)
270-5: Caerleon (gate by location). *Brit.* xv (1984), 337, no. 12

Diocletian and Maximian (297-305)
297-305: Housesteads (building probably, but not specified). *RIB* 1613
297-305: Birdoswald (*bal(neum), princ(ipia), praetor(ium)*). *RIB* 1912
297-305: Maryport, identification uncertain. *RIB* 844

5 Building dedications

These inscriptions and other references record specific buildings as new constructions or their rebuilding, either because the text states the building type, or its assocation with a structure makes it certain which building is referred to. Few in fact can be associated with surviving remains. The bias to religion in inscriptions is also reflected amongst those specifying buildings, to the extent that 'numerically, there are in fact more sacred constructions known from Britain than from [Gaul or Germany]' (Blagg 1990). These include structures such as arches.

Not a single major Romano-British public building is specified by name apart from references by Tacitus to facilities at Colchester in 60. Even the inscription from Brough-on-Humber refers to a theatre stage rather than the theatre itself. Only two forum-basilica complexes have yielded recognizable traces of inscriptions which appear to record their erection while other classes of public building, such as urban defences, baths or *macella* (markets), are not represented at all. In spite of fragments of inscriptions which might be all that remain of other such records (such as *RIB* 114 from Cirencester's forum), this is in marked contrast to the archaeological record which has, for example, demonstrated the existence of forum-basilica complexes in almost every major Romano-British town. Likewise, the building of the many hundreds of rural villas goes unrepresented in the epigraphic record.

In forts it seems that some structures were more likely to be commemorated than others. Anne Johnson notes that 'the provision or restoration of the fort aqueduct is often recorded by an inscription' (1983, 206). Some other classes of fort building, such as the hospital (*valetudinarium*), are not testified on inscriptions in Britain at all.

Many of the references to temples come from northern military sites, the source of most inscriptions. That tends to support the contention that religious dedications were favoured in Roman Britain, and that it is not entirely the product of chance. Were it otherwise, then we might expect more dedications of secular military structures from the same places. Beyond that it is difficult to analyse the material because so little of it is dated or datable. Of those that are, the dominant period is between *c.*175-265, reflected in the list of imperial dedications in Chapter 4.

Very fragmentary stones, such as *RIB* 466 from Chester, where the attribution to a specific building type wholly rests on the restoration are omitted.

Arcum — arch
Ancaster: dedication to the god Viridius by Trenico of an *arcum*. *JRS* lii (1962), 192, no. 7 (**36**)
Nettleham: a dedication to Mars Rigonemetos and the Numina Augustorum by Quintus Neratius, recording an *arcum*. *JRS* lii (1962), 192, no. 8
York: altar to Neptune(?), Genius loci and Numina Augustorum, recording an *[ar]cum et ianuam*

*36 Slab from Ancaster, found in a medieval grave, recording the gift of an arch (*arcum*) by Trenico to an otherwise-unknown god called Viridios. Undated but the style of lettering is consistent with other examples of the very late second or early third century. Width 0.7m. JRS lii (1962), 192, no. 7*

'arch and entrance-way', given by L. Viducius Placidus, from the Rouen region in Gallia Lugdunensis, in 221. *Brit.* viii (1977), 430, no. 18

Armamentaria — armoury
Lanchester: restoration of the *principia et armamentaria* under Gordian III (238-44), during the governorship of Maecilius Fuscus, by *cohors I L(ingonum) Gor(diana)* under their prefect, M. Aurelius Quirinus (see also *Balneum* below). *RIB* 1092 (**37**)

Aqua — water and aqueduct
Caernarvon: restoration of the *[rivos aq]uaeductium*, 'channels of the aqueduct', during the joint reign of Septimius Severus and Caracalla between 198-209. *RIB* 430
Chesters: *aqua adducta*, 'bringing of water', by *ala II Asturum* during the governorship of Ulpius Marcellus (c.177-84). *RIB* 1463 (**82**)
Chester-le-Street: see under *Balneum*
South Shields: provision of *aquam usibus*, 'water for uses', under, Severus Alexander, for *cohors V Gallorum* during the governorship of Marius Valerianus. *RIB* 1060

Ballistarium — artillery installation
High Rochester: building of a *ballist(arium?)*, once thought to be an artillery platform, i.e. a sloped earth mound. But this seems a strange thing to commemorate with an inscription. Other suggestions are that it was a covered facility for artillery, or that it was a workshop and stores for supporting the artillery engines on the fort. The date is 220 under Elagabalus, during the governorship of T. Claudius Paulinus, with the work by *cohors I fida Vardullorum*. *RIB* 1280
High Rochester: restoration of a *ballis(tarium)* during the governorship of Claudius Apellinus under Severus Alexander between 225-35, with the work by *cohors I fida Vardullorum*. This may be the same installation referred to above. *RIB* 1281 (**38**)

Balneum — baths
Beauport Park: restoration or extension work carried out on the *classis Britannica* bath-house by a *vil[icus]*, name lost, under the *c(uram) a(gens)*, Bass(us) or Bass(ianus). The stone was located beside the entrance and with no other buildings in the vicinity it is as good as certain that it was

37 *Slab from Lanchester, similar to another (6). This records the restoration by* coh(ors) I
L(ingonum) G(ordiana) *of the headquarters,* principia, *and armouries,* armamentaria, *and
the name of the governor, Maecilius Fuscus, between 238-44. Width 0.86m.* RIB 1092

once displayed by or over the bath-house entrance. *Brit.* ii (1971), 289, no. 2; *Brit.* xix (1988),
261
Birdoswald: restoration of a *praetor(ium)*, *princ(ipia)*, and *bal(neum)*, during the governorship of
Aurelius Arpagius between 297-305, under the command of the centurion in charge, Flavius
Martinus. There has been some debate about whether BAL is expandable here as *balneum* or
ballistarium. The former seems more likely, as the latter is otherwise only testified at High
Rochester. *RIB* 1912 (see *RIB* 95, p.792, note)
Bowes: restoration of a *balineum* (sic), destroyed by fire, during the governorship of Virius Lupus,
recorded on an altar to Fortuna. The work was carried out by Valerius Fronto, prefect of *ala
Vettonum* for *cohors I Thracum*. *c.*197-202. *RIB* states that LEG AVG (for *legatus Augusti*, as opposed
to *Augustorum*) proves the stone was carved before Caracalla's elevation to joint Augustus in May
198. This presupposes that the information would have reached Bowes when the stone was
carved and/or the mason included an extra G to denote *Augustorum*. Neither can be said with
certainty so it is safer to allocate the stone to the period of the whole governorship. *RIB* 730
Brougham: restoration of a *balneum*, destroyed by fire, recorded on a fragmentary stone at Cliburn,
thought to be from Brougham originally. *RIB* 791
Chester-le-Street: supposedly the provision of *aquam* and the erection of a new *balneum* for a cavalry
regiment (full name illegible) in 216 during the reign of Caracalla and, apparently, the
governorship of M. Antonius Gordianus (see Chapter 9). Neither *aquam* nor *balneum* survives
on the slab; they are inferred solely from the verb *induxit*, 'brought', i.e. 'brought [a water-
supply]'. *RIB* 1049
Kirkby Thore: implicit in the dedication to *Fort[un]a[e](?) Bal[n(eari)]*, 'Fortuna of the bath-house',
on an altar dedicated by G. Caledius Frontinus of a unit restored as *n(umeri) m(ilitum) S(yrorum)
s(agittariorum)*. *RIB* 764
Lancaster: restoration of *balineum [et] basilicam*, during the governorship of Octavius Sabinus, under

38 Slab from High Rochester recording the building of a ballis(tarium) *from the ground up (a* solo*)
by* coh(ors) I f(ida) Vard(ullorum) *during the governorship of Claudius Apellinus. Severus
Alexander (225-35) can be restored to the gaps and as other governors are known for 220-5 the
stone is attributed to 225-35. Width 0.90m.* RIB *1281*

the prefect of *ala Sebussiana [Postumiana?]* with Gallic Empire consular names for 262-6. *RIB* 605
Lanchester: building of a *balneum cum basilica*, 'baths with exercise hall', during the reign of Gordian
   III (238-44), the governorship of Egnatius Lucilianus, and the prefecture of M. Aurelius
   Quirinus, by *cohors I L(ingonum) Gor(diana)*. *RIB* 1091 (**6**)
Risingham: *explicito balineo*, 'with bath-house completed', recorded on an altar to Fortuna Redux
   dedicated by Julius Severinus, tribune of (probably) *cohors I Vangionum milliaria equitata*. The
   altar depicts a facade, possibly of a shrine within or integral to the bath-house (see also **61**). *RIB*
   1212

Basilica — hall, see also Forum-Basilica below
Lancaster: see under *Balneum* above
Lanchester: see under *Balneum* above
Reculver: see under *Templum/Aedes* below

Centuriae — barracks
Bainbridge: building of *centuriam* or *centurias* during the governorship of G. Valerius Pudens in the
   year 205 by *cohors VI Nerviorum* under their prefect L. Vinicius Pius. *JRS* li (1961), 192, no. 4,
   revised in *JRS* (1969) lix, 246
Caerleon: restoration of the seventh cohort's *centurias* between 255-60 in the reign of Valerian and
   Gallienus, and during the governorship of Desticius Juba while Vaetulasius Laetinianus was
   legate of the legion. *RIB* 334

Columna — column
Cirencester: base of an honorific *[col]umnam* to Jupiter Optimus Maximus, restored by Lucius
   Septimius [...], from Reims in Gaul, and now *pr(aeses)* and *rector* of *Prima Provincia* (= *Britannia
   Prima*). The text postdates Diocletian's division of Britain into four in 296. It seems unlikely to

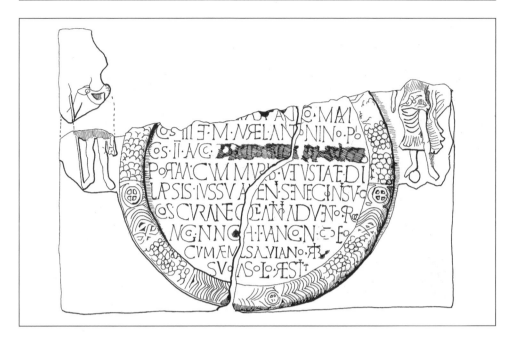

39 Slab from Risingham's south gate. Dedicated to Septimius Severus and Caracalla and Geta (erased) between 205-7/8. Portam cum muris, *'gate with walls', records the structure. The governor Alfenus Senecio is named and below him the procurator Oclatinius Adventus. Finally the unit,* cohors I Vangionum *is credited with the work. The text is remarkably stylish. Note how at the right-hand end of the penultimate line* TRIB, *for* trib(uno), *is formed as a monogram. Diameter 1.8m.* RIB *1234*

postdate the Edict of Milan in 313. However, Cirencester, alone amongst the principal cities of Roman Britain, has produced no evidence for urban Christianity either as in the form of a record of episcopal organization or structural remains of possible churches. As urban paganism is known to have persisted in some cities elsewhere in the Empire this restoration could have occurred after 313. *RIB* 103

Culmen from *columen* — gable, or projection
Moresby: fragmentary slab recording the success in building a *culminis. RIB* 799

Curia — senate house
Colchester: *curia* in existence by 60. Tacitus, *Annals* xiv.32

Exercitatoria baselica equester — cavalry drill hall
Netherby: building and completion of a *baselicam* (sic) *equestrem exercitatoriam* during the reign of Severus Alexander and the governorship of Marius Valerianus in 222. The text implies the project had been suspended, having been 'begun a long time ago' (*coeptam ... pridem*). *RIB* 978

Forum-Basilica
Verulamium: the dedication in 79 or 81 by the *[municipium] Ve[rulamium]* or the *[civitas Catu]ve[llaunorum]*, perhaps recording 'the building of the basilica', *[basilica or]nata*. The association of the building with the inscription is certain; the dedicating body responsible is not. *JRS* xlvi (1956), 146-7

Wroxeter: a dedication to Hadrian in 129-30 by the *civitas Cornov[iorum]* found shattered close to the east entrance of the forum. The date suggests the project may have been instituted at Hadrian's behest when he came to Britain in or about 119. *RIB* 288 (**34**)

Horreum — granary

Benwell: building dedication of the governorship of A. Platorius Nepos (*c.*122-6) by the *c[lassis] Britan(nica)*. Found in the granary portico. *RIB* 1340 (**21**)

Birdoswald: building of an *horreum* during the governorship of L. Alfenus Senecio, *c.*205-8, by *cohors I Aelia Dacorum* and *cohors I Thracum* under the tribune Aurelius Julianus. *RIB* 1909

Corbridge: building of an *horre[u]m* by a vexillation (unit name lost) during the governorship of G. Valerius Pudens or L. Alfenus Senecio between *c.*205-8. The stone is now built into the crypt of Hexham Abbey so a Corbridge origin is only assumed. *RIB* 1151

Greatchesters: restoration of an *horre[u]m* in 225 for *cohors II Asturum* during the reign of Severus Alexander and the governorship of [.....] Maximus, under the centurion Valerius Martialis. *RIB* 1738

Ianua — door, entrance, gate
see *Arcum*, York, above

Porta — gate

Birdoswald: recording building or restoration(?) at the east gate (where it was found) by *cohors I Aelia Dacorum* commanded by M. Claudius Menander during the governorship of Modius Julius. The exact date of this governor's term relies on interpretation of the butchered and re-cut *RIB* 980 from Netherby. However, it can only really be said that he was probably governor of *Britannia Inferior* during the early third century. *RIB* 1914

York: erection of (probably) the south-east gate of the fortress, near which it was found, by *IX Hispana* between 107-8 under Trajan. *RIB* restores *portam* but the original need not have been so specific. *RIB* 665

Porta cum muris — gate with walls

Risingham: rebuilding of a *portam cum muris* by *cohors I Vangionum*, by command of the governor L. Alfenus Senecio under the charge of Oclatinius Adventus, imperial procurator, and the tribune Aemilius Salvianus in the period *c.*205-8. Found by the south gate. *RIB* 1234 (**39**)

Porta cum turribus — gate with towers

Vindolanda: rebuilding of this *por[tam cum tu]rribus* in *c.*223 during the reign of Severus Alexander and the governorship of Claudius Xenophon (see Chapter 9 for his dates) by *[cohors IIII] Gallorum*. *RIB* 1706

Praetorium — commandant's house

Birdoswald: slab recording the restoration of a *praetor(ium)*, *princ(ipia)*, and *bal(neum)*, during the governorship of Aurelius Arpagius between 297-305, under the command of the centurion in command, Flavius Martinus. *RIB* 1912

Principia — headquarters

Birdoswald: slab recording the restoration of a *praetor(ium)*, *princ(ipia)*, and *bal(neum?)*, during the governorship of Aurelius Arpagius between 297-305, under the command of the centurion in command, Flavius Martinus. *RIB* 1912

Combe Down: resoration of a ruined headquarters by one Naevius, *lib(ertus) Aug(usti), adiut(or) proc(uratorum)*, 'imperial freedman and assistant to the procurators', under Caracalla (212-17), or Elagabalus (218-22) (the inscription gives PROCC, indicating a plural). The find-spot, close to a villa, has led to the suggestion that this was once the administrative centre of an imperial estate, supported by the finding of a lead seal reputedly of *Britannia Superior*. *RIB* 179 and 2411.37

Corbridge: building stone, of a headquarters(?), found in the headquarters strong-room by a vexillation of *VI Victrix* during the governorship of [Virius] Lupus, *c.*197-202. *RIB* 1163

Lanchester: see *armamentaria* above

40 *Dedication from Brough-on-Humber recording a new theatre stage,* proscaen[ium], *with the titles of Antoninus Pius for 140-61 (RIB gives a more precise date based on restoration, but the consular date does not survive). RIB's expansion of C in the triangular decoration on the side as part of* c(ivitas) P(arisii) *(assuming a matching P on the other side) is now rejected; the 'C' is probably part of the decoration. Diameter 0.66m.* RIB 707

Rough Castle: building of the *pri[nci]pia*, giving the titles for Antoninus Pius for the period 139-61. *RIB* 2145

Proscaenium — theatrical stage
Brough-on-Humber: presentation of a *proscaen(ium)* or *proscaen[ium]* by M. Ulpius Januarius, aedile of *Petuaria* some time between 140-61. *RIB* 707 (**40**)

Sepulcrum — tomb (see also *tumulus*)
Watercrook: slab from a tomb used by P. Aelius Bassus, veteran of *XX Valeria Victrix*, and others, erected by Aelius Surinus of *VI Victrix*, referring to the *sepulc(rum)*. *RIB* 754

Templum/Aedes/Fanum — temple/shrine
Bath: repair and repainting of a facade of the Four Seasons by Claudius Ligur. Stated in an inscription forming part of the facade and found on the site. *RIB* 141
Bath: lead 'curse' tablet recording a gift to *templum Marti*, 'temple of Mars', by Basilia. Cunliffe (1988), no. 97 (and various others)
Benwell: *templum* rebuilt about 238-44, recorded on a relief to the Matres Campestres and Genius alae I Hispanorum [...] Gordiana by the prefect T(erentius?) Agrippa. *RIB* 1334
Bewcastle: *templum* built and dedicated to Jupiter Optimus Maximus Dolichenus by an unknown individual or unit. *RIB* 992
Brough-on-Noe: restoration of a building, probably a temple (the inscription is damaged), on an altar to Hercules Augustus, dedicated by the prefect Proculus, probably commanding *cohors I Aquitanorum* (see *RIB* 283). *Brit.* xi (1980), 404, no. 3
Brougham: implicit on a fragmentary dedication by a member of *VI Victrix* referring to *instrumento* (shrine equipment). *RIB* 783
Caerleon: restoration of a *templ(um)* of Diana by T. Flavius Postumius [V]arus, *V(ir) C(larissimus)* (senator), and legate (of *II Augusta*?). Mid-third century (if the identification of Varus with the *praefectus urbi* in Rome in 271 is correct). *RIB* 316
Caerleon: restoration of an *(aedem)*? on a dedication to Jupiter Optimus Maximus and Genius by a legate (of *II Augusta*?), name lost, between the years 177-80. *Brit.* i (1970), 305, no. 1
Castlecary: building of an *(a)ed(em)* to Mercury by members of *VI Victrix*, 'citizens of Italy and Noricum' presumably between *c.*138-61. *RIB* 2148

41 *Altar from London, deity unknown, referring to the collapse (*conlabsum*) of, probably, a temple and its restoration by Aquilinus,* Aug(usti) lib(ertus), *and three others (Mercator, Audax, and Graec(us)). The style of the lettering is miserable, even taking into account the damage and weathering. Date unknown but probably third century. Found reused in the late riverside wall. Height 0.93m.* Britannia *vii (1976), 378, no. 1*

Castlesteads: restoration of a *templum* to the Matres Omnium Gentium by G. Julius Cupitianus, centurion commanding an unspecified unit. *RIB* 1988

Chichester: building of a *templum* to Neptune and Minerva between *c.*50-100 by the *collegium fabrorum*. *RIB* 91

Colchester: *templum divo Claudio*, 'temple to the deified Claudius', in existence by the year 60. Tacitus, *Annals* xiv.31

Dover: building of an *aedem* to the Matres Italicae by Olus Cordius, *st(rator) co(n)s(ularis)*. *Brit.* viii (1977), 426-7, no. 4

Hadrian's Wall (near mc 3): construction of, probably but not certainly, a temple or shrine to the god Digenis(?) by Julius Maximus, *sac(erdos)*. *RIB* 1314

Hadrian's Wall (mc 19): building of a *templ(um)* recorded on an altar to the Matres by a vexillation of *cohors I Vardullorum*. *RIB* 1421

Lincoln: dedication recording a *templum*, deity and dedicant, an *Aug(usti) lib(ertus)*, unknown. *Brit.* x (1979), 345, no. 5

London: restoration of, probably, a shrine dedicated to the Matres either by a woman called Vicinia, or the district, *vicinia* perhaps being a form of *vicus*(?). *RIB* 2

London: restoration of a collapsed structure, presumably a temple, to Jupiter Optimus Maximus by Aquilinus, *Aug(usti) lib(ertus)*, with Mercator, Audax and Graecus. *Brit.* vii (1976), 378, no. 1 (**41**)

London: *fanum Isidis*, 'temple of Isis', on a graffito on a late-first-century flagon from Southwark. *RIB* 2503.127

London: rebuilding of a *templ(u)m Isidis*, 'temple of Isis', by M. Martiannius Pulcher, governor of, presumably, *Britannia Superior*. *Brit.* vii (1976), 378, no. 2

Lydney Park: *templum [No]dentis*, 'the temple of Nodens', is recorded on a lead *defixio* composed by Silvianus. *RIB* 306

Netherby: *templum*, of an unknown deity, restored as a result of its recent collapse. The work may have been done during the reign of Severus Alexander (222-35), possibly by *cohors I Aelia Hispanorum*. *RIB* 979 (**42**)

Old Carlisle: restoration of a *te[mplum]* to the goddess A[...] by L. Vater[ius Mar]cellus, prefect of

42 Slab from Netherby recording a restored temple nu[per nimia vetus]tate conlabsum, *'recently collapsed because of its antiquity'. RIB restores* cohors I Aelia Hispanorum *in the first line (from other inscriptions of the unit at Netherby, e.g. RIB 978), followed by the deleted titles of Severus Alexander for 222. Height 0.56m.* RIB 979

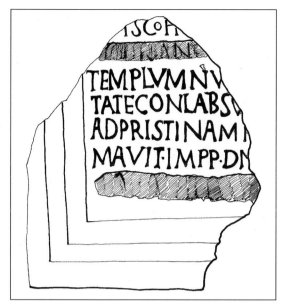

presumably *ala Augusta ob virtutem appellata. RIB* 886

Old Penrith: restoration of, probably, a temple to Jupiter Optimus Maximus by Aurelius At[tianus?], prefect of *cohors II Gallorum. RIB* 916

Old Penrith: restoration of an *ae[dem]* to the Matres Tramarinae, and the divine Severus Alexander and his mother Julia Mammaea some time between 222-35 by the [vexil]latio M[a]r[sacorum?]. *RIB* 919

Pagans Hill: *fanum* referred to on lead curse sheet. *Brit.* xv (1984), 336, no. 7

Reculver: dedication of an *aedem pr[inci]piorum cu[m b]asilica,* 'shrine in the headquarters building with hall', at Reculver between *c.*210-35. The governor's name is included but is very fragmentary. The most likely restoration is Q. Aradius Rufinus but even this is not certain. *Antiq. Journ.* xli (1961), 224; *JRS* li (1961), 191, no. 1; and *JRS* lv (1965), 220, no. 1 (**43**)

Ribchester: restoration of a *templum* between the years 225-35 by the centurion T. Floridius Natalis. The slab includes the name of the governor of (presumably) *Britannia Inferior,* V. Crescens Fulvianus, and traces of the name of Severus Alexander. The governors for the early part of the reign are known; therefore Fulvianus' term must be later. *RIB* 587

Rudchester: restoration of a *templ(um)* to Sol Invictus (i.e. Mithras) by the prefect T. Claudius Decimus Cornelius Antonius (found in the mithraeum). *RIB* 1396

Uley: *in templo Mercurii,* 'in the temple of Mercury', referred to in a defixio. *Brit.* xix (1988), 485-7, no. 2

Wallsend: construction of a *templum* recorded on a statue base by G. Julius Maximinus, centurion of *VI Victrix. RIB* 1305

Winchester: restoration of, presumably, a temple or shrine to the Matres, recorded on an altar dedicated by [A]ntonius [Lu]cretianus, *[b(ene)]f(iciarius) co(n)s(ularis). RIB* 88

York: erection of a *templum* to Serapis by Claudius Hieronymianus, legate of *VI Victrix.* Late second/early third century: see his biography in Chapter 9. *RIB* 658 (**74**)

York: restoration of an *aedem* to the Numen Augusti and the goddess Joug[...]. *RIB* 656

Theatrum — theatre
Colchester: *theatrum* in existence by 60. Tacitus, *Annals* xiv.32
See also *Proscaenium* above

Tumulus — tomb
Old Carlisle: *tumulum* mentioned on the tombstone of Amatius Ingenuus. *RIB* 906

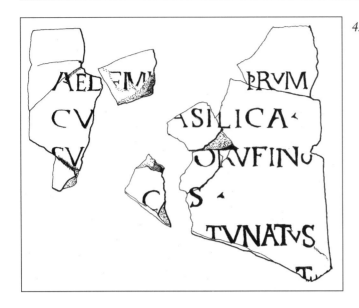

43 Damaged inscription from the headquarters at Reculver. That [For]tunatus dedicated or built the aedem p[rinci]piorum cu[m b]asilica, *'shrine of the headquarters with hall', is clear enough. The work seems to have occurred under* (sub) *the consular governor* (cos) *[..r(?)...]* Rufinus. *The various candidates all belong to the early third century. Width 305mm. JRS* li *(1961), 191-2, no. 1*

Turrem at castrum — tower and fort

Ravenscar: slab recording the construction of a *turr[e]m (et) castrum* by Justinianus, *p(rae)p(ositus)*, and Vindicianus, described as *masbier* (for *magister*, see Chapter 7). The style of the lettering is poor, like the datable milestones of the third and fourth century, and is assumed to be of fourth-century date. *RIB* 721

Vallum — rampart

Antonine Wall (Braidfield Farm nr Duntocher): 3240ft of *opus valli*, 'rampart work', by *VI Victrix*. *RIB* 2200

Bainbridge: erection of *[vallum cum?] bracchio caementicium*, '[rampart with?] irregular stonework', by *cohors VI Nerviorum* during the governorship of L. Alfenus Senecio and under the *praep[(ositus)* L. Vivius Pius, *c*.205-8. *RIB* 722

Carvoran: century of Silvanus *vallavit p(edes) CXII*, literally 'ramparted for 112 feet', during the prefecture of Flavius Secundus (datable to *c*.136-8 by *RIB* 1778, see Fortuna Augusta in Chapter 8). Similar usages at Carvoran on *RIB* 1816 and 1818 by different centuries (see also *RIB* 1822); the verb is otherwise unknown in Britain. *RIB* 1820

Hadrian's Wall (48m west of t 26b): 113 ft of *val(lum)*, by the *t(urma)* of Lucius A[..] Fanus. *RIB* 1445

6 Milestones

The milestones, or honorific pillars, of Roman Britain form a special category of inscribed stones. Largely datable they sometimes provide details of distances to and from places, and occasionally even of civic governments. But the majority provide just imperial titles. Most belong to the third and early fourth century, and in this respect they differ from all other classes of Roman inscriptions in Britain (**3**).

Their purpose seems to have been both to mark out roads, and publicise details of regimes. The texts are almost always more explicit than, for example, coin legends and a number of lesser emperors, such as Florinus (276), are represented who otherwise are unknown on Romano-British inscriptions. During the period of the Tetrarchies in the early fourth century almost all the various challengers are represented, often individually.

By definition these stones were installed outside Roman settlements. Not surprisingly, they are rarely located by excavation in their original sites. Roman roads are normally only surveyed, not excavated, so milestones are only likely to turn up by chance. A larger number have been found in contexts which make it clear they had been reused. The group from Bitterne (Hants) were almost all found in the late town walls. Although this helps us date the time after which the defences were built, it means also that milestones, as found, cannot accurately reflect their original distribution.

In a few instances there is some evidence for how milestones were administered. At Crindledykes Farm, near Vindolanda, a group was found buried together. This cache may be an accumulation of milestones, removed one by one when new milestones in the name of a new regime were installed, or they may represent a one-off post-Roman clearance. Either is possible, but some other milestones show clearly that, instead of being replaced, new inscriptions overlay old ones, or were carved elsewhere on the stone. These provide evidence for a rate of replacement. One from Castleford, incidentally found by the Roman road near the town, bears the titles of Trajan Decius (249-51) at one end, and at the other those of Gallus and Volusianus (251-3). As both could not be visible simultaneously it is clear that the Trajan Decius text could only have been on show for three to four years before the stone was inverted and a new inscription installed (*RIB* 2273, 2274). However, the text on one from Bitterne, originally carved for Gordian III (238-44), was overlain by one for Tetricus I (270-3). Here the original text escaped amendment for at least 26 years.

It is also true that most other Trajan Decius milestones were not inverted and recarved. Unfortunately, we have no way of knowing if they were physically replaced by new stones, though the small number of stones which were recarved, rather than replaced, suggests that there was at the very least a piecemeal tendency to update existing milestones. The Gordian III stone from Bitterne shows that this cannot have been ubiquitous and regimented, but we cannot say if it was common or rare. Certainly, none seem to have been replaced by new stones naming the same regime. Perhaps the only easy comparison is the British postbox, replaced when needed and bearing the cypher of the incumbent monarch, though of course these are not subject to political suppression, erasure and deliberate removal.

Milestones seem to survive either because they were located in remote places, or because excavations at other Roman sites have produced them in contexts which show they had been reused. The implication is, taking into account the small number of milestones known from more densely-populated and developed parts of Britain, they must once have been very widespread, though the possibility that some were made of wood should not be discounted. If there was at the very least a habit of replacing some as new regimes were established, then that helps explain the absence of first-century and the paucity of second-century examples. The numbers of third- and early-fourth century milestones may be explained by the shortness of many reigns, the political circumstances of the time which made it more likely that names and symbols of predecessors would be suppressed, and, finally, the cessation of milestone production no later than *c.*340 which meant that defacement or official removal of older stones would cease. However, they of course remained susceptible to unofficial removal, explaining the examples from the villa at Rockbourne.

Very few milestones state distance information or town names. There is no certain explanation for this. Perhaps the milestones were produced to standard formats in masons' yards and had mileage painted on them when installed. Texts on the stones are mainly crude and poorly carved onto the drum. In a few cases more care was taken, for example *RIB* 2303 of Constantinian date from Crindleykes near Chesters. Here a special bordered panel was carved to carry the text.

In order to provide milestone data in usable form they are listed twice below, firstly by date and then by county. The surviving rates per annum of reigns may, or may not, reflect the original rates of production in individual regimes. Milestones which cannot be accurately dated, for example *RIB* 2243 (bearing imperial titles which could belong to most of the second-century emperors) from about 10 miles south-west of Brough-on-Noe, are not included.

p = primary text
s = secondary text

BY REIGN

Hadrian
119-20: Leicester (Leics), 2 miles N. *RIB* 2244
119-38: Lancaster (Lancs), 4 miles ENE. *RIB* 2272
120-1: Caerhun (Gwynedd), 7 miles W. *RIB* 2265 (**44**)

Antoninus Pius
139-61: Bar Hill (AW), vicinity of, location and stone lost. *RIB* 2312

44 Milestone found nearly 7 miles (11km) west of the fort at Caerhun, Kanovium. The inscription includes Hadrian's titles for 120-1 and the distance a Kanovio *as 8 miles,* m(ilia) p(assum) VIII. *Height 2m. (Copyright © The British Museum).* RIB *2265*

140-4: Cramond (AW), vicinity of, location lost. *RIB* 2313 (see *RIB* 95, p. 800, note, for a new reading; previously thought to be Severan)

Severan
180-217: Bitterne (Hants), reused in the town wall. *RIB* 2228 (attribution to this period uncertain
198-209: Caerhun (Gwynedd), 7 miles W. *RIB* 2266

Caracalla
212-17: Caernarvon (Gwynedd), 7 miles NE. *RIB* 2264
213: Hadrian's Wall, E of mc 17. *RIB* 2298

Severus Alexander
222-3: Vindolanda (Northd), 1 mile E. *RIB* 2299
222-3: Hadrian's Wall, 200m ESE of mc 42. *RIB* 2306
231-5: Gwaenysgor (Clwyd). *JRS* xlvii (1957), 230, no. 19

Gordian III
238-44: Bitterne (Hants), probably reused in town wall. *RIB* 2222
238-44: Bitterne. *RIB* 2224p
238-44: Redruth (Cornwall), 1.25 miles E. *RIB* 2234
238-44: Kenchester (Hereford & Worcs), reused in town wall. *RIB* 2250
238-44: Port Talbot (W. Glam). *RIB* 2252 (same stone as 2253, 2256)
238-44: Ribchester (Lancs), original location lost. *RIB* 2269
238-44: Scalesceugh (Cumbria), 5 miles SE Carlisle. *RIB* 2289
238-44: Willington (Durham), NE of. *RIB* 2294

238-44: Lanchester (Durham). *RIB* 2295

238-44: Wonston (Hants). *Brit.* xvi (1985), 324, no. 3 — date of this example uncertain but like *RIB* 2222 it was erected by *r(es) p(ublica) B(eglarum)* and it is stylistically identical (see drawing in *RIB*, p. 692, and pl. xxviii in *Brit.* xvi)

Philip I

244-9: Lancaster (Lancs), 3 miles S. *RIB* 2270

244-6: Hangingshaw, Appleby (Cumbria), with Philip II as Caesar. *RIB* 2284

247: Old Carlisle (Cumbria), with Philip II as consul and Caesar prior to his elevation to joint Augustus that summer. *RIB* 2286

Trajan Decius

249-51: Caernarvon (Gwynedd), 5 miles E. *RIB* 2263

249-51: Ribchester (Lancs). *RIB* 598

249-51: Rbchester. original location lost. *RIB* 2268

249-51: Lancaster (Lancs), 3 miles S. *RIB* 2271

249-51: Aldborough (N. Yorks), 3 miles N. *RIB* 2276s (primary illegible)

249-51: Aldborough, S of N. gate. *RIB* 2277

249-51: Aldborough, 'near'. *RIB* 2278

249-51: Rockbourne (Hants). *JRS* lvi (1966), 219, no. 9

250-1: Castleford (W. Yorks), 0.5 miles S. *RIB* 2273 (same stone as 2274)

Trebonianus Gallus and Volusian (251-3)

251-3: Bitterne (Hants), reused in town wall. *RIB* 2223

251-3: Tintagel (Cornwall), exact original location lost. *RIB* 2230

251-3: Castleford (W. Yorks), 0.5 miles S. *RIB* 2274 (same stone as 2273)

251-3: Greta Bridge (Durham). *RIB* 2279

Valerian I (253-60)

253-60: Lincoln, 1 mile SW. *RIB* 2240

Postumus (259-68) (Gallic Empire)

259-68: Breage (Cornwall), exact original location lost. *RIB* 2232

259-68: Margam (W. Glam), 10 miles SE of Neath. *RIB* 2255

259-68: Trecastle Hill (Powys). *RIB* 2260

259-68: Brougham (Cumbria). *JRS* lv (1965), 224, no. 11 (**45**)

259-68: Dorchester (Dorset), reused in a late-Roman building 0.6 miles SE. *Brit.* xvii (1986), 435, no.7

261-2: Aber (Gwynedd). *JRS* l (1960), 238, no. 13; revised in *JRS* lii (1962), 195, no. 24p

Victorinus (268-70) (Gallic Empire)

268-70: Chesterton (Hunts). *RIB* 2238

268-70: Lincoln. *RIB* 2241

268-70: Pyle (W. Glam), 11 miles SE of Neath. *RIB* 2251

268-70: Trecastle Hill (Powys). *RIB* 2261 (same stone as *RIB* 2260)

268-70: Old Penrith (Cumbria). *RIB* 2287

268-70: Corbridge (Northd). *RIB* 2296

Tetricus I (270-3) and Tetricus II Gallic Empire

270-3: Bitterne (Hants). *RIB* 2224s

270-3: Bitterne. *RIB* 2225

270-3: Bitterne, reused in town wall. *RIB* 2226

272: Rockbourne (Hants), reused in the villa. *JRS* lii (1962), 195, no. 23

Claudius II (268-70)

268-70: Wall (Staffs). *RIB* 2246

45 *Milestone from Brougham, naming*
   Postumus (259-68), and dedicated by the
   R(espublica) C(ivitas) Car(vetiorum*)*.
   Height 0.76m. JRS *lv (1965), 224, no. 11*

Aurelian (270-5)
273-5: Bitterne (Hants). *RIB* 2227
273-5: Carvoran (HW), 0.5+ mile E. *RIB* 2309

Tacitus (275-6)
275-6: Dynevor, Llandeilo (Dyfed), original location lost. *RIB* 2262

Florianus (276)
276: Water Newton (Cambs), 1 mile S. *RIB* 2235
276: Castleford (W. Yorks). *RIB* 2275
276: Bowes (Durham), 2.5 miles W. *RIB* 2280p

Probus (276-82)
276-82: Bowes (Durham), 2.5 miles W. *RIB* 2280s
276-82: Vindolanda (Northd), 1 mile E. *RIB* 2300

Carus (282-3), Numerian (283-4), and Carinus as Caesar (283-5)
282-3: Carus. Bowes (Durham), 5 miles W. *RIB* 2281
282-3: Carus. Bowes, 5 miles W. *RIB* 2282
283-4: Numerian. Hadrian's Wall, 200m ESE of mc 42. *RIB* 2307
282-3: Carinus. Clanville (Hants), near the villa. *RIB* 98

Diocletian and Maximian (284-305)
284-305: Diocletian. Melin Crythan (W. Glam), 1.5 miles S of Neath. *RIB* 2257
286-305: Diocletian and Maximian. Port Talbot (W. Glam). *RIB* 2256 (same stone as 2252, 2253)
296-306: Constantius I. Brecon (Powys), 2.5 miles SE. *RIB* 2258 (same stone as 2259)

Carausius (286-93)
286-93: Gallows Hill (Cumbria), 1 mile S Carlisle. *RIB* 2291 (same stone as 2292)

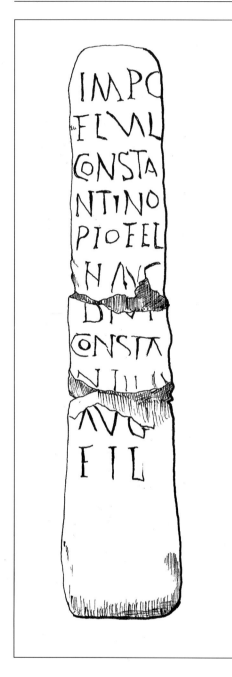

46 Milestone column from Caves Inn for Constantine I of 307-37. A large number of similar stones for this reign are known. Height 1.17m. JRS liv (1964), 179, no. 8

Second Tetrarchy 305-7

305: Diocletian. Hadrian's Wall at Old Wall nr mc59. *RIB* 2311

305-6: Flavius Severus (Caesar). Venn Bridge (Som), 5 miles SW of Ilchester. *RIB* 2229

305-6: Flavius Severus and Maximinus Daia (Caesars). Rochester (Kent), 3 miles W. *RIB* 2219

305-7: Galerius (or 305-11). Piercebridge (Durham). *RIB* 2293

305-7: Maximian (or 305-11). Vindolanda (Northd). *RIB* 2301 third text

306-7: Constantine I (Caesar). St Hilary (Cornwall), original location lost. *RIB* 2233

306-7: Constantine I (Caesar). Cambridge, 3 miles N. *RIB* 2237 (text repeated and superimposed)

306-7: Constantine I (Caesar). Gallows Hill (Cumbria), 1 mile S Carlisle. *RIB* 2292 (same stone as 2291)

306-7: Constantine I (Caesar). Vindolanda (Northd), 1 mile E. *RIB* 2303

306-7: Constantine I (Caesar). Carvoran (HW). *RIB* 2310

House of Constantine I, as Augustus (307-37)

307-37: West Worthing (W. Sussex). *RIB* 2220

307-37: Ancaster (Lincs), 0.25 mile N. *RIB* 2242

307-37: Worcester (Hereford & Worcs), 4 miles S. *RIB* 2249

307-37: Caerhun (Gwynedd), 4 miles W. *RIB* 2267

307-37: Bwlch-y-Ddeufaen, Caerhun (Gwynedd). *JRS* xlvi (1956), 148, no. 11

307-37: Brougham (Cumbria). *RIB* 2285

307-37: Hesket (Cumbria), 9 miles SE of Carlisle. *RIB* 2288

307-37: Vindolanda (Northd), 1 mile E. *RIB* 2302

307-37: Caves Inn (Leics). *JRS* liv (1964), 179, no. 8 (**46**)

307-37: Alcester (Warws). *JRS* lvi (1966), 220, no. 10

308-24: Port Talbot (W. Glam). *RIB* 2253 (same stone as *RIB* 2252, 2256)

309-13: Port Talbot, 5 miles SE of Neath. *RIB* 2254

309-13: Vindolanda, 1 mile E. *RIB* 2301 (fourth text)

317-26: Crispus (Caesar). Peterborough(?), original location lost. *RIB* 2239

308-24: Licinius I. Tintagel (Cornwall), original location lost. *RIB* 2231

309-13: Maximinus Daia. Corbridge (Northd). *RIB* 2297

317-37/40: Constantine II. Brecon (Powys), 2.5 miles SE. *RIB* 2259 (same stone as *RIB* 2258)

BY REGION

Southern England

Cornwall
238-44: Redruth, 1.25 miles E. *RIB* 2234
251-3: Tintagel, exact original location lost. *RIB* 2230
259-68: Breage, exact original location lost. *RIB* 2232
306-7: St Hilary, original location lost. *RIB* 2233
308-24: Tintagel, original location lost. *RIB* 2231

Dorset
259-68: Dorchester, reused in a late-Roman building 0.6 miles SE. *Brit.* xvii (1986), 435, no.7

Hants
180-217: Bitterne, reused in the town wall. *RIB* 2228 (attribution to this reign uncertain
238-44: Bitterne, probably reused in town wall. *RIB* 2222
238-44: Bitterne. *RIB* 2224p
238-44: Wonston. *Brit.* xvi (1985), 324, no. 3
249-51: Rockbourne. *JRS* lvi (1966), 219, no. 9
251-3: Bitterne, reused in town wall. *RIB* 2223
270-3: Bitterne. *RIB* 2224s
270-3: Bitterne. *RIB* 2225
270-3: Bitterne, reused in town wall. *RIB* 2226
272: Rockbourne, reused in the villa. *JRS* lii (1962), 195, no. 23
273-5: Bitterne. *RIB* 2227
282-3: Clanville, near the villa. *RIB* 98

Kent
305-6: Rochester, 3 miles W. *RIB* 2219

Somerset
305-6: Venn Bridge, 5 miles SW of Ilchester. *RIB* 2229

Sussex
307-37: West Worthing. *RIB* 2220

East Anglia

Cambridgeshire
276: Water Newton, 1 mile S. *RIB* 2235
306-7: Cambridge, 3 miles N. *RIB* 2237 (text repeated and superimposed)
317-26: Peterborough(?), original location lost. *RIB* 2239

Huntingdonshire
268-70: Chesterton. *RIB* 2238

Midlands and Welsh Marches

Hereford and Worcestershire
238-44: Kenchester, reused in town wall. *RIB* 2250
307-37: Worcester, 4 miles S. *RIB* 2249

Leics
119-20: Leicester, 2 miles N. *RIB* 2244
307-37: Caves Inn. *JRS* liv (1964), 179, no. 8 (**46**)

Staffs
268-70: Wall. *RIB* 2246

Warwickshire
307-37: Alcester. *JRS* lvi (1966), 220, no. 10

Northern Britain (including Lincs and Scotland)

Antonine Wall
139-61: Bar Hill, vicinity of, location and stone lost. *RIB* 2312
140-4: Cramond, vicinity of, location lost. *RIB* 2313 (see *RIB95*, p. 800, note, for a new drawing

Cumbria
238-44: Scalesceugh, 5 miles SE Carlisle. *RIB* 2289
244-6: Hangingshaw, Appleby. *RIB* 2284
247: Old Carlisle. *RIB* 2286
259-68: Brougham. *JRS* lv (1965), 224, no. 11 (**45**)
268-70: Old Penrith. *RIB* 2287
286-93: Gallows Hill, 1 mile S Carlisle. *RIB* 2291 (same stone as 2292)
306-7: Gallows Hill, 1 mile S Carlisle. *RIB* 2292 (same stone as 2291)
307-37: Brougham. *RIB* 2285
307-37: Hesket, 9 miles SE of Carlisle. *RIB* 2288

Durham
238-44: Willington, NE of. *RIB* 2294
238-44: Lanchester. *RIB* 2295
251-3: Greta Bridge. *RIB* 2279
276: Bowes, 2.5 miles W. *RIB* 2280p
276-82: Bowes, 2.5 miles W. *RIB* 2280s
282-3: Bowes, 5 miles W. *RIB* 2281
282-3: Bowes, 5 miles W. *RIB* 2282
305-7: Piercebridge. *RIB* 2293

Hadrian's Wall
213: E of mc 17. *RIB* 2298
222-3: Vindolanda, 1 mile E. *RIB* 2299
222-3: 200m ESE of mc 42. *RIB* 2306
273-5: Carvoran, 0.5+ mile E. *RIB* 2309

276-82: Vindolanda, 1 mile E. *RIB* 2300

283-4: 200m ESE of mc 42. *RIB* 2307

305: at Old Wall nr mc59. *RIB* 2311

305-7: Vindolanda. *RIB* 2301 third text

306-7: Vindolanda, 1 mile E. *RIB* 2303

306-7: Carvoran. *RIB* 2310

307-37: Vindolanda, 1 mile E. *RIB* 2302

309-13: Vindolanda, 1 mile E. *RIB* 2301 (fourth text)

Lancs

119-38: Lancaster, 4 miles ENE. *RIB* 2272

238-44: Ribchester, original location lost. *RIB* 2269

244-9: Lancaster, 3 miles S. *RIB* 2270

249-51: Ribchester. *RIB* 598

249-51: Ribchester, original location lost. *RIB* 2268

249-51: Lancaster, 3 miles S. *RIB* 2271

Lincs

253-60: Lincoln, 1 mile SW. *RIB* 2240

268-70: Lincoln. *RIB* 2241

307-37: Ancaster, 0.25 mile N. *RIB* 2242

Northumberland

268-70: Corbridge. *RIB* 2296

309-13: Corbridge. *RIB* 2297

N. Yorks

249-51: Aldborough, 3 miles N. *RIB* 2276s (primary illegible)

249-51: Aldborough, S of N. gate. *RIB* 2277

249-51: Aldborough, 'near'. *RIB* 2278

W. Yorks

250-1: Castleford, 0.5 miles S. *RIB* 2273 (same stone as 2274)

276: Castleford. *RIB* 2275

Northern Wales

Clwyd

231-5: Gwaenysgor. *JRS* xlvii (1957), 230, no. 19

Gwynedd

120-1: Caerhun, 7 miles W. *RIB* 2265 (**44**)

198-209: Caerhun, 7 miles W. *RIB* 2266

212-17: Caernarvon, 7 miles NE. *RIB* 2264

249-51: Caernarvon, 5 miles E. *RIB* 2263

307-37: Caerhun, 4 miles W. *RIB* 2267

307-37: Bwlch-y-Ddeufaen, Caerhun. *JRS* xlvi (1956), 148, no. 11

Southern Wales

Dyfed

275-6: Dynevor, Llandeilo (Dyfed), original location lost. *RIB* 2262

West Glamorgan

238-44: Port Talbot. *RIB* 2252 (same stone as 2253, 2256)

259-68: Margam, 10 miles SE of Neath. *RIB* 2255

268-70: Pyle, 11 miles SE of Neath. *RIB* 2251

284-305: Melin Crythan, 1.5 miles S of Neath. *RIB* 2257

286-305: Port Talbot. *RIB* 2256 (same stone as 2252, 2253)

308-24: Port Talbot. *RIB* 2253 (same stone as *RIB* 2252, 2256)

309-13: Port Talbot, 5 miles SE of Neath. *RIB* 2254

Powys

259-68: Trecastle Hill. *RIB* 2260

268-70: Trecastle Hill. *RIB* 2261 (same stone as *RIB* 2260)

296-306: Brecon, 2.5 miles SE. *RIB* 2258 (same stone as 2259)

317-37/40: Brecon, 2.5 miles SE. *RIB* 2259 (same stone as *RIB* 2258)

7 Posts and occupations

INTRODUCTION

As part of the Roman Empire, Britain had a full complement of Roman officials, administrators, soldiers, and civil occupations. Or so it would be reasonable to infer. But as usual the evidence is piecemeal. Leading officials have already been dealt with (Chapter 3). This chapter is concerned with lesser individuals holding posts for which they are often the only known examples in Roman Britain. Thus we have an aedile from the minor town of Brough but none from the major towns. Our problem is whether we assume that such individuals were exceptional, or whether the evidence which testifies them is exceptional. The latter is almost certainly the case and may be attributed to problems of survival as well as there having been fewer occasions on which such officials recorded themselves in Britain.

Lesser positions such as centurion, which are extremely widely known, are omitted. The division into Civil and Military is for guidance only. As a military province Britain's provincial administration was largely military in character and many of the governor's staff were soldiers on attachment. Military posts far outweigh civilian posts in the record, emphasizing the military indulgence in epigraphy.

Generally speaking the examples listed here are those recorded on inscriptions found in Britain. Some soldiers, either on tombstones or career inscriptions found abroad, record spells in some of these positions. These, however, rarely tell us where they held those posts. At least with the Romano-British examples we know where they were active or where they died when they were in the positions. Some interesting observations may be made about the distribution and type of posts testified on monuments found in Britain. For example, the post of *primus pilus* is much less well testified than that of *signifer*. In part this is obviously because there were many more standard bearers than senior centurions. On the other the testified *signiferi* are almost all known from tombstones whereas the handful of *primi pili* are not.

CIVIL POSTS

aedilis — aedile, magistrate with responsibility for civic amenities
Brough-on-Humber/North Ferriby: M. Ulpius Januarius, *aedilis*. 140-61. *RIB* 707 (**40**)

adiutor procuratorum — assistant of the procurators
Combe Down: Naevius, *lib(ertus) Aug(usti)* and *adiut(or) proc(uratorum)*, was responsible for rebuilding a *principia* (headquarters building) at Combe Down. The site was later occupied by a villa. His post has given rise to the suggestion that he helped administer an imperial estate,

supported by the find of a seal possibly of the province of *B(ritannia) S(uperior)* or *S(ancta)* on the site. 212-22. *RIB* 179 and *RIB* 2411.37
(see also *procurator* below)

arkarius/arcarius — treasurer
Chichester: an *ark(arius)* (name lost) seems to be recorded on an altar dedicated to the Matres Domesticae. *Brit.* x (1979), 339, no. 1

censitor Brittonum Anavion(ensium) — censor of the Anavionensian Britons
Foligno (Italy): tombstone of a man who held this post. His name is lost but T. Haterius Nepos (see Chapter 9) has been suggested. The location in Britain is unknown but his position as *censitor* of a local area is likely to have been matched at numerous other locations, probably in the military north or west. Believed to be Trajanic because this man's next post was as procurator in Armenia, annexed by Trajan in 114 but given up by Hadrian. *ILS* 1338

censitor civium Romanorum — censor of Roman citizens
Colchester: Gnaeus Munatius Aurelius Bassus at the Victricensian colony at Colchester. Undated. *ILS* 2740 (Nomentum)

comes sacrarum largitionum — count of sacred handouts
See *comes* in Chapter 4

curator — treasurer
Lincoln: G. Antistius Frontinus, on an altar dedicated to the Parcae Deae and Numina Augustorum. The body whose valuables he looked after is unknown, but he had been appointed to the position *ter(tium)*, 'for the third time'. *RIB* 247

curiales — late term for councillor, see *decurio* below

decurio — decurion, one of the 100 members of the *ordo*, town council (but see also the military *decurio* below)
Bath: part of a tomb of a *dec(urio) coloniae Glev[ensis]* (Gloucester), name lost, who died at Bath at the age of 80. *RIB* 161
Lincoln: tombstone of Volusia Faustina, citizen of *Lindum* (Lincoln), erected by her husband Aurelius Senecio, *dec(urio)*. *RIB* 250 (**47**)
Vindolanda: Lucius, *decurioni* from (place name lost), named on a wooden writing tablet. There is no indication that his post was a military one. *Tab. Vindol.* II.299
York: coffin of Flavius Bellator, *dec(urionis) col(oniae) Eboracens(is)*. *RIB* 674
York: coffin of Ant. Gargilianus (see *praefectus castrorum*), dedicated by Claudius Florentinus, *dec(urio)*. *Brit.* i (1970), 308, no. 14
York: coffin, name lost, *dec(urionis) col(oniae) Ebor[acensis]*. *Brit.* xviii (1987), 367, no. 5

legatus Augusti — Imperial legate, or governor. See Chapter 4

legatus uridicus — Imperial juridical legate. See Chapter 4

libertus Augusti — freedman of the emperor
Combe Down: see *adiutor procuratorum* above. *RIB* 179
Housesteads: altar, name lost of a *lib(ertus) A(ugusti)*. *RIB* 1610
Lincoln: on a dedication, name lost, of an *Aug(usti) lib(ertus)* recording a temple. *Brit.* x (1979), 345, no. 5
London: altar dedicated by Aquilinus, *Aug(usti) lib(ertus)*, and others, possibly to Jupiter Optimus Maximus and perhaps referring to a restored temple. *Brit.* vii (1976), 378, no. 1
York: Nikomedes on an altar to *Britannia*, describing himself as *Aug(ustorum) n(ostrorum) lib(ertus)*, which must place the date as not before 161, time of the first period of joint imperial rule. *RIB* 643

47 *Tombstone found reused in
Lincoln's Roman walls. Volusia
Faustina (left),* c(ivis)
Lind(um), *'citizen of
Lincoln', lived 26 years, one
month and 26 days,* merita
c(oniugi), *'well-deserving
wife' to Aurelius Senecio,*
dec(urio), *'councillor'.
Cl(audia) (right), possibly
daughter of one Catiotuus, lived
to at least 60. The womens'
hair-styles indicate early-third-
century date. The stone, a
standard husband-and-wife
blank, may have been adapted
for specific circumstances
involving the apparently-
unrelated womens' deaths.
Height 0.84m. (Copyright ©
The British Museum).* RIB
250

magistri vikanorum/vicanorum — masters of the villagers
Old Carlisle: altar to Jupiter Optimus Maximus and Vulkanus dedicated by the *vik(anorum)
mag(istri)*, using money contributed by those villagers. *RIB* 899

notarius — imperial secretary
In Britain: Paulus, *notarius*, sent to Britain in 353 in the aftermath of the Revolt of Magnentius (350-
3) to weed out Magnetius' erstwhile supporters. The purge turned into an uncontrolled and
vicious pogrom, which ruined many innocent families. Ammianus xiv.5.6-8

procurator (not to be confused with the equestrian procurators, see Chapter 3)
Tricomia (Phrygia): dedication to M. Aurelius Marcio, imperial freedman (*Aug(usti) liber(tus)*),
sometime *proc(urator) prov(inciae) Brit(anniae)* and working to the imperial equestrian procurator.
Undated but after *c.*161. *ILS* 1477
see also *adiutor procuratorum* above

quaestor — magistrate with financial duties
see under *senator* below

rationalis summae rei — officer in charge of financial affairs
The existence of this post, held by Allectus under Carausius (286-93), was formerly inferred from the exergue mark on Carausian silver and one of his medallions (RSR), and the reference to Allectus' position in charge of *summae rei* ('affairs of the highest importance'). However, the abbreviation is without parallel (RAT S R is more normal). It has now been shown that RSR and a further exergue mark on another medallion of Carausius, INPCDA, correspond to the sixth and seventh lines of the Fourth Eclogue of Virgil thus confirming the Virgilian references on other Carausian coinage. *Rationalis summae rei* in Britain may therefore now be discarded. Aurelius Victor, *de Caesaribus* xxxix.41, and see de la Bédoyère 1998

rex magnus — Great King
Chichester: T. Claudius Togidubnus, as *reg(is) mag(nis)* or *r(egis) lega[ti] Aug(usti)* apparently
(depending on the restoration) on a dedication slab recording the building of a temple to Neptunus and Minerva by a *collegium fabror(um)*. Late first century. Claudius recorded the submission of *reges Brit[anniae] XI*, 'eleven British kings', on an arch in Rome of the year 51. Client kings in Britain did not apparently outlive the first century. See Chapter 9 for Togidubnus for references and further discussion; *ILS* 216 (Rome arch)*RIB* 91 (and Bogaers 1979)

servus Augusti — Imperial slave
Old Carlisle: an altar from here was once believed to record this post, expanded thus *Aug(usti servus)*.
This has now, hardly surprisingly, been rejected along with much of the reading of the rest of the text. *RIB* 902

senator — councillor (fourth century)
Old Penrith: Flavius Martius, *sen(atori) in c(ivitate) Carvetior(um) quaestorio*, 'councillor of the Carvetian canton, [after] a quaestorship'. *RIB* 933

servus provincialis — [Slave] of the province
London: altar dedicated by Anencletus, restored as *(servus?) provinc(ialis)*, to his wife Claudia Martina. His position is therefore not confirmed. *RIB* 21

patroni provinciae Britanniae — patron of the province of Britain
C. Julius Asper. Consul in 212. Cited by Frere (1987, 197). No source supplied and untraced.
M. Vettius Valens, see his biography Chapter 9. *CIL* xi.383

MILITARY POSTS

This list covers the principal or unusual posts with the following exceptions: senior positions such as *legatus legionis* are given in Chapter 3 above; prolific positions such as *centurio*, *optio* and *miles* are not included.

actor praefecti — clerk to the prefect
Old Penrith: Julius Augustalis *actor Jul(ii) Lupi pr(a)ef(ecti)*, 'clerk of the prefect Julius Lupus', on an altar to Mars Belatucadrus and Numina Augustorum. *RIB* 918

actuarius/actarius — military clerk, subordinate to *cornicularius*
Ambleside: Flavius Romanus, *act(arius)*, on his tombstone recording that he was *in cas(tello) inte(rfectus) ab hosti(bus)*, 'killed in the fort, by the enemy'. *JRS* liii (1963), 160, no. 4
Caerleon: Ursus, *actar(io) [l]e[g(ionis)]*, in charge of an inscribed pilaster to Numina Augustorum and the Genius legionis II Augustae, at the behest of the *p(rimus) p(ilus)* on 23 September 244. *RIB* 327
Caernarvon: Aurelius Sabinianus, *act(arius)*, on an altar to Minerva. *RIB* 429
Chester: G. Valerius Justus, *actar[i]us leg(ionis) XX*. *RIB* 507

48 *Damaged altar or slab from Ebchester,*
dedicated to Minerva, ((Miner)vae, by Julius
Gr...nus, an actarius *of cohors IIII*
Br(eucorum?). The inclusion of Antoniana *in*
the unit's name dates it to Caracalla (213-17)
or Elagabalus (218-22). Height 0.56m. RIB
1101

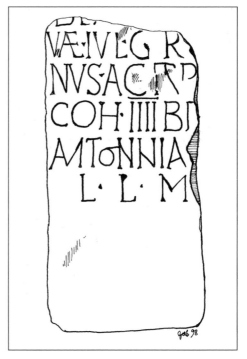

Ebchester: Julius Gr[...]nus, *actar[ius] cohors IIII Br[eucor(um)] Antonian[ae]*, on an altar to Minerva.
212-22. *RIB* 1101 (**48**)
aquilifer — bearer of the legionary eagle, subordinate to the centurion
Vindolanda: Vittius Adiutor, *aquilifer* with *II Augusta. Tab. Vindol.* II.189, no. 214
Wroxeter: T. Flaminius, *aq(uilifer)* with *XIV Gemina. c.*50-69. This revises the former reading in *RIB*.
RIB 292 (see *Brit.* xxvi (1995), 388-9, (b), and *RIB95*, p. 761, note)

archiereia (Greek) — priestess
Corbridge: altar to Heracles of Tyre by Diodora, *archiereia*). *RIB* 1129

architectus/arcitectus — legionary engineer
Birrens: Amandus, *arcitectus*, on a statuette to Brigantia. *RIB* 2091 (**49**)
Birrens: Gamidiahus, *arcit(ectus)*, on an altar to Harimella. *RIB* 2096
Carrawburgh: Quintus, *architect(us)*, on an altar to Minerva. *RIB* 1542

armatura — weapon instructor
Cramond: *c(enturio)* and *arm(atura)* (?), name lost, of *XX V(aleria) V(ictrix)* in charge of *cohors II*
Tungorum. RIB 2135 (see *RIB95*, p. 796)
Lydney Park: Flavius Abandinus on a bronze plaque to Mars Nodons (sic). *RIB* 305

beneficiarius — soldier on attachment
Birdoswald: [...]rinus, *b(ene)f(iciarius)*, on a dedication to Jupiter Optimus Maximus. *RIB* 1894

beneficiarius consularis — soldier attached to the governor's staff (see also *beneficiarius legati*
pro praetore below)
Binchester: Pomponius Donatus, *b(ene)f(iciarius) co(n)s(ularis)*, on an altar to Jupiter Optimus
Maximus and the Matres Ollotatae. *RIB* 1030
Binchester: T. Claudius Quintianus, *b(ene)f(iciarius) co(n)s(ularis)*, on altar to the Matres Ollotatae.
RIB 1031

49 *Gabled niche from Birrens depicting the goddess Brigantia. The dedicant was Amandus,* arc(h)itectus, *'engineer' of an unknown legion. Although* VI Victrix *built here, so did vexillations of* VIII Augusta *and* XXII Primigenia. *Height 0.91m.* RIB 2091

Catterick: Q. Varius Vitalis, *b(ene)f(iciarius) co(n)s(ularis)*, restoring an altar to the god of roads and paths in the year 191, previously dedicated by a *s(ingularis) c(onsularis)*. *RIB* 725

Catterick: Gaius N(...) O(...), *b(ene)f(iciarius)*, on an altar to the goddess Surio. *RIB* 726

Dorchester-on-Thames: M. Varius Severus, *b(eneficiarius) co(n)s(ularis)*, on an altar and screens to Jupiter Optimus Maximus and Numina Augustorum. *RIB* 235

Lancaster: Vibenius Lucius, *b(ene)f(iciarius) co(n)s(ularis)*, on an altar to Mars Cocidius. *RIB* 602

Lanchester: M. Didius Provincialis, *b(ene)f(iciarius) co(n)s(ularis)*, on an altar to Silvanus. *RIB* 1085

Housesteads: Litorius Pacatianus, *b(ene)f(iciarius) co(n)s(ularis)*, on an altar to Sol Invictus Mytras (Mithras). *RIB* 1599

Risingham: M. Gavius Secundinus, *b(ene)f(iciarius) co(n)s(ularis)*, on an altar to Mogons (or Mogonis) Cad... and Numen Augusti, during his first posting, at *Habitancum* (Risingham). *RIB* 1225

Winchester (Hants): Antonius Lucretianus, *[b(ene)]f(iciarius) co(n)s(ularis)*, on an altar to Matres. *RIB* 88

beneficiarius consularis provinciae superioris — soldier attached to the staff of the governor of
   Britannia Superior
Greta Bridge (N. Yorks): an altar, name and deity lost, giving the title *b(ene)f(iciarius) co(n)s(ularis)*
   provinci(a)e superior(is). As the findspot was in *Britannia Inferior* this has been taken as evidence that
   Inferior was subordinate to *Superior*. The date must lie somewhere in the third century. See also
   next entry. *RIB* 745
Vindolanda: Aurelius Modestus of *II Augusta*, on an altar to Silvanus, serving as *b(ene)f(iciarius)*
   co(n)s(ularis) provinciae superior(i)s (see *RIB* 745 above). *RIB* 1696

beneficiarius legati — soldier attached to the legionary legate's staff
Chester: Titineius Felix, *b(eneficiarius) leg(ati)*, of *XX V(aleria) V(ictrix)*. *RIB* 505

beneficiarius legati pro praetore — soldier attached to the governor's staff
Wroxeter (Salop): G. Mannius Secundus, *m(iles)* of *XX*, *ben(eficiarius) leg(ati) pr(o praetore)*. *RIB* 293

beneficiarius praefecti — soldier attached to a prefect's staff
Housesteads: Hurmius, *b(ene)f(iciario) praef(ecti)*, *mil(iti)* of *cohors I Tungrorum*. *RIB* 1619

beneficiarius tribuni — soldier attached to a military tribune's staff
Chester: G. Julius Marullinus, *b(ene)f(iciari) tribuni*. *RIB* 532
Chester: name lost, *b(ene)f(iciari) tr(ibuni)*. *RIB* 545
London: G. Pomponius Valentis, *[b(ene)f](iciarius) t[r]ib(uni)*, from *Victricens(is)* (Colchester). *JRS* lii
   (1962), 190-1, no. 1 (**27**)
Piercebridge: tombstone to, or an altar dedicated by, a legionary, name lost, serving as a
   b(ene)f(iciarius) trib(uni) from Germania Superior. *Brit.* xvii (1986), 438, no. 20

bucinator — trumpeter
Caernarvon: Januarius, *b(ucinatoris?)*, of the century of Victor, recorded on the base of a samian Form
   18 dish. *RIB* 2501.1
Carrawburgh: tombstone of Longinus, *buc(inatoris)*. *RIB* 1559

centurio praeposito — centurion in command
Birdoswald: Flavius Martinus, *cent(urione) p(rae)p(osito)*, dealing with rebuilding works at the fort
   between 297-305. *RIB* 1912

centurio regionarius — centurion in charge of the region
Bath: G. Severius Emeritus, *c(enturio) reg(ionarius)*, recording the restoration of a holy place which
   had been vandalised, on an altar dedicated to Virtus and Numen Augusti. *RIB* 152

comes maritimi tractus — Count of the maritime zone, see Chapter 4

cornicen? — horn blower
Cumberland quarries: Aelius Lucanus of *II Augusta*, his rank restored rather optimistically from a
   single R recorded in 1690, thus *[co]r(nicen)*. *RIB* 998

cornicularius — staff clerk
Bewcastle: Q. Peltrasius Maximus, promoted from *corniculario* to tribune of the Praetorian Prefects,
   on an altar to Cocidius. *RIB* 989
Greatchesters: tombstone of Aelius Mercurialis, *cornicul(ario)*. *RIB* 1742
York: L. Celerinius Vitalis, *corni(cularius) leg(ionis) VIIII His(panae)*, on an altar to Silvanus. Before
   120. *RIB* 659

curam agens — agent in charge
Beauport Park: Bassus/Bassianus, *c(uram) a(gens)*, of *classis Britannica(?)*. *Brit.* ii (1971), 289, no. 2;
   Brit. xix (1988), 261 (**50**)

50 *Slab found by the entrance of the* classis Britannica *bath-house at Beauport Park. It refers to a man called* Bass(us) *or* Bass(ianus), *the* c(uram) a(gens) *'in charge of the work', and a* vil(icus) *'foreman'. Width 280mm. Brit. ii (1971), 289, and xix (1988), 261-2*

Carriden: Ael(ius) Mansuetus, *curam agente*, of an altar erected by the vicus peoples of the fort of *Velunia*. *JRS* xlvii (1957), 229-30, no. 18

Cirencester: tombstone of a *[c]ura(m) a[gent(e)]*. *Brit.* v (1974), 461, no. 1

curator — the soldier of a cavalry *turma* responsible for supplies
Chesters: tombstone of Aventinus, *curator* of *ala II Asturum*. *RIB* 1480
Chesters: Marcus, *cur(ator)*, named on a samian Form 31 bowl dated to *c.*160-90. *RIB* 2501.5

custos armorum — custodian of arms and armour for a century
Haile: Primus, *cu(stos) ar(morum)*, on an altar to Hercules and Silvanus. *RIB* 796
Housesteads: name lost, *cus(tos) arm(orum)*, on an altar to Mars, Victory, and Numina Augustorum. *RIB* 1596

decurio princeps — centurion commanding a cavalry troop, *turma*
Castlesteads: Aurelius Armiger, *dec(urio) princ(eps)*, on an altar to Numen Augusti. *RIB* 1991

eques romanus — Roman knight
Colchester: tombstone of [...]o[...] Macr[...] [....]us, *Eq(ues) R(omanus)*. *RIB* 202

eques singularis Augusti — trooper of the imperial bodyguard
Malton: tombstone of Aurelius Macrinus, *eq(uite) sing(ularis) Au[g(usti)]*. *RIB* 714

eques singularis consularis — trooper of the governor's bodyguard
Carlisle: wooden writing tablet, name lost, *[eq(uiti) al]ae Sebosianae sing(ulari) Agricolae*, [trooper?] of *ala Sebosiana* and attached to Agricola's staff, *c.*78-84. *Brit.* xxix (1998), 74, no. 44
Catterick: undated lead sealing, *eq(uites) s(ingulares)*, no individual(s) named. *RIB* 2411.91

equisio consularis — groom on the governor's staff
Vindolanda: Veldeius, *equisioni co(n)s(ularis)*, apparently in London, addressee of a letter by his brother Chrauttius. *c.*95-105. *Tab. Vindol.* II.310

evocatus — soldier of the Praetorian Guard
Bewcastle: altar dedicated by Aurunceius Felicessemus, on an altar to Cocidius, tribune promoted from *evocato*. *RIB* 988

51 Tombstone from Kirkby Thore to a girl, whose father was an imaginifer. *See* **52**. *Width 0.76m.* RIB 769

Netherby: Paternius Maternus, on an altar to Cocidius, tribune of *cohors I Nervana* promoted from *evocato Palatino*. *RIB* 966 (possibly in fact from Bewcastle)

fabricensis legionis — armourer of the legion
Bath: tombstone of Julius Vitalis, *fabricie(n)sis leg(ionis) XX V(aleriae) V(ictricis)*, and a Belgic tribesman, paid for by the *col(l)egio fabrice(nsium)*. *RIB* 156

gubernator — pilot
York: M. Minucius Audens, *guber(nator)*, of *VI Victrix*. After 122. *RIB* 653
Unprovenanced: unnamed but a case involving a *gubernator* of the classis Britannica was dealt with by the *legatus iuridicus* of Britain, L. Javolenus Priscus. *Digest* xxxvi.1.48 (see E. Birley 1953, 51)

hiatros (Greek) — doctor
see *medicus* below

imaginifer — bearer of the imperial portrait standard
Bath (Avon): G. Jav[olenus Sa]tur[nal]is, *[i]m[a]g[in]n(iferi) leg(ionis) II Aug(ustae)*, on an altar to Sulis, erected by his freedman, L. Manius Dionisias. *RIB* 147 (see also the biography of L. Javolenus Priscus, *legatus iuridicus*, Chapter 9)
Carvoran: Julius Pastor, *imag(inifer) cohors II Delma(tarum)*, on an altar to Veteris. *RIB* 1795
Chester: tombstone of Aurelius Diogenes, *[ima]ginifer*. *RIB* 521
Kirkby Thore: Crescens, *imag(i)nif(e)ri*, on his daughter's tombstone. *RIB* 769 (**51, 52**)
London: name lost, *ima(giniferi)* of *leg(ionis) IX (Hispana)*, on a samian Form 18 dish 'of Flavian date'. *RIB* 2501.7

librarius — military clerk
Corbridge: T. Tertinius [...], *libr(arius)*, on a statuette base to Minerva. *RIB* 1134

magister — master
Ravenscar: Vindicianus, given as *masbier* which is either a misunderstanding by the mason or a phonetic representation of an otherwise-unknown colloquial variant, recording the building of a tower and fort. Fourth century? *RIB* 721

52 Detail of the tombstone in
51. RIB 769

magister primus — senior master
Chester: Furius Fortunatus, *mag(ister) pr(imus)*, on an altar to Minerva. *RIB* 457

masbier — see *magister*

medicus — surgeon (also the Greek *hiatros*)
Binchester: M. Aurelius [...]ocomas, *me[dicus]*, on an altar dedicated to Aesulapius and Salus for the
welfare of *ala Vettonum*. *RIB* 1028
Chester: Hermogenes, *hiatros* (= *medicus*), on an altar to Soteres. *RIB* 461 (in Greek)
Chester: altar dedicated by Antiochos, *hiatros* to Asklepios, Hygiaea and Panakeia. *JRS* lix (1969),
235, no. 3 (in Greek)

medicus ordinarius — surgeon of enlisted status
Housesteads: Anicius Ingenuus, *medico ord(inario)*, of *cohors I Tungrorum*. *RIB* 1618

mensor — surveyor
Piercebridge: Attonius Quintianus, *men(sor)*, on an altar to Mars Condates. *RIB* 1024

missicius — discharged soldier liable to be recalled
Chester: tombstone of a *missici(us)*, name lost, a former *benficiarius tribuni* (see above). *RIB* 545

pedites singularis consularis — soldier of the governor's bodyguard
Carlisle: undated lead sealings, marked with variations on *p(edites) s(ingularis) co(n)s(ularis)*. *RIB*
2411.92-3

praefectus castrorum — camp prefect
Caerleon: Julius [Ba]ssus, *praef(ectus) castror(um)* (of *II Augusta*?), on a dedication to Fortuna. *RIB*
317
Chester: tombstone of M. Aurelius Alexander, *praef(ectus) cast(rorum) leg(ionis) XX [V(aleriae)
V(ictricis)]*. *RIB* 490
Corbridge: Q. Terentius Firmus, *praef(ectus) castr(orum) leg(ionis) VI V(ictricis) P(iae) F(idelis)*, on an
altar to Apollo Maponus. *RIB* 1120
York: [A]nt. Gargilianus, formerly *[pr]a[e]f(ectus) leg(ionis) VI V(ictricis)*. *Brit*. i (1970), 308, no. 14
Unlocated: Poenius Postumus, *praefectus castrorum secundae legionis* (*II Augusta*), *c*.60-1. Tacitus (*Annals*)
xiv.37

praefectus legionis — prefect of the legion
Chester: tablet recording, name lost, *[pr]aef(ectus) leg(ionis) XX V(aleriae) V(ictricis)*. *JRS* lv (1965), 221, no. 5
Dalmatia: tombstone of L. Artorius Iustus, *praef(ectus) leg(ionis) VI*, presumably at York and perhaps under Commodus, recorded on an inscription from Dalmatia (see his biography, Chapter 9). *ILS* 2770

[praepositus] agens in praetentura — commander on frontier garrison duty
Corbridge: [Teren]tius, or [Arr]untius Paulinus, restored as *[p(rae)p(osito) a]g(ente) in praeten[tura]*. *RIB* 1152 (for this post and a discussion see *Brit.* xxix (1998), 356-9)

praepositus numeri et regioni — commander of the numerus and the region
Ribchester: T. Floridius Natalis, *c(enturio) leg(ionis) praep(ositus) n(umeri) et reg[ionis]*, on a slab recording the restoration of a temple during the later part of the reign of Severus Alexander (225-35; for more details of this stone, see Chapter 5). *RIB* 587

praepositus curam agens horreorum — officer in charge of the granaries
Corbridge: [...]norus, *[pr]aep(ositus) cu[ram] agens horr(eorum)* on an altar *tempo[r]e expeditionis felicissi(mae) Brittannic(ae)*, 'at the time of the successful expedition to Britain'; date unknown, but perhaps 209-11. *RIB* 1143

primus pilus — senior centurion of the legion
Caerleon: dedication by, name lost, *p(rimus) p(ilus) leg(ionis) [II Aug(ustae)?]*. *RIB* 385
Caerleon: name lost, *p(rimus) p(ilus)*, on a pilaster dedicated to the Numina Augustorum and the Genius of *II Augusta* on 23 September 244. *RIB* 327
Caerleon: Cn. Pompeius Homullus, *p(rimus) p(ilus) leg(ionis) II Aug(ustae)*. See his biography, Chapter 9.
Chester?: S. Flavius Quietus, *primus pilus* of *XX Valeria Victrix*. See his biography, Chapter 9.
London: M. Ulp(ius) Max(imus), *p(rimus) p(ilus)*, on a lead sealing from Billingsgate, London. *Brit.* xxi (1990), 369, no. 22
Vindolanda: Saturninus, *p(rimus) p(ilus)*, on the tombstone of his son Cornelius Victor, *s(ingularis) c(onsularis)*. *RIB* 1713
York: dedication(?) by, name lost, *p(rimus) p(ilus)*. *RIB* 698
Unlocated: P. Palpellius Clodius Quirinalis, *p(rimus) p(ilus) leg(ionis) XX*, presumably in Britain. By 56 he was *praef(ectus) classis* at Misenum, having held a military tribunate with *VII* in between. This means that he must have been with *XX* in the 40s during the Claudian campaign; but his career inscription from Trieste makes no mention of this. *ILS* 2702, Tacitus (*Annals*) xiii.30

princeps — second senior centurion of the legion
Chester: L. Elupius (or Elutrius) Praesans, *pri(nceps) leg(ionis) XX V(aleriae) V(ictricis)* on an an altar to Jupiter Optimus Maximus Tanarus, dedicated in 154. *RIB* 452
Castlesteads: Vic[...] Severus, *principi*, directing the erection of an altar to Jupiter Optimus Maximus by *cohors II Tungrorum*. *RIB* 1981
Castlesteads: Messius Obsequens, *p[r]inc[ipi]*, directing the erection of an altar to Jupiter Optimus Maximus by *cohors II Tungrorum*. *RIB* 1982
Castlesteads: P. Aelius Martinus, *princ(ipi)*, directing the erection of an altar to Jupiter Optimus Maximus and Numen Augusti by *cohors II Tungrorum* on 1st January 241. *RIB* 1983

princeps posterioris — fourth senior centurion of the legion
Hadrian's Wall (nr Stanwix): Julius Vitalis, *pr(incipis) pos(terioris)*, on a centurial stone. *RIB* 2023

signifer — standard bearer of a century
Caerleon: tombstone of G. Valerius Victor, *sig(nifer)* of *II Augusta*. *RIB* 365 (**53**)
Caerleon: tombstone of [...] Genialis [...], promoted? from *[signi]fero*, of *II Augusta*. *RIB* 367
Carrawburgh: tombstone of, name lost, *[signi]fero cohor(tis) I Batavorum*. *RIB* 1560
Chester: tombstone of [...]stus, *sig(nifer) [leg(ionis) XX] V(aleriae) V(ictricis)*. *RIB* 510

53 Tombstone, found near Caerleon, of Gaius Valerius Victor from Lyons (Lugduni), who served as a sig(nifer) *of* II Augusta. *He served 17 years before dying at 45. Width 1.19m. (Copyright © The British Museum).* RIB *365*

Chester: tombstone of D. Capienius Urbicus, *signiferi*, of *XX Valeria Victrix*? (no unit named): *RIB* 525

Chesters: [....]ens, *sig(niferi)*, on a samian Form 37 bowl. *RIB* 2501.12

Corbridge: tombstone of Flavinus, *eq(ues) alae Petr(ianae) signifer*, 'trooper of *ala Petriana* [and] *signifer*'. *RIB* 1172

Lancaster: name lost, *signiferi*, on a samian Form 18 dish. *RIB* 2501.11

Lincoln: tombstone of Gaius Valerius, *sign(ifer) c(enturiae) Hospitis*, 'signifer in the century of Hospes', and *mil(es) leg(ionis) IX*. *RIB* 257

Maryport: small stone inscribed *sig(nifer)* and accompanied by a sketch of a *signifer*. *RIB* 871

Mumrills: Cassius, *sign(ifer)*, on an altar to the Mother Goddesses. *RIB* 2141

Risingham: tombstone of Julius Victor, *sig(nifer)*, of *cohors I Vangionum?*). *RIB* 1247

Wroxeter: tombstone of Marcus Petronius, *sign(ifer)*, and *mil(es) leg(ionis) XIIII Gem(inae)*. *RIB* 294

York: tombstone of L. Duccius Rufinus, *signif(er) leg(ionis) VIIII*. *RIB* 673

singularis consularis/legati — bodyguard of the governor
(see also *eques singularis consularis* and *pedites singularis consularis*)
Catterick: Titus Irdas, *s(ingularis) c(onsularis)*, on an altar to the god of paths and roads, later restored in the year 191 (see *beneficiarius consularis* above). *RIB* 725

High Rochester: Julius Carantus, *s(ingularis) c(onsularis)*, on an altar to Minerva. *RIB* 1266

Ribchester: Julius Maximus, *s(ingularis) c(onsularis) alae Sar(matarum)*, on the tombstone of his wife Aelia Matrona. *RIB* 594

Vindolanda: Cornelius Victor, *s(ingularis) c(onsularis)*. *RIB* 1713

Vindolanda: name lost, on a wooden writing tablet from Vindolanda. *Tab. Vindol.* II.145

speculator — legionary detached as a secretary to the governor's staff
London: tombstone of [....]r Celsus, *[s]pec(ulator) leg(ionis) [II A]ug(ustae)*, erected by his fellow *sp[e]c(ulatores)* An[to]n(ius) Dardanus Cu[rso]r, Rubrius Pudens, and [....]s Probus. *RIB* 19

strator consularis — horse and stable overseer to the governor
Dover: Olus Cordius Candidus, *st(rator) co(n)s(ularis)*, recording on an altar the building of a shrine to the Italian Mother Goddesses. *Brit.* viii (1977), 426-7, no. 4

Irchester: tombstone of Anicius Saturninus, *strator co(n)s(ularis)*. *RIB* 233

tesserarius — keeper of the century's password
Caerleon: building stone by Primus, *te(s)era(rius)*. *RIB* 355
Ilkley: tombstone of Pude(ns), *tesser(arii)*, of *II A[ug(usta)]* or *II A(diutrix) [P(ia) F(idelis)]*. *RIB* 638

tribunus militum — military tribune
Brougham: dedication by, name lost, *[trib(unus)] mil(itum) leg(ionis) VIIII Aug(ustae)*. This may be by
   a man appointed from an auxiliary prefecture to the position and may not have served with *VIII
   Augusta* in Britain. *RIB* 782
Carlisle: dedication to Jupiter Optimus Maximus and various other gods by M. Aurelius Syrio,
   *trib(unus) mil(itum) leg(ionis) XX V(aleriae) V(ictricis) Antoninianae, c.*213-22. *Brit.* xx (1989), 331-3,
   no. 5
Chester: Flavius Longus, *trib(unus) mil(itum) leg(ionis) XX [V(aleriae) V(ictricis)]*, on an altar dedicated
   to imperial welfare and the Genius loci. *RIB* 450
Corbridge: dedication to Mars Ultor by *VI Victrix* during the governorship of Gn. Julius Verus
   through Lucius [....], *trib(unum) [mil(itum)]*, c.155-9. *RIB* 1132
Croy Hill: altar to the Nymphs dedicated by a *vexillatio leg(ionis) VI Vic(tricis) P(iae) F(idelis)* under
   Fa[b]ius L[i]bera[lus] who may have been a *trib(unus) milit(um)*. *RIB* 2160 (see *RIB95*, p. 797,
   note)
Old Penrith: tombstone of Ylas, foster-child of Claudius Severus, *trib(unus) milit(um)*. *RIB* 937
- see also Chapter 9 for the careers of Gn. Julius Agricola and the emperor Titus, and Tribunes under
   the individual legions in Chapter 2

veterinarius — animal doctor
Vindolanda: Virilis, *veterinarium*, apparently in London, in a letter from Chrauttius to Veldedeius.
   Tab. Vindol. II.310

vexillarius — flag-bearer
Corbridge: tombstone of [Ba]rathes of Palmyra, one time *vexil(l)a(rius)*. *RIB* 1171
Greatchesters: Quintus, *vex(illari)*, on a samian Form 31 bowl. *RIB* 2501.14

vilicus — foreman
Beauport Park: *vil(icus)*, name lost. *Brit.* ii (1971), 289, no. 2; *Brit.* xix (1988), 261

RELIGIOUS

episcopus — bishop
Lincoln?: Adelfius, *episcopus*, in 314. *Acta Concilii Arelatensis* (*PNRB*, 50)
London: Restitutus, *episcopus*, in 314. *Acta Concilii Arelatensis* (*PNRB*, 49)
Risley Park: Exsuperius, *episcopus*, inscribed on a silver lanx given to the church at *Bogium*
   (unknown). The lanx was cut up in 1729 but reconstituted, a mould taken and a reproduction
   cast from the original silver. The latter has turned up since *RIB* II, fasc 2, was published where
   the text is regarded as *alienum* and it has now been re-read. The nature of the lanx and the
   unknown location of *Bogium* means that Exsuperius may have been bishop almost anywhere.
   RIB 2414.40
Shavington: *Viventi [epis]copi*, '(property of) Bishop Viventius', on sheet lead fragments. *Brit.* xxix
   (1998), 436, no. 11
York: Eborius, *episcopus*, in 314. *Acta Concilii Arelatensis* (*PNRB*, 49)

haruspex — soothsayer
Bath: L. Marcius Memor, *harusp(ex)*. *JRS* lvi (1966), 217, no. 1 (and Cunliffe and Davenport, 1985,
   130, 9A.1) (**54**)

interpretor — interpreter (of dreams)
Lydney: Victorinus, *interp(r)[e]tiante*, on the temple mosaic. R.G. Collingwood preferred the idea
   that he was an 'interpreter on the Governor's staff' (Wheeler 1932, 103), a position which is
   difficult to reconcile either with the context, or common sense, and reflected the then

DEÆ SVLI
L·MARCIVS·MEMOR
HARVSP
D   D

54 *Base from the temple precinct at Bath, found in situ close to the sacrifical altar. The gift (presumably a statue) was given to Sulis by L(ucius) Marcius Memor, harusp(ex). The odd formation of harusp has been explained by the sculptor carving har first and adding usp later, perhaps because the post (of which this is the only example in Britain) was not understood. However, the addition is clearly in the same hand and the imbalance may have been a mistake. Height 0.9m. JRS lvi (1966), 217, no. 1*

preoccupation with military affairs. The new reading at least fits the context, but the only instance of a similar term recorded in *ILS* is the interpreting of Clarian Apollo (*ILS* 3230a). *RIB* 2448.3

magister primus — senior Master
Chester: Furius Fortunatus, *mag(ister) pr(imus)*, on an altar to Minerva. *RIB* 457

magister sacrorum — master of sacred ceremonies
Greetland: T. Aurelius Aurelianus, *mag(istro) s(acrorum)*, on an altar to Victoria Brigantia and Numina Augustorum in 208. *RIB* 627

praepositus religionis — director of the cult
Lydney: T. Flavius Senilis, *pr(aepositus) rel(igionis)*, on the temple mosaic. R.G. Collingwood rejected this as 'baseless, and not really Latin' (Wheeler 1932, 103), preferring Mommsen's *pr(aepositus) rel(iquationi) classis)*, 'officer-in-charge of a fleet supply-depot'. As with *interpretor* above, the suggestion was a bizarre case of ignoring common sense, given the context, resulting in an incongruous solution. *RIB* 2448.3

sacerdos — priest
Bath: tombstone of G. Calpurnius [R]eceptus, *sacerdos deae Sulis*, 'priest of the goddess Sulis. *RIB* 155
Hadrian's Wall (between Wallsend and Newcastle): Julius Maximus, *sac(erdos) d(ei)*, 'priest of the god (or goddess)', on an altar. The name of the deity has been suggested as Di(genis). *RIB* 1314
Hadrian's Wall (exact location unknown): altar to Nemesis by Apollonius, *sacerdos*. *RIB* 2065

sevir Augustalis — board member of the imperial cult
York: M. Verecundus Diogenes, *morit(ex?)*, 'shipper', named as *sevir col(oniae) Ebor(acensis)* on his coffin. *RIB* 678
York and Lincoln: M. Aurelius Lunaris, a *sevir Aug(ustalis) col(oniarum) Ebor(aci) et Lind(i)*, stated on an altar made of Yorkshire stone from Bordeaux of the year 237. *JRS* xi (1921), 102 (**29**)

55 Slab from Malton with a crude inscription wishing good fortune (feliciter) *to the Genius loci, 'Genius of this place', and an exhortation to a young slave* (servule) *to make use of his fortune in this goldsmith's shop* (tabernam aureficinam). *Width 330mm.* RIB 712

GENERAL OCCUPATIONS

The evidence for individual occupations is scattered amongst altars, dedications, tombstones, and the products of those occupations such as metalwork and pottery. In the case of the latter, which form by far the greatest body of evidence, very few actually provide a name for the occupation though its nature is usually obvious from the products. Instead they provide just a maker's name, often abbreviated, together with 'F' for *fecit*, 'made [this]', 'OF' for *officina*, 'workshop [of]'. Such makers' names are far too numerous to include in the following list which is limited to inscriptions or stamps which actually state a name for the occupation.

Individuals
aerarius — coppersmith
Colchester: Cintusmus, *aerarius*, on a bronze plaque to Silvanus Callirius. *RIB* 194
Fossdike: Celatus, *aerarius*, maker of a bronze statuette of Mars. *RIB* 274 (**67**)

artifices — skilled workers
Britain: in about 297 a number of these men were taken from Britain to work on the restoration of Britain *quibus illae provinciae redundabant*, 'with whom those provinces were overflowing'. *Panegyrici Latini* viii (v) 21.2 (in Mynors 1964, ed., p. 229)

aurificina taberna — goldsmith's shop
Malton: anonymous, on a building stone dedicated to the Genius loci wishing fortune to the slave of a *tabernam aurificinam*. *RIB* 712 (**55**)

curator — treasurer
Lincoln: altar dedicated to the Parcae and the Numina Augustorum by G. Antistius Frontinus described as *curator ter(tium)*, 'guild treasurer for the third time'. *RIB* 247

gynaecium — weaving works
Venta (Caerwent, Caistor-by-Norwich or Winchester): *procurator gynaecii in Britannis Ventensis*, 'the procurator of the weaving works in Britain at *Venta*'. Which *Venta* is meant is unknown. *ND* xi.60 (see *PNRB*, p. 492, Venta Belgarum, note)

lapidarius — stonemason
Bath: Priscus, *lapidariu[s]*, from Chartres, on an altar to Sulis. *RIB* 149

negotiator — trader
York: L. Viducius Placidus of Gallia Lugdunensis, *[n]egotiator*, on a dedication slab to Neptunus and Genius loci, recording the presentation of an arch and gate. *Brit.* viii (1977), 430, no. 18

negotiator Britannicianus — trader with Britain
Cologne: C. Aurelius Verus, *negotiator Britannicianus*, on an altar to Apollo. *ILS* 7522

negotiator cretarius Britannicianus — trader in pottery with Britain
Domburg (Holland): M. Secundinius Silvanus, *negotiator cretarius Britannicianus*, on an altar to Nehalennia. *ILS* 4751

scultor — sculptor
Bath: Sulinus, *scultor*, on a statue base dedicated to the Suleviae. *RIB* 151

sutoriis — shoemakers
Usk: the title *sutoriis* appears on an incomplete lead label. It was presumably attached to a package, either of completed goods, or raw materials. *RIB* 2410.13

tegulariae — tile kilns
London: tile stamped *tegul(ariae) D(ecimi) M(...) Val(...) (et) D(ecimi) M(...) P(...)*, 'tile kilns of Decimus M(....) Val(...) and Decimus M(...) P(...). The expansion of the complex ligatured stamp is uncertain. *Brit.* xx (1989), 340-1, no. 51

Firms (as opposed to individual concerns)
sociorum Lutudarensium Britannicum
Various: *socior(um) Lut(udarensium) Br(itannicum)*, 'British (lead) of the Lutudarensian company' on lead pigs from a variety of locations: *RIB* 2404.53 (Belby, Humberside), 2404.54 (Broomfleet, Humberside), 2404.55 (Brough-on-Humber), 2404.57 (Cave's Inn, Churchover, Warws), 2404.58 (Ellerker, Humberside), 2404.59-60 (Yeaveley, Derbs). For the name *Lutudarum* see the note to *RIB* 2404.39 and *PNRB*, 403-4. Ingots stamped with imperial titles were also produced here.

soc(iorum) or *soc(ietatis) Novaec(...)*
69-79: '(product) of the Novaec(..) company', on a lead pig from Bitterne (Hants) also bearing Vespasian's name. *RIB* 2404.6

soc(iorum) or *soc(ietatis) Nove(...)*
79: '(product) of the Nove(...) company', on a lead pig from Syde (Gloucs) also bearing Vespasian's titles for 79. *RIB* 2404.13

Collegia
A *collegium*, translated variously as a corporation or guild, was a body of individuals sharing a common trade, craft, or a religion. Several *collegia* are testified in Roman Britain. Not surprisingly they come from towns and forts, places where concentrations of population made guilds not only professionally advantageous but also provided social opportunities.

collegium
Caerwent: on a statue base at Caerwent to 'Mars Lenus or Ocelus Vellaunus', given by one Marcus
    Nonius Romanus in return *ob immunitat(em) collegni*, 'for freedom from liability of the college',
    in 152. *RIB* 309
Bath: *[c]olegio* (sic), on a frieze from the facade of Four Seasons in the temple precinct. *RIB* 141 (b)
High Rochester: on an altar dedicated by Caecilius Optatus, tribune, dedicated to the *Genius collegi*
    and Minerva. *RIB* 1268
York: on a building slab dedicated to the [Genius?] of the *collegi*, recording possibly the promotion
    of the *b(ene)f(iciarii)* of Gordianus. *Brit.* i (1970), 307, no. 12

collegium Apollinis
Burrow-in-Lonsdale (Overborough): on an altar recording a dedication to *Ge[ni]o colgf* (sic)
    [A]poll[i]nis. The abbreviation for *collegio* is probably due to a blundered reading of the altar in
    1684 prior to its loss. *RIB* 611

collegium conservorum — guild of fellow slaves
Haltonchesters: on the tombstone of an unknown slave of one Hardalio, erected by the *collegium
    conser(vorum)*. *RIB* 1436

collegium fabricensium — guild of armourers
Bath: tombstone of Julius Vitalis, *fabricie(n)sis* (armourer) of *XX V(aleria) V(ictrix)*, erected at the
    expense of the *col(l)egio fabrice(nsium)*. *RIB* 156

collegium fabrorum — guild of smiths
Chichester: *[colle]gium fabror(um)* on a dedication slab recording the building of a temple to
    Neptunus and Minerva during the time of Togidubnus, *c.*50-100. This is important evidence for
    the early appearance of Roman institutions even amongst artisans. *RIB* 91

collegium (Mercurionis?) — guild of worshippers of Mercury
Birrens: on a statue base to Mercury dedicated by Julius Crescens for the use of the *collign(ium)* (sic).
    RIB 2102
Birrens: on a statue base dedicated by the *cu[lt]ores colligni*, 'worshippers of the guild', to Mercury and
    Numen Augusti, under the charge of Ingenuius Rufus. *RIB* 2103

collegium peregrinorum — guild of provincials
Silchester: purportedly on three dedication slabs. The three stones have been heavily restored as
    follows to produce the name of the organization:
[collegio peregri]nor[u]m. RIB 69
con[legio pere]gr[i]norum ... Callevae. RIB 70 (**30**)
col[legio peregrin]orum. RIB 71

collegium Silvanianorum — guild of worshippers of Silvanus
Corbridge: a new reading of this damaged altar has produced *c[olle]g[ium] Si[l]vanianorum*,
    apparently drawn from the ranks of *II Augusta* who dedicated the stone. *RIB* 1136 (*RIB95*, p. 780,
    note)
Wendens Ambo: *col(legium) dei Sil(Vani)* on a bronze ring. *RIB* 2422.52

dendrophori Verulamiensium — branch bearers of Verulamium
Dunstable: colour-coated beaker bearing a graffito stating, *olla(m) dendrofororum Ve(r)(ulamiensium)
    Regillinus donavit*, 'Regillinus presented the pot of the Verulamiam branch-bearers'. Branch-
    bearers were associated with the cult of Cybele, and bore a pine tree in an annual procession to
    the temple. Their organizations resembled *collegia*. *RIB* 2503.114

8 Gods, goddesses, and cults

INTRODUCTION

The very large proportion of religious dedications known from Roman Britain has already been noted, and is a useful balance to the suggestion that other inscriptions have tended not to survive. It is difficult to avoid concluding that the Romano-British were more likely to use monumental inscriptions for religious purposes than anything else.

Almost all Romano-British sites produce evidence for what we would call religious practices of one sort or another. A few sites have yielded large quantities even if the primary purpose of the site was secular or military. The fort at Carrawburgh has, for instance, produced far more religious inscriptions than anything to do with the fort's prime function. *RIB* records 44 inscribed stones at Carrawburgh, of which 30 are altars or other religious dedications (many from the sacred spring by the fort, dedicated to Coventina), six are tombstones, and eight are imperial dedications or building stones (four of which are undatable centurial stones).

This bias reflects the enormous catholicity of the Roman world and the manner in which religious observances permeated every level of society. At one end were observations of official religious events. An extant, but incomplete, document from the fort at Dura-Europos in Syria lists the various occasions which the unit was obliged to celebrate during the years 224-235 (cited in L & R, II, 567). In January alone there were at least six, four of which involved celebrating the birthdays of past deified emperors and the person and family of the incumbent, Severus Alexander. Each one of these occasions might be commemorated by the erection of an altar. The fort at Maryport in Cumbria has produced a large number of well-preserved altars to Jupiter Optimus Maximus. These are almost certainly the remains of an annual ceremony during which the old altar was buried and a new one substituted.

Other religious dedications run from special dedications to emperors or major gods right down to barely-legible altars or reliefs erected to obscure local gods for whom there is no other evidence. In the Roman world any one god or goddess might be worshipped in a single place or hundreds of places. A local deity may be conflated with a classical deity. Mars was perhaps the most widely-adapted god, with many different partners or identifications in Britain.

These inscriptions have much to tell us about the flavour of Roman Britain, the gods and goddesses worshipped and the population. Although it has long been recognized that many minor, and some major, deities enjoyed very localized attention the following list makes this much clearer. That six inscriptions record the god Balatucadrus at Brougham suggests he was especially popular there. At Carvoran three of the eleven inscriptions to the Veteres are by one Necalames, presumably a soldier stationed there with a particular reverence for the shadowy deities. At Lanchester the altar to Garmangabis reflects the incumbent unit's veneration for a god from their nominal homeland. Or, there seem to have been certain individuals who favoured religious dedications. Marcus Cocceius Firmus, centurion with *II Augusta* at Auchendavy is known on four different altars from the site (*RIB* 2174-7) dedicated variously to Campestres, Diana, Epona, Mars, Minerva, Terra Britannicae and Victoria.

It is also obvious that much the greater part of all this evidence comes from the northern frontier, in particular the forts of Hadrian's Wall and those in the region, especially Corbridge and the forts of Cumbria. This must in part reflect survival and prolific antiquarian activity followed by excavations, but perhaps it was specially popular in remote windswept frontier settings to see gods and spirits in the hills, crags, rain, and storms of the edge of Empire.

The following catalogue lists testified deities by full name in alphabetical order, normally as testified on the original stones, and in their Latin form. Conflated gods are usually listed under the classical component, thus Mars Cocidius is followed by Mars Condates and so on even where the order is reversed on the inscription. However, where a local or Celtic deity is referred to on his/her own then the inscription is listed under that god's name. The only occasion where this practice has been diverted from is with Sulis-Minerva of Bath in deference to the fact that the deity is so well known in this form. British gods recorded elsewhere in the Empire are only recorded here if otherwise unknown in Britain.

Small, portable items of a personal nature, such as rings and spoons, are normally omitted because they are unreliable indicators of a place of worship and rarely add to the attested deities of Roman Britain. Where they do add a new form of a god or goddess they have been included but this is almost exclusively confined to Faunus and his various manifestations at Thetford.

Collegia, or religious guilds, are listed along with other *collegia* in Chapter 7.

Note that in the catalogue below, 'altar by ...' should be take to read 'altar dedicated by'; likewise 'altar to ...' should be taken to read 'altar dedicated to ...'. Names of deities are not normally included in the individual entries, except where spellings significantly vary, or where the reading relies on significant expansion of a very few letters. Dedications were generally made *to* gods, and therefore the expansion of names would normally be in the dative case. This is likely to create a certain amount of confusion, especially where comparisons are being made. I have therefore expanded names usually in the nominative case, making exceptions where only the dative ending of a name has survived to be expanded from.

A small number of inscriptions listed in *RIB* as dedications have been omitted where the god's name has been entirely restored (for example *RIB* 2059) and is therefore technically absent. The reader should also be aware that distribution of deities by inscriptions on which they are named does not complete the picture. There are also very many representations of gods from Roman Britain where there is no inscription, but where the identity of the deity is not in question. These are not included here, but a good example is the relief of Victory found at Bolton (E. Yorks; see *Brit.* xxix (1998), 322ff).

INDIVIDUAL DEITIES

Abandinus
Godmanchester: bronze plaque by Vatiaucus. *RIB* 2432.4

Aesculapius/Asklepios
Binchester: altar to [Aesc]ulapius by M. Aurelius [...]ocomas, *medicus*, for welfare of *ala Vettonum*. *RIB* 1028 (with Salus)
Burrow-in-Lonsdale (Overborough): altar by Julius Saturninus. *RIB* 609 (with Hygiaea (sic))
Chester: altar by Antiochos, *hiatros* (in Greek). *JRS* lix (1969), 235, no. 3 (with Hygiaea and Panakeia)
Chester: altar by the legate T. Pomponius Mamilianus. *RIB* 445 (with Fortuna Redux, and Salus)
Lanchester: altar to [Aescula]pius by the tribune T. Flavius Titianus with parallel Greek text (known from *RIB* 1083, Ebchester, to have been tribune of *cohors I Vardullorum* during the governorship of Antistius Adventus, *c.*175-8). *RIB* 1072
Maryport: slab by A. Egnatius Pastor (in Greek). *RIB* 808
South Shields: altar to Esculap(ius) by P. Viboleius Secundus. *RIB* 1052

Alaisiagae, see also **Beda, Baudihillia, Fimmilena, and Friagabis**
Housesteads altar by 'the Germans' of *cuneus Frisiorum Ver(covicianorum) Se(v)e(riani) Alexandriani* between 222-35. *RIB* 1594 (with Mars and Numen Augusti)

Ammilla Augusta Felix
London: miniature bronze warship prow. Identification uncertain, possibly the personification of a named ship. *RIB* 2432.1

Ancasta
Bitterne: altar by Geminus. *RIB* 97

Andate ('Victory')
Unlocated: referred to as the 'grave of Andate' by Dio and a place where the members of the Boudican Revolt conducted various sacrificial acts. Dio lxii.7

Andescociuoucus (see Mercury)

Anicetus, see Mithras

Anociticus, see **Antenociticus**

Antenociticus, also **Anociticus**
Benwell: altar by Aelius Vibius, centurion of *XX Valeria Victrix*. *RIB* 1327 (with Numina Augustorum) **(56)**
Benwell: altar by *cohors I Vangionum* under the prefect [...]c(ius) Cassi[anus]. *RIB* 1328
Benwell: altar to Anociticus by Tineius Longus, prefect of cavalry, between 177-80. *RIB* 1329

Apollo, see also **Genius collegii Apollinis**
Auchendavy: altar by M. Cocceius Firmus, centurion of *II Augusta*. *RIB* 2174 (with Diana)
Bar Hill: altar to [Apoll]in[i]. *RIB* 2165
Chester-le-Street: altar by Tertius. *RIB* 1043
Hadrian's Wall (near mc 42): altar by Melonius Senilis, *duplicarius* from Germania Superior. *RIB* 1665
Nettleton: bronze plaque by Decimius. *RIB* 2432.3
Newstead: altar by L. Maximius Gaetulicus, legionary centurion. *RIB* 2120
Scarcroft: altar. *JRS* lv (1965), 221, no. 6 (with Numen)
Whitley Castle: altar by Gaius [......]ius of *cohors [II] Nerviorum*. *RIB* 1198

56 Altar from Benwell, found in the temple of Antenociticus. It names the god as well as the Numina Augustorum and the dedicant Aelius Vibius, centurion with XX Valeria Victrix. Undated but found with RIB 1329, naming the governor Ulpius Marcellus in 177-80. Height 1.3m. RIB 1327

Apollo Anextiomarus
South Shields: bronze patera by Marcus A[...] Sab(inus). *RIB* 2415.55

Apollo Anicetus, see **Sol Apollo Anicetus**

Apollo Clarius, see **Clarius Apollo**

Apollo Cunomaglos
Nettleton: altar by Corotica, son or daughter of Iutus. *JRS* lii (1962), 191, no. 4 (and Wedlake 1982, 135-6, no. 1)

Apollo Grannus
Inveresk: altar by Q. Lusius Sabinianus, *procurator Augusti*. *RIB* 2132 (see also *ILS* 4649)

Apollo Maponus
Corbridge: altar by Q. Terentius Firmus, *praefectus castrorum* of *VI Victrix*. *RIB* 1120
Corbridge: altar by [Calp]urnius [...], tribune. *RIB* 1121
Corbridge: altar by Publius Aelius [...], centurion of *VI Victrix*. *RIB* 1122
Ribchester: shaft by Aelius Antoninus, centurion of *VI Victrix* and commander of *n(umerus) eq(uitum) Sar[m(atarum)] Bremetenn(acensium) [G]ordiani* between 238-44. *RIB* 583

Arciaco (with Numen Augusti)
York: altar by Mat... Vitalis, centurion. *RIB* 640 (with Numen Augusti) (**69**). But note the variant on Mercury (next entry) which may possibly explain this otherwise-unknown deity.

Arecurius see Corbridge under **Mercury** as **Arecurio**

Arimanes
York: statue by Volusius Irenaeus. *RIB* 641

Arnomecta
Brough-on-Noe: altar by Aelius Motio. *RIB* 281

Astarte
Corbridge: altar by Pulcher (in Greek). *RIB* 1124

Balatucadrus see **Belatucadrus**

Barrax, see **Mars Barrax**

Baudihillia et Friagabis (Alaisiagae)
Housesteads: altar by *numerus Hnaudifridi*. *RIB* 1576 (with Numen Augusti)

Beda et Fimmilena (Alaisiagae)
Housesteads: shrine door jam by 'Germans, citizens of Twenthe'. *RIB* 1593 (with Mars Thincsus, and Numen Augusti)

Belatucadrus and variants, see also **Mars Belatucadrus**
Bowness-on-Solway: altar to Belatocairo by Peisius, *m(iles)*. *RIB* 2056
Brougham: altar to B[a]latu(cadrus). *RIB* 772
Brougham: altar to Balatucairus by Baculo. *RIB* 773
Brougham: altar to Blatucairus by Audagus. *RIB* 774
Brougham: altar to Belatu[ca]drus by Julianus. *RIB* 775
Brougham: altar to Belatucadrus. *RIB* 776
Brougham: statue to Belatucadrus. *RIB* 777
Brougham: altar to Belatucabrous. *JRS* lix (1969), 237, no. 7
Burgh-by-Sands: altar to Belatucadrus. *RIB* 2038
Burgh-by-Sands: altar to Belatocadrus by Antr(onius) Auf(idianus?). *RIB* 2039
Burgh-by-Sands: altar to Belatucadrus. *RIB* 2044
Carlisle: altar to Belatucadrus. *RIB* 948
Carrawburgh: altar to Belleticaurus by Lunaris. *RIB* 1521
Carvoran: altar to Baliticaurus. *RIB* 1775
Carvoran: altar to Blatucadrus. *RIB* 1776
Castlesteads: altar to Belatugagrus by Minervalis. *RIB* 1976
Castlesteads: altar to Be[l]atuca[dr]us by Ullinus. *RIB* 1977 (and *Brit.* v (1974), 463, no. 10)
Kirkby Thore: altar to Belatucadrus by [...]iolus. *RIB* 759
Maryport: altar to Belatucadrus by Julius Civilis, optio. *RIB* 809
Old Carlisle: altar to Belatucadrus by Aurelius Tasulus, *vet(eranus)*. *RIB* 887
Old Carlisle: altar to Belatucadrus by Aurelius Diatova. *RIB* 888
Old Carlisle: altar to Belatucaurus. *RIB* 889
Old Penrith: altar to Bel[a]tuca[drus]. *RIB* 914
Old Penrith: altar to Balatocadrus. *Brit.* ix (1977), 474, no. 7
Old Penrith: altar to Belatucairus. *Brit.* ix (1977), 474, no. 8

Bellona
Old Carlisle: altar by Rufinus, prefect of *ala Augusta*, and his son Latinianus. *RIB* 890

Bona Dea Regina Caelestis (the Good Goddess, Queen, Caelestis), see also **Regina Caelestis** and **Virgo Caelestis**
Chesters: altar. *RIB* 1448

Bona Fortuna
Corbridge: altar to B(ona) F(ortuna). RIB 1135 (with Panthea)

Bonus Eventus et Fortuna
Caerleon: slab by Cornelius Castus and his wife Julia Belismicus. *RIB* 318
York: slab to [Bono Eventu]i et F[ortunae]? *RIB* 642 (*RIB* 703 is part of the same)

Braciaca, see **Mars Braciaca**

Bregans
Slack: altar by T. Aurelius Quintus. *RIB* 623 (and Numen Augusti)

Brigantia see also **Caelestis Brigantia, Nympha Brigantia, Brigantia Augusta**, and **Victoria Brigantia**
Adel: altar by Cingetissa. *RIB* 630
Birrens: figure in gabled relief by Amandus *arcitectus*. *RIB* 2091 (**49**)
South Shields: altar by Congeniccus. *RIB* 1053

Britannia
Balmuildy: altar by Q. Pisentius Justus, prefect of *cohors IIII Gallorum* between 138-61. *RIB* 2195
    (with Campestres)
York: altar by Nikomedes, imperial *libertus*. *RIB* 643

Caelestis Brigantia
Corbridge: altar by G. Julius Apolinaris, centurion of *VI Victrix*, his name, rank and unit replacing
    someone else's or else recarved to make a correction. *RIB* 1131 (with Jupiter Aeternus
    Dolichenus and Salus). See also *Brit.* xxvi (1995), 380, no. 7 for another possibility

Campestres (Goddesses of the Parade Ground), see also **Matres Campestres**
Auchendavy: altar by M. Cocceius Firmus, centurion of *II Augusta*. *RIB* 2177 (with Mars, Minerva,
    Hercules, Epona and Victoria)
Balmuildy: altar by Q. Pisentius Justus, prefect of *cohors IIII Gallorum* between 138-61. *RIB* 2195
    (with *Britannia*)
Gloster Hill: altar by *cohors I [...]*. *RIB* 1206
Newstead: altar by Aelius Marcus, *decurio* of *ala Augusta Vocontiorum*. *RIB* 2121

Camulus see **Mars Camulus**

Capitolinus, see **Jupiter Optimus Maximus Capitolinus**

Cautes (associate of Mithras)
Carlisle: altar by Julius Archietus. *RIB* 943

Cautopates (associate of Mithras)
Lanchester: altar to C(auto)p(ates). *RIB* 1082 (with Mithras and Sol Invictus)

Ceres Dea Suria (Ceres, the Syrian Goddess)
Carvoran: altar by M. Caecilius Donatianus, serving as tribune in the post of prefect, between 197-
    217. *RIB* 1791 (with Mater, Pax, and Virgo Caelestis)

Christos (represented by the XP 'Chi-Rho' monogram and/or A W 'Alpha' and 'Omega'), see also
    Deus
Ashton: lead tank bearing XP. *RIB* 2416.13
Biddulph: silver spoon bearing A XP W. *RIB* 2420.56
Brough: lead tank bearing IX, for Iesus Xristus. *Brit.* xxvi (1995), 318-22
Canterbury: silver spoons bearing XP. *RIB* 2420.60-1
East Stoke: lead tank bearing XP. *RIB* 2416.8
Gwent [found in 'Monmouthshire']: silver spoon bearing A XP W. *RIB* 2420.57
Icklingham: lead tanks bearing W XP A. *RIB* 2416.9
Icklingham: lead tanks bearing XP. *RIB* 2416.10

57 Votive silver leaf from the Water Newton treasure. The Christian symbolism of the Chi-Rho and A(lpha) and O(mega) is unequivocal even if votive leaves are more normally associated with pagan ritual. Length 157mm. RIB 2431.8

Lullingstone: wall-paintings bearing A XP W and images of people praying. *RIB* 2447.6-8
Maryport: stone plaque inscribed XP. *RIB* 856
Mildenhall: silver spoons bearing A XP W. *RIB* 2420.53-5
Traprain Law: silver spoons bearing XP. *RIB* 2420.58-9
Walesby: lead tank bearing XP. *RIB* 2416.14
Water Newton: silver bowl by Innocentia and Viventia, bearing A XP W. *RIB* 2414.1
Water Newton: silver bowl/cup bearing A XP W, and naming a sacred sanctuary. *RIB* 2414.2
Water Newton: silver strainers bearing A XP W. *RIB* 2414.3
Water Newton: silver strainers bearing XP and Iesus Xristus. *RIB* 2414.21
Water Newton: silver pan bearing XP W. *RIB* 2414.4
Water Newton: gold disc bearing A XP W. *RIB* 2430.3
Water Newton: silver plaque bearing W XP A. *RIB* 2431.1
Water Newton: silver plaques bearing A XP W. *RIB* 2431.4-11 (**57**)
Wigginholt: lead tank bearing XP. *RIB* 2416.12
Winchester: floor tile inscribed with XP. *Brit.* xxiv (1993), 316-17, no. 18

Clarius Apollo
Housesteads: altar recording the oracle of Clarian Apollo in Ionia by *cohors I Tungrorum*. There are
   various references in classical texts, for example Ovid, *Fasti* I.20. *RIB* 1579

Claudius Divus (the deified Emperor Claudius)
Colchester: *templum divo Claudio* in use by the year 60. Tacitus, *Annals* xiv.31

Cocidius, see also Mars Cocidius, Silvanus Cocidius and Vernostonus Cocidius
Bewcastle: altar by Annius Victor, legionary centurion. *RIB* 985
Bewcastle: silver plaque. *RIB* 986
Bewcastle: silver plaque by Aventinus. *RIB* 987
Bewcastle: altar by Aurunceius Felicessemus, tribune promoted from *evocatus*. *RIB* 988

Bewcastle: altar by Q. Peltrasius Maximus, tribune, promoted from *cornicularius* to the Praetorian Prefects. *RIB* 989

Birdoswald: altar by [Tere]ntius Valerianus, commanding *cohors I Aelia [Dacorum]*. *RIB* 1872

Birdoswald: primary dedication on an altar with secondary, and probably unrelated, dedication to Jupiter Optimus Maximus by Pomponius Desideratus, tribune commanding *cohors I Aelia Dacorum* between 270-3. *RIB* 1885

Hadrian's Wall (near milecastle 37): altar by Vabrius. *RIB* 1633

Hadrian's Wall (milecastle 52): altar by *II Augusta*. *RIB* 1955

Hadrian's Wall (milecastle 52): altar by *XX Valeria Victrix* between 262-6. *RIB* 1956

Hadrian's Wall (near milecastle 55): altar by a vexillation from *VI Victrix*. *RIB* 1961

Hadrian's Wall (near milecastle 55): altar to Co[cidius]. *RIB* 1963

Hadrian's Wall (near milecastle 60): altar by *VI Victrix*. *RIB* 2020

Housesteads: altar by Valerius, soldier with *VI Victrix*. *RIB* 1577 (with Genius praesidii)

Housesteads: altar by *II Augusta*. *RIB* 1583 (with Genius huius loci and Jupiter Optimus Maximus)

Netherby (or Bewcastle ?): altar by Paternius Maternus, tribune commanding *cohors I Nerviorum* and promoted from *evocatus Palatinus* (recorded at Netherby, probably erroneously). *RIB* 966

Risingham: altar. *RIB* 1207 (with Silvanus)

Vindolanda: altar by D. Caerellius Victor, prefect of *cohors II Nerviorum*. *RIB* 1683

Concordia legionis II Augusta et legionis XX (The Concord of *II Augusta* and *XX*)
Carlisle: base of sculptured relief. *Brit.* xx (1989), 331, no. 4

Concordia legionis VI Victrix Pia Fidelis et legionis XX (The Concord of *VI Victrix Pia Fidelis* and *XX Valeria Victrix*)
Corbridge: slab. *RIB* 1125

Condates, see **Mars Condates**

Conservatores (the Preservers-of-welfare Gods)
South Shields: altar dedicated 211-12. *RIB* 1054

Contrebis, see also **Ialonus Contrebis**
Burrow-in-Lonsdale (Overborough): altar by Vatta. *RIB* 610

Coventina, see also **Coventina Augusta**, and **Nympha Coventina**
Carrawburgh: altar to Conventina (sic) by Bellicus. *RIB* 1522

Carrawburgh: altar to Conveti(na) by Mausaeus, *optio* of *cohors I Frixiavonum*. *RIB* 1523

Carrawburgh: altar to Coventina by Aurelius Campester for *cohors I Cubernorum*. *RIB* 1524

Carrawburgh: altar to Coventina by Aurelius Crotus, a German. *RIB* 1525

Carrawburgh: altar to Coven(tina) by Vinomathus. *RIB* 1528

Carrawburgh: altar to Coventina by P[...]anus, *miles*. *RIB* 1529

Carrawburgh: altar to Covetine by Crotus. *RIB* 1532

Carrawburgh: altar to Covontina by Vincentius. *RIB* 1533

Carrawburgh: gabled relief to Covventina by Titus D(...) Cosconianus, prefect of *cohors I Batavorum*. *RIB* 1534 (**58**)

Carrawburgh: relief to Covven[ti(na)] by Aelius [...]pius, prefect of *cohors I Batavorum*. *RIB* 1535

Coventina Augusta
Carrawburgh: clay incense burner to Cove(n)tina Augusta made by Saturninus Gabinius. *RIB* 1530 and (revised) *RIB* 2457.2

Cuda(?)
Daglingworth: relief. *RIB* 129

Cultores (Gods of this Place)
Risingham: altar by Julius Victor, tribune (of *cohors I Vangionum*; see *RIB* 1217 under Jupiter Optimus Maximus below). *RIB* 1208

58 *Inscribed relief from Coventina's Well beside Carrawburgh. The text records the dedicant as T(itus) D(omitius?) Cosconianus, prefect of* cohors I Batavorum. *The stone was found with dozens of other altars and innumerable coins and artefacts. Height 0.74m. RIB 1534*

Custodes (Guardian Gods)
Vindolanda: altar by *cohors II[II] Gallorum* and Ve[...] Caecil[...]. *RIB* 1687 (with Jupiter Optimus Maximus and Genius)

Deus, see also **Mithras**, and **Mithras Invictus**
Caistor St Edmund: silver spoon bearing *Vivas in Deo*, in this case implicitly Christian in the phrasing of the exhortation. *RIB* 2420.49
Carvoran: pedestal or perhaps an unfinished altar recording the gift of a bracelet (*armilum*) from Binius. *RIB* 1806
Old Carlisle: altar to [D]eo by Flavius Aventinus. *RIB* 904
Rudchester: altar by L. Sentius Castus, (centurion?) of *VI Victrix*. In this case, the findspot in the fort mithraeum makes it certain that Mithras is meant. *RIB* 1398 (**59**)

Deus qui vias et semitas commentus est (God who devised roads and paths)
Catterick: altar by Titus Irdas, *singularis consularis*, and restored by Q. Varius Vitalis, *beneficiarius consularis*, in 191. *RIB* 725

Diana
Auchendavy: altar by M. Cocceius Firmus, centurion of *II Augusta*. *RIB* 2174 (with Apollo)
Bath: altar by Vettius B[e]nignus, *lib(ertus)*. *RIB* 138
Caerleon: slab recording restoration of a temple of Diana by T. Flavius Postumius [V]arus, senator and (legionary) legate, probably mid-third century if this is the man who was *praefectus urbi* in Rome in 271 (see *RIB*). *RIB* 316
Corbridge: altar by N[...]. *RIB* 1126
Risingham: altar by Aelia Timo. *RIB* 1209

59 *Altar from the* mithraeum *at Rudchester on Hadrian's Wall. The name of the god is merely given as Deo, 'To the God', but the figure and the bull makes it certain Mithras is meant. The dedicant is L(ucius) Sentius Castus of* VI Victrix. *Height 1.24m.* RIB *1398*

Diana Regina
Newstead: altar by G. Arrius Domitianus, centurion of *XX Valeria Victrix. RIB* 2122 (see this man again at Newstead under Jupiter Optimus Maximus and Silvanus)

Digenus?
Chester-le-Street: altar to Dig(enus?). *RIB* 1044
Hadrian's Wall (between Wallsend and Newcastle): altar to Di[genus?] (reading very doubtful). *RIB* 1314

Dis
Lincoln: on a tombstone of a 9-year-old girl. *RIB* 265

Disciplina/Discipulina Augusti/Augustorum (Discipline of the Emperor/Emperors)
Bertha: slab to Discipulinae Augusti. *JRS* xlix (1959), 136-7, no. 6
Bewcastle: altar to Discip(linae) Aug(usti) (secondary text). *RIB* 990
Birrens: altar by *cohors II Tungrorum c(ivium) L(atinorum). RIB* 2092
Castlesteads: altar of 209-11, rededicated 212-17, based on the text AUGGG, altered to AUG, i.e. for Severus and his sons, and then Caracalla alone. *RIB* 1978
Chesters: altar by *ala Augusta* for the Disciplina of Hadrian, 117-38. *Brit.* x (1979), 346, no. 7
Corbridge: base to Discipulinae Augustorum by *II Augusta. RIB* 1127
Corbridge?: slab to [Disci]p(ulinae) August[orum?] by *cohors I [fida Vardullor?]um* under [P. Calpu]rnius Victor. *RIB* asserts that this cannot predate 161-9, the first period of co-emperorship, but the relevant part of the text is not extant so this is only an inference. The same

applies to the dedicant's name. *RIB* 1128
Greatchesters: altar. *RIB* 1723

Dolichenus, see **Jupiter Optimus Maximus Dolichenus**, and **Jupiter Dolichenus**

Domesticae, see **Matres Domesticae**

Domina Nemesis (Lady Nemesis)
Caerleon: lead curse (anonymous). *RIB* 323

Domus Divina (Divine Imperial House)
Castlesteads(?): altar to Brigantia in honour of Caracalla and his divine house by M. Cocceius
    Nigrinus, *[pr]oc(urator) Aug(usti)*, between 212-17. *RIB* 2066 (with Nympha Brigantia)
Chichester: column base. *RIB* 89 (with Jupiter Optimus Maximus)
Chichester: slab recording the building of a temple to Neptune and Minerva in honour of the
    Domus Divina by the guild of smiths on a site given by [...]ens, son of Pudentinus, and by the
    authority of T. Claudius Togidubnus (see Chapter 9). *RIB* 91 (with Neptune and Minerva)
Old Penrith: slab to D(omus) D(ivinae) recording the rebuilding of a temple by Aurelius
    At[tianus?], prefect of *cohors II Gallorum*. *RIB* 916 (with Jupiter Optimus Maximus Dolichenus)
Vindolanda: altar by vicus inhabitants at Vindolanda. *RIB* 1700 (with Numina Augustorum and
    Volcanus)

Epona
Auchendavy: altar by M. Cocceius Firmus, centurion of *II Augusta*. *RIB* 2177 (with Campestres,
    Mars, Minerva, Hercules, and Victoria)
Carvoran: altar by P[...] So[...]. *RIB* 1777

Fatum Bonum (Good Fate)
Maryport: altar by G. Cornelius Peregrinus, tribune of the cohort and *decurio* of Saldae in
    Mauretania Caesariensis. *RIB* 812 (with Fortuna Redux, Genius loci, and Roma Aeterna)

Faunus (all on silver spoons unless otherwise mentioned)
Thetford: as Faunus Andicrose. *RIB* 2420.11
Thetford: as Faunus Ausecus (Faunus prick-ear/long-ear?). *RIB* 2420.12-13
Thetford: as Faunus Blotugus (Faunus Bringer of Spring Blossom or Fosterer of Corn?). *RIB*
    2420.14
Thetford: as Faunus Cranus. *RIB* 2420.15-16
Thetford: as Faunus Medigenus (Faunus the Mead-Begotten?). *RIB* 2420.17-19
Thetford: as Faunus Narius (Faunus the Lord), see also **Narius** below. *RIB* 2420.20-1
Thetford: as Faunus Saternius (Faunus, Giver of Plenty?). *RIB* 2420.22

Fersomeri, see **Unseni Fersomeri**

Fimmilena et Beda (Alaisiagae)
Housesteads: shrine door jam by 'Germans, citizens of Twenthe'. *RIB* 1593 (with Mars Thincsus,
    and Numen Augusti)

Fontes (the Fountains)
Chester: altar by *XX Valeria Victrix*. *RIB* 460 (with Nymphs)

Fortuna
Balmuildy: altar by Caecilius Nepos, tribune. *RIB* 2189
Binchester: altar by M. Valerius Fulvianus, prefect of cavalry. *RIB* 1029
Birdoswald: altar. *RIB* 1873
Birrens: altar by *cohors I Nervana Germanorum*. *RIB* 2093
Birrens: statue pedestal by Celer, *libertus*, for P. Campanius Italicus, prefect of *cohors I[I] Tungrorum*.
    RIB 2094

60 *Small altar from the bath-house by Carrawburgh, and typical of the myriad of personal dedications found along or near Hadrian's Wall. Vitalis made,* fecit, *this altar willingly and deservedly,* lib(ens) mer(ito), *to the goddess Fortuna (D(e)ae For(tunae)). Height 355mm.* RIB *1537*

Birrens: altar. *RIB* 2095

Bowes: altar by Virius Lupus, governor, restored a bath-house for *cohors I Thracum*; work in charge of Valerius Fronto, prefect of *ala Vettonum*, between *c.*197-202. *RIB* 730

Caerleon: block by Julius [Ba]ssus, *praefectus castrorum* of (*II Augusta*?). *RIB* 317

Carlisle: miniature clay altar inscribed (on the top). *Brit.* xxiv (1993), 316, no. 6

Carrawburgh: altar by M. Flaccinius Marcellus, prefect of *cohors I Batavorum*. *RIB* 1536

Carrawburgh: altar by Vitalis. *RIB* 1537 (**60**)

Carvoran (probably): altar by Audac(ilius) Romanus, centurion of *VI*, *XX*, and *II Augusta*. *RIB* 1779

Castlecary: altar by vexillations of *II Augusta* and *VI Victrix*. *RIB* 2146

Greatchesters: altar to [F]or[t]u(nae) by a *vexillatio G(aesatorum) R(a)eto(rum)* commanded by the centurion Tabellius Victor. *RIB* 1724

Haltonchesters: altar. *RIB* 1423

Risingham: altar by G. Valerius Longinus, tribune. *RIB* 1210 (for this man again see Hercules, *RIB* 1214) (**61**)

Slack: altar by G. Antonius Modestus, centurion of *VI Victrix*. *RIB* 624

York: altar by Sosia Juncina, wife of Q. Antonius Isauricus, imperial (legionary) legate, between. *RIB* 644 (**71**)

York: statue base by Metrob[ianus?], *li[b(ertus)*, for the benefit of Publius [Maesius] Auspicatus (Maesius is restored from the name of the beneficiary's son on the stone). *RIB* 645

Unprovenanced (British origin): altar. *RIB* 2217 (with Numina Augustorum)

Fortuna Augusta (the Emperor's Fortune)

Carvoran: altar dedicated for Lucius Aelius Caesar by T. Flavius Secundus, prefect of *cohors I Hamiorum sagittaria*, between 136-8. *RIB* 1778

Lanchester: altar by P. Aelius Atticus, prefect. *RIB* 1073

Risingham: altar by Aelia Proculina. *RIB* 1211

61 Altar from Risingham bath-house, dedicated by the tribune Valerius Longinus to Fortuna. A temple(?) facade is depicted. Another altar to Fortuna Redux (RIB 1212), also from Risingham bath-house, depicts an almost identical facade, suggesting the building was within or integral to the bath-house. Height 1.02m. RIB 1210

Fortuna Balnearis
Kirkby Thore: altar to Fort[un]a Bal[n(eari)] by G. Caledius Frontinus of *n(umerus) m(ilitum) S(yrorum) s(agittariorum)*. *RIB* 764

Fortuna et Bonus Eventus see Bonus Eventus et Fortuna above

Fortuna Conservatrix (Fortune the Preserver)
Chesters: altar by Venenus, a German. *RIB* 1449
Manchester: altar by L. Senecianius Martius, centurion of *VI Victrix*. *RIB* 575
Netherby: altar by M. Aurelius Salvius, tribune of *cohors I Aelia Hispanorum* (also named on *RIB* 978 at Netherby, in 222), about 222. *RIB* 968

Fortuna Populi Romani (Fortune of the Roman People)
Vindolanda: altar to Fortuna P(opuli) R(omani) by G. Julius Raeticus, centurion of *VI Victrix*. *RIB* 1684

Fortuna Redux (Fortune the Home-Bringer)
Chester: altar by the legate (presumably of *XX Valeria Victrix*) T. Pomponius Mamilianus. *RIB* 445 (with Aesculapius, and Salus)
Maryport: altar by G. Cornelius Peregrinus, tribune of the cohort and *decurio* of *Saldae* in Mauretania Caesariensis. *RIB* 812 (with Fatum Bonum, Genius loci, and Roma Aeterna)
Maryport: votive pillar. *RIB* 840 (with Roma Aeterna)
Risingham: altar by Julius Severinus, tribune, on completion of a bath-house. *RIB* 1212

Fortuna Servatrix (Fortune the Deliverer)
Kirkby Thore: altar by Antonia Stratonis following a vision. *RIB* 760

*62 Altar found close to the fort at Lanchester, naming the goddess Garmangabis and vexillatio Sueborum Lon(govicianorum) Gor(dianae). Gordian III's name in the unit title, dates the text to 238-44 (see also **6, 37**). Height 1.37m. RIB 1074*

Friagabis et Baudihillia, Alaisiagae
Housesteads: altar by *numerus Hnaudifridi. RIB* 1576 (with Numen Augusti)

Garmangabis
Lanchester: altar by *vex(illatio) Sueborum Lon(govicianorum) Gor(dianae)* between 238-44. *RIB* 1074 (with Numen Augusti of Gordian III) (**62**)

God (in Hebrew form of Jahweh)
Caernarvon: amulet by Alphianos in Greek, apparently to the Hebrew God. *RIB* 436. See *Brit.* xxvii (1996), 456 for a revised translation of the text

Genius
Caerwent: altar. *Brit.* ii (1971), 353, no. 9
Chichester: altar by Lucullus. *RIB* 90
Cirencester: base by Attius [....?]. *RIB* 101
Ebchester: altar. *RIB* 1099
Old Carlisle: altar by Aurelius Martialis and Aurelius E[b]uracio(?). *RIB* 891
Vindolanda: altar by *cohors II[II] Gallorum. RIB* 1687 (with Jupiter Optimus Maximus and Custodes)

Genius alae primae Hispanorum Asturum (Genius of the ala)
Benwell: altar by Terentius Agrippa, prefect of *ala I Hispanorum Asturum. RIB* 1334 (with Matres Campestres)

Genius centuriae (Genius of the century)
Carlisle: altar by the century of Bassilius Crescens. *RIB* 944
Chester: altar. *RIB* 446
Chester: altar by Julius Quintilianus for the century of Aurelianus. *RIB* 447

Genius cohortis (Genius of the cohort)
Gloucester: altar by Orivendus (reading revised in *RIB95*). *RIB* 119
High Rochester: altar by T. Licinius Valerianus, tribune, for *cohors I fida Vardullorum*. *RIB* 1263 (with Signa cohortis)
Lanchester: altar by *cohors I Vardullorum* during the governorship of Antistius Adventus in *c.*175-6. *RIB* 1083, at the expense of the tribune Flavius Titianus (with Numen Augusti)

Genius collegii (Genius of the guild)
High Rochester: altar by Caecilius Optatus, tribune. *RIB* 1268 (with Minerva)

Genius collegii Apollinis (Genius of the college of Apollo)
Burrow-in-Lonsdale (Overborough): altar by [B]ellinus. *RIB* 611 (with Numina Augustorum)

Genius Domini Nostri/Dominorum Nostrorum (Genius of our lord/lords)
High Rochester: altar by Egnatius Lucilianus, governor, for the *Signa* of *cohors I Vardul[l(orum)* and *n(umerus) Explorator(um) Brem(eniensium) Gor(diani)* under the charge of Cassius Sabinianus, tribune, between 238-44. *RIB* 1262 (with Signa)
Old Penrith: altar by *cohors [II?] Gallo[r(um)]*, *for Philip I and II, between 244-9*. *RIB* 915 (with Jupiter Optimus Maximus)

Genius Eboraci (Genius of York)
York: altar to Gen(io) Eb[or(aci?)]. *RIB* 657 (with Numen Augusti)

Genius huius Loci (Genius of this place)
Carrawburgh: altar by the Texandri and Suevae from a vexillation of *cohors II Nerviorum*. *RIB* 1538
Housesteads: altar by members of *II Augusta* on garrison duty. *RIB* 1583 (with Cocidius and Jupiter Optimus Maximus)

Genius Imperatorum? (Genius of the Emperors)
Caerleon: slab recording the possible restoration of a temple between 177 and 180. *Brit.* i (1970), 305, no. 1 (and Jupiter Optimus Maximus)

Genius legionis II Augustae (Genius of *legio II Augusta*)
Caerleon: pilaster given by [...], *primus pilus*, in 244 under the charge of Ursus, *actarius*, of *II Augusta*. *RIB* 327 (with Numina Augustorum)

Genius legionis XX Valeria Victrix D[eciana?] 'Genius of the XX legion'
Chesters: altar by Titus Vet[...] between 249-51. *RIB* 449

Genius loci (Genius of the Place), see also Genius huius Loci
Bath: altar by Torianus(?) of *VI Victrix?*. *RIB* 139
Binchester: altar by *ala Vettonum*. *RIB* 1032 (with Matres Ollotatae)
Carlisle: altar. *RIB* 945
Carrawburgh: altar by M. Hispanius Modestinus, prefect of *cohors I Batavorum*. *JRS* li (1961), 193, no. 9 (with Nymphae)
Castlesteads: altar by G. Verecundius Severus. *RIB* 1984 (with Jupiter Optimus Maximus)
Chester: altar by Flavius Longus, *tribunus militum* of *XX [Valeria Victrix]*, and his son Longinus, from Samosata. *RIB* 450
Clifton (found at Brougham?): altar by Subrius Apollinaris, *princeps* of *cohors I V[angionum?]*. *RIB* 792 (with Jupiter Optimus Maximus)
Daglingworth: slab. *RIB* 130 (with Matres)

63 Altar from Vindolanda to Jupiter Optimus Maximus, 'other immortal gods', and Genius praetori, 'Genius of the commandant's house'. Dedicated by Q. Petronius Urbicus, prefect of cohors IIII Gallorum with a suffix which must be either Antoniniana *(213-22),* Severiana *(222-35),* Deciana *(249-51), or* Postumiana *(259-68). Height 1.37m.* RIB *1686*

Lincoln: altar. *RIB* 246

Malton: panel of exhortation to the slave of the *taberna aureficinam*. *RIB* 712 (**55**)

Maryport: altar by G. Cornelius Peregrinus, tribune of the cohort and *decurio* of Saldae in Mauretania Caesariensis. *RIB* 812 (with Fatum Bonum, Fortuna Redux, and Roma Aeterna)

Tilston: altar. *Brit.* xv (1984), 341, no. 14

Vindolanda: altar by Lupulus. *Brit.* iv (1973), 329, no. 10 (with Mogons)

York: altar. *RIB* 646

York: stone. *RIB* 647

York: altar by Q. Crepereius Marcus. *Brit.* iv (1973), 325-9, no. 5

Genius numeri Maurorum Aurelianorum Valeriani Gallienique (Genius of the *numerus* of Aurelian Moors of Valerian and Gallienus)

Burgh-by-Sands: altar by Caelius Vibianus, tribune of *numerus Maurorum Aurelianorum Valeriani Gallienique*, under the direction of Julius Rufinus, *princeps* between 253-8. *RIB* 2042 (with Numina Augustorum; the primary dedication to Jupiter Optimus Maximus is entirely restored in *RIB*)

Genius praesidii (Genius of the guard/garrison)

Housesteads: altar by Valerius, *miles* with *VI Victrix*. *RIB* 1577 (with Cocidius)

Genius praetorii (Genius of the commandant's house)
Lanchester: base by Cl. Epaphroditus Claudianus, tribune of *cohors I Lingonum. RIB* 1075
Vindolanda: altar by Pituanius Secundus, prefect of *cohors IIII Gallorum. RIB* 1685
Vindolanda: altar by Q. Petronius Urbicus, prefect of *cohors IIII Gallorum. RIB* 1686 (with Jupiter
    Optimus Maximus and 'other immortal gods') (**63**)
Vindolanda: altar by *cohors IIII Gallorum. RIB* 1687 (with Custodes and Jupiter Optimus
    Maximus)

Genius sanctus centuriae (Holy Genius of the century)
Chester: altar by Aelius Claudianus, *optio. RIB* 448

Genius sanctus huius loci (Holy Genius of this place)
Cirencester: altar. *RIB* 102

Genius signiferorum legionis XX Valeria Victrix (Genius of the standard-bearers of *XX Valeria
    Victrix*)
Chester: base by T. Flavius Valerianus for his colleagues. *RIB* 451

Genius Terrae Britannicae (Genius of the Britannic land)
Auchendavy: altar by M. Cocceius Firmus, centurion of *II Augusta. RIB* 2175

Genius [...]vali (Genius of [...]valium; perhaps *Luguvalium*, i.e. Carlisle))
Hadrian's Wall (near mc 59): altar by [...] Martius, centurion of *cohors I Batavorum. RIB* 2015 (with
    Mars Cocidius)

Hammia
Carvoran: altar made by Sabinus. *RIB* 1780

Harimella
Birrens: altar by Gamidiahus, *arcit(ectus). RIB* 2096

Herakles Tyrioi (Heracles, i.e. Hercules, of Tyre)
Corbridge: altar to Heracles of Tyre by Diodora the priestess (in Greek). *RIB* 1129

Hercules
Auchendavy: altar by M. Cocceius Firmus, centurion of *II Augusta. RIB* 2177 (with Campestres,
    Epona, Mars, Minerva, and Victoria)
Brancaster: bronze tablet. *RIB* 2432.5
Burgh-by-Sands: altar by *cohors [....]. RIB* 2040 (with Numen Augusti)
Carvoran: inscription to (H)erc(u)l[i]. *RIB* 1781
Haile: altar by Primus, *custos armorum. RIB* 796 (with Silvanus)
High Rochester: altar to Herculens (sic). *RIB* 1264
Housesteads: altar by P. Aelius Modestus, prefect of *cohors I Tungrorum. RIB* 1580 (**64**)
Old Carlisle: altar by Sigilius Emeritus, or Sigilius, the *emeritus*, recording a division of spoils with
    the god. *RIB* 892
Risingham: altar by Julius Paullus, tribune. *RIB* 1213 (named as tribune of *cohors I Vangionum* at
    Risingham on *RIB* 1241)
Risingham: altar to (H)e[r]cul[i] by G. Valerius Longinus. *RIB* 1214 (see also *RIB* 1210 under
    Fortuna above for his full name)
Whitley Castle: altar by G. Vitellius Atticianus, centurion of *VI Victrix. RIB* 1199
York: slab by T. Perpet[...] Aeternus of York. *RIB* 648

Hercules Augustus (Imperial Hercules)
Brough-on-Noe: altar by the prefect Proculus, possibly referring to the restoration of a temple. *Brit.*
    xi (1980), 404, no. 3

64 Altar from Housesteads to Hercules, dedicated by the prefect Publius Aelius Modestus of cohors I Tungrorum. Height 1.07m. RIB 1580

Hercules Invictus (Invincible Hercules)
Carlisle: arched slab by Publius Sextanius, prefect of *ala Augusta*, celebrating the slaughter of a band of barbarians. *RIB 946*
Risingham: altar by L. Aemilius Salvianus, tribune of *cohors I Vangionum*. *RIB 1215*

Hercules Magusanus (Hercules the magician?)
Mumrills: altar by Valerius Nigrinus, *dupli(carius)* of *ala (I) Tungrorum*. *RIB 2140*

Hercules Saegon[...]
Silchester: slab by T. Tammonius Vitalis. *RIB 67*

Hercules Victor (Victorious Hercules)
Whitley Castle: altar. *RIB 1200* (with Menerva (sic))

Hospitales (Gods of Hospitality)
Newcastle-upon-Tyne: altar. *RIB 1317* (with Jupiter Optimus Maximus and Numen Augusti)
York: altar by P. Aelius Marcianus, prefect of *cohors [.....]* (*I Augustae Bracarum* has been suggested on the evidence of this man as its prefect on *ILS 2738*). *RIB 649* (with Jupiter Optimus Maximus and Penates)

Hveterus/Hviteres, and variants. See also **Veteris** etc.
Carrawburgh: altar to the Hviteres. *RIB 1549*
Hadrian's Wall (exact location unknown): altar to the Hvitires. *RIB 2069*
Housesteads: altar to Hveteris by Superstes and Regulus. *RIB 1602*
Housesteads: altar to Hvitris by Aspuanis. *RIB 1603*
Netherby: altar to Hveterus. *RIB 973*

65 Altar from London recording the restoration of a temple of Isis by M(arcus) Martiannius Pulcher, v(ir) c(larissimus*)? (senator), and propraetorian legate of the Emperors of, presumably,* Britannia Superior. *The altar had been used in the fourth-century riverside wall, thus providing no location for the temple other than that it was in London. Height 1.22m. Brit. vii (1976), 378-9, no.2*

Hygiaea
Burrow-in-Lonsdale (Overborough): altar by Julius Saturninus. *RIB* 609 (with Asclepius)
Chester: altar by Antiochos, *hiatros*. *JRS* lix (1969), 235, no. 3 (with Asklepios and Panakeia)

Hypermenes (Saviour Gods)
Chester: altar by Hermogenes, a doctor (in Greek). *RIB* 461

Ialonus Contrebis, see also Contrebis
Lancaster: altar by Julius Januarius, *emeritus*, former *decurio*. *RIB* 600

Invictus, see Hercules Invictus, Mithras Invictus, Silvanus Invictus, and Sol Invictus

Ioug[...]
York: slab to *Dea Ioug[...]* by *[...]sius, recording restoration of the shrine*. *RIB* 656 (with Numina Augustorum)

Isis
London: flagon of late-first-century type recording the address *Londini ad fanum Isidis*, 'at London, by the temple of Isis'. The inscription could be much later than the vessel, which has survived intact, and thus could have been inscribed at any date during the Roman period. *RIB* 2503.127
London: altar recording the rebuilding of a temple of Isis by M. Martian[n]ius Pulcher, *leg(atus) Aug(ustorum)*, at some point in the third century. *Brit.* vii (1976), 378-9, no. 2 (**65**)

Iu[..]teris Fortunat[us]
Netherby: altar. *RIB* 969

Juno Regina
Carlisle: 213-22 — altar by M. [Aurelius?] Syrio, military tribune with *XX Valeria Victrix. Brit.* xx (1989), 331-3, no. 5 (with Jupiter Optimus Maximus, Minerva, Mars, and Victoria)

Jupiter/Juppiter
Colchester: statuette by P. Oranius Felix. *RIB* 2432.8
Stony Stratford: silver plate by Vassinus. *RIB* 215 (with Volcanus)

Jupiter Aeternus Dolichenus (Eternal Jupiter of Doliche)
Corbridge: altar by G. Julius Apolinaris (sic), centurion of *VI Victrix*, his name replacing someone else's. *RIB* 1131 (with Caelestis Brigantia and Salus)

Jupiter Augustus
Maryport: altar by M. Censorius Cornelianus, centurion of *[X Fr]etensis*, commander of *cohors I Hispanorum. RIB* 814

Jupiter Optimus Maximus (Jupiter, Best and Greatest)
Auchendavy: altar by M. Cocceius Firmus, centurion of *II Augusta. RIB* 2176 (with Victoria Victrix)
Aldborough: altar. *RIB* 708 (with Matres)
Binchester: altar by Pomponius Donatus, *b(ene)f(iciarius) co(n)s(ularis). RIB* 1030 (with Matres Ollototae sive Transmarinae) (N.B. another possibility at *Brit.* xxiii (1992), 314, no. 10)
Birdoswald: altar by *cohors I Aelia Dacorum* under the tribune Ammonius Victorinus. *RIB* 1874
Birdoswald: altar by *cohors I Aelia Dacorum* under the tribune Aurelius Faustus in 237. *RIB* 1875
Birdoswald: altar by *cohors I Aelia Dacorum* under Aurelius Saturninus. *RIB* 1876
Birdoswald: altar by *cohors I Aelia Dacorum* under Aurelius [....]. *RIB* 1877
Birdoswald: altar by *[cohors I A]el(ia) Da[corum]* under F[l(avius) .....]. *RIB* 1878
Birdoswald: altar by *cohors I Aelia Dacorum* under the tribune Funisulanus Vettonianus. *RIB* 1879
Birdoswald: altar by *cohors I Aelia Dacorum* under Julius Marcellinus, centurion of *II Augusta. RIB* 1880
Birdoswald: altar by *cohors I Aelia Dacorum* under the tribune Julius Saturninus. *RIB* 1881
Birdoswald: altar by *cohors I Aelia Dacorum*, commanded by the tribune Marcius Gallicus, around the period 255-75 (see next entry for this man in post under Postumus). *RIB* 1882 (with Numen Augusti)
Birdoswald: altar by *cohors I Aelia Dacorum Postumiana*, commanded by the tribune Marcius Gallicus between 259-68. *RIB* 1883
Birdoswald: altar with by Pomp[oni]us D[eside]rat[us], tribune commanding *cohors I Aelia Dacorum Tetricianorum* between 270-3 (with primary anonymous dedication to Cocidius). *RIB* 1885
Birdoswald: altar by *cohors I Aelia Dacorum Postumiana* under the tribune Probius Augendus between 259-68. *RIB* 1886
Birdoswald: altar by *cohors I Aelia Dacorum* under the tribune Statius Longinus. *RIB* 1887
Birdoswald: altar by *cohors I Aelia Dacorum* under the tribune [...]us Con[...]. *RIB* 1888
Birdoswald: altars by *cohors I Aelia Dacorum* under [...]. *RIB* 1889-91
Birdoswald: altar by *cohors I Aelia Dacorum Antoniniana* between 213-22. *RIB* 1892
Birdoswald: altar by *cohors I Aelia Dacorum Gordiana* between 238-44. *RIB* 1893
Birdoswald: altar by *cohors I Aelia Dacorum* in the charge of [...]rinus, *beneficiarius. RIB* 1894
Birdoswald: altar by *cohors I Aelia Dacorum* under the tribune [...]. *RIB* 1895
Bowness-on-Solway: altar by Sulpicius Secundianus, tribune, between 251-3. *RIB* 2057 (and *RIB* 2058 recorded with an identical text)
Caerleon: slab recording the possible restoration of a temple between 177 and 180. *Brit.* i (1970), 305, no. 1 (and Genius Imperatorum?)
Cappuck: altar by *ve[x]il(l)atio R(a)etorum Gaesat(orum)* commanded by the tribune Julius Severinus. *RIB* 2117
Cardewlees: altar by (?), for the *numina* of Valerian I, Gallienus, and Valerian II as Caesar under the charge of G. [C]arinius Aurelianus, centurion of *II Augusta*, between 253-5. *RIB* 913 (with Numina Dominorum Nostrorum)
Carlisle: altar by M. [Aurelius?] Syrio, military tribune with *XX Valeria Victrix*, between 213-22. *Brit.* xx (1989), 331-3, no. 5 (with Juno, Minerva, Mars, and Victoria)

Carriden: altar by the *vicus* peoples of the fort of *Velunia* under the charge of Aelius Mansuetus. *JRS* xlvii (1957), 229-30, no. 18

Castlesteads: altar by *cohors IIII Gallorum* commanded by the prefect of cavalry Volcacius Hospes. *RIB* 1980

Castlesteads: altar by *cohors II Tungrorum* commanded by the prefect Albius Severus, directed by Vic(...) Severus, *princeps*. *RIB* 1981

Castlesteads: altar by *cohors II Tungrorum* commanded by the prefect Aurelius Optatus, directed by Messius Opsequens, *princeps*. *RIB* 1982

Castlesteads: altar by *cohors II Tungrorum Gordiana*, commanded by the prefect T. Claudius Claudianus, work directed by [P.?] Aelius Martinus, *princeps*, in 241. *RIB* 1983 (with Numen Augusti Nostri)

Castlesteads: altar by G. Verecundius Severus. *RIB* 1984 (with Genius loci)

Castlesteads: altar. *RIB* 1985

Chichester: column base, and honouring the *Domus Divina*. *RIB* 89

Cirencester: column base by L. Septimius, *v(ir) p(erfectissimus) pr(aeses)*, and *rector*, of *Britannia Prima*. *RIB* 103 (**26**)

Clifton: altar by Subrius Apollinaris, *princeps* of *cohors I V[angionum?]*. *RIB* 792 (with Genius loci)

Dorchester-on-Thames: altar *cum cancellis* ('with screens') by M. Varius Severus, *beneficiarius consularis* of the governor. *RIB* 235 (with Numina Augustorum)

Godmanstone (nr Dorchester, Dorset): altar by Titinius Pines, of *[XX V(aleria)] V(ictrix)*(?). *JRS* lv (1965), 220-1, no. 2

Hadrian's Wall (between t 7b and mc 8): altar. *RIB* 1366

Housesteads: altar. *RIB* 1581

Housesteads: altar by *milites* of *II Augusta*. *RIB* 1582

Housesteads: altar by *milites* of *II Augusta* on garrison duty. *RIB* 1583 (with Cocidius and Genius loci)

Housesteads: altar by *cohors I Tungrorum*, under the prefect Q. Julius Maximus. *RIB* 1584 (with Numina Augustorum)

Housesteads: altar by *cohors I Tungrorum*, under the prefect Q. Julius [Cur?]sus. *RIB* 1585 (with Numina Augustorum)

Housesteads: altar by *cohors I Tungrorum*, under the prefect Q. Verius Superstis. *RIB* 1586 (with Numina Augustorum)

Housesteads: altar by (?), under the prefect [...]rius [.]upe[...]. *RIB* 1587 (with Numina Augustorum)

Housesteads: altar by [.....], prefect. *RIB* 1588 (with Numina Augustorum)

Housesteads: altar, anonymous dedication on behalf of Desidienius Ae[mi]lianus, prefect, in 258. *RIB* 1589

Lanchester: altar by *cohors I Lingonum* under the prefect [F]ulvius [Fel]ix. *Brit.* xix (1988), 492, no. 10

London: altar posssibly recording the rebuilding of a temple by Aquilinus, imperial *libertus*, Mercator, Audax, and Graecus. The dedication is not certain and may instead have been to Mithras or the Matres. *Brit.* vii (1976), 378, no. 1

Maryport: altar by [...]iana Hermione. *RIB* 813 (formerly read as Iuno)

Maryport: altar by *cohors I Hispanorum*, Hadrianic. *RIB* 815 (with Numen Augusti)

Maryport: altar by *cohors I Hispanorum*, commanded by the prefect L. Antistius Lupus Veranius. *RIB* 816

Maryport: altar by *cohors I Hispanorum*, commanded by the tribune G. Caballius Priscus. *RIB* 817

Maryport: altars by G. Caballius Priscus, tribune. *RIB* 818-20

Maryport: altar by P. Cornelius Ur[...], prefect of *cohors I Hispanorum*. *RIB* 821

Maryport: altar by Helstrius Novellus, prefect of *cohors I Hispanorum*. *RIB* 822

Maryport: altar by M. Maenius Agrippa, tribune of *cohors I Hispanorum*. *RIB* 823

Maryport: altar by M. Maenius Agrippa, tribune. *RIB* 824 (with Numen Augusti)

Maryport: altar by Maenius Agrippa, tribune. *RIB* 825 (with Numen Augusti)

Maryport: altar by Maenius [Agrippa], tribune. *RIB* 826

Maryport: altar by [L.?] Cammius Maximus, prefect of *cohors I Hispanorum* and tribune of *cohors XVIIII Voluntariorum*. *RIB* 827

Maryport: altars by L. Cammius Maximus, prefect of *cohors I Hispanorum*. *RIB* 828-9

Maryport: altar by T. Attius Tutor, prefect of *cohors I Baetasiorum*. *RIB* 830

Maryport: altar by L. Caecilius Vegetus, prefect of *cohors I Dalmatarum. RIB* 831
Maryport: altar by [Postumius] Acilianus, prefect of *[cohors I Dalmatarum]* between 138-61. *RIB* 833
　　(see *RIB* 832 under Jupiter Optimus Maximus Capitolinus)
Maryport: altar by [...], prefect of *cohors [...]. RIB* 834
Maryport: altar. *RIB* 835 (with Volcanus?)
Moresby: altar by *cohors II T(h)racum*, commanded by the prefect Mamius Nepos. *RIB* 797
Netherby: altar. *RIB* 969 (with Iu[...]teris Fortunatus?)
Newcastle-upon-Tyne: altar. *RIB* 1316 (with Victoria Augusti)
Newcastle-upon-Tyne: altar. *RIB* 1317 (with Hospitales and Numen Augusti)
Newstead: altar by G. Arrius Domitianus, centurion of *XX Valeria Victrix. RIB* 2123 (see this man
　　again at Newstead under Diana Regina and Silvanus)
Old Penrith: altar by *cohors [II] Gallorum* between 244-9. *RIB* 915 (with Genius Dominorum
　　Nostrorum)
Shakenoak: altar. *Brit.* ii (1971), 353, no. 8
Vindolanda: altar by Q. Petronius Urbicus, prefect of *cohors IIII Gallorum [Antoniniana]* or
　　[Severiana], between 213-35. *RIB* 1686 (with Genius Praetori) (**63**)
Vindolanda: altar by *cohors IIII Gallorum. RIB* 1687 (with Custodes and Genius)
Vindolanda: altar by *[c]oh(ors) IIII G[al]l(orum)* under the prefect L. [...]gius Pudens. *RIB* 1688
Vindolanda: altars. *RIB* 1689-90
Hadrian's Wall (exact place unknown but probably Vindolanda): altar by *cohors IIII Gallorum* under
　　the prefect Naevius Hilarus. *RIB* 2062
York: altar by P. Aelius Marcianus, prefect of *cohors [.....]* (*I Augustae Bracarum* has been suggested on
　　the evidence of this man as its prefect on *ILS* 2738). *RIB* 649 (with Hospitales and Penates)
Unprovenanced: altar by Vitalis (reading of Jupiter Optimus Maximus in *RIB95*). *RIB* 1017 (with
　　Mars Cocidius)

Jupiter Optimus Maximus Capitolinus
Maryport: altar by Postumius Acilianus, prefect of *cohors I Dalmatarum* between 138-61. *RIB* 832

Jupiter Optimus Maximus Conservator (Jupiter, Best and Greatest, the Preserver)
Old Carlisle: altar. *RIB* 898

Jupiter Optimus Maximus Dolichenus (Jupiter, Best and Greatest, of Doliche)
Benwell: altar by M. Liburnius Fronto, centurion of *II Augusta*, between 139-61. *RIB* 1330 (with
　　Numina Augustorum for the welfare of Antoninus Pius and *II Augusta*)
Bewcastle: slab recording the building of a temple. *RIB* 992
Birdoswald: altar to Jupiter Optimus Maximus [D(olichenus)?] by *cohors I Aelia Dacorum*, under the
　　tribune Flavius Maximianus. *RIB* 1896
Birdoswald: altar by *cohors I Aelia Dacorum Maximini*, under the tribune Flavius Maximianus,
　　between 235-8. *JRS* xlvii (1957), 229, no. 17
Birrens: altar to [Jupiter Optimus Maximus] Dol[iche]nus by Magunna. *RIB* 2099
Caerleon: altar by Fronto Aemilianus [...] Rufilianus, *legatus Augustorum* (possibly 161-9), of *II
　　Augusta*(?). *RIB* 320
Carvoran: altar. *RIB* 1782
Chesters: altar by Galerius Ver[ecundus?] for the welfare of *Augustorum Nostrorum*, 'our emperors'.
　　RIB 1452
Croy Hill: relief to [Jupiter Optimus Maximus Dolic]henus. *RIB* 2158
Duntocher: altar. *RIB* 2201
Greatchesters: altar by L. Maximus Gaetulicus, centurion of *XX Valeria Victrix. RIB* 1725
Greatchesters: altar by Regulus for(?) [...]ina, daughter of Sabinus. *RIB* 1726
Old Carlisle: altar to Jupiter Optimus Maximus [D(olicheno)?] by *ala Augusta* under the prefect
　　Egnatius Verecundus about 197. *RIB* 895
Old Penrith: slab recording the rebuilding of a temple by Aurelius Attianus, prefect of *cohors II
　　Gallorum*, and in honour of *D(omus) D(ivina). RIB* 916
Piercebridge: altar by Julius Valentinus, centurion from Upper Germany, in 217. *RIB* 1022
Piercebridge: uncertain fragment, dedication conjectural. *RIB* 1023
Piercebridge: statue base by a vexillation of *VI Victrix*, the army of Germany, under the supervision

66 Statue base from Piercebridge, recording Jupiter Optimus Maximus Dolichenus, and dedicated by a vexillation of VI Victrix and the 'army of the Germanies' (exer(citus) G(ermaniae)) under the charge of M(arcus) Loll(ius) Venator, centurion of II Augusta. The stone apparently forms one of a series of inscriptions, including one dated to 217 (RIB 1022) from the site which refer to a gathering of forces, at Piercebridge towards the close of Caracalla's reign. JRS lvii (1967), 205, no, 16 (see also Britannia xvii (1986), 438, no. 20).

of M. Lollius Venator, centurion of *II Augusta. JRS* lvii (1967), 205, no. 16 (**66**)
Risingham: slab. *RIB* 1219
Risingham: altar to [Jupiter Optimus Maximus] Dolochenus by G. Julius Publilius Prius, tribune. *RIB* 1220

Jupiter Optimus Maximus Heliopolitanus (Jupiter, Best and Greatest, of Heliopolis)
Carvoran: altar by Julius Pollio. *RIB* 1783

Jupiter Optimus Maximus Tanarus
Chester: altar by L. Elupius (or Elutrius) Praesens, of the Galerian voting tribe at Clunia (*Hispania Tarraconensis*), *princeps* of *XX Valeria Victrix*, in 154. *RIB* 452

Jupiter Serapis, see also **Serapis**
Kirkby Thore: altar by Lucius Alfenus Pal[...]. *RIB* 762

Lamiae Triades (Three witches)
Benwell: altar. *RIB* 1331

Latis
Birdoswald: altar. *RIB* 1897
Burgh-by-Sands: altar by Lucius. *RIB* 2043

Lenus Mars, see **Mars Lenus**

Loucetius Mars, see **Mars Loucetius**

Magusanus Hercules, see **Hercules Magusanus**

67 *Statuette of Mars found in the Fossdike at Torksey. The statue plinth bears an inscription on two panels. The panel states the names of the donors, Bruccius and Caratius Colasunus, who had paid 100 sesterces for it. A side panel (not visible) adds that Celatus, aerarius (coppersmith), made the statue from 3 denarii-worth of bronze. Height 283mm. (Copyright © The British Museum). RIB 274*

Maponus, see also **Apollo Maponus**
Hadrian's Wall (exact location unknown): altar by Durio, Ramio, Trupo, and Lurio, all Germans. *RIB* 2063 (with Numen Augusti)
Vindolanda: silver pendant. *RIB* 2431.2

Mars
Auchendavy: altar by M. Cocceius Firmus, centurion of *II Augusta*. *RIB* 2177 (with Campestres, Minerva, Hercules, Epona and Victoria)
Balmuildy: altar to [Ma]rti. *RIB* 2190
Bath: lead 'curse' tablet recording a gift to the temple of Mars by Basilia. Cunliffe (1988), no. 97
Benwell: altar by Lenuanus. *RIB* 1332
Birdoswald: altar by [...], tribune of *cohors I Aelia Dacorum*. *RIB* 1898
Birdoswald: altar by Aurelius Maximus. *RIB* 1899 (with Victoria)
Birrens: altar by *cohors II Tungrorum* under the prefect Silvius Auspex. *RIB* 2100 (with Victoria Augusti)
Brough-on-Noe: altar. *RIB* 282
Brougham: altar to [Ma]rti. *RIB* 779 (with Victoria)
Brougham: altar by Januarius of the *numerus equitum [St]ratonicianorum*. *RIB* 780
Carlisle: 213-22 — altar by M. [Aurelius?] Syrio, military tribune with *XX Valeria Victrix*. *Brit.* xx (1989), 331-3, no. 5 (with Jupiter Optimus Maximus, Juno, Minerva, and Victoria)

Castlesteads: altar by Venustinus Lupus. *RIB* 1986
Castlesteads: altar by Paconius Saturninus, prefect of cavalry. *RIB* 1987 (with Numen Augusti)
Croy Hill: altar by Gaius D[...] B[...]. *RIB* 2159
Ebchester: altar. *RIB* 1100 (with Numen Augusti)
Fossdike: statuette by Bruccius and Caratius Colasunus. *RIB* 274 (with Numina Augustorum) (**67**)
Gloucester: altar. *RIB* 120
Greta Bridge: altar by Enemn[o]genus. *RIB* 742
Greta Bridge: altar. *RIB* 743
Housesteads: statue base. *RIB* 1590
Housesteads: altar by Q. Florius Maternus, prefect of *cohors I Tungrorum*. *RIB* 1591
Housesteads: altar by Vi[....]anus. *RIB* 1592
Housesteads altar by 'the Germans' of *cuneus Frisiorum Ver(covicianorum)* between 222-35. *RIB* 1594
    (with Numen Augusti and Alaisiagae)
Housesteads: altar. *RIB* 1595 (with Victoria)
Housesteads: altar by [...], *custos armorum*. *RIB* 1596 (with Victoria and Numina Augustorum)
Housesteads: altar by Calve[...], a German. *RIB* 1597
Lancaster: altar by Sabinus, *praepositus*, and *numerus Barcariorum*. *RIB* 601
Lanchester: altar by Ascernus. *RIB* 1078
Lanchester: altar by Caurus. *RIB* 1079
Lanchester: altar by Sancidus. *RIB* 1080
Lanchester: altar. *RIB* 1081
Lincoln: altar to Ma[r]t[i]. *RIB* 248
Newtown: circular stone with incised image of the god and inscribed Matri, for Marti. *RIB* 2453.3
Old Carlisle: altar. *RIB* 900
Ribchester: base. *RIB* 585 (with Victoria)
Silchester: slab to Marti[...] (either the god or naming an individual) by guild of peregrini. *RIB* 71
Staincross Common: altar for the welfare of D(ominorum) N(ostrorum) Imp(eratorum)
    Aug(ustorum). *RIB* 622
Stony Stratford: silver plate. *RIB* 216
Stony Stratford: bronze plate. *RIB* 217
York: altar by G. Agrius Auspex. *RIB* 650
York: altar. *RIB* 651

Mars Alator
Barkway: silver-gilt plaque by Dum(...?) Censorinus. *RIB* 218
South Shields: altar by G. Vinicius Celsus. *RIB* 1055

Mars Augustus (Imperial Mars)
Birdoswald: altar. *RIB* 1900
Lanchester: gold plate by Auffidius Aufidianus. *RIB* 1077

Mars Barrex
Carlisle: altar by Januarius Ri[o?]reg[.]iau[...]. *RIB* 947

Mars Belatucadrus (with variant spellings) see also **Belatucadrus**
Bewcastle: altar. *JRS* xlvii (1957), 228, no. 11
Burgh-by-Sands: altar. *RIB* 2044
Carlisle: altar. *RIB* 948
Carvoran: altar to Mars Belatucairus. *RIB* 1784
Netherby: altar by [A]ur(elius?) [Ni]ca[n]or(?). *RIB* 970
Old Penrith: altar by Julius Augustalis, *actor* of Julius Lupus. *RIB* 918 (with Numina Augustorum)

Mars Braciaca
Bakewell: altar by Q. Sittius Caecilianus, prefect of *cohors I Aquitanorum*. *RIB* 278

Mars Camulus
Bar Hill: altar by *II [Au]g(usta)*. *RIB* 2166

Mars Cocidius see also **Cocidius**
Bewcastle: altar by Aelius Vitalianus. *RIB* 993
Cumbria (exact find-spot unknown): altar by Vitalis. *RIB* 1017 (with Jupiter Optimus Maximus; reading revised in *RIB95*)
Hadrian's Wall (near milecastle 59): altar by [...] Martius, centurion of *cohors I Batavorum*. *RIB* 2015 (with Genius [...]valium])
Hadrian's Wall (near milecastle 65): altar by members of two centuries of *II Augusta* commanded by the centurion Aelianus, work in the charge of Oppius Felix, *optio,*. *RIB* 2024
Lancaster: altar by Vibenius Lucius, *beneficiarius consularis*. *RIB* 602

Mars Condates
Bowes: altar by Arponatus. *RIB* 731
Chester-le-Street: altar by V[e]robnus. *RIB* 1045
Cramond: altar to M(ars) Con[dates]. *Brit.* ix (1978), 475, no. 15
Piercebridge: altar by Attionus Quintianus, *mensor* and *evocatus*. *RIB* 1024

Mars Conservator (Mars the Preserver)
Chesters: altar. *RIB* 454

Mars Corotiacus
Martlesham: bronze statue base, made by Glaucus, dedicated by Simplicia. *RIB* 213

Mars Lenus
Caerwent: statue base to Mars Lenus *sive* ('or') Ocelus Vellaunus by Nonius Romanus in 152. *RIB* 309 (with the Numen Augusti of Marcus Aurelius)
Chedworth: altar to [L]en(o) M[arti] with relief of the god. *RIB* 126

Mars Loucetius
Bath: altar by Peregrinus from Trier. *RIB* 140 (with Nemetona)

Mars Medocius Campesium (Mars Medocius of the Parade Ground?)
Colchester: bronze plaque by Lossio Veda, a Caledonian, between 222-35. *RIB* 191 (with Victoria of Severus Alexander)

Mars Militarus (Military Mars)
Maryport: altar by *cohors I Baetasiorum* under the prefect T. Attius Tutor (his full name appears on *RIB* 842, see Maryport under Victoria Augusti below). *RIB* 837
Maryport: altar by *cohors I Baetasiorum* under the prefect Ulpius Titianus. *RIB* 838

Mars Nodens/Nodons/Nudens, see also **Nodens**
Cockersand Moss: statuette by Aurelius [...]cinus. *RIB* 616
Cockersand Moss: statuette to M(ars) N(odens) by Lucianus for his colleague Aprilius Viator. *RIB* 617
Lydney Park: bronze plate by Flavius Blandinus, *armatura*. *RIB* 305
Lydney Park: bronze plate by Pectillus to Nudente M(arti). *RIB* 307
Lydney Park: mosaic by T. Flavius Senilis, *pr(aepositus) rel(igionis)*, helped by Victorinus, *interp(r)[e]tor*. *RIB* 2448.3

Mars Ocelus see also **Ocelus Vellaunus**
Caerwent: altar by Aelius Augustinus, *optio*. *RIB* 310
Carlisle: slab dedicated between 222-35. *RIB* 949 (with the Numen of Severus Alexander and Julia Mamaea)

Mars Olludius
Custom Scrubs, Bisley: gabled relief. *RIB* 131

Mars Pacifer (Mars the Peacemaker)
Ribchester: altar. *RIB* 584

Mars Pater (Father Mars)
Birdoswald: inscribed fragment to [Mar]ti Pat[ri...]. *RIB* 1901

Mars Rigas
Malton: base by Scirus. *RIB* 711

Mars Rigisamus
West Coker: bronze plaque by Iventius Sabinus. *RIB* 187

Mars Rigonemetos (Mars, King of the Grove)
Nettleham: slab by Q. Neratius Proxsimus, recording his arch. *JRS* lii (1962), 192, no. 8 (with Numina Augustorum)

Mars Sediarum (Mars of the Sediae — presumably a place or tribe)
Markyate: on a small bronze or brass tablet with an inscription reading 'tessera of Mars of Sediae'. *RIB* 2408.1

Mars Thincsus
Housesteads: shrine door jam by 'Germans, citizens of Twenthe'. *RIB* 1593 (with the Alaisiagae: Beda and Fimmilena)

Mars Toutatis
Barkway: plaque by T. Claudius Primus, *liber(tus)*. *RIB* 219

Mars Ultor (Mars the Avenger)
Corbridge: altar to [Deo Marti] Ul[tori]? by L(ucius) [...], *trib(unum)* *[militum]*, during the governorship of Gn. Julius Verus (c. 155-9). *RIB* 1132

Mars Victor (Mars the Victorious)
Benwell: altar by Vindex. *RIB* 1333
Carlisle: inscription recorded before 1125 on a Roman building. *RIB* 950
Risingham: altar by [J]ul(ius) Publilius [P]ius, tribune. *RIB* 1221
Risingham: altar by [...], under the charge of Au[r(elius)]. *RIB* 1222
Risingham: altar to [Mars Vi]ctor by [...], *libertus*. *RIB* 1223
Vindolanda: panel by [...] Caninius, commanding [....] (unit name lost but *RIB* restores *cohors III Nerviorum* from earlier readings). *RIB* 1691

Mater Div(or)um (Mother of the Gods)
Carvoran: altar by M. Caecilius Donatianus, prefect serving as tribune. *RIB* 1791 (with Virgo Caelestis, Pax, Virtus, and Ceres Dea Suria)

Matres (Mother Goddesses)
Aldborough: altar. *RIB* 708 (with Jupiter Optimus Maximus)
Binchester: altar by Gemellus. *RIB* 1033
Binchester: altar. *RIB* 1034
Carrawburgh: altar by Albinius Quartus, *miles*. *RIB* 1540
Castlecary: altar. *RIB* 2147
Cirencester: altar. *Brit.* iv (1973), 324, no. 1 (with Mercury)
Daglingworth: altar. *RIB* 130 (with Genius loci)
Hadrian's Wall (near milecastle 79): altar. *RIB* 2055
London: plinth recording restoration of, possibly, a shrine. *RIB* 2
Newcastle-upon-Tyne: altar. *Brit.* ix (1978), 475, no. 13
Ribchester: altar dedicated by M. Ingenuius Asiaticus, *dec(urio)*, to the Matres (dependent on Camden's reading in 1580). *RIB* 586

Ribchester: altar by Marulla (wife?) of Insequens. *Brit.* xxv (1994), 298. no. 3
Vindolanda: altar. *RIB* 1692 (with Numen Domini Nostri)
York: altar by M. Rustius Massa. *RIB* 654

Matres (variously) **Afrae, Britanniae, Italicae/Italae, Gallae, Germanae**
Dover: altar recording the building of a temple to the Matres Italicae by Olus Cordius, *strator consularis. Brit.* viii (1977), 426-7, no. 4
Winchester: altar to Matres Italae Germanae Gal(lae) Brit(annae) by Antonius Lucretianus, *beneficiarius consularis. RIB* 88
York: altar to Mat(res) Af(rae) Ita(lae) Ga(llae) by M. Minucius Audens, *miles* and *gubernator* of *VI Victrix. RIB* 653

Matres Alatervae(?)
Cramond: altar by *cohors I Tungrorum*, directed by [...], centurion of *XX Valeria Victrix. RIB* 2135 (with Matres Campestres)

Matres Brittiae (British Mother Goddesses)
Xanten (Germany): altar dedicated by L. Valerius Simplex of *XXX Ulpia Victrix. ILS* 4789

Matres Campestres (Mother Goddesses of the Parade Ground), see also **Campestres**
Benwell: altar by T(erentius?) Agrippa, prefect of *ala I Hispanorum Asturum*, in 238. *RIB* 1334 (with Genius alae I Hispanorum Asturum)
Cramond: altar by *cohors I Tungrorum*, directed by [...], centurion of *XX Valeria Victrix. RIB* 2135 (with Matres Alatervae)

Matres Communes (Mother Goddesses living everywhere)
Carrawburgh: altar. *RIB* 1541
Chesters: altar dedicated for the *decuria* commanded by Aurelius Severus. *RIB* 1453

Matres Domesticae (Household Mother Goddesses)
Catterick: altar by Julius Victor. *JRS* l (1960), 237, no. 6
Chichester: altar by ..., *arkarius. Brit.* x (1979), 339, no. 1
Hadrian's Wall (near milecastle 73): altar by a vexillation of *VI [Victrix]. RIB* 2050
Stanwix: altar by Asinius Senilis. *RIB* 2025
York: altar by G. Julius Crescens. *RIB* 652

Matres Germaniae (German Mother Goddesses)
Hadrian's Wall (exact provenance lost): altar by M(arcus) Senec[ia]nius. *RIB* 2064

Matres Ollototae (Mother Goddesses from other peoples)
Binchester: altar by Matres Ollototae *sive* ('or') Transmarinae by Pomponius Donatus, *beneficiarius consularis. RIB* 1030 (with Jupiter Optimus Maximus)
Binchester: altar to Matres O[l]lot(otae) by T. Claudius Quintianus, *beneficiarius consularis. RIB* 1031
Binchester: altar to [M]atres O[llotatae] by *ala Vettonum. RIB* 1032 (with Genius loci)
Heronbridge: altar by Julius Secundus and Aelia Augustina. *RIB* 574

Matres Omnium Gentium (Mother Goddesses of all races)
Castlesteads: altar to [Mat]ribu[s] Omnium Gentium by G. Julius Cupitianus, centurion commanding, on the restoration of a temple. *RIB* 1988

Matres Parcae (Mother Goddesses, the Fates), see also **Parcae**
Carlisle: base dedicated for Sanctia Gemina. *RIB* 951
Skinburness: altar. *RIB* 881

Matres Suleviae, see also **Suleviae**
Colchester: slab by Similis of the *Cant(iaci). RIB* 192

Matres Tramarinae (Mother Goddesses from Overseas)
Binchester: altar to Matres Ollototae *sive* ('or') Transmarinae by Pomponius Donatus, *beneficiarius consularis*. *RIB* 1030 (with Jupiter Optimus Maximus)
Castlesteads: altar. *RIB* 1989
Old Penrith: slab by *[vexil]latio M[a]r[sacorum?]* between 222-35. *RIB* 919 (with Numen of Severus Alexander and Julia Mammaea)
Old Penrith: slab by *vexillatio Germa[no]r(um) V[o]r[e]d(ensium)*. *RIB* 920
Risingham: altar by Julius Victor (tribune of *cohors I Vangionum*; see for example *RIB* 1217 under Jupiter Optimus Maximus above). *RIB* 1224

Matres Tramarinae Patriae (Mother Goddesses of the Overseas Homeland)
Newcastle-upon-Tyne: altar by Aurelius Juvenalis. *RIB* 1318

Matunus
High Rochester: altar by [G. Julius Marcus (deleted)?], governor, through Caecilius Optatus, tribune (of *cohors I Vardullorum*; see *RIB* 1272 under Mithras Invictus below), in 213. *RIB* 1265

Mercury
Birrens: statue base by Julius Crescens for the benefit of the *collegium*. *RIB* 2102
Birrens: statue base by a *collegium* of Mercury under the charge of Ing(enuius) Rufus. *RIB* 2103 (with Numen Augusti)
Caerleon: statuette from Cur[...] and erected by Severus. *RIB* 321
Caister-on-Sea: bronze tablet by Aurelius Atticia[n]us. *RIB* 2432.2
Carlisle: relief to M(ercurius) by C(...) I(....) S(....). The incorporated *caduceus* confirms the expansion. *RIB* 952
Castlecary: altar by *milites* of *VI Victrix*, citizens of Italy and Noricum. *RIB* 2148
Cirencester: altar. *Brit.* iv (1973), 324, no. 1 (with Matres)
Corbridge: relief to Arecurio (sic), attributed to a mason misreading instructions, by Apollinaris. *RIB* 1123
Corbridge: relief. *RIB* 1133
Lincoln: inscription recording a guild of Mercury. *RIB* 270
Lincoln: face-pot with the inscription D(e)o Mercurio. *RIB* 2499.1
Old Harlow: lead sheet to Mercurius (on reverse) by the lover of Eterna. *Brit.* iv (1973), 325, no. 3
Uley: bronze plaque from Severa [...] Felix. *RIB* 2432.6
Uley: bronze fragment. *RIB* 2432.7
Vindolanda: relief. *RIB* 1693
Wallsend: relief recording the dedication of a statuette of M(ercurius) by *cohors II Nerviorum*. The inclusion of a goat on the relief confirms the expansion of the deity's name. *RIB* 1303
Wallsend: slab to M(ercurius). *RIB* 1304
York: relief. *RIB* 655

Mercury Andescociuoucus
Colchester: slab by Imilico, *libertus* of Aesurilinus. *RIB* 193 (with Numina Augustorum)

Mercury Propitius (Mercury the Favourer)
Leicester: inscription on column. *RIB* 244 (the authenticity of the inscription has been questioned)

Minerva, see also **Sulis Minerva**
Auchendavy: altar by M. Cocceius Firmus, centurion of *II Augusta*. *RIB* 2177 (with Campestres, Epona, Hercules, Mars, and Victoria)
Benwell: altar by Primus. *JRS* xlviii (1958), 151, no. 8
Birrens: altar by *cohors II Tungrorum*, under the prefect G. Silvius Auspex. *RIB* 2104
Caernarvon: altar by Aurelius Sabinianus, *actarius*. *RIB* 429
Carlisle: altar by M. [Aurelius?] Syrio, military tribune with *XX Valeria Victrix*, between 213-22. *Brit.* xx (1989), 331-3, no. 5 (with Jupiter Optimus Maximus, Juno, Mars, and Victoria)
Carrawburgh: altar by Quintus, *architectus*. *RIB* 1542
Carrawburgh: altar by Venico. *RIB* 1543

68 Altar (restored) from the mithraeum at Carrawburgh. The god Mithras is depicted as Sol Invictus, and the dedication is by M(arcus) Simplicius Simplex, prefect of an unnamed unit. His citizen's name, where both nomen *and* cognomen, *is believed to indicate he was a romanized Celt. Height 1.24m. RIB 1546*

Carvoran: slab to [Mi]ner[vae] or Nep[tuno]. *RIB* 1788

Chester: altar by Furius Fortunatus, *magister primus*. *RIB* 457

Chichester: slab recording the building of a temple to Neptune and Minerva in honour of the Domus Divina by the guild of smiths on a site given by [...]ens, son of Pudentinus, and by the authority of T. Claudius Togidubnus (see Chapter 9). *RIB* 91

Corbridge: statuette base to M[inerva] by Titus Tertinius, *librarius*. *RIB* 1134

Ebchester: altar to [Miner]va by Julius Gr[...]nus, *actarius* of *cohors IV Breucorum Antoninianae*, between 213-22. *RIB* 1101

High Rochester: altar by Julius Carantus, *singularis consularis*. *RIB* 1266

High Rochester: altar by Flavius Severinus, tribune. *RIB* 1267

High Rochester: altar by Caecilius Optatus, tribune (of *cohors I Vardullorum*; see *RIB* 1272 under Mithras Invictus below), about 213. *RIB* 1268 (with Genius collegii)

Stonea: gold plaque to Mi(ne)rva. *RIB* 2430.1

Whitley Castle: altar to Menerva (sic). *RIB* 1200 (with Hercules Victor)

Minerva Sulis, see **Sulis Minerva**

Mithras, see also **Deus**, **Mithras Invictus**, **Sol Invictus**

Lanchester: altar to M(ithras). *RIB* 1082 (with Cautopates and Sol Invictus)

London: relief of Mithras (unnamed) to Ulpius Silvanus, *emeritus* of *II Augusta*. *RIB* 3

London: panel. *RIB* 4 (with Sol Invictus)

Mithras Invictus, see also **Deus**, **Mithras Invictus**, **Sol Invictus**, Sol Invictus Mithras Saecularis

Caerleon: base to [In]victus [Mit]hras by [...]s Iustus of *II Augusta*. *RIB* 322

Carrawburgh: altar to Inv(ictus) M(ithras) by L. Antonius Proculus, prefect of *cohors I Batavorum Antoninianae* between 213-22. *RIB* 1544

Carrawburgh: altar to In(victus) M(ithras) by A. Cluentius Habitus, prefect of *cohors I Batavorum*, after 198-211 on the evidence of the Severan titles in his home town's name. *RIB* 1545

Carrawburgh: altar to Invictus Mitras by M. Simplicius Simplex, prefect. *RIB* 1546 (**68**)

High Rochester: slab to Invictus by L. Caecilius Optatus, tribune of *cohors I Vardullorum*. *RIB* 1272 (with Sol)

Rudchester: altar to Invictus Mytras by P. Aelius Titullus, prefect. *RIB* 1395

Rudchester: altar to Anicetus (= Invictus) [Mithras] by Aponius Rogatianus. *RIB* 1397 (with Sol Apollo)

Mogons (N.B. there are several variants on this name, listed below, usually derived from the dative form *Mogonti*)

Old Penrith: altar to Mog(on)s. *RIB* 921

Vindolanda: altar by Lupulus. *Brit.* iv (1973), 329, no. 10 (with Genius loci)

Mogons/Mogonis Cad[...] see also **Mounus Cad(...)**

Risingham: altar to Mogonito Cad[...] by M. G(avius?) Secundinus, *[b](ene)f(iciarius) co(n)s(ularis)*, on his first posting at *Habitancum* (Risingham). *RIB* 1225 (with Numen Domini Nostri Augusti)

Risingham: altar by Inventus to Mounus Cad(...). *RIB* 1226

Mogons Vitiris

Netherby: altar by Aelius [....]. *RIB* 971

Mountis/Mountes

High Rochester: altar by Julius Firminus, *dec(urio)*. *RIB* 1269

Old Penrith: altar. *RIB* 922

Mounus see **Mogons Cad[...]**

Narius see also **Faunus Narius** above

Thetford: silver spoon. *RIB* 2420.23

Nemesis, see also **Domina Nemesis**

Chester: altar by Sext(ius) Marcianus, centurion, following a vision. *JRS* lvii (1967), 203, no. 5

Hadrian's Wall (exact location unknown): altar by Apollonius, *sacerdos*. *RIB* 2065

Nemetona

Bath: altar by Peregrinus from Trier. *RIB* 140 (with Mars Loucetius)

Neptune

Birrens: altar by Claudius [...]. *RIB* 2105

Castlecary: altar by *cohors I Vardullorum* under the prefect Trebius Verus. *RIB* 2149

Castlesteads: altar to [N]ep[tuno]. *RIB* 1990

Chichester: slab recording the building of a temple to Neptune and Minerva in honour of the Domus Divina by the guild of smiths on a site given by [...]ens, son of Pudentinus, and by the authority of T. Claudius Togidubnus (see Chapter 9). *RIB* 91 (with Neptune)

Lympne: altar by L. Aufidius Pant[h]era, prefect of *classis Britannica*, *c.*115-40. *RIB* 66 (**72**)

Maryport: altar appropriated by L(ucius) Cass(ius) (secondary text). *RIB* 839

Newcastle-upon-Tyne: altar by *VI Victrix* (with *RIB* 1320, see Oceanus). *RIB* 1319

Vindolanda: altar. *RIB* 1694

York: arch and gateway to L. Viducius Placidus, *negotiator* from Rouen, in 221. *Brit.* viii (1977), 430, no. 18 (with Genius loci and Numina Augustorum; N.B. Neptune is restored on the stone and an alternative reading is IOM for Jupiter Optimus Maximus)

Nodens, see also **Mars Nodens**

Lydney Park: lead curse made by Silvianus against the ring-thief Senicianus. *RIB* 306

69 Altar found built into a medieval church in York naming the otherwise-unknown god Arciaco, along with the Numen Augusti. Dedicated by the ord(inatus) *(centurion), Mat... Vitalis. Height 0.61m. RIB 640*

Numen

Netherby: altar to the Numen of Caracalla by *cohors I Aelia Hispanorum*, during the governorship of [G. Julius Marcus?] in *c.*213. *RIB* 976

Vindolanda: slab to the Numen of Severus Alexander(?) by *cohors IIII Gallor(um) [Severianae Alexandrianae]*, commemorating the restoration of a gate during the governorship of Claudius Xenephon between 222-35 (see Chapter 9 for Xenephon's dates). *RIB* 1706

Numen Augusti/Numina Augustorum/Numen Domini Nostri (The Spirit of Augustus/Spirits of the Augusti/Spirit of our Lord)

Bath: altar to Numina Augustorum by G. Curiatius Saturninus, centurion of *II Augusta*. *RIB* 146 (with Sulis Minerva)

Bath: altar to Numen Augusti by G. Severius Emeritus, *c(enturio) reg(ionarius)*, recording the restoration of the holy place. *RIB* 152 (with Virtus)

Benwell: altar to Numina Augustorum by Aelius Vibius, centurion of *XX*. *RIB* 1327 (with Antenociticus) (**56**)

Benwell: altar to Numina Augustorum, and naming Antoninus Pius, by M. Liburnius Fronto, centurion of *II Augusta*, between 139-61. *RIB* 1330 (with Jupiter Optimus Maximus Dolichenus)

Birdoswald: altar to Numen Augusti by *cohors I Aelia Dacorum*, commanded by the tribune Marc(ius?) Gallicus, around the period 255-75 (see *RIB* 1883 under Jupiter Optimus Maximus for this man in post under Postumus). *RIB* 1882 (with Jupiter Optimus Maximus)

Birdoswald: statue base to Numen Augusti by *cohors I Aelia [Dacorum?]*. *RIB* 1904 (with Signa)

Birrens: statue base of Mars(?) to Numen Augusti by a *collegium* of Mercury under the charge of Ingenuius Rufus. *RIB* 2103 (with Mercury)

Bollihope Common: altar to [Numina August]orum (primary text; for secondary, see Silvanus Invictus below). *RIB* 1041 (**70**)

Brough-on-Humber: slab to Numina Augustorum M. Ulpius Januarius, *aedilis* of the vicus of *Petuaria*, to commemorate the new stage (*proscaenium*) for the theatre between 140-61. *RIB* 707 (with Domus Divina of Antoninus Pius) (**40**)

Burgh-by-Sands: altar to Numen Augusti by *cohors [....]*. *RIB* 2040 (with Hercules)

Burgh-by-Sands: altar to Numina Augustorum by Caelius Vibianus, tribune of *numerus Maurorum Aurelianorum Valeriani Gallienique*, under the direction of Julius Rufinus, *princeps*, between 253-8. *RIB* 2042 (with Genius *numeri Maurorum Aurelianorum Valeriani Gallienique*; the dedication to Jupiter Optimus Maximus is entirely restored in *RIB*)

Burrow-in-Lonsdale (Overborough): altar to Numen Augusti by Bellinus. *RIB* 611 (with Genius collegii Apollinis)

Caerleon: pilaster to Numina Augustorum by [...], *primus pilus* in 244. *RIB* 327 (with Genius legionis II Augustae)

Caerleon: altar to Numina Augustorum. *Brit.* viii (1977), 429-30, no. 16

Caerwent: statue base of Mars Lenus(?) and to Numen Augusti by Nonius Romanus in 152. *RIB* 309 (with Mars Lenus and Ocelus Vellaunus)

Cardewlees: altar to [N(umina)] D(ominorum) N(ostrorum) Va[leri]ani et G[allie]ni et Vale[ria]ni nob(ilissimi) C(a)es(ari) P(iorum) F(elicium) Augustor(um) by *numerus [...]* under the charge of G. [C]arinius Aurelianus, centurion of *II Augusta*, between 255-9. *RIB* 913 (with Jupiter Optimus Maximus)

Carlisle: altar to Numen Imp(eratoris) Alexandri Aug(usti) in 222-35. *RIB* 949 (with Mars Ocelus)

Carvoran: altar to Numina [Aug(ustorum)] by Julius Pacatus and Pacutius C[...], commemorating a new building. *RIB* 1786 (with Mars?)

Castlesteads: altar to Numen [Aug(usti)] by *cohors II Tungrorum Gordiana*, under the prefect T. Claudius Claudianus, in 241. *RIB* 1983 (with Jupiter Optimus Maximus)

Castlesteads: altar to Numen Augusti by Paco[ni]us Satur[ni]nus, prefect of cavalry. *RIB* 1987 (with Mars)

Castlesteads: altar to Numen Augusti by Aurelius Armiger, *decurio princeps*. *RIB* 1991 (with Vanauns)

Colchester: slab to Numina Augustorum by Imilco, *libertus* of Aesurilinus. *RIB* 193 (Mercury Andescociuoucus)

Chester: slate tablet to Numen Augusti. *RIB* 458

Chester: altar(?) to Numina Augustorum. *RIB* 459

Dorchester-on-Thames: altar *cum cancellis* ('with screens') to Numina Augustorum by M. Varius Severus, *beneficiarius consularis*. *RIB* 235 (with Jupiter Optimus Maximus)

Ebchester: altar to Numen Augusti. *RIB* 1100 (with Mars)

Fossdike: statuette of Mars and dedicated to Numina Augustorum by Bruccius and Caratius Colasunus. *RIB* 274 (with Mars) (**67**)

Greetland: altar to Numina Augustorum by T. Aurelius Aurelianus, *magister sacrorum*, in 208. *RIB* 627 (with Victoria Brigantia)

Hadrian's Wall (exact location unknown): altar to Numen Augusti by Durio, Ramio, Trupo, and Lurio, all Germans. *RIB* 2063 (with Maponus)

Haltonchesters: altar to Numina Augustorum. *RIB* 1425

Housesteads: altar to Numen Augusti by *numerus Hnaudifridi*. *RIB* 1576 (with Baudihillia and Friagabis)

Housesteads: altar to Numina Augustorum by *cohors I Tungrorum*, under the prefect Q. Julius Maximus. *RIB* 1584 (with Jupiter Optimus Maximus)

Housesteads: altar to Numina Augustorum by *cohors I Tungrorum*, under the prefect Q. Julius [...]sus. *RIB* 1585 (with Jupiter Optimus Maximus)

Housesteads: altar to Numina Augustorum by *cohors I Tungrorum*, under the prefect Q. Verius Superstis. *RIB* 1586 (with Jupiter Optimus Maximus)

Housesteads: altar to Numina [Augustorum], under the prefect [...]rius [.]upe[...]. *RIB* 1587 (with Jupiter Optimus Maximus)

Housesteads: altar to [Numina A]ug(ustorum). *RIB* 1588 (with Jupiter Optimus Maximus)

Housesteads: shrine door jam to Numen Augusti by 'the Germans'. *RIB* 1593 (with Beda,

Fimmilena, and Mars Thincsus)

Housesteads altar to Numen Augusti by 'the Germans' of the cuneus Frisiorum Vercovicianorum between 222-35. *RIB* 1594 (with Mars and the Alaisiagae)

Housesteads: altar to Numina Augustorum by [...], *custos armorum*. *RIB* 1596 (with Mars and Victoria)

Lanchester: altar to N(umen) Gor[di]ani Aug(usti) N(ostri) by *vexillatio Sueborum Lon(govicianorum) Gor(diana)* between 238-44. *RIB* 1074 (with Garmangabis) (**62**)

Lanchester: altar to Numen Augusti by *cohors I Vardullorum* during the governorship of Antistius Adventus, at the expense of the tribune Flavius Titianus (with Genius cohortis), about 175-8. *RIB* 1083

Lincoln: altar to Numina Augustorum by G. Antistius Frontinus, *curator*. *RIB* 247 (with Parcae)

London: slab to Numen C[aes(aris) Aug(usti)?]. *RIB* 5

London (Greenwich Park): slab dedicated to Nu[mini Aug?]. See next entry for the evidence that this is plausible. *RIB* 38

London (Greenwich Park): small slab dedicated to [...Nu]min[i Aug...?] by [...Cae]ciliu[s...]cus. If the identification is correct another slab from this site may now be expanded (see previous entry). Minerva remains an alternative, but less likely, possibility. Unpublished but forthcoming (found 15 July 1999)

Maryport: altar to Numen Augusti by *cohors I Hispanorum*. *RIB* 815 (with Jupiter Optimus Maximus)

Maryport: altar to Numen Augusti by M. Maenius Agrippa, tribune. *RIB* 824 (with Jupiter Optimus Maximus)

Maryport: altar to Numen Augusti by (M.) Maenius Agrippa, tribune. *RIB* 825 (with Jupiter Optimus Maximus)

Nettleham: slab to Numina Augustorum by Q. Neratius Proxsimus, recording his arch. *JRS* lii (1962), 192, no. 8 (with Mars Rigonemetos)

Nettleton: altar to Numen [A]ug(usti) N(ostri) by Aurelius Pu[...]. Wedlake (1982), 136, no. 2 (with Silvanus)

Newcastle-upon-Tyne: altar to [Nu]men [Augusti?]. *RIB* 1317 (with Hospitales and Jupiter Optimus Maximus)

Old Penrith: altar to Numina Augustorum by Julius Augustalis, *actor* of Julius Lupus. *RIB* 918 (with Mars Belatucadrus)

Old Penrith: slab to N(umen) Imp(eratoris) Alexandri Aug(usti) by the *vexillatio Marsacorum* between 222-35. *RIB* 919 (with Matres Tramarinae)

Old Penrith: altar to [Num(ina) A]ug(ustorum) by a vexillation of *[X]X [Val](eria) Vic(trix)*. *RIB* 940

Risingham: altar to N(umen) D(omini) N(ostri) Aug(usti) by M. G(avius?) Secundinus, *beneficiarius consularis*. *RIB* 1225 (with Mogons Cad[...])

Risingham: altar to Numina Augustorum by *cohors IIII Gallorum*. *RIB* 1227

Scarcroft: altar to Num(en) [Aug(usti)?]. *JRS* lv (1965), 221, no. 6 (with Apollo)

Slack: altar to N(umen) Aug(usti) by T. Aurelius Quintus. *RIB* 623 (with Bregans)

Somerdale Keynsham: altar to Num(ina) Divor(um) Aug(ustorum) by G. Indutius Felix in the year 155. *RIB* 181 (with Silvanus)

South Shields: frieze to Numin[a Aug(ustorum)?] by Domitius Epictetus, recording a *templu[m]*. *RIB* 1056 (with another deity, name lost)

Ty Coch, near Bangor: milestone/honorific column dedicated to Num(ina) Aug(ustorum?) during the reign of Caracalla between 212-17. *RIB* 2264

Vindolanda: altar to Numina Augustorum by *vicus* inhabitants at Vindolanda. *RIB* 1700 (with Domus Divina and Volcanus)

Vindolanda: altar to Numen d(omini) n(ostri). *RIB* 1692 (with Matres)

York: altar to N(umen) Aug(usti) by Mat(...) Vitalis, centurion. *RIB* 640 (with Arciaco) (**69**)

York: slab to Numen Augusti by [...]sius, recording restoration of the shrine. *RIB* 656 (with Ioug[...])

York: altar to Numen Augusti. *RIB* 657 (with Genius Eboraci?)

York: slab recording an arch and gateway dedicated to Numina Augustorum by L. Viducius Placidus, *negotiator* from the Rouen region, in 221. *Brit.* viii (1977), 430, no. 18 (with Genius loci and Neptune)

Unprovenanced (British origin): altar to Numina Augustorum. *RIB* 2217 (with Fortuna)

Nympha/Nymphae
Carrawburgh: altar to the [Nymp]hae by a vexillation of *[VI] Victrix. RIB* 1547
Carrawburgh: altar to the Nymphae by M. Hispanius Modestinus, prefect of *cohors I Batavorum. JRS*
li (1961), 193, no. 9 (with Genius loci)
Carvoran: altar to the Nymphae by Vettia Mansueta and daughter Claudia Turianilla. *RIB* 1789
Castleford: slab to the Nymp(h)ae. *Brit.* xiv (1983), 337, no. 11
Chester: altar to the Nymphae by *XX Valeria Victrix. RIB* 460 (with Fontes)
Croy Hill: altar to the Nymphae by a vexillation of *VI Victrix* under Fabius Liberalis. *RIB* 2160
Greta Bridge: altar by Brica and daughter Januaria (name of the specific local Nymph unresolvable
from the record of this stone). *RIB* 744
Risingham: altar to the Nymphae by the unnamed wife of Fabius. *RIB* 1228

Nympha Brigantia
Castlesteads(?): altar to Nympha Brigantia in honour of Caracalla and his divine house by M.
Cocceius Nigrinus, *[pr]oc(urator) Aug(usti) n(ostri)*, 'procurator of our Emperor', between 212-17.
RIB 2066 (with Domus Divina)

Nympha Coventina
Carrawburgh: altar to Nimfa (sic) Coventina by Maduhus, a German. *RIB* 1526
Carrawburgh: altar by [...]tianus, *decurio. RIB* 1527

Ocelus Vellaunus, see also Mars Ocelus
Caerwent: statue base by Nonius Romanus in 152. *RIB* 309 (with Mars Lenus and the Numen
Augusti of Marcus Aurelius)

Oceanus/Ocianus
Newcastle-upon-Tyne: altar to Ocianus by *VI Victrix* (with *RIB* 1319, see Neptune). *RIB* 1320
York: bronze plate, texts in Greek, by Demetrius. *RIB* 663 (with Tethys) (attached to *RIB* 662,
dedicated to Theoi Hegemonikos, 'gods of the governor's headquarters')

Panakeia
Chester: altar by Antiochos, *hiatros. JRS* lix (1969), 235, no. 3 (with Asklepios and Hygeia)

Panthea, see also Silvanus Pantheus
Corbridge: altar. *RIB* 1135 (with Bona Fortuna)

Parcae (Fates), see also Matres Parcae
Carlisle: altar by Donatalis for his son Probus. *RIB* 953
Lincoln: altar by G. Antistius Frontinus, *curator. RIB* 247 (with Numina Augustorum)

Pax (Peace)
Carvoran: altar by M. Caecilius Donatianus, tribune serving as prefect. *RIB* 1791 (with Virgo
Caelestis, Mater, Virtus, and Ceres Dea Suria)
High Rochester: base by the tribune Julius (Silvanus) Melanio. *RIB* 1273, see *RIB95*, p. 781

Penates
York: altar by P. Aelius Marcianus, prefect of *cohors [.....]* (*I Augustae Bracarum* has been suggested on
the evidence of this man as its prefect on *ILS* 2738). *RIB* 649 (with Hospitales and Jupiter
Optimus Maximus)

Priapus
Birrens: slab inscribed *[P]riapi m(entula)*, 'phallus of Priapus', and a face of a god. The phrase seems
to be exceedingly rare to the point of being unparalleled but Lewis and Short note *Priapo
mentulatior* in a series of anonymous erotic poems collected for an 1878 edition of Catullus. The
text is so unusual that some scepticism about its authenticity must be noted. *RIB* 2106 (but note
also *RIB* 983 which is a specific and authentic reference to a phallus — *mentula*)

Ratis
Birdoswald: altar. *RIB* 1903
Chesters: altar. *RIB* 1454

Regina (Queen Goddess), see also **Diana Regina**, and **Salus Regina**
Lanchester: altar by Misio. *RIB* 1084
Lemington: relief to Dea Regina. *RIB* 125

Regina Caelestis (The Queen Caelestis), see also **Bona Dea Regina Caelestis, Caelestis Brigantia** and **Virgo Caelestis**
Carvoran: relief of altar by Aurelius Martialis. *RIB* 1827 (re-read, see *RIB95*)

Ricagambeda
Birrens: altar by men from *pagus Vellaus* ('Vellavian district'), currently with *cohors II Tungrorum*. *RIB* 2107

Roma
High Rochester: altar to D(eae) R(omae) by *dupl(icarii)* of the *numerus exploratorum Bremeniensium*, under the charge of the tribune Caepio Charitinus. *RIB* 1270

Roma Aeterna (Eternal Rome)
Maryport: altar by G. Cornelius Peregrinus, tribune of the cohort and *decurio* of *Saldae* in Mauretania Caesariensis. *RIB* 812 (with Fatum Bonum, Fortuna Redux, and Genius loci)
Maryport: votive pillar. *RIB* 840 (with Fortuna Redux)

Romulus
Custom Scrubs, Bisley: relief made by Juventinus and by Gulioepius. *RIB* 132

Salus (Health)
Binchester: altar by M. Aure[lius ...]ocomas, *me[dicus]*, for welfare of *ala Vet[tonum]*. *RIB* 1028 (with Aesculapius)
Chester: altar by the *liberti* and *familia* of the legate T. Pomponius Mamilianus (see Chapter 9). *RIB* 445 (with Aesculapius and Fortuna Redux)
Corbridge: altar by G. Julius Apolinaris, centurion of *VI Victrix*, his name replacing someone else's. *RIB* 1131 (with Caelestis Brigantia and Jupiter Aeternus Dolichenus)
Ribchester: altar during the governorship of Gordianus(?) (see Gordian I in Chapter 9) in *c*.216. *RIB* 590 (with Victoria of Caracalla)

Salus Regina (Queen of Health)
Caerleon: altar by P. Sallienius Tha[la]mus, prefect of *II Augusta*, about 198-209 (see *RIB* 326). *RIB* 324

Sattada or **Satiada**
Vindolanda?: altar by the *curia* of the Textoverdi. *RIB* 1695

Serapis, see also **Jupiter Serapis**
York: relief by Claudius Hieronymianus, legate of *VI Victrix*, recording the dedication of a temple, late second/early third century. *RIB* 658 (**74**)

Setlocenia
Maryport: altar by Labareus, a German. *RIB* 841

Signa (Standards)
Birdoswald: statue base by *cohors I Aelia [Dacorum?]*. *RIB* 1904 (with Numen Augusti)
High Rochester: altar to *Signa cohors I Vardullorum* by Egnatius Lucilianus, propraetorian legate for the *cohors I Vardullorum* and *numerus Exploratorum Brem(enensium)* under the charge of Cassius Sabinianus, tribune, between 238-44. *RIB* 1262 (with Genius Domini Nostri)

Signa cohortis (Standards of the cohort)
High Rochester: altar by T. Licinius Valerianus, tribune, for cohors I Vardullorum. *RIB* 1263 (with
  Genius cohortis)

Silvanae [et] Quadrvae Caelestis (The Heavenly Silvanae nymphs and Quadruae)
Westerwood, Cumbernauld: altar by Vibia Pacata, wife of Flavius Verecundus, centurion of *VI
  Victrix*. *JRS* liv (1964), 178, no. 7

Silvanus see also **Vinotonus Silvanus**
Auchendavy: altar. *RIB* 2178
Bar Hill: altar by [C]aristanius [J]ustianus, prefect of *cohors I Hamiorum*. *RIB* 2167
Birdoswald: altar by venatores Bannie(n)sses. *RIB* 1905 (formerly believed to refer to Bewcastle)
Cadder: altar by L. Tanicius Verus, prefect. *RIB* 2187 (see *ILS* 8759b for a possible ancestor of this
  man in 80-1 in Egypt)
Carvoran: altar by Vellaeus. *RIB* 1790
Cirencester: altar by Sabidius Maximus. *RIB* 104
Colchester: bronze plate by Hermes. *RIB* 195
Corbridge: altar by a vexillation of *II Augusta* and *cuneus [...]*. *RIB* 1136
Eastgate: altar by Aurelius Quirinus, prefect of *cohors I Lingonum* at Lanchester, between *c.*238-44.
  RIB 1042 (datable from *RIB* 1091-2, naming this man under Gordian III) **(70)**
Hadrian's Wall (milecastle 49): altar to [Si]l[v]an[us] by Flavius Marcellinus, *decurio*. *RIB* 1870
Haile (find-spot unknown): altar made by Primus, *custos armorum*. *RIB* 796 (with Hercules)
Kirkby Thore: altar by Ael[...]. *RIB* 763
Lanchester: pedestal by M. Didius Provincialis *beneficiarius consularis*. *RIB* 1085
Moresby: altar by *cohors II Lingonum*, commanded by G. Pompeius Saturninus. *RIB* 798
Netherby: altar. *RIB* 972
Nettleton: altar by [A]ur(elius) Pu[...]. *JRS* lix (1969), 235, no. 1, and Wedlake (1982), 136, no. 2
  (with Numen Augusti)
Newcastle-upon-Tyne: altar by G(aius) Val(erius). *RIB* 1321
Newstead: altar by G. Arrius Domitianus, centurion of *XX Valeria Victrix*. *RIB* 2124 (see this man
  again at Newstead under Diana Regina and Jupiter Optimus Maximus)
Old Penrith: altars. *RIB* 923-4
Risingham: altar to Sil[vanus]. *RIB* 1207 (with Cocidius)
Somerdale Keynsham: altar by G. Indutius Felix in 155. *RIB* 181 (with Numina divina
  Augustorum)
Vindolanda: altar by Aurelius Modestus of *II Augusta*, and *beneficiarius consularis superioris Britannia
  Superior*. *RIB* 1696
York: altar by L. Celerinius Vitalis, *cornicularius* with *IX Hispana* before 120. *RIB* 659
Unprovenanced (now at Hereford): altar. *RIB* 303

Silvanus Callirius
Colchester: bronze plate by Cintusmus, *aerarius*. *RIB* 194

Silvanus Cocidius
Housesteads: altar by Q. Florius Maternus, prefect of *cohors I Tungrorum*. *RIB* 1578

Silvanus Invictus (Unconquerable Silvanus)
Bollihope Common: altar by G. Tetius Veturius Micianus, prefect of *ala Sebosiana*, recording a boar
  kill (secondary text). *RIB* 1041 (primary text for Numina Augustorum)

Silvanus Pantheus
High Rochester: altar to Silvanus [Pa]ntheus by Eutychus, *libertus*, for [Ru]fin[us], tribune
  commanding *[cohors I Vardullorum]* (from *RIB* 1288) and his wife (Julia) [L]ucilla. *RIB* 1271
  (Rufinus' tombstone, *RIB* 1288, appears to record his wife's full name and by implication his
  career though in fact the deceased's name is lost)

Silvanus Vinotonus, see **Vinotonus**, and **Vinotonus Silvanus**

Sol (The Sun)
Housesteads: altar by Herion. *RIB* 1601

Sol Apollo Anicetus [Mithras] where *Anicetus* is the Greek for *Invictus*
Rudchester: altar by Aponius Rogatianus. *RIB* 1397

Sol Invictus (The Unconquerable Sun) (sometimes as Mithras)
Castlesteads: altar by S. Severius Salvator, prefect. *RIB* 1992
Castlesteads: altar by M. Licinius Ripanus. *RIB* 1993
Corbridge: slab by a vexillation of *VI Victrix* during the governorship of S. Calpurnius Agricola, c.163-6. *RIB* 1137
High Rochester: slab recording a building by L. Caecilius Optatus, tribune of *cohors I Vardullorum*, about 213. *RIB* 1272 (conflated with Mithras Invictus)
Lanchester: altar dedicated to S(ol) I(nvictus). *RIB* 1082 (with Mithras and Cautopates)
London: panel dedicated to [Sol] Invictus. *RIB* 4 (with Mithras?)
Rudchester: altar by T. Claudius Decimus Cornelius Antonius, prefect, to Mithras as Sol Invictus on the restoration of the mithraeum. *RIB* 1396

[Sol Invictus Elagabalus] (this name of the emperor, deified in his lifetime, is entirely restored on the inscription by *RIB*)
Chesters: slab recording the restoration of a building and by Septimius Nilus, prefect of *ala II Asturum* during the governorship of Marius Valerianus in 221. *RIB* 1465

Sol Invictus Mitras/Mytras Saecularis (The Unconquerable Sun, Mithras, Lord of the Ages)
Castlesteads: altar to Sol [Invi]ctus M[ith]r[a]s by M. Licinius Ripanus, prefect. *RIB* 1993
Housesteads: altar by Litorius Pacactianus, *beneficiarius consularis*. *RIB* 1599
Housesteads: altar by Publicius Proculinus, centurion, in 252. *RIB* 1600

Sol Mitras (sic)
Castlesteads: altar. *RIB* 1994

Soteres (Greek Saviour Gods)
Chester: altar by Hermogenes, *hiatros* (= *medicus*). *RIB* 461

Sucabus
Hadrian's Wall?: slab by Cunovindus. *Brit.* ii (1971), 292, no. 14

Suleviae, see also **Matres Suleviae**
Bath: statue base by Sulinus, *scultor*, son of Brucetus. *RIB* 151 (see Cirencester below)
Binchester: altar dedicated by the *[ala] Vett[onum]*. *RIB* 1035
Cirencester: altar by Sulinus, son of Brucetus. *RIB* 105 (see Bath above). *RIB* 151, and under Sulis Minerva below. *RIB* 150)
Cirencester: altar by [P]rimus. *RIB* 106

Sulis
Bath: altar by Aufidius Eutuches, *libertus* of and for the good of M. Aufidius Maximus, centurion of *VI Victrix*. *RIB* 143 (see next entry)
Bath: altar by M. Aufidius Lemnus, *libertus* of and for the good of (M.) Aufidius Maximus, centurion of *VI Victrix*. *RIB* 144 (see previous entry)
Bath: altar by L. Manius Dionisias, *libertus*, for the good of G. Jav[olenus Sa]tur[nal]is (see L. Javolenus Priscus in Chapter 9), *imaginifer* of *II Augusta*. *RIB* 147
Bath: altar by Q. Pompeius Anicetus. *RIB* 148
Bath: altar by Priscus, *lapidarius*, from the Carnutes tribe (in Gaul, around Chartres), and son of Toutius. *RIB* 149

*70 Altar found near a stream feeding the
River Wear at Eastgate, naming
Silvanus and the dedicant Aurelius
Quirinus,* pr(aefectus)*, between 238-
44 (see **6, 37**). Height 0.91m.* RIB
1042

Sulis Minerva
Bath: fragment of inscribed frieze recording repairs at the expense of Claudius Ligur[...]. *RIB*
141(d)
Bath: altar by G. Curiatius Saturninus, centurion of *II Augusta*. *RIB* 146 (with Numina
Augustorum)
Bath: altar by Sulinus, son of Maturus. *RIB* 150
Bath: base by L. Marcius Memor, *haruspex* of Sulis. *JRS* lvi (1966) 217, no. 1 (and Cunliffe and
Davenport, 1985, 130, 9A.1) **(54)**

Suria, see also **Ceres Dea Suria**
Carvoran: altar by Lic[in]ius [Cl]em[ens], prefect of *[co]h(ors) I Ha[miorum]*, during the
governorship of Calpurnius Agricola, between *c.*163-6. *RIB* 1792
Catterick: altar by Gaius N[...] O[...], *beneficiarius*. *RIB* 726

Tanarus, see **Jupiter Tanarus**

Terra Batavorum (Land of the Batavians) — now rejected
The sole instance of this supposed deity, on *RIB* 902, is now re-read as Brigantia Augusta. See above
and *RIB95*

Tethys
York: bronze plate, texts in Greek, by Demetrius (see *RIB* for this man who may be a figure
mentioned by Plutarch). *RIB* 663 (with Oceanus) (attached to *RIB* 662, see next entry)

Theoi Hegemonikoi (Greek: Gods of the governor's headquarters)
York: bronze plate, texts in Greek, by Scribonius Demetrius. *RIB* 662 (attached to *RIB* 663 dedicated
to Oceanus and Tethys)

Tridam[...]
Unprovenanced (now at Michaelchurch, Herefords): altar by Bellicus. *RIB* 304

Tutela Brigantia Augusta (Guardian Brigantia Augusta)
Old Carlisle: altar to T(utela) B(rigantia) A(ugusta) by T. Aurelius. *RIB* 902 (re-reading in *RIB95* of a stone formerly thought to refer to Terra Batavorum)

Unseni Fersomeri
Old Penrith: altar by Burcanius, Arcavius, Vagdavarcustus, and Pov[.]c[.]arus. *RIB* 926

Vanauns
Castlesteads: altar by Aurelius Armiger, *decurio princeps*. *RIB* 1991 (with Numen Augusti)

Verbeia
Ilkley: altar by Clodius Fronto, prefect of *cohors II Lingonum*. *RIB* 635

Vernostonus Cocidius
Ebchester: altar by Virilis, a German. *RIB* 1102

Veter/Veteres/Vheteris/Viter/Vitiris/Votris, variously male or female, singular or plural, and numerous other variants. See also **Hueeteris**, and **Mogons Vitiris**
Benwell: altar to Vetris. *RIB* 1335
Benwell: altar to the Vitires. *RIB* 1336
Carrawburgh: altar to Veteris by Uccus. *RIB* 1548
Carvoran: altar to Veteris by Necalames. *RIB* 1793
Carvoran: altar to Veteris by Necalames. *RIB* 1794
Carvoran: altar to Vetiris by Julius Pastor, *imaginifer* of *cohors II Delmatarum*. *RIB* 1795
Carvoran: altar to Vetiris by Andiatis. *RIB* 1796
Carvoran: altar to Veteris. *RIB* 1797
Carvoran: altar to Viteris. *RIB* 1798
Carvoran: altar to Vitiris by Menius Dada. *RIB* 1799
Carvoran: altar to Vitiris by Milus and Aurides. *RIB* 1800
Carvoran: altar to Vitiris by Ne[ca]limes (sic, but see 1793-4 above). RIB 1801
Carvoran: altars to the Veteres. *RIB* 1802-4
Carvoran: altar to the Vitires by Deccius. *RIB* 1805
Catterick: altar to Vheteris by Aurelius Mucianus. *RIB* 727
Chester-le-Street: altar to Vitiris by Duihno. *RIB* 1046
Chester-le-Street: altar to the goddesses the Vitires by Vitalis. *RIB* 1047
Chester-le-Street: altar to the goddesses the Vit(ires). *RIB* 1048
Chesters: altar to Vitiris by Tertulus. *RIB* 1455
Chesters: altar to the Veteres. *RIB* 1456
Chesters: altar to Vitiris. *RIB* 1457
Chesters: altar to Votris. *RIB* 1458
Corbridge: altar to Vetiris. *RIB* 1139
Corbridge: altar to Vitiris. *RIB* 1140
Corbridge: altar to Vit(iris) by Mitius. *RIB* 1141
Ebchester: altar to Vitiris by Maximus. *RIB* 1103
Ebchester: altar to Vitiris. *RIB* 1104
Greatchesters: altar to Vetiris. *RIB* 1728
Greatchesters: altar to the Veteres by Romana. *RIB* 1729
Greatchesters: altar to the Veteres. *RIB* 1730
Hadrian's Wall (exact location unknown): altar to Veteris. *RIB* 2068
Housesteads: altar to the Veteres. *RIB* 1604
Housesteads: altar to the Veteres. *RIB* 1605
Housesteads: altar to the Veteres by Aurelius Victor. *RIB* 1606
Lanchester: altar to Vit(iris). *RIB* 1087
Lanchester: altar to Vitiris by [....], *princeps*. *RIB* 1088

Piercebridge: altar to Veteris. *Brit.* v (1974), 461, no. 3
South Shields: altar to Vitiris by Cr[...]. *Brit.* xviii (1987), 368, no. 7
Thistleton: silver plaque to Vete[ris] by Mocux[s]oma. *RIB* 2431.3
Vindolanda: altar to [V]ete[r]is. *RIB* 1697
Vindolanda: altar to Veteris. *RIB* 1698
Vindolanda: altar to the Veteres by Senaculus. *RIB* 1699
Vindolanda: altar to the Veteres by Longinus. *Brit.* iv (1973), 329, no. 11
Vindolanda: altar to the Veteres by Senilis. *Brit.* iv (1973), 329, no. 12
Vindolanda: altar to Vetir. *Brit.* vi (1975), 285, no. 6
Vindolanda: altar to Ve[ter]. *Brit.* vi (1975), 285, no. 7
Vindolanda: altar to the Vitirum. *Brit.* x (1979), 346, no. 8
York: altar to Veter by Primulus. *RIB* 660

Vicres
Old Penrith: altar by T(...) S(....). *RIB* 925

Victor, see **Hercules Victor** and **Mars Victor**

Victoria (Victory)
Auchendavy: altar by M. Cocceius Firmus, centurion of *II Augusta*. *RIB* 2177 (with Campestres, Epona, Hercules, Mars, and Minerva)
Birdoswald: altar by Aurelius Maximus. *RIB* 1899 (with Mars)
Brougham: altar. *RIB* 779 (with Mars)
Carlisle: altar by M. [Aurelius?] Syrio, military tribune with *XX Valeria Victrix*, between 213-22. *Brit.* xx (1989), 331-3, no. 5 (with Jupiter Optimus Maximus, Juno, Mars, and Minerva)
Colchester: statue in existence by 60. Tacitus, *Annals* xiv.32
Colchester: bronze plaque to Victoria of Severus Alexander by Lossio Veda, a Caledonian, between 222-35. *RIB* 191 (with Mars Medocius Campesium)
Hadrian's Wall (1.25 miles south of mc 51): crag inscription recording *aurea per caelum volitat Victoria pennis*, 'golden Victory flies through the sky on her wings'. *RIB* 1954
High Rochester: base by Julius Silvanus Melanio. *RIB* 1273, see *RIB95*, p. 781 (with Pax)
Housesteads: altar by [...], *custos armorum*. *RIB* 1596 (with Mars and Numina Augustorum)
Lanchester: altar by Ulpius. *RIB* 1086
Ribchester: base. *RIB* 585 (with Mars)
Ribchester: altar to the Victoria of Caracalla during the governorship of Gordianus(?) (see Gordian I in Chapter 9) in *c.*216. *RIB* 590 (with Salus)
Rough Castle: altar by *cohors VI Nerviorum*, commanded by Flavius Betto, centurion of *XX Valeria Victrix*. *RIB* 2144

Victoria Augusti/Augustorum (Victoria of the Emperor/Emperors)
Benwell: altar by *ala I Asturum*, during the governorship of Alfenus Senecio, between *c.*205-8. *RIB* 1337
Birrens: altar by *cohors II Tungrorum* under the prefect Silvius Auspex. *RIB* 2100 (with Mars)
Castlesteads: relief. *RIB* 1995
Corbridge: altar by L. Julius Juli[anus]. *RIB* 1138
Greatchesters: altar by *cohors VI Nerviorum*, under the prefect G. Julius Barbarus. *RIB* 1731
Maryport: altar by *cohors I Baetasiorum*, under the prefect T. Attius Tutor. *RIB* 842
Maryport: altar by *cohors I Baetasiorum*, under the prefect Ulpius Titianus. *RIB* 843
Newcastle-upon-Tyne: altar. *RIB* 1316 (with Jupiter Optimus Maximus)

Victoria Augustorum Dominorum Nostrorum (Victoria of the Emperors, our Lords)
Maryport: altar. *RIB* 844

Victoria Brigantia (Victorious Brigantia)
Castleford: altar by Aurelius Senopianus. *RIB* 628
Greetland: altar by T. Aurelius Aurelianus, *magister sacrorum*, in 208. *RIB* 627 (with Numina Augustorum)

Victoria legionis VI Victricis (Victory of *VI Victrix*)
Tunshill Farm: silver plate dedicated by Valerius Rufus. The find-spot in a quarry makes it likely it
had been removed from elsewhere in antiquity, perhaps York. *RIB* 582

Victoria Victrix (Victorious Victory)
Auchendavy: altar by M. Cocceius Firmus, centurion of *II Augusta*. *RIB* 2176 (with Jupiter Optimus
Maximus)

Vinotonus
Scargill Moor, Bowes: altar by L. Caesius Frontinus, prefect of *cohors I Thracum*. *RIB* 733
Scargill Moor, Bowes: altar by V[inotono]. *RIB* 737

Vinotonus Silvanus
Scargill Moor, Bowes: altar by Julius Secundus, centurion of *cohors I Thracum*. *RIB* 732

Vinotonus Silvanus Augustus
Scargill Moor, Bowes: altar by T. [O]rbius Pri[mia]nus, prefect of *[cohors I Thracum?]*. *Brit.* xix
(1988), 491, no. 7

Viradecthis
Birrens: altar by the Condrusi (a German tribe) serving in *cohors II Tungrorum*, under the prefect G.
Silvius Auspex. *RIB* 2108

Virgo Caelestis (for Julia Domna) see also **Bona Dea Regina Caelestis, Caelestis Brigantia**,
and **Regina Caelestis**
Carvoran: altar by M. Caecilius Donatianus, prefect, between 197-217. *RIB* 1791 (with Virtus,
Mater, Pax, and Ceres)

Viridius
Ancaster: slab by Trenico, recording his making an arch. *JRS* lii (1962), 192, no. 7 (**36**)

Virtus (Virtue)
Bath: altar by G. Severius Emeritus, *c(enturio) reg(ionarius)*. *RIB* 152 (with Numen Augusti)
Carvoran: altar by M. Caecilius Donatianus, prefect. *RIB* 1791 (with Virgo Caelestis, Mater, Pax,
and Ceres)
Chesters: altar by *ala II Asturum* in 221-2. *RIB* 1466
Duntocher: relief of 139-61 by a vexillation of *VI Victrix*. *RIB* 2200
Maryport: altar by [...]iana Hermoniae, daughter of Quintus. *RIB* 845

Volcanus Vulcan
Barkway: silver votif leaf to Nu(mini) [Vo]lc(an)o. *RIB* 220
Maryport: altar to V[olcano?] (or Victoria). *RIB* 835 (with Jupiter Optimus Maximus)
Maryport: altar by Helstrius Novellus, prefect (of *cohors I Hispanorum*, see *RIB* 822 under Jupiter
Optimus Maximus above). *RIB* 846
Old Carlisle: altar to V(o)lk(ano) by the *magistri* of the *vicus* inhabitants between 238-44. *RIB* 899
(with Jupiter Optimus Maximus)
Stony Stratford: silver plate to [Vo]lca(no) by Vassinus. *RIB* 215 (with Jupiter)
Vindolanda: altar by *vicus* inhabitants at Vindolanda. *RIB* 1700 (with Domus Divina and Numina
Augustorum)

DEITIES BY LOCATION

The following catalogue lists sites alphabetically together with the names of deities to which dedications have been found at each location. To find details of those dedications, turn to the alphabetic catalogue of deities above.

Sites are not distinguished between find-spots, villas, towns, settlements and forts. Some inscriptions or smaller finds may well have been removed in antiquity. Tunshill Farm, for example, is extremely unlikely to have had anything to do with the Victory of *VI Victrix* in antiquity.

Adel (W. Yorks)
Brigantia

Aldborough (N. Yorks)
Matres

Ancaster (Lincs)
Viridius

Ashton (Northants)
Christ

Auchendavy (AW)
Apollo
Campestres
Diana
Epona
Genius Terrae Britannicae
Hercules
Jupiter Optimus Maximus
Mars
Minerva
Silvanus
Victoria
Victoria Victrix

Bakewell (Derbys)
Mars Braciaca

Balmuildy (AW)
Britannia
Campestres
Fortuna
Mars

Bar Hill (AW)
Apollo
Mars Camulus
Silvanus

Barkway (Herts)
Mars Alator
Mars Toutatis
Volcanus

Bath (Avon)
Diana
Genius loci
Mars
Mars Loucetius
Minerva
Nemetona
Numen Augusti/Numina Augustorum
Suleviae
Sulis
Sulis-Minerva
Virtus

Benwell (HW)
Antenociticus
Campestres
Genius ALAE
Jupiter Optimus Maximus Dolichenus
Lamiae
Mars
Mars Victor
Matres Campestres
Minerva
Numen Augusti/Numina Augustorum
Veter/Veteres/Viter/Vitiris/Votris
Victoria

Bertha (Perth)
Disciplina

Bewcastle (Cumbria)
Cocidius
Disciplina
Jupiter Optimus Maximus
Mars Belatucadrus
Mars Cocidius

Binchester (Durham)
Fortuna Sancta
Genius loci
Jupiter
Matres
Matres Ollotatae
Salus
Suleviae

Birdoswald (HW)
Cocidius
Fortuna
Jupiter Optimus Maximus Dolichenus
Latis
Mars
Mars Augustus
Mars Pater
Numen Augusti/Numina Augustorum
Ratis
Signa
Silvanus
Victoria

Birrens (Dum & Gall)
Brigantia
Disciplina
Fortuna
Harimella
Jupiter Optimus Maximus Dolichenus
Mars
Mercury
Minerva
Neptune
Numen Augusti/Numina Augustorum
Priapus
Ricagambeda
Victoria
Viradecthis

Bitterne (Hants)
Ancasta

Bollihope (Durham)
Numen Augusti/Numina Augustorum
Silvanus Invictus

Bowes (Durham)
Fortuna
Jupiter Optimus Maximus
Vinotonus
Vinotonus Silvanus

Bowness-on-Solway (HW)
Belatucadras
Matres

Brough-on-Humber (East Riding of Yorkshire)
Numen Augusti/Numina Augustorum

Brough-on-Noe (Derbys)
Arnomecta
Hercules Augustus
Mars

Brougham (Cumbria)
Belatucadrus
Mars
Victoria

Burgh-by-Sands (HW)
Belatucadrus
Genius numeri Maurorum Aurelianorum Valeriani Gallienique
Hercules
Jupiter Optimus Maximus
Latis
Mars Belatucadrus
Numen Augusti/Numina Augustorum

Burrow-in-Lonsdale (Lancs)
Aesculalpius
Contrebis
Genius collegii Apollinis
Hygiaea
Numen Augusti/Numina Augustorum

Cadder (AW)
Silvanus

Caerleon (Gwent)
Bonus Eventus et Fortuna
Diana
Domina Nemensis
Fortuna
Genius legionis II Augustae
Jupiter Optimus Maximus
Jupiter Optimus Maximus Dolichenus
Mercury
Mithras
Numen Augusti/Numina Augustorum
Salus

Caernarvon (Gwynedd)
God
Minerva

Caerwent (Gwent)
Genius
Mars Lenus
Mars Ocelus
Numen Augusti/Numina Augustorum
Ocelus Vellaunus

Caister-on-Sea (Norfolk)
Mercury

Cappuck
Jupiter Optimus Maximus

Cardewlees (Cumbria)
Jupiter Optimus Maximus

Numen domini nostri/Numina dominorum
nostrorum

Carlisle (Cumbria)
Belatucadrus
Cautes
Genius centuriae
Genius loci
Hercules
Jupiter Optimus Maximus
Juno
Mars
Mars Barrex
Mars Belatucadrus
Mars Ocelus
Mars Victor
Matres Parcae
Minerva
Numen Augusti/Numina Augustorum
Parcae
Victoria

Carrawburgh (HW)
Belatucadrus
Coventina
Coventina Augusta
Fortuna
Genius huius loci
Hviteres
Mater
Matres Communes
Minerva
Mithras
Mithras Invictus
Nympha/Nymphae
Nympha Coventina
Veter/Veteres/Viter/Vitiris/Votris

Carriden (West Lothian)
Jupiter Optimus Maximus

Carvoran (HW)
Belatucadrus
Ceres Dea Suria
Epona
Fortuna Augusta
Hammia
Hercules
Jupiter Optimus Maximus Dolichenus
Jupiter Optimus Maximus Heliopolitanus
Mars Belatucadrus
Mater
Minerva
Numen Augusti/Numina Augustorum
Nympha/Nymphae
Pax
Regina Caelestis

Silvanus
Suria
Veter/Veteres/Viter/Vitiris/Votris
Virgo Caelestis
Virtus

Castlecary (AW)
Fortuna
Matres
Mercury
Neptune

Castleford (W. Yorks)
Nymphs
Victoria Brigantia

Castlesteads (HW)
Belatucadrus
Disciplina
Genius loci
Jupiter Optimus Maximus
Mars
Matres Omnium Gentium
Matres Tramarinae
Mithras
Numen Augusti/Numina Augustorum
Sol Invictus
Sol Mithras
Vanauns
Victoria

Catterick (N. Yorks)
Matres Domesticae
Suria
Veter/Veteres/Viter/Vitiris/Votris

Chedworth (Gloucs)
Mars Lenus

Chester (Ches)
Aesculapius
Fortuna Redux
Genius centuriae
Genius loci
Genius sancta centuriae
Genius signiferorum legionis XX Valeria Victrix
Hypermenes
Hygiaea
Jupiter Taranus
Mars Conservator
Nemesis
Numen Augusti/Numina Augustorum
Nympha/Nymphae
Panakeia
Salus
Soteres

193

Chester-le-Street (Durham)
Apollo
Digenis
Veter/Veteres/Viter/Vitiris/Votris

Chesters (HW)
Bona Dea Regina Caelestis
Disciplina
Fortuna Conservatrix
Genius legionis XX Valeria Victrix D[eciana]
Jupiter Optimus Maximus Dolichenus
Matres Communes
Ratis
Regina Caelestis
Sol Invictus Elagabalus
Veter/Veteres/Viter/Vitiris/Votris
Virtus

Chichester (West Sussex)
Genius
Jupiter Optimus Maximus
Matres Domesticae
Minerva
Neptune

Cirencester (Gloucs)
Genius
Genius sancta huius loci
Jupiter Optimus Maximus
Matres
Mercury
Silvanus
Suleviae

Clifton (Cumbria)
Genius loci
Jupiter Optimus Maximus

Cockersand Moss (Lancs)
Mars Nodens

Colchester (Essex)
Claudius Divus
Mars Medocius Campesium
Matres Suleviae
Mercury Andescociuoucus
Numen Augusti/Numina Augustorum
Silvanus
Silvanus Callirius
Victoria

Corbridge (Northd)
Arecurio (Mercury)
Apollo Maponus
Astarte
Brigantia
Concordia legionis VI Victrix et legionis XX
Diana

Disciplina
Hercules
Jupiter Dolichenus
Jupiter Optimus Maximus
Mercury
Minerva
Panthea
Salus
Silvanus
Victoria
Veter/Veteres/Viter/Vitiris/Votris

Cramond (Lothian)
Mars Condatis
Matres Alatervae
Matres Campestres

Croy Hill (AW)
Mars
Nympha/Nymphae

Custom Scrubs (Gloucs)
Mars Olludius
Romulus

Daglingworth (Gloucs)
Cuda?
Genius loci
Matres

Dorchester-on-Thames (Oxon)
Jupiter Optimus Maximus
Numen Augusti/Numina Augustorum

Dover (Kent)
Matres Italicae

Duntocher (AW)
Jupiter Optimus Maximus
Virtus

East Gate (Durham)
Silvanus

East Stoke (Notts)
Christ

Ebchester (Durham)
Genius
Mars
Minerva
Numen Augusti/Numina Augustorum
Vernostonus

Fossdike (also Fossdyke) (Lincs)
Mars
Numen Augusti/Numina Augustorum

194

Gloster Hill (Northd)
Campestres

Gloucester
Genius cohortis
Mars

Godmanchester (Cambs)
Abandinus

Godmanstone (Dorset)
Jupiter Optimus Maximus

Greatchesters (HW)
Disciplina
Fortuna
Jupiter Optimus Maximus Dolichenus
Victoria
Veter/Veteres/Viter/Vitiris/Votris

Greetland (W. Yorks)
Numen Augusti/Numina Augustorum
Victoria Brigantia

Greta Bridge (N. Yorks)
Mars
Nympha/Nymphae

Hadrian's Wall (see also under individual
   fort names)
Apollo
Genius [...]vali
Hvitires
Jupiter Optimus Maximus
Jupiter Optimus Maximus Dolichenus
Maponus
Mars Cocidius
Matres
Matres Domesticae
Nemesis
Numen Augusti/Numina Augustorum
Nympha Brigantia
Silvanus
Veter/Veteres/Viter/Vitiris/Votris

Haile (Cumbria)
Hercules
Silvanus

Haltonchesters (HW)
Fortuna
Numen Augusti/Numina Augustorum

Harlow (Essex)
Numen Augusti

High Rochester (Northd)
Genius
Genius domini nostri
Hercules
Matunus
Minerva
Mithras
Mountes
Pax
Roma
Signa
Signa cohortis
Silvanus Pantheus
Sol Invictus
Victoria

Housesteads (HW)
Alaisiagae
Baudihillia
Beda
Clarius Apollo
Cocidius
Fimmilena
Friagabis
Genius huius loci
Genius praesidii
Hercules
Hveteris
Hvitris
Jupiter Optimus Maximus
Mars
Mars Thincsus
Numen Augusti/Numina Augustorum
Silvanus Cocidius
Sol
Sol Invictus Mithras Saecularis
Veter/Veteres/Viter/Vitiris/Votris

Icklingham (Suff)
Christ

Ilkley (W. Yorks)
Verbeia

Inveresk (Lothian)
Apollo Grannus

Kirby Hill
Divus Antoninus

Kirkby Thore (Cumbria)
Belatucadrus
Balnearis Fortuna
Fortuna Servatrix
Jupiter Serapis
Silvanus

Lancaster (Lancs)
Ialonus Contrebis
Mars
Mars Cocidius

Lanchester (Durham)
Aesculapius
Cautopates
Fortuna Augusta
Garmangabis
Genius cohortis
Genius praetorii
Jupiter Optimus Maximus?
Mars
Mars Augustus
Mithras
Numen Augusti/Numina Augustorum
Regina
Silvanus
Sol Invictus
Victoria
Veter/Veteres/Viter/Vitiris/Votris

Leicester (Leics)
Mercury Propitius

Lemington (Gloucs)
Regina

Lincoln
Dis
Genius loci
Mercury
Numen Augusti/Numina Augustorum
Parcae

London (including Greenwich)
Isis
Jupiter Optimus Maximus
Matres
Mithras
Numen Caesaris Augusti
Sol Invictus

Lydney (Gloucs)
Mars Nodens
Nodens

Lympne (Kent)
Neptune

Malton (N. Yorks)
Genius loci
Mars Rigas
Manchester
Fortuna Conservatrix

Martlesham (Suffolk)
Mars Corotiacus

Maryport (Cumbria)
Aesculapius
Belatucadrus
Christ
Fatum Bonum
Fortuna Redux
Genius loci
Jupiter Augustus
Jupiter Optimus Maximus
Jupiter Optimus Maximus Capitolinus
Mars Militarus
Neptune
Numen Augusti/Numina Augustorum
Roma Aeterna
Setlocenia
Victoria
Virtus
Volcanus

Moresby (Cumbria)
Jupiter Optimus Maximus
Silvanus

Mumrills (AW)
Hercules Magusanus

Netherby (Cumbria)
Fortuna Conservatrix
Iu[...]teris Fortunatus
Jupiter Optimus Maximus
Mars Belatucadrus
Mogons Vitiris
Numen
Numen Augusti/Numina Augustorum

Nettleham (Lincs)
Mars Rigonemetos
Numina Augustorum

Nettleton (Wilts)
Apollo Cunomaglos
Silvanus

Newcastle-upon-Tyne
Hospitales
Jupiter Optimus Maximus
Matres
Matres Tramarinae Patriae
Neptune
Numen Augusti/Numina Augustorum
Oceanus
Silvanus
Victoria

Newstead (Roxburghs)
Apollo
Campestres
Diana

Old Carlisle (Cumbria)
Belatucadrus
Bellona
Deus
Genius
Hercules
Jupiter Optimus Maximus Conservator
Jupiter Optimus Maximus Dolichenus
Mars
Mars Belatucadrus
Tutela Brigantia Augusta
Volcanus

Old Harlow (Essex)
Mercury

Old Penrith (Cumbria)
Belatucadrus
Genius dominorum nostrorum
Jupiter Optimus Maximus
Jupiter Optimus Maximus Dolichenus
Mars Belatucadrus
Matres Tramarinae
Mogons
Mountis
Numen Augusti/Numina Augustorum
Silvanus
Unseni Fersomeri
Vicres

Overborough — see **Burrow-in-Lonsdale**

Piercebridge (Durham)
Jupiter Optimus Maximus Dolichenus
Veter

Ribchester (Lancs)
Apollo Maponus
Mars
Mars Pacifer
Matres
Mithras
Victoria

Risingham (Northd)
Cocidius
Cultures
Diana
Fortuna
Fortuna Augusta
Fortuna Redux
Hercules

Hercules Invictus
Jupiter Optimus Maximus Dolichenus
Mars Victor
Matres Tramarinae
Mogons Cad[...]
Mounus Cad[...]
Numen Augusti/Numina Augustorum
Numen domini nostri/Numina dominorum
   nostrorum
Nympha/Nymphae
Silvanus

Rough Castle (AW)
Victoria

Rudchester (HW)
Deus (Mithras)
Sol Apollo Anicetus Mithras
Sol Invictus

Scarcroft (W. Yorks)
Apollo
Numen

Shakenoak (Oxon)
Jupiter Optimus Maximus

Silchester (Hants)
Hercules Saegon[...]
Mars

Skinburness (Cumbria)
Matres Parcae

Slack (W. Yorks)
Bregans
Fortuna
Numen Augusti/Numina Augustorum

Somderdale Keynsham (Somerset)
Numen Augusti/Numina Augustorum
Silvanus

South Shields (Tyne & Wear)
Aesculapius
Apollo Anextiomarus
Brigantia
Conservatores
Mars Alator
Numen Augusti/Numina Augustorum
Vitiris

Staincross Common (S. Yorks)
Mars

Stanwix (HW)
Matres Domesticae

Stonea (Cambs)
Minerva

Stony Stratford (Bucks)
Jupiter
Mars
Volcanus

Thetford (Norfolk)
Faunus

Thistleton (Leics)
Veteris

Tilston (Cheshire)
Genius loci

Tunshill Farm (Lancs)
Victoria legionis VI Victricis

Ty Coch (Gwynedd)
Numen Augusti/Numina Augustorum

Uley (Gloucs)
Mercury

Vindolanda (Chesterholm) (Northd)
Cocidius
Custodes
Fortuna Populi Romani
Genius
Genius praetorii
Jupiter Optimus Maximus
Maponus
Mars Victor
Matres
Mercury
Mogons
Neptune
Numen
Numen Augusti/Numina Augustorum
Sattada
Silvanus
Veter/Veteres/Viter/Vitiris/Votris
Volcanus

Walesby (Lincs)
Christ

Wallsend (HW)
Mercury

Water Newton (Cambs)
Christ

West Coker (Somerset)
Mars Rigisamus

Westerwood (AW)
Silvanae and Quadriviae

Whitley Castle (Northd)
Apollo
Hercules
Hercules Victor
Minerva

Wigginholt (West Sussex)
Christ

Winchester (Hants)
Matres Italiae Germanae Gallae Britanniae

York
Arciaco
Arimanes
Bonus Eventus et Fortuna
Britannia
Dis
Fortuna
Genius Eb[oraci?]
Genius loci
Hercules
Hospitales
Ioug[...]
Jupiter Optimus Maximus
Mars
Matres
Matres Afrae Italae Gallae
Matres Domesticae
Mercury
Numen Augusti/Numina Augustorum
Oceanus
Penates
Serapis
Silvanus
Tethys
Veter/Veteres/Viter/Vitiris/Votris

DATED ALTARS AND OTHER RELIGIOUS DEDICATIONS

The following chronological summary of altars or religious dedications (including buildings) are approximately datable either because the texts carry imperial titles, military units adopting the name of the current emperor (for example *Gordiana* for Gordian III), details of consuls, or were by individuals known from elsewhere. The list is therefore rather random but it does at least show, yet again, the significant preponderance of examples unequivocally attributable to the first half of the third century (see **3**). As these include many private dedications it seems probable that this group is an approximate reflection of all such inscriptions which of course dominate the record. More details of the individual dedications will be found in Chapter 8 by simply consulting the deity/deities concerned and the alphabetical list of places under each. Examples listed where the deity's name is lost have been included because the stone concerned is either an altar or part of a statue base which makes its religious nature fairly unequivocal. Other instances have been omitted. It will be seen that almost all the dedications were made by military individuals or in the name of a military unit. Even those which make no such specification can usually be assumed, by location, to have been made by a soldier or a unit.

(m) = indicates that the dedicant(s) specify themselves as a military individual or unit.

50-100
c. 50-100: Chichester. *RIB* 91 (Neptune et Minerva)

100-150
c. 115-35: Lympne (m). *RIB* 66 (Neptune)
117-38: Chesters (m). *Brit.* x (1979), 346, no. 7 (DA for Hadrian)
136-8: Carvoran (m). *RIB* 1778 (Fortuna Augusta)
138-61: Moresby (m). *RIB* 832 (IOM)
139-61: Benwell (m). *RIB* 1330 (IOM et NA)

150-200
152: Caerwent. *RIB* 309 (Mars Lenus/Ocelus Vellaunus et NA)
154: Chester (m). *RIB* 452 (IOM Tanarus)
155: Somerdale Keynsham. *RIB* 181 (NA)
158: Corbridge (m). *RIB* 1132 (Mars Ultor)
c. 163-6: Corbridge (m). *RIB* 1137 (Sol Invictus)
c. 163-6: Carvoran (m). *RIB* 1792 (Suria)
c. 163-6: Carvoran (m). *RIB* 1809 (deity's name lost)
167: Stanwix. *RIB* 2026 (deity's name lost)
c. 175-8: Lanchester (m). *RIB* 1083 (NA and Genius cohortis)
177-85: Benwell (m). *RIB* 1329 (Anociticus)
180-92: Carlisle (m). *RIB* 946 (Hercules [...] Invictus)

185: Old Carlisle (m). *RIB* 903 (deity's name lost)
188: Old Carlisle (m). *RIB* 893 (IOM)
c. 190-210: York. *RIB* 658 (Serapis)
191: Old Carlisle (m). *RIB* 894 (IOM)
191: Catterick (m). *RIB* 725 (Deus qui vias et semitas commentus est)

200-250
198-209: Caerleon (m). *RIB* 324 (Salus Regina)
205-8: Benwell (m). *RIB* 1337 (Victoria Augustorum)
208: Greetland. *RIB* 627 (Victoria Brigantia et NA)
209-11: Castlesteads. *RIB* 1978p (DA)
210-35: Reculver. *Antiq. Journ.* xli (1961), 224; *JRS* li (1961), 191, no. 1; and *JRS* lv (1965), 220, no. 1
211-12: South Shields (m). *RIB* 1054 (Conservatores)
211-17: Risingham (m). *RIB* 1237 (deity's name lost)
212-17: Castlesteads. *RIB* 1978 (Disciplina Augustorum)
212-17: Hadrian's Wall area. *RIB* 2066 (Nympha Brigantia and NA)
212-17: Ty Coch. *RIB* 2264 (NA)
213: High Rochester (m). *RIB* 1272 (Sol Invictus)
c. 213: High Rochester (m). *RIB* 1268 (Minerva et Genius collegi)
213-22: Ebchester (m). *RIB* 1101 (Minerva)
213-22: Carrawburgh (m). *RIB* 1544 (Mithras

199

Invictus)

213-22: Carlisle (m). *Brit.* xx (1989), 331-3, no. 5 (IOM et alia)

213-22: Birdoswald (m.). *RIB* 1892 (IOM)

c. 216: Ribchester. *RIB* 590 (Salus and Victoria Augusti)

217: Piercebridge (m). *RIB* 1022 (IOM Dolichenus)

221: York. *Brit.* viii (1977), 430, no. 18 (*arcum et ianuam* to Neptune, Genius loci and NA)

221-2: Chesters (m). *RIB* 1466 (Virtus)

c. 222: Netherby (m). *RIB* 968 (Fortuna Conservatrix)

222-25: Colchester. *RIB* 191 (Mars Medocius et Victoria Augusti, for Severus Alexander)

222-35: Old Penrith (m). *RIB* 919 (Numen Augusti and Matres Tramarinae)

222-35: Carlisle. *RIB* 949 (Mars Ocelus and Numen imperatoris of Severus Alexander)

222-35: Housesteads (m). *RIB* 1594 (Mars et Alaisiagae et NA for Severus Alexander)

234: Caerleon. *RIB* 328 (deity's name, if the stone was religious, lost)

235 (or less likely 289): Camerton. *RIB* 180 (deity's name lost)

c. 235-8: Birdoswald. *RIB* 1896 (IOM Dolichenus)

235-8: Birdoswald (m). *JRS* xlvii (1957), 229, no. 17 (IOM Dolichenus)

237: Birdoswald (m). *RIB* 1875 (IOM)

238-41: High Rochester (m). *RIB* 1262 (Genius domini et Signa cohortis)

238-44: Lanchester (m). *RIB* 1074 (Garmangabis and NA)

238-44: Old Carlisle. *RIB* 899 (IOM and Vulkanus)

238-44: Benwell (m). *RIB* 1334 (Matres Campestres et Genius alae)

238-44: Birdoswald (m). *RIB* 1893 (IOM)

241: Papcastle (m). *RIB* 882 (deity's name lost)

241: Castlesteads (m). *RIB* 1983 (IOM et NA)

242: Old Carlisle (m). *RIB* 897 (IOM)

244: Caerleon (m). *RIB* 327 (NA et Genius legionis)

244-9: Papcastle (m). *RIB* 883 (deity's name lost)

244-9: Old Penrith (m). *RIB* 915 (IOM et Genius DN)

250-300

c. 250-70: Caerleon. *RIB* 316 (Diana)

251-3: High Rochester. *RIB* 1273 (Victoria et Pax)

251-3: Bowness-on-Solway (m). *RIB* 2057 (IOM)

251-3: Bowness-on-Solway (m). *RIB* 2058 (deity's name lost)

252: Housesteads (m). *RIB* 1600 (Sol Invictus Mitras Saecularis)

255-9: Cardewlees (m). *RIB* 913 (IOM and *NDN*)

255-75: Birdoswald (m). *RIB* 1882 (IOM and NA)

259-68: Birdoswald (m). *RIB* 1883 (IOM)

259-68: Birdoswald (m). *RIB* 1886 (IOM)

259-68: Burgh-by-Sands (m). *RIB* 2042 (NA)

258: Housesteads (m). *RIB* 1589 (IOM)

262-6: Hadrian's Wall (m). *RIB* 1956 (Cocidius)

270-3: Birdoswald (m). *RIB* 1885s (IOM)

c. 296-313 (or later): Cirencester. *RIB* 102 (IOM)

9 People of Roman Britain

The criteria for inclusion in this chapter include evidence for an official role of significance in Britain (for example, command of a legion), a social, commercial, political or religious role of importance, or archaeological significance. Individuals only known from brief epigraphic references to have held a military tribunate in Britain, or the command of an auxiliary unit are, for example, generally omitted. Their names will be found under the names of the military units they commanded, or the religious dedications they made.

Names are usually listed by *nomina* but where this would divert from more familiar forms, the latter have been preferred. Thus Gnaeus Julius Agricola is listed under A. Similarly, where an individual is known only by part of his name then that is what he or she is listed under. Characters referred to in **bold** type have their own entries.

Adelphius

Bishop of *colonia Londiniensium* (the surviving versions of the text provide several variants) in attendance at the Council of Arles in 314. The name of his city has long since been recognized to be corrupt (a bishop of London is also listed at Arles, see **Restitutus**), and was most probably Lindensium (Lincoln).

Source: *PNRB* 49ff

Adminius

A son of Cunobelinus, exiled to the Continent, who presented himself and a small group of supporters to Caligula around the year 39. Adminius tried to persuade Caligula to attempt an invasion of Britain. Caligula initially presented this to the Roman people as evidence of Britain's spontaneous submission but it nevertheless led to his abortive plans for a British campaign in 40.

No reason is supplied for the exile of Adminius. Perhaps he had either challenged or compromised the territorial ambitions of his father. He is never heard of again. Two other brothers, **Caratacus** and **Togodumnus**, actively opposed the Roman invasion as their father's heirs.

Source: Suetonius (*Caligula*) xliv.2

Aelius Brocchus

Known only from the correspondence of his wife **Claudia Severa** and Sulpicia Lepidina, wife of **Flavius Cerialis**. Brocchus was prefect of an unknown auxiliary unit at a place called *Briga* (also unknown, but probably on the northern frontier) between about 92 and 103. Amongst the little known about him is a request to him from Cerealis for a loan of hunting-nets. He went on to command the *ala contariorum* in Pannonia.

Source: *Tab. Vindol.* II.233, 248, 291, 292 (most easily found in Bowman 1994, nos. 16, 18, 21-22, and Bowman and Thomas 1994); see also Bowman 1994 in general for this man, especially p. 55; *CIL* iii.4360

M. Aemilius Papus

Legate of an unnamed legion in Britain under Hadrian but perhaps more remarkable for his full name, Marcus Cutius Marcus Priscus Messius Rusticus Aemilius Papus Arrius Proculus Julius Celsus.

Sources: *CIL* ii.1283, 1371 (and Birley, A., 1979, 170)

Agricola

Gnaeus Julius Agricola first served in Britain under **Suetonius Paullinus** where, as a tribune, he was appointed to the governor's staff. Subsequently he became quaestor in Asia and tribune of the plebs in Rome.

The turmoil of the Year of Four Emperors (68-9) found him initially associated with Galba but **Vespasian**'s appearance in the conflict led Agricola to side with him. This may have had something to do with Vespasian's time in Britain and Agricola's early career. It was a sensible decision as it turned out, and in 69 Agricola was granted command of *XX Valeria Victrix* with which he will have been familiar during the Boudican campaign. *XX* had been reluctant to swear allegiance to Vespasian, largely because their legate in 68 (**Roscius Coelius**) had allied himself with Vitellius.

The appointment was obviously a move by Vespasian to provide *XX* with a commander whom they would have difficulty rejecting. In this capacity Agricola served under **Vettius Bolanus** and **Petillius Cerialis**. The governorship of Aquitania and a consulship interceded before he became governor of Britain in 77 or 78, a term which lasted until 83 or 84.

Year 1 (78)

Agricola succeeded **S. Julius Frontinus** and seems to have been immediately confronted by a rising in Wales of the Ordovices who had seized the opportunity of the interregnum to destroy an auxiliary regiment. Destruction of the tribe was followed by an impulsive campaign into Anglesey and its surrender. The appearance of lead pipes bearing his name and imperial titles for 79 suggest that the new fortress at Chester was begun, or at any rate continued at this time, to create a permanent base to control north Wales.

The military campaign was followed by a policy of preventing future war. This was done by ceasing to delegate to freedmen or slaves and instead taking personal control of provincial administration. Various practices had been devised to allow those who collected tribute to rake-off huge profits. These were, in theory, compulsorily ceased.

Year 2 (79)

The military campaign of the second season was personally supervised throughout by Agricola, but Tacitus omits to say where it took place. The description of exploring river estuaries and forests is too vague for certain attribution.

In the winter the policy of romanization was advanced by educating the Britons into Latin language and culture as well as Roman social practices of dress and recreation. This may be the year in which the Verulamium forum was dedicated but it has often been pointed out that it must surely have been begun long before Agricola arrived and that therefore both the inscription and Tacitus are being disingenuous.

Dio states that events in Britain led to the award of the title *Imperator* for the 15th time to Titus. This occurred in the year 79 but he appears to be describing events more applicable to 81 or 82.

Year 3 (80)

The campaign in this year advanced as far as the Tay (*Taum*). No battles were fought, the enemy (or perhaps more likely, the Romans) being discouraged by appalling weather, but forts were established along the way.

Year 4 (81)

This is the year of Tacitus' cryptic remark that the perfect frontier between the Clyde and Forth (*Clota et Bodotria*) was reached and would have been consolidated if only the irrepressible spirit of the army and Rome's glory had permitted the Empire to accept an end to her dominions. The line and the land to the south was garrisoned and secured.

Year 5 (82)

Agricola made a crossing by ship prior to a series of battles against unknown tribes. Where he crossed is not stated but as he is also said to have lined the coast which faces Ireland (Galloway) with troops this suggests the crossing was over the Solway. The crossing of the Forth did not come until Year 6.

Year 6 (83)

The advance over the Forth stimulated the Caledonian tribes into action. Agricola divided his army into three and continued. The tribes attacked *IX Hispana*, said by then to be the weakest of the legions involved. No others are named at any point in the campaign by Tacitus, but it is generally assumed from his earlier career that *XX* was the principal legion in the Caledonian campaign. The weakness may have been that a number of legionaries had been detached to build and garrison forts further south. *IX* was rescued by cavalry and infantry but the tribes proceeded to regroup and organize themselves for more war.

Year 7 (84)

Agricola now marched to Mons Graupius, location unknown, to force the Caledonian tribes into a set-piece battle. The campaign was opened with the fleet sent ahead to foment fear by raiding along the coast. The battle was a Roman victory, fought by the auxiliaries against superior numbers. In the aftermath the remains of the tribes spirited themselves away into the highlands and Agricola withdrew to the land of the 'Boresti' and ordered the fleet to circumnavigate Britain. Dio confirms the latter and states that Agricola learned that Britain was an island; however, this was already well-known to the ancients as Caesar's description makes clear.

The eventual outcome of Agricola's career is not relevant here apart from the fact that he was withdrawn from Britain after his exceptionally long tenure and never returned. Dio says that he had achieved more than was appropriate to his station, the implication being that he was perceived as a possible threat by the paranoid Domitian who eventually had him murdered.

Only archaeology has been the source of evidence that Agricola's conquests north of the Tyne-Solway area were very largely given up in the next few years. The most eloquent evidence is the systematic dismantling of the fortress at Inchtuthil. It is unavoidably the case that, though a broad picture of Agricola's activities can be compiled from archaeological excavation and aerial photography, Tacitus does not provide enough factual or topographical detail for the exact procession of events to be reconstructed.

One recent piece of evidence is the writing tablet from Carlisle, recording a *singularis* detached from *ala Sebosiana* on Agricola's staff.

Sources: Tacitus (*Agricola*) passim; Dio Cassius lxvi.20.1-3; *JRS* xlvi (1956), 146-7 (Verulamium forum); *RIB* 2434.1-2 (Chester lead pipes bearing imperial titles for 79 and Agricola's name as governor); wooden writing tablet from Carlisle from a *singularis* of *ala Sebosiana* detached to Agricola. *Brit.* xxix (1998), 74, no. 44

Alban

The Christian martyr Albanus was executed outside the eastern walls of Verulamium. He had replaced another Christian who was being pursued by the authorities. The post-Roman drift of settlement to the east of the Roman city and the site of modern St Albans may be attributed to a martyrium which presumably lies beneath the medieval abbey church. The date of the event has been linked to the time of **Septimius Severus'** campaigns in Britain around the year 209. Gildas' account describes a Britain ruled by a Caesar who, after the execution, ordered a cessation of the persecution without recourse to the 'emperors'. During the campaign Severus ruled jointly with his eldest son **Caracalla** and both were in the north fighting. Britain was left in the control of his younger son **Geta** who only held the rank of Caesar until 209 when he too was elevated to the position of Augustus. Nevertheless it is quite possible that Gildas had conflated or confused a variety of accounts of different martyrdoms. Albanus may have been killed much later.

Sources: Gildas x-xi; Bede (*Hist. Eccl.*) I.7

Albinus, see Clodius Albinus

L. Alfenus Senecio

Governor between *c*.205-8 and named on a large number of inscriptions which testify to extensive building activity in the north and on the northern frontier during his tenure. At least some of this may be attributed to preparation for the impending campaign by Septimius Severus.

Sources: *RIB* 722, 723 (Bainbridge), 740 (Bowes), 746 (Greta Bridge), 1151(?) (Corbridge), 1234 (Risingham), 1337 (Benwell), 1462 (Chesters), 1909 (Birdoswald); *JRS* lvii (1967), 205, no. 17 (Housesteads) in a highly-optimistic restoration

Allectus

Emperor in Britain from 293-6, known almost entirely from his coinage. Aurelius Victor is said to have described him as having been in charge of **Carausius**' financial department (*summa res*). The Latin can mean any official matters of the highest importance so is not as precise as presented by some historians in translation. The interpretation of the Carausian coin exergue-mark RSR as *Rationalis Summae Rei* was based on this text but this and another Carausian exergue mark (INPCDA) have now been shown to represent Virgilian texts (*Eclogues* iv.6-7).

Whatever Allectus' true position, in 293 he participated in a plot to kill the British usurper Carausius and reigned in his place until 296. In that year a campaign led by **Constantius Chlorus** led to his defeat at the hands of **Asclepiodotus** somewhere in southern Britain.

Allectus is untestified on any inscription. The association of a monumental quayside structure in London with his reign is entirely based on the premise that timbers used were felled between 293-6. This of course only tells us the building was erected after this date and may be discarded as evidence for his 'headquarters'.

Allectan coinage lacked the imaginative zeal of the types issued by Carausius although in general the coins were better manufactured and of more regular shape and size. However, he appears to have introduced a small bronze coin, *quinarius*, the reverse of which invariably depicts a galley. It was not maintained after his defeat.

Sources: Aurelius Victor (*De Caesaribus* xxxix.41; Eutropius ix.22.2. See also Casey (1996)

Alypius

In 363 Alypius, who came from Antioch, was placed in charge of rebuilding the Temple at Jerusalem. Before this date he had been *pro praefectis* of Britain, succeeding **Martinus**.

Source: Ammianus xxiii.1.2-3

Q. Antistius Adventus (also known as **Postumius Aquilinus**)

That this man was governor of Britain is stated on an undated dedication from Lanchester. Earlier in his career he had participated in the Parthian expedition of Marcus Aurelius which finished in 166. After this he governed Arabia and Germania Inferior, recorded on an inscription which takes us no further. However, this allows for a governorship of Britain to start about 175 or later. The Lanchester dedication mentions only a single emperor who is un-named, but which must be Marcus Aurelius. Until 169 Aurelius ruled jointly with Lucius Verus, and again with Commodus from 177. A diploma of 23 March 178 states the governor to be **Ulpius Marcellus**. Therefore, the governorship of Antistius Adventus must fall between 169-77, with 174-7 being the most likely block.

Sources: *RIB* 1083 (Lanchester); *ILS* 1091, 8977

M. Antius Crescens Calpurnius

Rose to become proconsul of Macedonia after his time in Britain as *legatus iuridicus*. Interestingly, the inscription from Italy which records his career adds that he simultaneously acted as vice-propraetorian legate; that is, he was also vice-governor of Britain. Fortunately for us the text includes the information that he was one of the overseeing priests at the Saecular Games apparently held in 204. This must place his time in Britain to late in Commodus' reign at the earliest. A logical time for him to have acted as vice-governor might have been during the war of 184 when the governor, **Ulpius Marcellus**, was obliged to fight a campaign.

Source: *ILS* 1151

M. Antonius Gordianus Sempronianus Romanus, afterwards Gordian I

Possibly governor of *Britannia Inferior* in *c*.216. He was well-known for his intellectual powers and his moral judgement. These attributes led him to the proconsulship of Africa where he was persuaded to declare himself emperor in 238 in response to the brutality meted out by the emperor Maximinus on possible rivals. However, Gordian's son, Gordian II, was defeated and killed in Africa by supporters of Maximinus. Gordian I committed suicide. In 238 Gordian's grandson by his daughter Maecia Faustina became emperor as Gordian III. This followed the murders of Balbinus and Pupienus who had reigned themselves for only 98 days after the death of Maximinus.

Gordian III's murder in 244 was probably followed by the systematic erasure of his grandfather's names from inscriptions. In Britain at least three are thought to have borne Gordian I's name as governor but only one (*RIB* 1049) is partly legible, supplying *[...]diani*. This stone carries the name of the consuls for 216, giving us a date for his governorship which goes unmentioned in the imperial biographies (*SHA*).

Sources: *RIB* 590 (? erased; Ribchester), 1049 (Chester-le-Street), 1279 (? erased; High Rochester)

Q. Antonius Isauricus

Legate of (probably) *VI Victrix*, known only from an altar found in York and by the goddess Fortuna by his wife Sosia Juncina. The stone cannot be accurately dated because his title is stated merely as *leg(atus) Aug(usti)*. It could conceivably belong to any point in the second century, including *IX Hispana*'s tenure though the style of the stone makes this unlikely. Isauricus would probably have been more explicitly described as governor if the stone had post-dated the division of Britain. His post must then date to somewhere between 122-215.

Sources: *RIB* 644 (York) (**71**)

71 *Altar from York, recording a dedication to Fortuna by Sosia Juncina, (wife) of Q. Antonius Isauricus,* leg(atus) Aug(usti). *The location and title makes it highly likely he was commander of* VI Victrix *in the second century. Height 0.69m.* RIB 644

Q. Aradius Rufinus

Either Aulus Triarius Rufinus (consul 210), Quintus Aradius Rufinus, or another, is named on the headquarters inscription from Reculver as being incumbent at the time the new shrine was erected. Quintus Aradius Rufinus is normally assumed to be the correct man but this does not provide a precise date. An inscription from *Bullia Regia* in North Africa, possibly naming the same man, makes the reign of Severus Alexander a possibility (222-35).

Source: *JRS* li (1961), 191, no. 1, and *JRS* lv (1965), 220, no. 1

L. Artorius Justus

Prefect and thus an equestrian, of *VI Victrix* in Britain, stated on his tombstone found in Dalmatia. The post would normally have been held by a *legatus*, of senatorial rank. The only ready explanation for this apparent anomaly is the statement in the fourth-century life of Commodus (180-92) that during the war in Britain he had sacked 'certain' senators and installed equestrians in command of the troops in their place. If this is correct then Artorius Justus' command of *VI Victrix* would belong to the years *c.*182-8. He went on to lead a force of British legions 'against the Armoricans' but this statement is unverifiable from any other source. Another *praefectus legionis* is apparently testified at Chester though in his case the post appears to have occurred before 170.

Sources: *ILS* 2770 (Dalmatia); *SHA* (Commodus) vi.2; *JRS* lv (1965), 221, no. 5 (Chester)

J. Asclepiodotus

Praetorian prefect in north-west Gaul in 296. He led one of the two waves against **Allectus** in Britain that year. The other was led by **Constantius Chlorus**. The principal account of the campaign, a panegyric on Constantius, omits any named mention of Asclepiodotus and allocates all the glory to Constantius. What actually seems to have happened is that Asclepiodotus lead the first wave that landed near the Solent. He marched inland to confront and defeat Allectus. Eutropius is unequivocal in attributing the victory to Asclepiodotus. Constantius merely arrived in London to reap the harvest.

Source: Aurelius Victor xxxix.39; Eutropius ix.14 (both are most readily located in Casey, 1996, 197)

M. Atilius Metilius Bradua

Known to have been governor of Britain from a single Greek inscription. This names him as governor under Hadrian of *Germanias kai Bretannias*. His term is normally attributed to around 115-19; however, there is no mention of Trajan on the inscription. But as **Q. Pompeius Falco** is known to have been completing his term in 122 and all other Hadrianic governors are attested it must have been the case that Metilius Bradua was finishing his tenure around 118-9, thus beginning in 114-15. There is a possibility he was related to P. Metilius/Maecilius Nepos, governor in 98.

Sources: *ILS* 8824a

L. Aufidius Panthera

Lucius Aufidius Pant[h]era's remote family origins can be traced to an ancestor called Aufidius who had introduced panthers to the circus. In Britain he is known from a dedication to Neptune found at Lympne. This altar provides no information about his date but a diploma names him as *praefectus* of an *ala milliaria* in Upper Pannonia on 2 July 133. This post is likely to have preceded his fleet command, so it may be assumed that he was promoted during the last few years of Hadrian's reign or the first few years of the reign of Antoninus Pius.

Sources: *RIB* 66 (see Chapter 2; Lympne) (**72**); *CIL* xvi.76

Aurelius Arpagius

Governor (*pr(aeses)*), probably of *Britannia Inferior*, between 297-305. He is known only from a slab found at Birdoswald recording extensive rebuilding work under the Tetrarchy.

Source: *RIB* 1912 (Birdoswald)

M. Aurelius Lunaris

His name indicates that citizenship was probably acquired by his father or grandfather during the reign of Aurelius (161-80). In 237 Lunaris was a *sevir Augustalis* at the colonies of York and Lincoln, and was involved in trading goods in and out of Bordeaux. There he set up an altar, thanking the goddess 'Boudig' for her protection. It also records that York

72 *Altar found in the east gate at the Saxon Shore fort of*
   Lympne. Weathering and barnacle damage showed that
   it had spent time in the sea, appropriate considering it
   was dedicated to Neptune by L(ucius) Aufidius
   Pantera, praefect(us) *of the British fleet,* clas(sis)
   Brit(annica). *Height 0.89m.* RIB 66

and Lincoln were in *Britannia Inferior*. Interestingly the stone itself was from Yorkshire showing that it had been shipped from Britain, either for the symbolic importance of its origin or as ballast.

Source: *JRS* xi (1921), 102 (Bordeaux) (**29**)

Q. Aurelius Polus Terentianus

Legate of *II Augusta* under Commodus, recorded on an inscription from Mainz which also describes him as legate of *XX Primigenia*. Otherwise difficult to explain, the occasion may have been celebration of a new legionary command for him in Britain, necessitated by a mutiny. Infuriated by the power-crazy commander of the Praetorian Guard, Perennis, the troops in Britain had appointed one of their legates, **Priscus**, as emperor. Priscus rejected his unsolicited elevation but a number of soldiers went to Rome to see Commodus. Commodus allowed the Praetorian Guard to kill Perennis but sent **Pertinax** to restore discipline in Britain in about 185.

Sources: *AE* 1965.240 (Mainz); Birley (1971), 338; Dio lxxii.9

M. Aurelius Quirinus

Prefect of *cohors I Lingonum* at Lanchester under Gordian III (238-44). He is one of the few auxiliary commanding officers to leave us with evidence of his leisure activities. He left an altar by a stream at Eastgate (also Durham) dedicated to Silvanus. It probably followed a hunting expedition in the woods.

The stylistic similarity of three stones from Lanchester, two of which name Quirinus, suggest he patronized a talented mason amongst his garrison. The two building stones are the only building-specific stones of the reign from Britain and help illustrate the randomness of the epigraphic record.

Source: *RIB* 1042 (Eastgate, **70**), 1074, 1091, 1092 (Lanchester, **6, 37, 62**)

Aurelius Ursicinus

Recorded as the principal owner of material included in the Hoxne (Suffolk) treasure discovered in 1992. His name appears ten times on silver spoons in the form *Aur(elii) Ursicini*, '[the spoon] of Aurelius Ursicinus'. The treasure included around 15,000 coins, the latest of which are dated to 408. Ursicinus clearly lived at the time of the hoard or earlier, but we have no way of assessing if he was the hoarder, the hoarder's ancestor, the victim of a thief, or an earlier owner entirely unknown to the hoarder.

Although the name Ursicinus is known from literary sources it is not possible to say whether this man was the same as any of them, or if he was related (see, for example, Ammianus Marcellinus on the vice-prefect Ursicinus in Rome in 368). Other names recorded in the treasure include Faustinus, Juliana, Peregrinus, and Silvicola. These individuals may have been members of the same family but it is also possible that the treasure was made up of official requisitions from several families and buried by a third party.

Sources: Bland and Johns (1993); Ammianus Marcellinus xxviii.1.44-5

T. Avidius Quietus

Known only as governor of Britain on an incomplete diploma of 98 from Flémalle. This places him at the beginning of Trajan's reign and he was, perhaps, a new appointment. He was well known, and admired by Pliny the Younger.

Sources: *CIL* xvi.43; Pliny vi.29.1

Q. Baienus Blassianus

Known from a career inscription, recording his command of the *classis Britannica*. He was eventually elevated to the prefecture of Egypt, a post of immense prestige for an equestrian. Only the prefecture of the Praetorian Guard was superior. However, the only 'tag' by which his career can be dated is an Egyptian papyrus which refers to his presence in Egypt in the year 168. His command of the British fleet may have occurred at any point in the preceding 25 years.

Sources: *AE* 1974.123

Boudica/Boudicca/Boudouica

Widow of Prasutagus, King of the Iceni. Prasutagus, who died in about 59 or 60, made his daughters joint heirs with Nero. The idea was that this would lead to a peaceable transfer of power. It did not. Boudica was flogged and her daughers raped. Their relatives were enslaved while other Iceni estates were seized.

Their humiliation became a focus for the mounting resentment felt by East Anglian tribes at Roman high-handedness, oppression, and brutality. The progress of the ensuing Revolt is well-known: with Boudica at their head the rebels burst out of East Anglia, sacking Colchester, London, and Verulamium as well as, presumably, other Roman settlements in the vicinity, before being defeated by **Suetonius Paullinus**.

The chaos of tribal rebellion was unlikely to have proved attractive to some of the British population who may have already begun to accept Roman rule as a more stable and predictable way of life. This may explain why the defeat and suppression of the Revolt was followed by almost permanent peace in the south and east.

Sources: Tacitus (*Agricola*) xvi, (*Annals*) xiv.31ff

Caesius Nasica

Legate of a legion (unnamed) in Britain during the governorship of **Didius Gallus**. Tacitus describes him in the context of supporting **Cartimandua** but he is rather cryptic about the legion's precise involvement. Roman military force seems to have intervened with a worrying start but successful outcome. Tacitus' main agenda is, however, to criticise Didius Gallus.

It has been suggested (Birley 1973, 181), that this man and the governor **Q. Petillius Cerealis Caesius Rufus** were brothers.

Source: Tacitus (*Annals*) xii.40

S. Calpurnius Agricola

Recorded in the life of Marcus Aurelius as the governor leading a war against the Britons in about the year 163. This supplies a context for an undated stone from Carvoran by Hadrian's Wall, recording a dedication to the Dea Suria by *cohors I Hamiorum sagittaria* during Calpurnius Agricola's tenure. The stone is interpreted as evidence for reoccupation at Carvoran following withdrawal from the Antonine Wall. A further undated stone names him at Corbridge. Unfortunately, a more explicit slab also naming him has required significant restoration to produce a date of 163. In fact, the extant portions of the stone lack most of the year-specific dating information and in reality it can only be attributed to the reign of Marcus Aurelius during the lifetime of his intended heir, Lucius Verus, between 161-7. Prior to his appointment to Britain he was governor of Germania Superior, testified in the year 158.

Sources: *SHA* (Marcus Aurelius) viii.7-8; *RIB* 1792 (Carvoran); 1137, 1149 (Corbridge); *AE* 1986.523

Calvisius Rusonus (or **Rufus**)

Governor of *Britannia Inferior* at some time during the reign of Severus Alexander (222-35). As the governors of 220-5 are testified he must belong to 225-35. He is recorded on a dedication for *cohors II Gallorum Severiana Alexandriana* at Old Penrith. The visible latter part of his name is more compatible with Rus(onus) rather than Ruf(us) so the former is to be preferred.

Sources: 225-35. *RIB* 929 (see *RIB* I (1995), 776, and *RIB* 2491.83)

Caracalla (73)

Caracalla, or correctly, Marcus Aurelius Antoninus (and before that Bassianus), was the eldest son of **Septimius Severus** and brother of **Geta**. He was born in 188 and in 198 was created joint Augustus with his father. In 208 he accompanied Severus, who was anxious to distract him from the fleshpots of Rome, and Geta to Britain for the Caledonian campaign. In 211 Severus died at York, possibly hurried along by his ambitious eldest son. Caracalla succeeded with Geta who had been promoted to Augustus as well. Caracalla made peace in Britain, terminated the campaign and withdrew. Thereafter he conducted a reign of terror in Rome.

In 212 Caracalla murdered Geta. In 213 inscriptions swearing allegiance to Caracalla were erected in Britain apparently at the behest of the governor **G. Julius Marcus**. These, however, were subsequently defaced both because Marcus had probably earned Caracalla's opprobrium and because of the *damnatio memoriae* which was enforced after Caracalla's murder in 217. Restoration and interpretation of inscriptions of this reign are sometimes complicated by Caracalla's official name, also used by Elagabalus (218-22).

Sources: Herodian iii.14.1, 3-10; Dio lxxvi.15.1-3, lxxvii.1.1; *SHA* (Caracalla) passim

Caratacus

When the Roman invading force landed in 43, **Cunobelinus** of the Catuvellauni was already dead. Before 41 one of his sons, **Adminius** had been exiled, probably for pro-Roman tendencies. His other sons, Caratacus and Togodumnus, led the post-invasion resistance despite suffering initial defeats. Togodumnus was killed but Caratacus fled west and took over the leadership of the Silures in south Wales and moved north into the territory of the Ordovices gathering support for a battle. Despite selecting a position which provided his local forces with advantages he was defeated by **Ostorius Scapula**. Nevertheless he escaped to seek sanctuary with **Cartimandua** of the Brigantes. In the year 51 he was handed over to the Roman command and transported to Rome. His dignity in defeat won him his freedom and that of his family.

Sources: Dio lx.20; Tacitus (*Annals*) xii.33-8

Carausius (86)

Marcus Aurelius Mausaeus Carausius, as he styled himself, was appointed by Maximian to lead a fleet against pirates in the English Channel. He had been born in Menapia (Belgium) in the middle years of the third century, spending much of his formative life under the Gallic Empire. He trained as a sailor but later joined the army. Carausius came to fame in 284 when he fought in a war against vagrant rebels in Gaul called the Bagaudae.

Mausaeus is an unusual name but it also appears on an altar from Carrawburgh

73 Caracalla, who ruled from 198-211
with his father Septimius Severus, and
his brother Geta from 208. From 211-
12 he ruled jointly with Geta until
murdering him. He ruled alone until
his own assassination in 217. The
portrait does not conceal his brutality.

dedicated to Coventina (*RIB* 1523) by an *optio* of *cohors I Frisiavonum*. The only source of
Carausius' full name is a milestone from near Carlisle.

Carausius' success led to his fleet appointment but his activities aroused imperial
suspicions. Stories circulated that he waited for pirates to raid towns and villas and then
ambushed them on their way home, making off with the loot himself. It is no less likely
that Maximian promoted the stories, having been disturbed by Carausius' popularity.

In or around 286 Carausius rebelled and established an imperial enclave in Britain and
northern Gaul. His regime was presented as a kind of rumbustious restoration of Roman
imperial values, buoyed up with the soundest coinage for decades and Virgilian slogans.
This propaganda campaign has left a legacy in the abundant coinage which he issued from
London and another mint, perhaps at Colchester or Cirencester.

Early attempts to topple Carausius foundered on the beaches of Gaul as the imperial
fleet was destroyed by storms. Carausius maintained power until 293, altering his stance
to one of unsolicited membership of an imperial college of emperors with Diocletian and
Maximian. In 293 Carausius was murdered by his associate, an official called **Allectus**
who ruled the rebel empire until 296.

Sources: *RIB* 2291. Latin sources may be found in Mynors (1964) but summaries of coins, sources
and other data are Casey (1994) and de la Bédoyère (1998).

C. Caristanius Fronto

Legate of *IX Hispana* in Britain. His career inscription from Antioch in Pisidia states that this occurred during the reign of **Vespasian** (69-79). Subsequently, during the reigns of **Titus** and Domitian, he went on to become governor of Pamphylia. He evidently died during the reign of Domitian. Caristanius Fronto is unrecorded in Britain.

Sources: *ILS* 9485 (Antioch)

Cartimandua

Cartimandua was queen of the Brigantes. She consolidated her position as a Roman client monarch in 51 when she handed over **Caratacus** to Rome. The tribal territory approximated to what is now known as northern England. As a result she ruled a client kingdom in the north thereafter which brought her wealth and over-confidence. In around the years 68-9 her husband Venutius was supplanted from her side by her lover, and his aide, Vellocatus. She made Vellocatus her consort in an act of folly which alienated her entire tribe.

Venutius was initially loyal to the Romans, and he was admired for his skill in warfare. What began as a private falling-out with his wife and a divorce, was eventually translated into wholesale opposition to Rome. Venutius moved swiftly, gathering support from within and without the tribe, forcing Cartimandua to flee with limited Roman assistance, probably during the governorship of **Vettius Bolanus**.

Petillius Cerealis was responsible between 71-4 for the ending of Brigantian ambitions, though Tacitus' brief description of this episode in the *Agricola* makes no mention of Cartimandua or Venutius. Considering how much he made of Venutius in the *Annals* and the *Histories* this is interesting. Talk of the 'last stand' of Venutius at the hillfort of Stanwick is thus an archaeological inference based on approximately contemporary finds and its exceptional size for the region.

Sources: Tacitus (*Histories*) iii.45, (*Annals*) xii.36, 40, (*Agricola*) xvii

Chrysanthus

Vicar of Britain in the very late fourth century. He went on to become bishop in Constantinople.

Sources: Socrates (*Hist. Eccl.*) vii.12 and 17 (cited by Frere, 1987, 350, n. 31)

Civilis

Sent to Britain about the year 367 to govern Britain as deputy prefect at the request of Theodosius. Ammianus calls him *pro praefectis*, a title which seems to be interpreted as a synonym for *vicarius* though various books dealing with the period in Roman Britain make no comment on the different name. Civilis was said to have a considerable temper but was respected for his sense of justice and incorruptibility.

Sources: Ammianus xxvii.8.10

Classicianus

Gaius Julius Alpinus Classicianus succeeded **Decianus Catus** as *procurator provinciae Britanniae* in 61. He was a high-born Gaul whose family had benefited from selective awards of Roman citizenship in earlier times. He was critical of Roman imperial policy and as a result of his recommendations the governor **Suetonius Paullinus** was recalled, though the dispute may be a literary fabrication by Tacitus. His father-in-law, Julius Indus, had earlier opposed a revolt in Gaul led by Julius Florus of the Treveri in 21, during the reign of Tiberius. Classicianus' tombstone erected by his wife Julia Pacata, daughter of Indus, found in London, is now in the British Museum.

His status did not prevent the destruction of his tomb and its integration into fourth-century defences. It was found in two major fragments, in 1852 and 1935. Not until 1935 was it confirmed that this was the man mentioned by Tacitus (see Chapter 1).

Classicianus presumably died in office, probably in the mid- to late 60s.

Sources: Tacitus (*Annals*) iii.42 (for Indus), xiv.38 (for Classicianus); *RIB* 12 (London)

Claudia Severa

Wife of **Aelius Brocchus**, commander of an auxiliary unit around 92-103. Her handwriting on a tablet found at Vindolanda is the earliest instance of female Latin handwriting known. She lived with her husband and son at the unknown fort of *Briga* and corresponded with her friend Sulpicia Lepidina, wife of **Flavius Cerealis**, prefect of *cohors IX Batavorum* at Vindolanda.

Sources: *Tab. Vindol.* II.291-2 (see Bowman 1994, nos. 21, 22)

Claudius (83)

Claudius succeeded in 43, following the murder (in which he was not implicated) of Caligula. His principal need was to consolidate power. The arrival of **Verica** around now, seeking help to return him to power in Britain provided a pretext. Caligula's plans for an invasion supplied the means.

Claudius did not participate in the invasion. Anxious that the troops were unwilling to embark across the sea he sent his freedman Narcissus to encourage them. Narcissus was mocked but the soldiers set sail.

Claudius waited for news from **Aulus Plautius** that headway had been made but that opposition was too strong to continue. This was presumably a device to allow Claudius the chance to win his glory. He duly arrived, met the army at the Thames, and led the march to seize Colchester. Claudius received the surrender of the Britons, including 11 kings. These and other details were recorded on two triumphal arches in Rome. Part of the inscription of one survives and coins also record their existence.

On his return Claudius was awarded a triumph. He celebrated the success by naming his son Britannicus and awarded an ovation to Aulus Plautius, a means of rewarding a general without upstaging the emperor.

Altogether Claudius had spent sixteen days in Britain. He was later honoured in a temple of classical form at Colchester which may or may not have been complete by the time of its destruction in 60. It was afterwards rebuilt. There is a single life-sized bronze statue bust of Claudius which is extant. Found in a Suffolk river and evidently hacked from a full-sized figure, possibly mounted, it may have once been displayed in Colchester. The theory that it was mutilated and disposed of by Boudican rebels will remain unproven but the context and its find-spot make this a serious possibility.

Sources: Dio lx.19-23; Suetonius (*Claudius*) xvii, xxiv; *ILS* 216 (arch of Claudius), 2648 and 2701 (M. Vettius Valens and G. Gavius Silvanus, praetorians decorated in the invasion), 2696 (P. Anicius Maximus, *praefectus castrorum* of *II Augusta* decorated in the invasion).

Claudius Apellinus

Named as *leg(atus) Aug(ustorum)* of (presumably) *Britannia Inferior* on a slab from High Rochester by *cohors I Vard(ullorum)*. The emperor's name has been erased, and is normally restored as Severus Alexander but this cannot be absolutely certain. If correct, Apellinus' governorship may be attributed probably to somewhere between 225-35.

Source: *RIB* 1281 (High Rochester)

T. Claudius Augustanus

Tiberius Claudius Augustanus was procurator of Britain, recorded in an inscription from Verona. His son is said to be known as a senator from Pliny the Younger's letters, which must mean that the father's procuratorship in Britain had occurred before *c*.85 but after the testified Neronian procuratorship of **Classicianus** between *c*.61-5.

Sources: *CIL* v.3337; Birley (1979, 49)

A. Claudius Charax

Legate of *II Augusta c*.143, and later a well-known historian. This may mean he was closely involved with the legion's building work on the Antonine Wall.

Source: *AE* 1961.320

T. Claudius Cogidubnus, see **Togidubnus**

Claudius Hieronymianus

Claudius Hieronymianus, legate of *VI Victrix* at York, built a temple to Serapis. The style of the dedication stone and the nature of the god are considered to suggest a date during the reign of Septimius Severus. As with **Q. Antonius Isauricus** it must pre-date the division of the province into *Superior* and *Inferior*; otherwise Hieronymianus would be named as governor of *Inferior*. He is usually identified with a man of the same name referred to as governor in Cappadocia between *c*.180-220 in an obscure work by the Christian apologist Tertullian (see *RIB* for this and another reference by Ulpian).

Source: *RIB* 658 (York) (**74**)

DEO·SANCTO
SERAPI
TEMPLVM·A·SO
LO·FECIT
CL·HIERONY
MIANVS·LEG
LEG·VI·VIC

*74 Slab from York recording the building of a temple dedicated to Serapis by the legate of VI Victrix,
Claudius Hieronymianus. That he is not named as governor means that the stone must predate
the division of Britain by Severus. The style and subject matter suggests the late second century.
Width 0.9m. RIB 658*

Ti. Claudius Paulinus

Tiberius Claudius Paulinus was governor of *Britannia Inferior* in 220, recorded on an
inscription from High Rochester and approximately fixed by the supposed dates of his
predecessor **Modius Julius** and successor **Marius Valerianus**, governor in 221. He had
formerly commanded *II Augusta* at Caerleon, recorded on a statue base from Caerleon, a
post which he must have held not long before 220. The text of a letter to his friend Titus
Sennius Sollemnis, and written during his time as governor in Britain, has survived,
preserved on a monument to Sollemnis in Vieux. It accompanied gifts which seem to have
been offered in return for assistance in avoiding prosecution in Rome, recorded on
another part of the same monument.

Sources: *RIB* 311 (Caerwent) (**75**), 1280 (High Rochester); *CIL* xiii.3162 (letter, Vieux; partly
translated by Birley, 1979, 43, and another section in L & R, source 120, p.445)

Claudius Xenophon/Xenephon

Governor of *Britannia Inferior* under Severus Alexander (222-35). Two milestones from the
Hadrian's Wall area show his governorship included the year December 222 to December
223.

Sources: *RIB* 1706 (Vindolanda), 2299 (Stanegate near Vindolanda), 2306 (Hadrian's Wall near mc 42)

75 *Statue(?) base from Caerwent, recording a dedication made by council decree of the cantonal government of the Silures* (ex decreto ordinis, res publica civitatis Silurum) *to Paulinus, legate of* II Augusta *and proconsul of the province of* (Gallia) Narbonensis. *His full name, Tiberius Claudius Paulinus, can be restored from a slab of 220 found at High Rochester (*RIB 1280*) by which time he was governor of* Britannia Inferior. *Height 1.19m.* RIB 311

D. Clodius Albinus

D. Clodius Septimius Albinus was governor in Britain in 192 when Commodus was murdered. Pertinax succeeded Commodus. Within three months Pertinax too was murdered. The brief reign of Didius Julianus which followed led to a new civil war.

Septimius Severus realized he could not defeat both his rivals, Clodius Albinus and Pescennius Niger, simultaneously. One report is that he sent a man called Heraclitus to secure Britain. Evidently this failed. Therefore Severus offered Albinus the post of Caesar (which the *SHA* claim had already been offered by Commodus) before setting out to defeat Niger. Albinus fell into the trap and Severus proceeded to defeat and kill Niger in 194.

Severus' plans to dispose of Albinus were thwarted when Albinus realized he was being duped. He moved his army into Gaul, even collecting reinforcements from governors of other provinces. Severus obtained from the Senate a declaration that Albinus and his supporters were public enemies.

When the final battle came, at Lyons in 197, Albinus had reputedly amassed up to 150,000 troops. Far more than the British garrison could have provided, it still suggests Albinus had seriously denuded Britain of troops. The campaign had not gone all Severus' way, and nor did the battle which came close to a catastrophe for him when his soldiers fell into hidden trenches. The timely arrival of Severan cavalry proved decisive. Albinus realized the game was lost and committed suicide.

The outcome seems to have been the division of Britain in order to prevent a repeat.

But Herodian's statement does not date the event closely and contradicts later descriptions by him of the nature of government in Britain. It is possible that it was not implemented until later in the reign or until Caracalla's reign.

Sources: Dio lxxiii.14.3, 15.1; lxxv.4.1; Herodian ii.15, iii.6; *SHA* (Severus) vi.9-10; x.1ff; *SHA* (Clodius Albinus) *passim*

M. Cocceius Nigranus?

Marcus Cocceius Nigrinus was *[pr]oc(urator) Aug(usti)* during the reign of Caracalla. He is known only from a manuscript record of a lost dedication made between 212 and 217 to Caracalla and Victoria Brigantia.

Source: *RIB* 2066 (uncertain provenance, possibly Castlesteads)

Cogidubnus, see Togidubnus

Constans

Constans was one of the sons and heirs of Constantine I. By the terms of his father's will he inherited control of the Balkans, Italy, and Africa in 337. However, in 340 he fought with his elder brother Constantine II who had inherited control of Gaul, Spain, and Britain. Constantine II was killed and Constans took control of Britain.

In the winter of 342-3 Constans sailed to Britain. The plan, a risky one, seems to have been to establish his power before a revolt broke out. He was apparently successful, despite reputedly only bringing a hundred men with him. A lead seal from London, bearing Constans' head, is the only rather tenuous archaeological evidence for the occasion.

Sources: Julius Firmicus Maternus (*De Errore Profanum Religionum*) xxviii.6; Libanius (*Oration*) lix.139, 141; RIB 2411.23 (London lead seal)

Constantine I, the Great (76)

Constantine was the only son of the first marriage of his father, **Constantius Chlorus**. When the time came for Constantius and Galerius to appoint their junior emperors and heirs (*see* Constantius Chlorus below), Galerius decided to promote his own family and had already appointed both the new Caesars, one of whom was his nephew. Constantine felt his birthright was being stolen and set out to Britain to meet Constantius, being detained on the way by Galerius. However, he escaped to Britain arriving in time to witness his father's death from sickness. Constantine I was declared emperor at York in the summer of 306. By 324 he had defeated his rivals and colleagues to rule alone.

A series of coins of the London mint, which operated until about 325, bears the reverse *Adventus Aug(usti)*, thought to indicate visits by him to the province in 307, 312, and 314, to secure troops for these wars. Zosimus certainly says that he levied troops in Britain. Eusebius states that he came to subjugate Britain but adds no details of what was going on or why.

76 *Bronze coins of Constantine I from the London mint. The reverse (from a different coin) depicts the emperor on horseback with the legend* Adventus Aug(usti)*. The type is interpreted as proof of Constantine's visits to London during his reign*

Milestones survive in Britain in greater numbers from the first few years of Constantine's reign than any other (**46**). This may be because the practice of renewing stones later died out and these were not replaced. Alternatively he may have instigated road repairs as an effective way of consolidating his regime and also maximizing government control of remote regions.

Sources: Aurelius Victor (*Liber de Caesaribus*) xl.2-4; Eutropius x.1-3, 2.2; Zosimus ii.8.2, 9.1, 15.1; Eusebius (*de Vita Constantini*) I.8, 25; milestones (see Chapter 6)

Constantine III (77)

A series of usurpers were installed in Britain in the early fifth century beginning with Marcus, who was declared emperor by the British garrison. He was quickly replaced by a man called Gratian. He too was rapidly ousted and a soldier called Constantine was chosen, helped by the symbolism of his name. Constantine III, as he is known, crossed to Gaul immediately taking with him his sons Constans and Julian and his British general Gerontius. His coinage was all struck on the continent and some carry the reverse *Victoria Auggg* to denote his unsolicited membership of the legitimate college of emperors.

Constantine attempted to take advantage of the chaos in Gaul, and the ineffectual imperial government holed up in Ravenna, to establish a new Gallic empire of Britain, Gaul, and Spain. However, Constantine's troops sacked the provinces they passed through and barbarians exploited the disorder to launch new raids. By 410 Constantine's regime was falling apart. Gerontius had revolted in Spain when Constantine III expanded his ambitions to attempt the conquest of Italy; meanwhile, the Britons had thrown out any imperial officials they could find and sorted out their own defences, which suggests that

77 Gold coin of Constantine III (407-11)

Constantine III had never enjoyed wide popular support in Britain. Many years later in Gaul Ecdicius, a member of the imperial house and friend of Sidonius, used his own means and those of other 'great men' to raise a 'public army' which confronted Goths much more successfully than the official forces. This may have been what happened in Britain. Honorius seized the advantage and ordered his army to engage Constantine III, then besieged at Arles. Constantine was defeated, and executed. His short reign marks the end of Roman Britain.

Sources: Orosius (*Adversum Paganos*) vii.40.4, 42.1-4; Zosimus vi.1-5

Constantius I (Constantius Chlorus)
Diocletian became emperor in 284. In 286 he divided the Empire between himself in the East and Maximian in the West. In 293, to ease further the responsibilities, two junior partners were appointed, Galerius for the East and Constantius Chlorus in the West. The idea was that Diocletian and Maximian would abdicate, the latter two would succeed and appoint their own junior partners and heirs.

Constantius was immediately charged with suppressing the revolt in Britain. First he seized Boulogne and then, following the murder of **Carausius** and the accession of **Allectus**, he began the construction of a fleet which was used in 296. One wing was led by **Asclepiodotus** while Constantius brought up the rear. Asclepiodotus defeated Allectus and Constantius made the triumphal entry into London, emulating Claudius' own triumphal entry into Colchester 253 years before.

Around the year 305 Constantius returned to Britain for a campaign into Scotland. The events are little more than alluded to in the sources and the absence of contemporary inscriptions in the north makes it impossible to verify them. He seems to have been seriously ill and died at York in 306. He had already been joined by his son **Constantine** who had great misgivings about the management of Diocletian's imperial collegiate system which was about to oust him permanently.

Sources: Panegyric for Constantius Caesar vi.1-2 (Boulogne), xiii-xx (the campaign); Panegyric on Constantine v.3, vii.1-2

Constantine II See under Constans above

V. Crescens Fulvianus

Valerius Crescens Fulvianus was governor of *Britannia Inferior* probably between 225-35, if the restoration of the name of Severus Alexander to the single stone bearing his name is correct. The stone, from Ribchester, records the restoration of a temple.

Sources: *RIB* 587 (Ribchester)

Cunobelinus

Cunobelinus was king of the Catuvellauni, a tribe which occupied territory north of the Thames centred on an area very approximately equivalent to Middlesex and Hertfordshire. He was dead by 43 but his territorial aggrandizement created tensions in Britain that provided Claudius with a pretext for invasion. His power was such that Suetonius describes him as *rex Britannorum* ('King of the Britons').

The Catuvellaunian tribal centre originally seems to have been Verulamium, marked VER on a variety of coins of his father Tasciovanus (*c*.20BC-AD10). However, it is evident from the coins of Cunobelinus not only that he was the successor of Tasciovanus but also that his principal centre was now *Camulodunum* (Colchester), marked CAMU on his coins. Dio even says that this was the capital of Cunobelinus.

Plainly the Catuvellauni had expanded at the expense of the Trinovantes to the east while the evidence concerning **Verica** suggests they had also expanded westwards. Dio, in his account of the invasion, states that the 'Bodunni' (recte, Dobunni) were subject to the Catuvellauni. As the Dobunnian tribal zone was centred on the area around where Cirencester is now it is clear that Cunobelinus had been highly successful

Sources: Suetonius (*Caligula*) xliv.2; Dio lx.20, 21, 33

Decianus Catus

Imperial procurator of Britain in 60-1. His base, perhaps already in London, is not specified by Tacitus but it was not at Colchester, where he sent only about 200 ill-equipped men to help resist Boudica. No doubt this inadequate performance was responsible for his replacement by **G. Julius Alpinus Classicianus** in the aftermath of the Revolt.

Sources: Tacitus (*Annals*) xiv.32, 38; Dio lxii.2

Desticius Juba

Governor *(leg(atus) Aug(ustorum))* of (presumably) *Britannia Superior* in *c*.255-60, as recorded on a building inscription from Caerleon in the reigns of Valerian and Gallienus.

Source: *RIB* 334 (Caerleon)

A. Didius Gallus

Aulus Didius Gallus was governor between 52-7, appointed on the death in office of **Ostorius Scapula**. Didius Gallus was an experienced senior soldier who had participated in the invasion of Britain. His instructions seem to have been to hold, control, and consolidate the Welsh frontier and to avoid campaigning deep within Wales. For this important but unspectacular work he received Tacitus' opprobrium, even though his long tenure in the post suggests he was competent and successful. Didius Gallus was also confronted with a split between the pro-Roman Brigantian queen **Cartimandua** and her anti-Roman husband Venutius.

Sources: Tacitus (*Agricola*) xiv, (*Annals*) xii.40, xiv.29

Dulcitius

Dulcitius, with the rank of *dux*, was sent to Britain in about 367 to assist Civilis in governing Britain on the request of **Theodosius**. He was famous for his knowledge of warfare.

Sources: Ammianus xxvii.8.10

Eborius

Bishop of York, in attendance at the Council of Arles in 314.

Source: *PNRB* 49ff

Egnatius Lucilianus

Egnatius Lucilianus is named as *leg(atus) Aug(usti)* on a slab from Lanchester recording building work by *coh(ors) I L(ingonum) Gor(dianae)*, thus attributable to the reign of Gordian III (238-44). Lucilianus can be assumed to have governed *Britannia Inferior*. See also **Nonius Philippus**, testified as governor in 242, and **Maecilius Fuscus**, on a similar stone from Lanchester for this reign.

Sources: *RIB* 1091 (Lanchester) (**6**), 1262 (High Rochester)

M. Favonius Facilis

The well-known tombstone of Marcus Favonius Facilis, centurion with *XX*, was found to the west of Colchester and is normally taken as evidence that *XX* was the legion stationed at Colchester between approximately 43 and 49. The date of the stone is assumed from the lack of the title *Valeria Victrix*, won in 60 during the Boudican Revolt, and the

223

knowledge that a legion was moved west in about 49 (but see *XX* in Chapter 2 for several examples of post-60 inscriptions lacking these titles).

Facilis was a member of the Pollian voting tribe and the stone was erected by his freedmen Verecundus and Novicius. Exceptionally the tombstone was found in close association with cremated remains and pottery that can be associated with the period prior to the Boudican Revolt.

Sources: *RIB* 200 (Colchester); Tacitus (*Annals*) xii.32

Flavius Cerialis

Prefect of *cohors IX Batavorum* at Vindolanda about 92-103, and known from numerous letters found at Vindolanda. See also L. Neratius Marcellus and Aelius Brocchus.

Source: *Tab. Vindol.*, for example, II.225, 233, 234, 248, 255 (also Bowman 1994, nos. 15-20, and passim for this man) (**78**)

Flavius Martinus

Centurion in charge of works carried out by an unnamed cohort at Birdoswald *c*.297-305, during the governorship of **Aurelius Arpagius**. He is one of the last named and dated ordinary soldiers of the Roman army in Britain.

Source: *RIB* 1912 (Birdoswald)

T. Flavius Postumius Varus

Titus Flavius Postumius Varus names himself as *v(ir) c(larissimus)* (senator) and legate, presumably of *II Augusta*, on stone dedication from Caerleon recording the restoration of a temple of Diana. Although undated the man is thought to be identifiable with a Postumius Varus who was *praefectus urbi* ('city prefect') of Rome in 271. His time at Caerleon will have preceded this post and probably dates to the 250s.

Sources: *RIB* 316 (Caerleon); *ILS* 2940 (Rome)

S. Flavius Quietus

Sextus Flavius Quietus died probably in Rome where his tombstone records his military career. Elevated to the post of *primus pilus* with *XX* in Britain, probably having worked his way up from being an ordinary legionary, he was eventually appointed *praefectus* of the *classis Britannica*. His career cannot be dated and he is not otherwise testified in Britain. The mid-second century has been suggested.

Sources: *AE* 1960.28

Flavius Sanctus

Described as *praeses* (governor) of *Rutupinus ager* in a short poem by Ausonius. The 'Rutupinian land' is presumably Britain, based on the name of the port of Richborough,

78 *Writing tablet from Vindolanda (back half). It names Vindolanda (third line from bottom, lower right of main section) and was a copy of a letter written by Flavius Cerealis to his friend Crispinus. The top line includes the word Marcellum, and is a reference to the governor L. Neratius Marcellus. (Copyright © The British Museum).* Tab. Vindol. *II.234*

Rutupiae. The work is attributed to the period 379-82 and records the death of Sanctus at the age of 80. It may therefore be assumed that he was governor of one of the British provinces some time around the middle years of the fourth century.

Source: Ausonius (*Parentalia*) xviii.8

Fullofaudes

Fullofaudes was *dux* in Britain in the year 367. He was ambushed and imprisoned by members of the notorious *barbarica conspiratione* ('barbarian conspiracy'). His fate is unknown.

Sources: Ammianus xxvii.8.1

C. Gavius Silvanus

Besides recording that he was decorated for his part in the British war by Claudius, this man's career stone adds that he was at the time tribune of *cohors XII Praetorianorum*. This provides useful information for the participation of the Praetorians in the invasion of Britain.

Source: *ILS* 2701 (Turin)

Gerontius

A general (*comes*) of British birth who served under **Constantine III** during his rebellion between 407-11. He turned against Constantine III and killed his son Constans. Despite elevating his own nominee, Maximus, as emperor Gerontius was killed in the traditional fashion by his own troops.

Sources: Zosimus vi.2.2ff, Orosius vii.42.4ff

Geta

Born in 189, Publius Septimius Geta was younger son of **Septimius Severus** and brother of **Caracalla**. In 198 he was elevated to the status of Caesar. In 208 he arrived with his father and brother in Britain in order to participate in the Caledonian campaign. Geta was left in charge of governing Britain and to mete out justice. In 209 he was created Augustus as well and in 210 coins in his name bearing the legend *Victoriae Brittanicae* were also issued.

In 211 Severus died and the Empire passed to the joint rule of Caracalla and Geta. In 212 Geta was murdered by Caracalla who had no wish to share his power. His time in charge of the civil administration of Britain is thought to have been by some when the martyr **Alban** was executed.

Sources: Herodian iii.14.3-10, 15.6-7; *SHA* (Geta) *passim*

Gordian I, see M. Antonius Gordianus

Gratianus

Gratian the Elder, also known as Funarius on account of his strength (from *funarius*, meaning of, or belonging to a rope, i.e. a rope could not be ripped from his hands), was father of Valentinian I. He was born in Pannonia about the year 321. He reached the position of *comes* in charge of the army in Africa where he was accused of theft; he left and was appointed *comes* of the army in Britain at some unspecified point between about 330-50. After retirement to Pannonia his property was confiscated by Constantius II for allegedly having supported the usurper Magnentius (350-3).

Sources: Ammianus xxx.7.2-3

Hadrian (79)

Publius Aelius Hadrianus (117-38) made his celebrated visit to Britain in or about the year 119. The occasion was part of his empire-wide tour and he arrived from Germany where sloppy practices amongst the troops, particularly the officers, shocked him. Hadrian immediately instituted reforms and a return to discipline.

In Britain similar decadence may have led to the building of the Wall, but there is some historical and epigraphic evidence for war on the northern frontier. The Wall itself was begun by the early 120s and is credited to the governorship of Hadrian's friend, **Aulus Platorius Nepos**, known from diplomas to have been in office in 122 and 124.

79 Coin of Hadrian (struck 128-38)

Sources: *SHA* (Hadrian), v.2, xi.2, and xii.6; *CIL* xvi.69-70 (diplomas); *RIB* (examples) 1340 (Benwell) (**21**), 1427 (Haltonchesters), 1638 (mc 38) (**12**)

Haterianus

Possibly [...]isus Claudius [Aem]ilius Quintus Julius Haterianus, and recorded as *legatus Augusti* of Cilicia on a single inscription (now lost) from Caerleon. It has been inferred that the text may be explained that he was celebrating his appointment to the governorship as a promotion from his present post as legate of *II Augusta*, though the latter post is entirely speculative. He may have been a visiting dignitary. The style suggests the second century.

Sources: *RIB* 335 (Caerleon)

T. Haterius Nepos

This man rose to be prefect of Egypt. He is tentatively identified as the man who served as *censitor Brittonum Anavion[en(sium)]*, according to a tombstone found at Foligno in Italy. The basis for this inference is other inscriptions naming the family at Foligno, and because he is named as prefect of Egypt on another. As this *censitor's* next post after Britain was as procurator in Armenia, annexed by Trajan in 114 but given up by Hadrian, he must have served under Trajan.

The regional name has survived in the name of the River Annan in south-west Scotland, and indicates that this was where he worked. As his tombstone seems to indicate a career during the reign of Trajan this is interesting evidence for Roman administrative influence beyond the line along which Hadrian's Wall would subsequently be built.

Source: *ILS* 1338 (Foligno), 9060; Birley (1979), 52

P. Helvius Pertinax, see **Pertinax**

L. Javolenus Priscus

G. Octavius Tidius Tossianus Lucius Javolenus Priscus, *legatus iuridicus* of Britain and successor to **G. Salvius Liberalis**, had a distinguished career with two legionary commands before his British appointment in the late first century, and afterwards several provincial governorships (by 91 for instance he was governor of Germania Superior).

One of the cases over which he presided was enshrined in the Digest of Roman law. The estate of a helmsman (*gubernator*) of the British fleet was in dispute because his son had predeceased him.

G. Jav[olenus Sa]tur[nal]is, *imaginifer* of *II Augusta*, recorded on an altar at Bath has been suggested as someone who may have gained his citizenship from Javolenus Priscus. The name is sufficiently rare to make such a suggestion more plausible than normal.

Sources: *ILS* 1015 (Dalmatia; translation in Ireland, p. 84); *Digest* xxxvi.1.48 (see E. Birley 1953, 51); *RIB* 147 (Bath); *ILS* 1998 (diploma, listing his governorship in 91)

Jovinus, see **Severus.**

Julia Domna

Wife and Empress of **Septimius Severus**. She accompanied him to Britain during his campaigns of 208-11 and was the subject of several dedications in Britain made under **Caracalla.**

Sources: *SHA* (Septimius Severus) passim; *RIB* 590 (Ribchester), 976 (Netherby), 1235 (Risingham), 1791 (Carvoran); *Brit.* xi (1980), 405, no. 6 (Newcastle)

Gn. Julius Agricola, see **Agricola**

G. Julius Alpinus Classicianus, see **Classicianus**

S. Julius Frontinus

Sextus Julius Frontinus succeeded **Petillius Cerealis** as governor in about 73 or 74. His activities in Britain are only known from the *Agricola* by Tacitus. Frontinus is said to have subdued the Silures in Wales in a highly effective campaign in which he mastered the difficult terrain. The end of his term of office, depending on Tacitus' precise meaning, took place in 73 or 74. He was succeeded by Agricola.

Source: Tacitus (*Agricola*) xvii.2

L. Julius Julianus

Lucius Julius Julianus was legate of *II Augusta*. A lost altar from near Hexham only names him and gives no information about his post, recorded on a career inscription from

Interamna in Italy. He is considered probably to have held his post in the Severan period, but apparently prior to the division of Britain.

Sources: *CIL* xi.4182; *RIB* 1138 (Hexham)

G. Julius Marcus

Gaius Julius Marcus was governor of Britain in 213. An unusually large number of military inscriptions from this year in Britain are known, each of which declares unswerving loyalty to Caracalla. Given the latter's murderous paranoia this was perhaps a judicious act but in Julius Marcus' case it did not save him. His name has only come down to us in a record of a milestone, now lost but found close to milecastle 17 on Hadrian's Wall. In most other cases his name was erased but the precise dating information allows them to be attributed to his governorship.

It can only be concluded that Julius Marcus was arrested on Caracalla's orders and convicted on some charge of treason. In 213 Caracalla is reputed to have murdered the proconsular governor of Gallia Narbonensis and proceeded to enact 'many measures directed against persons and in violation of the rights of communities'. One might even speculate that the inscriptions of 213 were ordered by Julius Marcus when news reached him of events in Narbonensis. We will never know and nothing else is known about him.

Sources: *SHA* (Caracalla) v.1-3; *RIB* 905 (Old Carlisle), 976, 977 (Netherby), 1202 (erased) (Whitley Castle), 1235 (erased) (Risingham), 1265, 1278 (both erased) (High Rochester), 1551 (uncertain; Carrawburgh), 2298 (milestone near mc 17 Hadrian's Wall); *Brit.* xi (1980), 405, no. 6 (erased) (Newcastle); *Brit.* xvi (1985), 325-6, no. 11 (erased) (South Shields)

S. Julius Severus

Sextus Julius Severus was governor of Britain around the years 130-3/4. The stone from Carrawburgh, purported to record building at the fort during his governorship, is so fragmentary as to be effectively useless and it should be discounted as reliable evidence. A stone from Bowes, now lost, provides more convincing traces of his name and Hadrian's titles for the period 128-38. Fortunately, his career stone lists his achievements during the reign of Hadrian, and states that he was propraetorian legate of Britain. Before Britain he had governed Moesia Inferior and went on to govern Judaea. The transfer to Judaea is stated by Dio to have taken place under Hadrian following the Jewish revolt of 132 and immediately followed his British governorship.

Sources: *RIB* 739 (Bowes), 1550(?) (Carrawburgh); *ILS* 1056; Dio lxix.13.2

L. Julius Vehilius

L. Julius Vehilius Gratus Julianus was an equestrian with a distinguished career. He rose to become prefect of the Praetorian Guard in Rome. Along the way he was appointed *procurator Augusti in command of a vexillation tempore belli [Britannici]*, 'at the time of the British war', though the word *Britannici* has been restored. As he was decorated for valour in the Parthian war by Antoninus Pius and Lucius Verus, and also for the German and

Sarmatian wars by Marcus Aurelius and Commodus, it may be assumed that the supposed war in Britain referred to is either that under Pius, *c.*154, or under Marcus Aurelius, *c.*163.

Sources: *SHA* (M. Aurelius) viii.7-8; *ILS* 1327 (*CIL* vi.31,856)

Gn. Julius Verus

Gnaeus Julius Verus was governor of Britain around 158, recorded on several inscriptions. The most intriguing is the slab from the Tyne at Newcastle which refers to reinforcements of *II Augusta*, *VI Victrix* and *XX Valeria Victrix* and the two German provinces. Whether the text is describing contributions from the legions being sent *to* Germany, or whether reinforcements were arriving *from* Germany, is unknown. Julius Verus had been governor of Germania Inferior so the reinforcements may have accompanied him.

If so, this has implications for interpreting events on the northern frontier. Julius Verus may have presided over the aftermath of a war implicit on *Britannia* coins of 154, perhaps leading to the abandonment of the Antonine Wall. Only the Birrens slab provides a point to fix Julius Verus' term. It carries details of Antoninus Pius' 21st tribunician power (December 157-December 158). Verus was certainly out of the post by 161 (*see* M. Statius Priscus) and possibly as early as 159. This means his term began in *c.*155-7.

Sources: *RIB* 283 (Brough-on-Noe), 1132 (Corbridge), 1322 (Newcastle), 2110 (Birrens); *Brit.* xxviii (1992), 463-4, no. 28 (diploma); *ILS* 1057 and 8974 (two parts of the same slab)

C. Junius Faustinus

Caius Junius Faustinus Placidus Postumianus is a possible early-third-century governor of Britain (*Superior?*) and a former *comes* of Septimius Severus. He is untestified in Britain itself.

Source: *CIL* viii.597 (see Birley 1979, p. 37)

D. Junius Juvenalis

This man, who may be the Roman poet Juvenal, spent part of his career as tribune of *cohors I Delmatarum* in Britain. The stone recording the man's name is from *Aquinum*, Juvenal's home town. His career ran from the end of the reign of Domitian right on into Hadrian's time. The unit is testified in Britain from 122 and by 138-61 was at Maryport. Juvenal himself makes a passing reference to Britain's short nights and the 'conquest' of the Orkneys. If the identification with the tribune of *cohors I Delmatarum* is correct this is one of the very few surviving personal comments on the experience of life in Britain.

Source: *ILS* 2926 (Aquinum); Juvenal (*Satires*) ii.161 (short British nights and Orkneys), iii.319 (*Aquinum*)

L. Junius Victorinus Flavius Caelianus

This man was legate of *VI Victrix* and recorded his exploits north of Hadrian's Wall on an altar found at Kirksteads, near Kirkandrews upon Eden. He can be inferred to have gone on to be legate of Germania Superior from a dedication at Stockstadt to Jupiter Optimus Maximus and his personal Genius by a member of the governor's staff, the *beneficiarius consularis* G. Secionius Senilis. Date is uncertain, but should precede the division of Britain, therefore *c.*122-212.

Source: *RIB* 2034 (Kirksteads); *RIB95*, 794, note to 2034; *CIL* xiii.6638 (Stockstadt)

Justinianus
One of the very few named officials from later Roman Britain, Justinianus is named as *p(rae)p(ositus)* in charge of construction works at Ravenscar in an exceptional instance of late-Romano-British epigraphy. The date is uncertain but the archaeology of the site suggests fourth century.

Source: *RIB* 721 (Ravenscar)

Q. Lollius Urbicus
Quintus Lollius Urbicus was governor of Britain between about 138-42. The *SHA* states that Lollius Urbicus subdued and repelled the Britons, and built a turf wall. This is an exceptional instance of a man and events testified in literary and epigraphic sources. However, Urbicus is mentioned on few of the building stones from the Antonine Wall, most of which provide dates no more precise than 139-61 and give no details of the governor. It cannot therefore be automatically assumed that the construction of the new frontier was confined to his term.

Sources: *SHA* (Antoninus Pius) v.4; *RIB* 1147, 1148 (probably) (Corbridge), 1276 (High Rochester), 2191, 2192 (Balmuildy); *CIL* viii.7606

Lupicinus
In 360 Lupicinus was *magister armorum*, or commander-in-chief, under Julian (360-3). He was sent to resolve a breakdown of the peace between the Romano-British and the Scots and Picts. He sailed from Boulogne to Richborough and then marched to London. Lupicinus was said to be arrogant and supercilious. The accounts add nothing about what he did. He was soon recalled and arrested to prevent him siding with Constantius II against Julian.

Sources: Ammianus xx.1.1-3, 4.3, 4.6, 4.9, 9.9

Q. Lusius Sabinianus
Quintus Lusius Sabinianus names himself as *proc(urator) Aug(usti)* on two dedications found at Inveresk, near Edinburgh. One, now lost, was to Apollo Grannus. The other confirms Sabinianus' title. The location suggests that his term must have been during the time the Antonine Wall was held, about 139-60.

Sources: *RIB* 2132; *Brit.* viii (1977), 433, no. 30 (Inveresk)

Maecilius Fuscus

Maecilius Fuscus is named as *leg(atus) Aug(usti)* on a slab from Lanchester recording building work by *coh(ors) I L(ingonum) Gor(dianae)*, attributable to the reign of Gordian III (238-44). Fuscus presumably governed *Britannia Inferior*.

Source: *RIB* 1092 (Lanchester) (**37**)

M. Maenius Agrippa

Marcus Maenius Agrippa came from Camerinum in Italy. Most of his career was spent in Britain during the reign of Hadrian. He commanded the following units in Britain in this order, having been selected by Hadrian to participate in an expedition (of uncertain date) to Britain. He rose finally to be the province's procurator:

prefect of *cohors II Flavia Brittonum equitata*
tribune of *cohors I Hispanorum* (at Maryport, *RIB* 823)
prefect of *ala Gallorum et Pannoniorun catafractata*
prefect of *classis Britannica*
procurator of *provinciae Britanniae*

Sources: *RIB* 823 (Maryport); *ILS* 2735 (Camerinum; see also Jarrett 1976, 147-8)

Magnentius

Usurper in the West from 350-3 during the reign of Constantius II. In 350 Magnentius, an army commander under Constans and possibly of British descent, seized the West, exploiting Constans' decadence and contempt for his soldiers. Constans fled towards Spain but was murdered near the Pyrenees. In 351 Magnentius was defeated by Constantius II, leaving him only Gaul and Britain. In 353 he was defeated again and committed suicide. The revolt of Magnentius had repercussions for Britain. Constantius II sent **Paulus** to deal with supporters of Magnentius in the British garrison. The implication is that Magnentius' forces had been largely drawn from Britain and that he had enjoyed considerable support there.

Sources: Ammianus xiv.5.6-8

Magnus Maximus

Magnus Maximus, a Spaniard, was a military commander in Britain who had successfully campaigned against barbarians in the early 380s. His popularity led either to his troops proclaiming him emperor, or his own personal declaration of the fact (the sources vary), in 383. Maximus began a continental campaign, and was joined by more and more of Gratian's army. Gratian, the legitimate emperor, was killed by one of his own officers.

Much of Maximus' army was made up from the British garrison, and he may have returned briefly to engage the Picts and Scots in 384. In 388 Maximus was defeated and executed in Italy by Theodosius I who restored Valentinian II in the West.

Magnus Maximus makes an appearance in contemporary accounts because of his effect on mainstream events. Maximus used Britain as an exploitable resource, not as an

80 Slab found by the east gate at Birdoswald. It records work under the governor Modius Julius by
cohors I Aelia Dacorum and its tribune Cl(audius) Menander. The slab may have been
matched by another bearing the emperor's name. Modius Julius' dates are not known for certain
and theories depend on interpretations of a butchered and recut slab from Netherby (see text).
Width 0.96m. RIB *1914*

ideological, or actual, base. Despite this, Maximus was remembered fondly as a popular
hero. In Wales, historical lineages of Dark Age kingships were traced back to a Macsen
Wledig who may or may not have been Maximus.

The sixth-century chronicler Gildas castigated Maximus for robbing Britain of her
defences and exposing her to barbarian assaults from the Scots and Picts. He relates how
the Britons appealed to Rome for assistance which came in the form of a 'legion'.

Sources (all most easily found in Ireland 1986): Orosius (*Adversum Paganos*), vii.34.9-10; Zosimus
iv.35.2-6, 37.1-3, 37.10; Sozomenus (*Eccl. Hist.*) vii.13; Prosper Tiro (*Chronicon*) 1191; Gildas (*De
Excidio Britanniae*) xiv-xv

G. Manlius Valens

According to Dio, G. Manlius Valens was aged 89 in the year 96. He can thus be identified
as the Manlius Valens, said by Tacitus to have commanded a legion when **A. Didius
Gallus** became governor in 52. The legion (presumably *II Augusta*) had been defeated by
the Silures. By 69 he was still commanding a legion in Gaul.

Sources: Tacitus (*Annals*) xii.40.1, (*Histories*) i.64; Dio lxvii.14.5

Marius Valerianus

Governor of *Britannia Inferior* in 221 and 222, dates fixed by three dated inscriptions from Chesters (30 October 221), Netherby (222), and South Shields (222). All refer to the restoration of buildings or the provision of new facilities which suggests he may have presided over or instigated a phase of military renewal.

Sources: *RIB* 978 (Netherby), 1060 (South Shields), 1465 (Chesters)

M. Martian(n)ius Pulcher

This man's name says he was of senatorial rank *(v(ir) c(larissimus)* — the reading here is uncertain), and *leg(atus) Aug(ustorum)* on an altar recording the rebuilding of a temple of Isis in London (**65**). His exact status is a matter for debate thanks to damage to the inscription which cannot be precisely dated, though is thought to be third century. He was, presumably, governor of *Britannia Superior*.

Source: *Brit.* vii (1976), 378-9, no. 2

Martinus

Vicarius of Britain in 353 under Constantius II. Following the defeat of **Magnentius** that year **Paulus** was sent to Britain to weed out supporters. Martinus led the backlash against Paulus' vindictive tactics and attempted to assassinate him. He failed and committed suicide. He was considered to have been a wise and effective governor.

Sources: Ammianus xiv.5.6-8

Melania

Melania the Younger, a Christian heiress, was born in the late fourth century. In 404 she decided to dispose of her estates in Italy, Sicily, North Africa, Spain and (probably) Britain. Christian women were especially susceptible to being persuaded to do this by influential male Christian leaders. The information comes from a later 'Life' of Melania which traced her path to sainthood. Such accounts cannot be trusted for detail, especially the lands in Britain, but this is useful evidence for some villa estates in Britain belonging to absentee continental landlords. One of Melania's Italian estates was said to contain 62 villages, each with 400 inhabitants. Under imperial law all these people were tied to the estate and their jobs.

Source: *vita Melania* x

Metilius Bradua, see Atilius

P. Maecilius (or Metilius) Nepos

Named as the previous governor of Britain in the year 98, by which time T. Avidius Quietus had taken over, on a diploma found in Belgium. The diploma is incomplete and supplies only '... Nepos'. He may be the P. Maecilius Nepos who appears in the letters of

Pliny the Younger and is described as someone about to become governor 'of an important province' (*maximae provinciae*).

Source: *CIL* xvi.43 (diploma; see *RIB* II, fasc. I, table I); Pliny (*Letters*) iv.26.2

L. Minicius Natalis

Lucius Minicius Natalis Quadronius Verus was legate of *VI Victrix* under Hadrian and perhaps during the governorship of **S. Julius Severus**. His career stone is explicit in stating that he was *legatus Augusti* of *VI Victrix in Britannia*. He was wealthy, lived near Hadrian's estate at Tivoli and had enjoyed a triumphant athletic career as a charioteer.

Sources: *ILS* 1061

Modius Julius

Modius Julius was governor of (presumably) *Britannia Inferior* in the early third century, and normally stated to be around the year 219. The interpretation of the butchered and adulterated inscription from Netherby as including this man's name, that of Elagabalus, and an unprecedented form of the second consulship of Elagabalus (in 219) is rather optimistic. However, the names of Modius Julius and Elagabalus (or Caracalla) on this stone are not implausible. Moreover, considering that many governors of *Britannia Inferior* and their dates are known, there are few other times at when he could have been governor. See **T. Claudius Paulinus** and **Marius Valerianus** for other governorships of the reign. Modius Julius is, however, unequivocally named as governor on an undated inscription of early-third-century style from Birdoswald.

Sources: *RIB* 980 (Netherby), 1914 (Birdoswald) (**80**)

P. Mummius Sisenna and P. Mummius Sisenna Rutilianus

Someone called [...] Sisenna, identifiable as the P. Mummius Sisenna who was consul in 133, is named as governor of Britain on a diploma found at Wroxeter and dated 14 April 135. He had succeeded **S. Julius Severus**, known to have been moved to Judaea about 133-4. A similar name, P. Mummius Sisenna Rutilianus, son of P(ublius), is recorded on a career inscription as having been legate of *VI Victrix* prior to his own consulship in 146. As the latter makes no mention of a British governorship for which, in any case, he would not have been qualified until after 146, it seems only reasonable to suggest that they were father and son.

This is now accepted to have been the case, though it is quite clear that it cannot be absolutely certain. The situation may have prevailed, therefore, where the father was governor and his son a legionary legate under him. However unusual, this would not have been unprecedented.

No inscriptions or events can be attributed to the governorship though Sisenna may have presided some of the warfare which **Lollius Urbicus** was sent to suppress in or about 138.

Sources: *RIB* 2401.8 (*CIL* xvi.82; diploma); and Birley 1979, 37 and 173; *ILS* 1101 (legate of *VI Victrix*)

Q. Natalius Natalinus et Bodeni

This name appears on a fourth-century mosaic at Thruxton. In this respect he appears to be the only Romano-British villa owner or tenant who names himself for us. His citizen's name has been created from the root Natalis but included the phrase *et Bodeni*, which seems to indicate that he was also known as Bodenus, a name of Celtic origin. However, this word is in the genitive, 'of Bodenus' which presents a problem; perhaps it indicates his father's name, i.e. '(son) of Bodenus'.

Either way it seems likely that his family origins had been British but that he or his ancestors had adopted a Roman name as part of their integration into a romanized way of life.

The mosaic is displayed at the British Museum in London.

Source: *RIB* 2448.9

Nectaridus

Nectaridus is named by Ammianus as *comes maritimi tractus* ('count of the maritime area') in Britain in the year 367. He was killed. Name and title are otherwise untestified and it may be an alternative for *comes litoris Saxonici* ('count of the Saxon shore').

Sources: Ammianus xxvii.8.1

L. Neratius Marcellus

Governor of Britain between roughly 102-6 under Trajan. He is named as such on a diploma of 19 January 103. An inscription from his home town, *Saepinum*, mentions a governor of Britain, but the name is lost. He also appears in the letters of Pliny the Younger as the source of a post as military tribune, presumably in Britain. The diploma helps date the Vindolanda tablets because Marcellus appears to be mentioned on one of them, described as *Marcellum clarissimum consularem meum*, 'my governor [...] Marcellus, that distinguished man'. Like the record in Pliny, Marcellus is here also seen as a potential source of favourable positions. The writer, **Flavius Cerialis** is seeking help from the addressee, Crispinus, to intercede with the governor.

Sources: *RIB* 2401.1 (diploma, *CIL* xvi.98; the same text also appears at *ILS* 2001, *CIL* vii.1193); Pliny, Letters, iii.8.1; *ILS* 1032 (Saepinum); *Tab. Vindol.* II.225 (see Bowman 1994, 121, no. 15) (**78**)

Nonius Philippus

Nonius Philippus is named as *leg(atus) Aug(usti)* on a dedication to Jupiter Optimus Maximus by *ala Augusta* at Old Carlisle. Conveniently, the stone carries the consuls for the year, making it datable to 242 under Gordian III. Nonius Philippus must have been governor of *Britannia Inferior*. **Egnatius Lucilianus** and **Maecilius Fuscus** are both also testified as governors in this reign on the less specific evidence of the unit title at Lanchester.

Sources: *RIB* 897 (Old Carlisle)

M. Oclatinius Adventus

Proc(urator) Aug(ustorum) under **Alfenus Senecio**, governor during the reign of Septimius Severus between *c.*205-8. Dio describes Oclatinius Adventus as a man who had risen from the soldiery, despite being illiterate. As such, his elevated status was a presage for the future.

Sources: *RIB* 1234 (Risingham), *RIB* 1462 (Chesters); Dio lxxviii.14.1; see also Rankov 1987

Octavius Sabinus

Named as *praeses* (governor) and *v(ir) c(larissimus)* (of senatorial rank) on a slab from Lancaster recording building work by *ala Sebussiana* (*ala Gallorum Sebosiana*). The text mentions two Gallic Empire consuls, Censor and Lepidus, attributed to the period 262-6. This allows his governorship, presumably of *Britannia Inferior*, to be fixed in that period and the restoration of the titles of Postumus (259-68) to the rest of the inscription including the unit's name.

Source: *RIB* 605 (Lancaster)

P. Ostorius Scapula

Publius Ostorius Scapula was governor in Britain between 47-52. On arrival he was immediately faced with a revolt by the (then) client tribe of the Iceni. With this problem suppressed he moved north-west to split British resistance in the west and north, relying on support from **Cartimandua** and her kingdom of the Brigantes in the north. His principal campaign was in Wales against **Caratacus**. Caratacus was defeated but escaped and fled to Cartimandua who handed him over to the Romans. Despite this the Welsh tribes, mainly the Silures, maintained their opposition and in 52 Ostorius died, it was said, of exhaustion.

Sources: Tacitus (*Agricola*) xiv; (*Annals*) xii.31-39

Gn. Papirius Aelianus

Governor of Britain at some point in the mid-140s, named on a diploma from Chesters dated between 10 December 145 and 9 December 146. Unlike his predecessor **Lollius Urbicus** he is untestified on any inscriptions and nothing of note is known about him.

Sources: *RIB* 2401.10 (*CIL* xvi.93)

L. Papius Pacatianus

Vicar of Britain on 20 November 319 under Constantine I.

Source: *Cod. Theod.* xi.7.2

Paulus

Notarius (imperial secretary) to Constantius II. In 353, following the defeat of **Magnentius**, Paulus was sent to Britain to flush out supporters of Magnentius. Paulus initiated a vicious pogrom by producing trumped-up charges. **Martinus**, the governor, was powerless to stop him and even tried to assassinate him. Paulus' activities may have ruined many landowners though it is not possible to state in any one instance that a villa was abandoned for this reason.

Source: Ammianus xiv.5.6-8

Pelagius
Leader of a Christian heresy that took root in the late fourth century and occasioned a crisis which lasted into the fifth. Bede describes it beginning in the year 394, and Pelagius himself arrived in Rome between 399-401. Pelagius believed that human beings were responsible for their own morality, and that human perfection was an attainable and unavoidable goal for Christians. Pelagius was, by all accounts, from Britain (or Ireland) even though much of his teaching and activity was carried out on the continent. Major church leaders like Augustine and Jerome attacked Pelagius with their pens adding the customary personal abuse to theological objections.

Sources: Augustine (*Letters*) 50.3-5 (Loeb edition); Bede (*Hist. Eccl.*) i.10, 17, 21

Pertinax
Publius Helvius Pertinax was sent to Britain in *c.*185 to resolve problems of discipline (*see* Q. Aurelius Polus Terentianus). He dealt ruthlessly with mutinies, but his strict disciplinarian approach earned him hostility from the British legions. He asked to be returned to Rome where the same habit cost him his life in 193 when he was made Emperor following the murder of Commodus. He had reigned just 86 days.

Sources: *SHA* (Pertinax) iii.5-10

Q. Petillius Cerialis
Quintus Petillius Cerialis Caesius Rufus, governor in Britain between 71-4, was earlier legate of *IX Hispana* during the Revolt of **Boudica** in 60-1. Leading his cavalry from the legionary base or bases in the East Midlands to confront the menace he hopelessly underestimated the scale of the rebellion and was routed. Tacitus said he was better at hating his enemies than defending himself against them.

Subsequently he found fame in the campaign against the revolt of Civilis in 70 prior to his appointment as governor of Britain apparently in 71 to succeed the Vitellian supporter **Vettius Bolanus**. His dates as governor are provided by the sequence listed by Tacitus and the consulships he held in 70 and 74; the governorship must lie between them. Petillius Cerialis may or may not have brought the newly-raised *II Adiutrix* with him. Inferences drawn from tombstones at Lincoln stating service life of legionaries and its known date of activation in about 69, suggest it was there by 76 at least.

Petillius Cerialis, Tacitus said, proceeded to act where Vettius Bolanus had failed. He marched into Brigantian territory, presumably against Venutius (see Cartimandua), and succeeded in annexing much of the region.

Due to his earlier career with *IX Hispana* it has been assumed that the legion formed the backbone of Petillius Cerialis' campaign. This is not testified and is merely a reasonable inference. The foundation of York as a fortress for *IX Hispana* is attributed to this governorship but there is no epigraphic or literary confirmation of this.

Birley (1973, 181) has suggested that this man and the legate Caesius Nasica were brothers.

Sources: Tacitus (*Annals*) xiv.32 (Boudica), (*Histories*) iv.68, 71, v.16 (against Civilis, Cerialis' character, and *II Adiutrix*), (*Agricola*) xvii (against Brigantes); *see II Adiutrix* in Chapter 2; *CIL* xvi.20 for his full name; Birley (1973), provides a detailed analysis of his career and family

P. Petronius Turpilianus

Publius Petronius Turpilianus was governor of Britain between 61 and 63. He succeeded **Suetonius Paullinus**, removed on the pretext that he had lost a few ships, and thus was charged with reconstructing Britain after the Boudican Revolt. Tacitus states that his term began shortly after serving his consulship, attested in the first half of 61. Tacitus derided him for indulging in laziness and passing this off as peace though in reality a policy of aggressive suppression would have been suicidal for the Roman authorities. He will have worked closely with **Classicianus**, the new procurator.

There is a problem in interpreting Tacitus with respect to dates. At *Annals* xiv.29 he states that the Boudican Revolt broke out in the year of Turpilianus' consulship, which was 61. At xiv.39 he describes Turpilianus' becoming governor of Britain, having just finished as consul. This seems not enough time to allow for all the events of the Boudican Revolt and its aftermath. It is now assumed that Tacitus was in error and that the Revolt started in 60 (see Frere 1987, 79, n. 37).

Sources: Tacitus (*Agricola*) xvi, (*Annals*) xiv.29, 39

Polyclitus

Polyclitus, an imperial freedman, was sent to Britain in the aftermath of the Boudican Revolt to settle the differences between the governor, **Suetonius Paullinus** and the new procurator, **Classicianus**, and also to reduce any further temptations to rebellion. The Britons were fascinated that an ex-slave exercised such power over a governor and his army.

Source: Tacitus (*Annals*) xiv.39

A. Platorius Nepos

Aulus Platorius Nepos was *legat(us) Aug(usti) pro praet(ore) provinc(iae) Britannia* stated on his career inscription from Aquilea. His term in Britain was between approximately 122 and 126. A number of inscriptions from Hadrian's Wall name him as governor in the reign of Hadrian. He was clearly charged with operating the primary construction of Hadrian's Wall. Nepos was a personal friend of Hadrian and had served as joint consul with him in 119. Later they fell out. Although mentioned in *SHA* (Hadrian) no connection with Britain is included, a good example of the inadequacy of some literary sources.

Precise dates are provided by two diplomas which name him as governor of Britain on 17 July 122 and 15(?) September 124.

Sources: *ILS* 1052 (Aquilea); *CIL* xvi.69 (*RIB* II, fasc. I, Table I, diploma of 122); *RIB* 2401.6 (*CIL* xvi.70, diploma of 124); *RIB* 1051 (Jarrow), 1340 (Benwell) (**21**), 1427 (Haltonchesters), 1634 (Hadrian's Wall, mc 37), 1637, 1638 (Hadrian's Wall, near mc 38) (**12**), 1666 (Hadrian's Wall, mc 42), 1935 (Hadrian's Wall, near TW mc 50); *SHA* (Hadrian) iv.2, xv.2, xxiii.4; that *RIB* 995 from Bewcastle also names him is argued convincingly by Tomlin in *Brit.* xxix (1999), 443, (a), and note 73

A. Plautius

Aulus Plautius is known only from several literary sources as the commander of the Claudian invasion force in 43 and remained as governor until 47. He thus presided over the movement of forces across southern Britain to take Camulodunum, fighting a major river battle along the way, the arrival of Claudius, and the subsequent fanning out of legions across Britain.

Sources: Dio lx.19-22; Suetonius (Claudius) xxiv, (Vespasian) iv.1; Tacitus (*Agricola*) xiv.1

Poenius Postumius

Praefectus castrorum of *II Augusta*, probably then based at Exeter or dispersed amongst vexillation fortesses in the area, in 60-61. He refused to respond to **Suetonius Paullinus'** orders to confront the Boudican Revolt. This deprived the legion of the chance to earn battle honours and was followed by his suicide. His dithering may have been due to the legion being away or otherwise indisposed (hence no reference to a legate), and that he was so intimidated by the prospects of engaging the revolt that he was prepared to disobey orders.

Sources: Tacitus (*Annals*) xiv.37

Q. Pompeius Falco

Quintus Pompeius Falco was governor of Britain around 118-22. He must have succeeded **M. Atilius Metilius Bradua** and is named as predecessor to **A. Platorius Nepos** on a diploma of 17 July 122 and confirmed as governor of Britain under Hadrian in a career inscription from Tarracina which carries his remarkable full name of Quintus Roscius Sex(ti) F(ilius) Quir[..] Coelius Murena Silius Decianus Vibullius Pius Julius Eurycles Herculanus Pompeius Falco.

As Falco is never named on any surviving inscription in Britain it may be assumed that he therefore played no significant part in the inception and construction of Hadrian's Wall.

Sources: *CIL* xvi.69 (*see RIB* II, fasc. I, Table I, diploma of 122); *ILS* 1035 (Tarracina)

Cn. Pompeius Homullus

Cnaeus Pompeius Homullus Aelius Gracilis Cassianus Longinus rose to be *proc(urator) Aug(usti) provinciae Brittaniae* during a long career which began in the army. He served as *primus pilus* in both *II Augusta* and *X Fretensis*, the former presumably after it arrived in Britain. Prior to his procuratorship he served in the Rome garrison as a tribune and was decorated in an unspecified war. After Britain he went on to be procurator in the twin provinces of Lugdunum and Aquitania. Unfortunately there is no means of accurately dating his time in Britain. Birley (1979, 50), suggests the war he was decorated in was under Domitian and thus attributes his period as procurator to the late 80s or 90s; however, it could equally well have been significantly later.

Sources: *ILS* 1385

T. Pomponius Mamilianus

Titus Pomponius Mamilianus Rufus Antistianus Funisulanus Vettonianus was a legionary legate, presumably of *XX*(?). His position is recorded on an undated altar at Chester, dedicated to Fortuna Redux, Aesculapius, and Salus by his freedmen and slaves. An approximate date comes from Pliny the Younger who had a friend called Mamilianus *turba castrensium negotiorum*, 'beset with military affairs', in the year 100 and employs a metaphor based on Mamilianus' legionary standards, *aquilas*. However, another man with a similar name (only differing in the lack of Mamilianus) was consul in 120.

Sources: *RIB* 445 (*see RIB* 1879 (Birdoswald) for a possible descendant); Pliny (*Letters*) ix.25

M. Pontius Laelianus

Marcus Pontius Laelianus Larcius was military tribune with *VI Victrix* when it was transferred from Germany to Britain, stated on the stone recording his career. This is thought normally to have occurred in the early part of Hadrian's reign when *VI Victrix* turns up building Hadrian's Wall. The legion probably accompanied the new governor, **A. Platorius Nepos**, compatible with Pontius Laelianus' consulship in 144.

Sources: *ILS* 1094, with a fuller version on *ILS* 1100 (the name is lost on the latter but enough detail survives to show that it must be the same man)

T. Pontius Sabinus

Primus pilus of *III Augusta*, sent to Britain in command of vexillations of *VII Gemina*, *VIII Augusta*, and *XXII Primigenia* at some unspecified date apparently in Hadrian's reign. See also **M. Maenius Agrippa**.

Sources: *ILS* 2726B

Prasutagus

King of the Iceni, and husband of **Boudica**, during the early part of the Roman conquest. He made Nero the joint beneficiary of his will with his daughters in the hope that this would guarantee the security of the Iceni. The outcome following his death in *c*.59-60 was quite the opposite. *See* **Boudica** above for references.

Priscus

Only known from Dio to have been a legionary legate in Britain in about 182-5. See **Q. Aurelius Polus Terentianus**.

Restitutus

Named as *ex civitate Londiniensium episcopus*, 'bishop from the civitas of Londinium' at the Council of Arles in 314 and listed in the *Acta*.

Source: *PNRB* 49-50

M. Roscius Coelius

Legate of *XX* in 69. Tacitus describes the intense personal animosity between him and the governor **Trebellius Maximus**, and how the circumstances of civil war allowed this explosive relationship to break free. Only the description in the *Histories* names him. Roscius was relieved of his command for having been slow to show allegiance to **Vespasian** and was succeeded by **Agricola**.

Sources: Tacitus (*Agricola*) xvi.3-4, (*Histories*) i.60

C. Sabucius Major Caecilianus

Leg(atus) iurid(icus) prov(inciae) Britanniae, proclaimed on his career inscription. His tenure in the post is said to have occurred during the 170s, an inference the basis of which is not immediately evident from the text of his inscription (see Birley 1979, 48).

Source: *ILS* 1123 (and also 1123a, which may provide a basis for the late-second-century date)

P. Sallienius Thalamus

Praef(ectus) of *II Augusta* at Caerleon at some point during the reign of **Septimius Severus** between 198-209, which presumably means he was *praefectus castrorum*, then serving in command of the legionary base in the absence of the legate. The second of two stones from Caerleon which name him carries the titles of Septimius Severus and **Caracalla** as Augusti and **Geta** as Caesar, thus fixing the period.

Sources: *RIB* 324, 326 (Caerleon)

Sallustius Lucullus

Britanniae legatum ('governor of Britain') under Domitian and executed by the paranoid emperor for being stupid enough to design a new spear which he named the *Lucullean* after himself. It can only assumed that he was governor at some point between roughly 84 and 94. An inscription naming him, purportedly found in Chichester in the mid-seventeenth century and now lost, is believed to have been a fake (*RIB* 2334). However, Chichester is one of the few sources of high-quality first-century inscriptions in Britain and the text is convincing enough; unfortunately, no illustration has survived. Even so, it provides no assistance with dating.

Sources: Suetonius (*Domitian*) x.3

C. Salvius Liberalis

Caius Salvius Liberalis Nonius Bassus was *legatus iuridicus* of Britain. He may have been appointed around the beginning of the reign of Titus. His career inscription records that he served in his posts under both the deified Vespasian and Titus (69-81).

Sources: *ILS* 1011

P. (or L.) Septimius Geta (ii) See Geta.

Septimius Severus (81)

Lucius Septimius Severus was born in 146 at Leptis Magna in north Africa. His military career was highly successful and by 192 he was governor of Upper Pannonia. After the murder of Commodus, Severus sided with **Pertinax** but the latter's assassination precipitated a civil war. Severus was a willing participant in the race for the purple. By 197 he had defeated his last rival, **Clodius Albinus**, governor of Britain. The civil war had provided opportunities for barbarian attacks on the northern frontier in Britain, problems which were passed to **Virius Lupus** and **L. Alfenus Senecio** to sort out. Lupus was obliged to bribe barbarians for peace due to Severus being engaged in warfare in the east.

Herodian states that having settled affairs in Britain Severus divided Britain into two separate commands, later known as *Britannia Superior* and *Britannia Inferior*. It is not clear when this came into force but the purpose was evidently to prevent a repeat performance of Clodius Albinus' bid for power. The first specific reference to one of the new names is on a slab from Vindolanda of 222-3. It is normally assumed that the new arrangements were activated by 216 at the latest.

Rome provided opportunities for Severus' sons **Caracalla** and **Geta** to indulge in wasteful and decadent pastimes. Severus brought them to Britain to harden them up in a frontier war. The campaign began in 208 and lasted until 211-12.

The extensive rebuilding of Hadrian's Wall has forever complicated the archaeology of the structure and even led to the belief in antiquity that he had been responsible for its original erection. A vast series of coins of all denominations commemorated the campaign with the legend *Victoriae Brittanicae*, struck in the names of Severus and his sons.

However, the campaign shattered the emperor. He died in York in 211. Caracalla abandoned the campaign shortly afterwards, giving up forts and territory, and returned to Rome where he murdered his brother and ruled alone.

Sources: Dio lxxiii.14.3, 15.1-2, lxxv.4.1, 6-7 (the civil war), lxxv.5.4 (Lupus buys peace), lxxvi.11.1, 13, 15.1-2 (the British campaign); Herodian ii.15.1-5, iii.5.2-8 (the civil war), iii.8.2 (the division of Britain), iii.14.1-10, 15.1-3 (the British campaign); *SHA* (Severus) x.1-2; Eutropius viii.19.1 (Severus and the Wall); *RIB* 1706 (Vindolanda)

L. Septimius [...]

Pr(aeses) (governor) of *Britannia* Prima after the reorganization of Britain into four provinces in or around 296. He dedicated a column to Jupiter in Cirencester. He was therefore a pagan or felt it was expedient to appeal to a pagan enclave in the town. Although this might make the dedication likely to belong to the period 296-313 or 360-3

81 Septimius Severus (193-211), victor of the civil war after the death of Commodus. Severus' British campaign did not begin until 208 but the preceding three or four years saw a considerable amount of building work, much performed during the governorship of Lucius Alfenus Senecio between 205-8

(during the reign of Julian the Apostate), it is also true that Cirencester is the most significant city of Roman Britain for which there is no documentary or archaeological evidence of a church of Roman date. In the fourth century it was not unusual for some cities to maintain a completely pagan character. Given this, the inscription cannot be tightly dated at all and could belong to any time in the fourth century. (**26**)

Source: *RIB* 103 (Cirencester)

Severus

In 367, during the barbarian conspiracy, Severus was *comes domesticorum* ('count of the household troops'). Severus was despatched to Britain by Valentinian I when news of the disaster reached him. However, he was soon recalled and replaced by one Jovinus who in 366 was *comes equitum* ('count of the cavalry'). Jovinus established that a bigger army was needed and command passed to **Theodosius**.

Sources: Ammianus xxvii.2.1, 8.2

P. Sextianus [....]

Prefect of *ala Augusta* at Carlisle where he commemorated the unit's success over a band of barbarians which involved slaughtering the latter. The stone, a decorative window or niche, seems to date to about 180-92, in which case the event recorded might have occurred during the war which ended in 184.

Source: *RIB* 946 (Carlisle)

M. Statius Crispus

Governor of Britain around 161. He is only known from an inscription which helpfully states that his career began under Hadrian when he took part in the campaign to suppress a Jewish rebellion. After holding a consulship in 159 he rose to the governorship of Britain and then Cappadocia during a joint emperorship. This first occurred between 161-9 when Marcus Aurelius ruled with Lucius Verus. **S. Calpurnius Agricola** is also known to have governed Britain in this period, but there are difficulties with his precise dates. Statius Crispus was probably in Britain around 160/1-3. His series of prestige military appointments show that he must have been sent to Britain because circumstances there merited his skills. But nothing more detailed is known about his time in Britain.

Source: *ILS* 1092 (Rome)

Stilicho

In 395 Theodosius I died. The Empire was divided between his sons Arcadius, who took the East, and Honorius, then only twelve years old, in the West. Real power lay with a Vandal general called Flavius Stilicho, *magister militum* ('master of soldiers'). Stilicho's contribution to Britain is only described in a panegyric by Claudian of the year 400 which refers to his efforts to protect her from Scots, Picts, and Saxons. A possible link is the invasion described by Gildas which followed the return home of the 'legion' sent after the fall of Maximus in 388. But Gildas is unreliable and Claudian's poem may be no more than a routine trotting out of standard achievements, so there is little point in trying to fabricate a detailed narrative. Claudian also makes a more general comment about the perception of 'wild Britain' as the home of fierce and terrible people.

Stilicho wanted to increase the territories controlled by the Western Empire but was unwilling to deal decisively with the Visigoths. This gave the Visigoths the idea that they might succeed in their territorial ambitions in 401, leading to yet further withdrawals of the British garrison to prop up Stilicho's army in 402. According to Claudian this involved 'the legion that had been left to guard Britain', perhaps the one described by Gildas. Not surprisingly, this sustained reduction of the British garrison led to further attempts at usurpation (see **Constantine III**).

Sources: Claudian (*in Eutropium*) i.391-3, (*de consulatu Stilichonis*) ii.247-55; Gildas (*de Excidio Britanniae*) xvi-xvii

G. Suetonius Paullinus

In office between *c.*58-61, Gaius Suetonius Paullinus is the most notorious governor of Roman Britain. Despatched to pick up the pieces after **Quintus Veranius**' premature death in office, he embarked on a campaign against the Silures, followed by an advance on the Druid stronghold and psychological powerbase in Anglesey in 60. In the middle of this successful holocaust he learned that **Boudica** had risen in East Anglia and begun a violently destructive march against the principal towns of the south-east. She had been provoked by her treatment following the death of her husband, Prasutagus and found support amongst the Iceni and Trinovantes who profoundly resented the oppressive and exploitative Roman regime, including the calling in of loans, for example by the procurator **Decianus Catus**. *IX Hispana* was also decimated and nearly cost the life of the legate **Petillius Cerialis**.

Although Suetonius raced back he lacked manpower and was forced to leave Colchester, London, and Verulamium to their fates. Suetonius fell back and waited for the infantry to catch up. In the ensuing battle the Boudican Revolt was comprehensively quashed.

The garrison of Britain was reinforced and forts built across East Anglia to clamp the eastern tribes with an iron hand. Suetonius Paullinus quarrelled with the more conciliatory new procurator, **Classicianus**. An imperial freedman, Polyclitus, was sent to Britain to sort out the argument. Eventually Paullinus was returned to Rome on the pretext of having lost a few ships and was replaced by **Petronius Turpilianus**.

Sources: Dio lxii.7-8; Tacitus (*Agricola*) v, xiv-xv, (*Annals*) xiv.29-39

Theodosius

Flavius Theodosius, *comes*, was chosen to lead the force to Britain in 367 sent to defeat the 'barbarian conspiracy'. Enjoying a substantial military reputation he sailed to Richborough and waited for his main forces of Batavians, Herulians, Jovians and Victores to catch up. Then he marched to London where he dispersed his troops who, being fresh and presumably largely mounted, apprehended bands of barbarians slowed down by booty. Ammianus does not refer to any other parts of Britain, or cities by name, which suggests that Theodosius was mainly concerned with the south-east (corresponding to the province of *Maxima Caesariensis*).

Loot was returned to its owners, and prisoners were released. Theodosius withdrew to London, received the usual ovation, and then set about repairing the province. Using intelligence gathering he realized the barbarians were too coordinated to be defeated by a single battle; also, provincial disruption was evident from the large numbers of army deserters. Theodosius recalled them by issuing pardons. He then asked that **Civilis**, an irritable, but just, man, be installed as Vicar of the Britons, assisted by **Dulcitius** as Duke.

Theodosius also 'restored' (*restituit*) towns and forts though no archaeology of the period has been tied to this event. Some late-Roman defensive features at towns, such as London's bastions, may be his work. But there is no perceptible 'destruction' level which can be associated with 367.

'Restoration' may have just meant restoring systems and government (see *Valentia* in Chapter 3). Theodosius was also faced by treacherous frontier scouts called the Areani (or Arcani). Established under Constans to patrol border country and spy on barbarians they had, allegedly, been bribed to tell the barbarians about Roman troop movements. Theodosius ejected them from their bases.

Theodosius was described by Ammianus as the returning hero when he was recalled in 369. Yet Ammianus also describes other events in Britain which show that his popularity was far from universal. A Pannonian called Valentinus, exiled to Britain because of some unmentioned crime, started to foment opposition to Theodosius. He made overtures to the army and to other exiles. Theodosius used an effective intelligence operation to apprehend Valentinus.

Following his British posting Theodosius was promoted to commander of the imperial cavalry. By 378 his son was emperor as Theodosius I.

Sources: Ammianus xxvii.8, xxviii.3

Titus

Son of **Vespasian** and emperor 79-81. Titus served as *tribunus laticlavius* in Britain and Germany. This post was normally held just before the age of 25 and as he was born in 41 this must have occurred towards the latter part of Nero's reign just prior to his service in the Jewish War of 67 with his father.

It is not known which legion Titus served with, though given his father's career *II Augusta* is possible. What is particularly interesting is that Suetonius states his personal popularity was such that a large number of statues and busts of him were erected in Britain and Germany. The archaeological record has produced none of these at all, the closest being one of the possible readings of the Verulamium forum inscription. He presided over part of **Agricola**'s campaigns.

Source: Suetonius (*Titus*) iv.1

Togidubnus

Tacitus says that *quaedam civitates*, 'certain cantonal areas', were given to a king called Cogidubnus or Cogidumnus. The name is now recognized to be a mistranscription of a Celtic form which should start with T. Togidubnus, or Togidumnus, evidently a quisling by any other name, 'has remained faithful continuously to our time' (*ad nostram usque memoriam fidissimus mansit*), a cryptic statement which could mean the time Tacitus was writing or a time he could recall.

Either way Togidubnus was alive in the late first century. This is difficult to reconcile with the context in Tacitus where it seems to be clear that the granting of lands had taken place in or around the year 50. However, if he was a young, impressionable, and easily-bought 20-year-old in the year 50 (and Tacitus says he was exploited as one of the kings used as *instrumenta servitutis*, ('tools of enslavement') then it is quite possible Togidubnus was still alive 50 years later.

Happily, Togidubnus makes an appearance on an inscription from Chichester. He acquired some of Claudius' names and is said to have called himself Tiberius Claudius Togidubnus. Strictly speaking the stone is incomplete: TI for Tiberius is missing and only GIDUBNI survives of his main name.

The same problem afflicts his title. Long ago the inscription was read and restored to create the title *r(egis) le[gat(us) Au]g(usti) in Brit(annia)* ('King, and imperial legate in Britain'). It has since been suggested that a correct reading is *re[g(is) ma]gn(i)*, or 'Great King'. The latter fits better and accords with Tacitus, though as ever there cannot be certainty.

The stone records the dedication of a temple to Neptune and Minerva by a local guild of smiths but is undated. On the assumption that this is the man mentioned by Tacitus, and also the restored title which would not have endured after his lifetime, it can be assumed this belongs to the period c.50-100. It serves to show how parts of Britain were ruled as client states, a convenient form of subsidiary government which left conquered areas in a state of transition between independence and absorption into the Empire.

There is no demonstrable connection with the well-known late-first-century house at Fishbourne, near Chichester. That it was Togidubnus' residence and headquarters is a reasonable inference but it remains no more than that. It is equally possible, and perhaps more likely, that it was a home for the provincial governor. But this too is entirely unsubstantiated.

Sources: Tacitus (*Agricola*) xiv; *RIB* 91 (Chichester); Bogaers 1979

Togodumnus
Son of **Cunobelinus**. See **Caratacus** and **Claudius** above.

M. Trebellius Maximus
This governor is known only from Tacitus. He succeeded **Petronius Turpilianus** in about 63. Tacitus thought him ineffectual and handicapped by greed, meanness, and a lack of military experience. This is probably Tacitus seeking to elevate the achievements of Agricola, his father-in-law, though he repeated the allegations in the *Histories*. But there may be some truth because Tacitus adds that the army mutinied (led by **Roscius Coelius**, legate of *XX*) and forced Trebellius Maximus into hiding.

In the *Histories* Tacitus says Trebellius Maximus fled to join Vitellius in the civil war, leaving Britain without a governor. Eventually Vitellius despatched **Vettius Bolanus** to succeed him. In the *Agricola* Tacitus omits any mention of Trebellius Maximus fleeing and says he and the British garrison eventually negotiated an arrangement in which they let him live and they did as they pleased.

Trebellius Maximus had a relatively long period in the governorship between 63-9, which seems odd given his failings. But the background is the deterioration in imperial power during the last four years of Nero's rule and his descent into vice, followed by the civil wars of 68-9 which may have made his replacement impossible.

Sources: Tacitus (*Agricola*) xvi.3-4, (*Histories*) i.60.2, ii.65.2

L. Trebius Germanus

[Lucius?] Trebius Germanus was governor of Britain on 20 August 127, named on a diploma owned by Itaxa, soldier in *cohors II Lingonum*, which surfaced in 1997. He is otherwise unknown in Britain but he probably succeeded **Aulus Platorius Nepos** in or around 124-6. A man called L. Trebius Germanus was consul with C. Calpurnius Flaccus, recorded on a tombstone from Rome. The latter may be the otherwise-unknown friend of Pliny the Younger's which would make this Trebius Germanus either the governor of Britain or his father. This pair of consuls is otherwise unknown but the association with Pliny the Younger is compatible with a Hadrianic date for Germanus' governorship.

Source: M. Roxan (pers. comm.); *ILS* 7912; Pliny (*Letters*) v.2

A. Triarius Rufinus See Q. Aradius Rufinus above

M. Ulpius Januarius

Aedile of the vicus of *Petuaria* (Brough-on-Humber? — there is some doubt about the identification of the name with the find-spot) during the reign of Antoninus Pius. The inscription which records his name commemorates his gift of a new stage at his own expense. The damage to the stone means that it could at best date between 140 and 161, not 140-1 as claimed by *RIB*. The stone is exceptionally interesting because Ulpius Januarius was a minor official in a minor town and yet he is one of only a handful of private individuals to have recorded their civic munificence on an inscription in Britain. Either he was exceptional in providing such private funds, or he was exceptional in recording it, or his stone's survival is exceptional and misleading in this respect.

Sources: *RIB* 707 (**40**)

Ulpius Marcellus

Testified as governor on a diploma of 178, and leading the Roman army in a British war of about 184 under Commodus by Dio. He also appears on an inscription from Chesters recording *aqua adducta*, 'the bringing of water' by *ala II Asturum* during his governorship. He thus served under Marcus Aurelius (161-80), and Commodus (180-96), and during their period of joint rule (177-80) explaining an inscription from Benwell where he is named as serving under unspecified joint emperors.

Prior to the discovery of the diploma of 178 such a long tenure was thought impossible. Therefore, it was suggested Dio's Marcellus and the Marcellus of the inscriptions were two different men. A second Marcellus was thus postulated, and assigned to 211-12 in the joint reign of Caracalla and Geta (governors of the joint rule of Severus and Caracalla being generally accounted for). The residence of the Asturians and the building of the aqueduct were thus also assigned to that period. The theory was widely accepted without question, but is now discounted.

Dio describes him as incorruptible and frugal but given to arrogance. He was, however, more interested in Marcellus' ability to do without sleep and his reliance on special bread.

Sources: Dio, lxxiii.8.1-2; diploma 23 March 178 (*RMD* 184, via M. Roxan); *RIB* 1329 (Benwell, and see *RIB*, 1995, p. 783 note for *RIB* 1329), 1463-4 (Chesters) (**82**); *JRS* xlvii (1957), 229, no. 14 (Chesters) (**23**); Birley 1981 (for Ulpius Marcellus i and ii); Frere 1987 (e.g. 152, n. 31)

C. Valerius Pansa

Procurator in Britain, believed to have held the post no earlier than the mid-second century. None of the authorities who cite this man supply a reason for this statement.

Source: *CIL* v.6513

G. Valerius Pudens

Gaius Valerius Pudens was governor of Britain in 205. He is named as *amplissimi co(n)sularis* ('of distinguished consular rank' — no term for governor is supplied, despite some translations) and presiding over building work on a complete inscription dated to 205 and recording the building of barracks. It was found in 1960 in the east gateway of Bainbridge fort.

Sources: *JRS* li (1961), p. 192, no. 4 (Bainbridge)

Sex. Varius Marcellus

Proc(urator) prov(inciae) Brit(anniae), recorded on an inscription erected by his wife. He can be approximately dated because his wife, Julia Soaemias Bassiana, was related to **Julia Domna**, empress of **Septimius Severus**. He must therefore have held the post some time at the very end of the second or early third century.

Sources: *ILS* 478 (Velitrae)

Venutius see Cartimandua

Q. Veranius

Governor of Britain in 57. As the first new governor of Britain under Nero he was, apparently, charged with a change in policy: the total conquest of Wales. However, he died within the year and what he had achieved, if anything, is unknown though he had bragged to Nero that two years would be enough to subdue all Britain; whether that meant the existing province or the whole island is unclear. Tacitus says that he indulged in a few raids against the Silures.

Veranius' tombstone survives, confirming that he died in office as governor of Britain. He is one of the very few historically-testified officials of the first century in Roman Britain whose career can be verified from a tombstone or other inscription. Unfortunately, the section that refers to Britain only states that he was governor and died in office.

Sources: Tacitus (*Agricola*) xiv.3, (*Annals*) xiv.29.1; *AE* 1953.251

AQVA•ADDVCTA
ALAE•II•ASTVR•
SVB•VLP•MARCELO
LEG•AVG•PR PR

82 Slab from Chesters recording the bringing of water (aqua adducta) *into the fort by* ala II
Asturum *during the governorship of Ulpius Marcellus (177-84). It was found reused and is
thought to have once been displayed on a cistern by the south-east gate. Width 0.99m.* RIB 1463

Verica

According to Dio, 'Berikos' was forced to leave Britain as a result of a rebellion and fled
to Rome where he persuaded **Claudius** to mount an invasion of Britain. Berikos may be
reasonably identified as the Verica of the Celtic coinage series, where he names himself for
example as VERIC COM.F, or *Verica, Commii filius*, 'Verica, son of Commius'. Other coins
in the series name *Calleva* (Silchester). Together with the distribution of the coins they
mean he can be associated with the Atrebates in central southern Britain.

However, Commius 'the Atrebate' is known from Caesar and the historian Frontinus
to have been a major player in Caesar's invasions of 55 and 54 BC as a pro-Roman. His
son can hardly have been active more than 90 years later. The only conclusion can be that
Verica was referring to his descent from Commius or that another, otherwise-unrecorded,
Commius had lived in the meantime.

Verica's reign is normally attributed to *c.*10-40, based on the numbers of his coins and
the Roman models which had been utilized for designs. Coins of Cunobelinus of the
Catuvellauni and his brother Epaticcus, provide evidence of a sort for what happened. The
Atrebates, like the Trinovantes to the east, apparently suffered steady encroachment on
their territory. This, it may be assumed, was what led Verica to flee. He is never heard of
again.

Sources: Dio lx.19.1; Caesar (*De Bello Gallico*) iv-viii, passim; Frontinus (*Strategematica*) ii.13.11

Vespasian

Titus Flavius Vespasianus was an Italian provincial whose senatorial career led to the command of *II Augusta* in the invasion of Britain in 43, a favour acquired for him by the imperial freedman Narcissus (see **Claudius** above).

The reference by Tacitus to this post is the only direct testimony for any specific legion's participation in the invasion. Suetonius adds the information that Vespasian's activities in the invasion led to the subjugation of two unnamed tribes, 20 'towns' (*oppida*), and the Isle of Wight.

Vespasian was awarded *triumphalia ornamentalia* and in the year 51 he was consul. It seems likely then that he spent at least five to six years in Britain. Thereafter he lived in retirement until 63 when he was made proconsul of Africa and afterwards was sent to suppress the revolt in Judaea in 67. His success meant he was well-placed to compete in the civil war which followed Nero's death in 68. In the summer of 69 he was declared emperor and ruled until 79.

In archaeological terms Vespasian and his short-lived dynasty are associated with the most comprehensive phase of romanization in Britain, manifested in the early forum-basilica complexes of towns like London, Verulamium and Silchester and substantial quantities of imported goods. The campaigns of **S. Julius Frontinus** and the first part of **Agricola's** belong to the reign of Vespasian.

Sources: Suetonius (*Vespasian*), passim, but especially iv; Tacitus (*Histories*), passim, but especially iii.44

M. Vettius Bolanus

Appointed governor of Britain in about 69 by Vitellius who was killed by the late summer that year. **Vespasian** appointed **Q. Petillius Cerealis** in his place by about 71.

Tacitus considered Vettius Bolanus' style of government to be too placid for a violent frontier province like Britain, supposedly forcing **Agricola**, then legate of *XX*, to moderate his ambitions. In a further device to elevate the achievements of Agricola, Tacitus said that Vettius Bolanus never achieved peace, a harsh judgement on a man who was in post so briefly.

Around this time the Brigantes in northern Britain split between **Cartimandua** and Venutius. Vettius Bolanus provided Cartimandua with a military escort out, leaving the area to Venutius for the meantime. Vettius Bolanus was only able to use auxiliary cavalry and infantry units. This probably reflects the participation by vexillations of the legions in the civil war theatre and, perhaps, their suspect loyalties. But a poem by the poet Statius was dedicated to Vettius Bolanus' son and describes a British war in which forts were built and a breastplate won from a British king.

Sources: Tacitus (*Histories*) ii.65, ii.97, iii.44-45, (*Agricola*) viii.1; Statius (*Silvae*) v.2.149

M. Vettius Valens (i)

The career inscription of Marcus Vettius Valens from Rimini, with a consular date for 66, records that he served as *beneficiarius* with the praetorian guard, acting as the imperial bodyguard, during the British war when he was decorated. This must be the invasion of 43. His career included a term as military tribune with *XIV Gemina Martia Victrix*, which must have occurred after 60 (see Chapter 2), and is useful evidence for the legion's full titles.

Sources: *ILS* 2648 (Rimini)

M. Vettius Valens (ii)

Marcus Vettius Valens (ii) was *legatus iuridicus* of Britain sometime between roughly 130-50 (guesses vary). He bore the same name as a man decorated in the invasion of 43 (above) and was thus probably the latter's descendant. He went on to become *patroni provinciae Britanniae*, 'patron of the province of *Britannia*'.

Source: *CIL* xi.383

Victorinus (i)

Under Probus (276-82) Victorinus, of Moorish origin, advised the appointment of an unnamed governor of Britain, though whether this was *Britannia Superior* or *Inferior* is not specified. The governor led a rebellion and, as it was regarded his responsibility, Victorinus was sent to Britain. He ousted the rebel by means of a trick which is not described.

Source: Zosimus I.66.2

Victorinus (ii)

Vicar of Britain in the last few years of the fourth century.

Source: Rutilianus Namatianus (*de reditu suo*) 493-510

L. Viducius Placidus

This man came from near Rouen (*Rotomagus*) in Gaul. At the mouth of the Scheldt in Holland he left an altar dedicated to the goddess Nehalennia. He also dedicated an arch and gate at York in 221 to Genius loci and Numina Augustorum as well as, possibly, Neptune (or Jupiter Optimus Maximus). Placidus calls himself a trader (*[n]egotiator*) and was probably dealing in goods transported across the North Sea between Holland and eastern Britain.

The inscription from York is incomplete but, like that of **M. Aurelius Lunaris**, he may have added that he was a priest. If so, that would reflect the traditional association of wealth with civic and public religious responsibilities in the Roman world. Another altar, of similar date, from the mouth of the Scheldt, and also dedicated to Nehalennia, records the name of Marcus Secund(inius) Silvanus, a trader in pottery with Britain (*negotiator cretarius Britannicianus*).

Source: *Brit.* viii (1977), 430, no. 18 and Hassall 1978, 46; *ILS* 4751 (Domburg, Holland; M. Secundinius Silvanus)

Virius Lupus

Legatus Augusti of Britain between *c*.197-202. His predecessor, **Clodius Albinus**, is thought to have removed much of the British garrison during the civil war, exposing the northern frontier to tribal raids. To Virius Lupus fell the task of restoring Britain's garrison. Dio says that Lupus had to buy peace from the *Maeatae*, a tribe in the southern uplands of Scotland then in league with the Caledonians further north.

Several inscriptions under Virius Lupus' governorship mention rebuilding in the north and this might suggest, but not confirm, that the *Maeatae* had exploited any troop removals by Clodius Albinus. The suggestion that very few units are testified in the same place before and after this period, demonstrating the reorganization of the garrison by Lupus is misleading because relatively few units are testified at any place in both periods (see Chapter 2).

The inscriptions from Ilkley (long lost and surviving only as a transcription) and Corbridge make no reference to damage by violence. The Bowes stone states that the bath-house was destroyed by fire but does not attribute the fire to any cause — in any case a bath-house was more likely to be destroyed by an accidental fire than anything else. An undated stone, probably from Brougham, seems to record a similar event.

Sources: Dio lxxv.5.4; *RIB* 637 (Ilkley), 730 (Bowes), 791 (Brougham?), 1163 (Corbridge)

Vitulasius Laetinianus

The last-known legionary legate in Britain, commanding *II Augusta* at Caerleon between 255-60 during the joint reigns of Valerian and Gallienus. This is recorded on an explicit and complete late inscription referring to the building of new barracks (*centuriae*).

Source: *RIB* 334 (Caerleon)

10 Coins

INTRODUCTION

Roman coins resemble monumental inscriptions in their succinct, sometimes cryptic, statements about personalities or events. Being numerous, datable and small they are the most reliable and widespread archaeological evidence because they are more immune from subjective inferences. If, for instance, a coin of Trajan bears titles associated with the year 105 (no Roman coin, apart from an exceptional issue of Hadrian, carries a numerical date), then that was when it was struck and the layer in which it is found (assuming there has been no contamination) cannot predate that year.

What concerns us here is the information which a coin carries, and what that tells us about the history of Roman Britain. So long as a coin is a genuine product of a Roman mint then this information is available regardless of where the coin was found.

Roman coins were produced in an endless series of limited editions. The coin was a convenient medium for publicizing the name and appearance of the incumbent emperor, sometimes with alarming realism. Caracalla and Maximinus I, for example, are shamelessly depicted as thugs, but the imagery matched the age and its symbols of power. The reverses were used to illustrate a limitless series of themes, ranging from innocuous imperial 'virtues' such as Fortuna, Hilaritas, Felicitas, and Pax, to explicit commemorations of new buildings or military victories.

Thanks to the plethora of imperial titles it is generally possible to date coins fairly closely during the first and second centuries. In the third century and therafter the holding of offices was less often notified on coins but the brevity of most of the reigns still restricts many coins to a few years.

However, Roman Britain, together with a few other provinces such as Spain, had little impact on Roman coinage. The erection of triumphal arches to celebrate the invasion in 43 was recorded on a large number of Claudian silver and gold coins but the terse two-word legends tell us nothing new. The surviving component of one of the arch inscriptions in Rome is far more important.

The events in Britain throughout the rest of the first century and up to 117 go unmentioned. The suppression of the Boudican Revolt and the Agricolan march into Scotland are ignored. In one sense this is remarkable. On the other, neither event was wholly triumphant. Boudica nearly cost Rome the new province, and the Agricolan conquests were rapidly given up. Britain was of minimal significance to the Roman world. While Agricola marched north Domitian was more concerned with the dangerous German frontier. Successes here were commemorated on coins. Trajan's Dacian and Parthian wars diverted his attention completely.

Not until Hadrian and his subsequent tour of the Empire and its borders do coins start to feature Britain. But, apart from the bronze asses of *c.*119-22 (**84**), the British coins of Hadrian are spectacularly rare and do no more than depict her in military female form. They record Hadrian's visit and speech to the army in a stock series of similar coins turned out to record similar events in other provinces. Those which depict *Britannia* alone can only be inferred to record some sort of military activity but it could hardly be said that this was explicit. While Trajan had celebrated a series of major civil and military building projects on his coins, Hadrian's Wall and all of Hadrian's other Empire-wide projects, go unmentioned.

Similarly, the Antonine Wall was ignored on coinage though various issues record what appear to be victories in Britain, for example the *Britannia* coins of 143. This is probably the first instance of coinage actually supplying information about Romano-British history which is not totally evident from other sources. The coins of 154-5, apparently circulated more or less only in Britain, are especially interesting in their depiction of a *Britannia* (**84**) which implies a period of otherwise-unrecorded warfare. Issues recording British victories under Commodus were followed by a major series under Septimius Severus and his sons (**84**). But Britain makes virtually no subsequent appearances on coins.

Only the reigns of Carausius and Allectus between 286 and 296 bring coinage into its own. Without it we would have very little idea about the character of this turbulent decade. Analysis of the coinage and its mint marks has made it possible to reconstruct some of the events during this dynamic period. The revelation that Carausius was the only Roman emperor of all time to use explicit textual references to the celebrated poetry of Virgil has shown that Romano-British pretensions to classical credibility were more ambitious than had perhaps been realized.

With the exception of London's use as a mint from 286 until about 325 the fourth century is almost a blank as far as Romano-British history from coins is concerned. Despite the increasing violence and would-be usurpers the events in Britain and everywhere else in the Empire go untestified on coins which were now produced in vast quantities of standard banal issues.

COINS AS HISTORICAL EVIDENCE

Claudius (41-54) (83)

Rome
Claudius issued a series of gold aurei and silver denarii from the mint of Rome with a common reverse type from the year 46. The reverse invariably depicts a triumphal arch bearing the inscription: *de Britann[is]*, 'From Britain', perhaps referring to the source of the bullion.

The arch may be identified as one of the pair erected to commemorate the campaign, recorded by Dio Cassius (lx.22.1). One survives in fragments in Rome and enough of its inscription remains to show that it was dedicated in or around the year 51 (*ILS* 216). An exceedingly rare sestertius issue depicts Claudius' son Britannicus (murdered in 55), renamed after the conquest of Britain.

83 Sestertius *of Claudius (struck 42-54), but making no mention of any British victory. News of this was confined to silver and gold.*

Caesarea, Cappadocia. This eastern mint issued a series of silver *didrachmae* of Claudius with a reverse depicting the emperor in a quadriga (chariot drawn by four horses) and the legend *de Britannis*, 'from Britain'. Unlike the Rome issues there is not enough specific information on the obverse to date these coins precisely.

Hadrian (117-38)

Rome 119-22

These bronze asses are the first coins to bear a representation of *Britannia*. The legends give Hadrian's titles for the period 119-28 but they are normally dated on style to the early part of that decade (**84**).

The reverse depicts *Britannia* seated facing left on a pile of stones and holding a spear and shield. In the exergue the legend *Britannia* identifies her as the province. The coins probably record a military defeat but the image is too oblique to be certain.

Rome 134-8

A variety of brass sestertii, belonging to Hadrian's long series of province issues, include Britain. The legends confine the coins to the period 128-38 but are normally attributed to the last four years.

Some depict *Britannia* in a similar posture to the asses of 119-22, now accompanied by a much briefer legend. Others show Hadrian being greeted by *Britannia* and the legend *Adventui Aug Britannia*, 'the arrival of the Emperor in Britain', and a further series shows Hadrian greeting the army of the province, *Exerc(itus) Brit(anniae)* .

The latter two types are exceptionally rare and, apart from the wording, are identical to issues naming other provinces. All these coins all postdate Hadrian's actual visit to Britain and only confirm the event.

Antoninus Pius (138-61)

Rome 143-4

A variety of sestertii of this period depict *Britannia* seated, but in a more heroic pose than under Hadrian, and Victory. All of the legends include Pius' third consulship (140-4) and some add his second acclamation as Imperator (143-61), thus fixing the coins to 143-4 (**84**).

Unlike Claudius and Hadrian the inclusion of Victory types makes it clear that a military victory in Britain has been won.

Rome(?) 154-5

The bronze asses of this year, all depicting *Britannia* and recording the eighteenth tribunician power of Antoninus Pius (February 154 — February 155), seem to indicate a further victory (**84**).

It has been long observed that these coins, often ill-struck, are mostly found in Britain. But they seem to have been distributed simultaneously with a very innocuous issue of the same date in the name of Marcus Aurelius as imperial heir. As these seem to have served no purpose other than as cash it is difficult to see whether the *Britannia* coins were very important. The description of *Britannia* here as 'dejected' or 'defeated' is very subjective. When a province was shown as defeated it was usually accompanied by an explicit legend, such as *Iudaea capta*, 'Judaea captured'.

This may mean that the coins were struck in Britain for local circulation but there is no evidence to support the contention. There was nothing new about special issues for provinces. For example, Domitian's asses of 86, with no special legends, were also widely distributed in Britain. Coins of this issue, when found in 'as struck' condition are also sometimes demonstrably poor in style and execution.

Commodus (180-92)

Rome 184-5

Two kinds of brass sestertii were issued by Commodus which refer to Britain. The first depicts *Britannia* standing with Commodus' titles for 184 and the exergue legend *Britt[annia]* (sic). The other shows a seated Victory preparing to inscribe a shield together with Commodus' titles for 184 and 185 (depending on the year of issue), and in the exergue *Vict(oriae) Brit(annicae)*. These coins thus record a military victory in the year 184 or just before (**84**).

Rome 184-5+

Silver denarii of Commodus from this date onwards include *Brit(annicus)* amongst his imperial titles.

84 Second-century 'British victory' coins (reverses only)

    a. As *of Hadrian, c. 122 depicting* Britannia

    b. Sestertius *of Antoninus Pius for 143 with* Britannia

    c. Sestertius *of Antoninus Pius for 143 with Victory and field legend* Bri - tan(nia)

    d. As *of Antoninus Pius for 154 depicting* Britannia

    e. Sestertius *of Commodus for 184 with Victory inscribing a shield and exergue legend*
Vict(oria) Brit(tannica*)*

    f. Sestertius *of Caracalla for c. 209-11 with two Victories and legend* Victoriae Brittannicae

Septimius Severus 193-211

Rome 208-11

The *Victoriae Brittannicae* (sic) coins of Septimius Severus and his sons Caracalla and Geta are the most prolific British series of Roman coins. There are innumerable minor variations on the same theme: a Victory in Britain on coins datable to 206 and afterwards. Severus however did not arrive in Britain to prosecute the campaign until 208, so the series began with the governorship of L. Alfenus Senecio (*c*. 205-8).

The various types were also the first recording British victories to be issued in gold, silver, brass and bronze in all denominations (**84**). None postdate 212, the year in which Caracalla murdered Geta and when the Severan dynasty's interest in Britain ceased.

Although the Victory coins are generally specific in the sense that they refer to Britain there are other coins of this period which are sometimes taken to allude to the campaign. One of these is a bronze type issued in the name of Caracalla with his titles for 209. Bearing a reverse depicting soldiers crossing a bridge of boats, it carries the word *traiectus*, 'crossing'. Either this is an allegorical theme which simply alludes to the act of setting out on an expedition or it is a literal description of bridge-building in the campaign in Britain (see for example Robertson 1980). As the type does not specifically refer to Britain the evidence is, frankly, of marginal significance. One might have assumed that bridge-building took place during the campaign anyway and, as the coinage does not tell us where any such bridge was, it adds nothing to what was already obvious.

Victorinus (268-70)

This short-lived ruler of the Gallic Empire issued a rare series of legionary gold aurei, presumably intended as donatives. Each depicts a legionary emblem together with the titles of that legion. They include one for *XX Valeria Victrix*, then presumably stationed at Chester (see Chapter 2). The absence of *II Augusta* and *VI Victrix* from the series may simply be due to the rarity of the coins.

Carausius (286-93)

For numismatists the coinage of the rebel emperor Carausius is the most interesting and dynamic of all types relating to Roman Britain. Carausius was an opportunist, an idealist, and a propagandist. He saw his coinage as a means of promulgating his image and dogma. By issuing coins of improved standards, including an exceptional series of silver types which restored a level of purity unknown since Nero's time, he created an aura of legitimacy and revived traditional values. The range of types is extensive and is being added to all the time as finds proliferate.

The Carausian mints

At the time of the revolt exergue marks, normally used for mint marks, were in their infancy. They appeared on the reverse, beneath the main field. Most of these can be attributed to two mints, only one of which can be identified with reasonable certainty. Other marks seem to have had exceptional meanings, including literary allusions.

85 Bronze radiate of Carausius (286-93) with galley and legend Felicitas Aug(usti). *In the exergue* CXXI, *i.e. the 'C' mint followed by a statement of value.*

London

The London mint is the only certain Carausian mint. The mint marks are almost without exception ML. Other coins of identical style and sometime sharing obverse dies carry no mint mark yet must have been struck in London.

Much of the silver, and some scarce bronze types, also carry RSR in the exergue. Die links and style also make these certain products of London. However, these belong to the Virgilian series (see below).

The 'C' mint

Some other coins of Carausius bear M C, or M CL, in place of M L. Style distinguishes these from the London coins so they must have originated in a different mint. However, there are several possible candidates for the mint site, including Colchester and Gloucester.

Carausian coin types

Carausius et Fratres Sui: this issue depicts Carausius with Diocletian and Maximian on the obverse, and a reverse legend including AVGGG. It denoted Carausius' self-appointment to a triumvirate imperial college with the legitimate regime then ruled by Diocletian in the East and Maximian in the West. The mint marks have been interpreted as evidence for a date in the last 2-3 years of the reign and as such suggest an attempt at conciliation.

Allusive types: a variety of Carausian coins refer to broad literary themes of renovation, restoration, tradition and stereotypical Roman virtues (**85**). They characterize the regime for us and show that Carausius was interested in creating an image of old Rome revived in Britain. No attempt was made to revive or invent a British Celtic theme. A recent discovery of a *denarius* of Carausius, acquired by the British Museum in 1998, depicts

261

Neptune (or Oceanus) as a bust on the reverse with the legend *Lae(titia) Carausi Aug(usti)*, 'The Joy of Carausius Augustus'. The maritime element is obvious, considering Carausius' origins, but Laetitia was often associated on coins with a maritime theme. The design here, however, is entirely innovative and in this respect typical of the vigorous imagination behind many Carausius types.

Legionary types: number of Carausian coins have reverses carrying the title and emblems of selected legions. Of the three British legions *VI Victrix* is omitted though several continental legions are included, such as *I Minervia*, then on the Rhine. The coins were not high value, being bronze, and it is notable that with a single exception they were omitted from the silver series. It is therefore unlikely that they were issued to buy troop loyalty. The absence of *VI Victrix* is curious; the idea that perhaps the legion had spurned the regime would surely make it more likely that the type would have been produced if loyalty-buying was the purpose. On the other hand the inclusion of continental legions suggests the opposite.

The Virgilian series
The best-known of the Carausian coins, mostly silver, which allude to Virgilian slogans bears the legend *expectate veni*, 'the awaited one is come', long recognized to reflect a line in Virgil's Aeneid (ii.283). Oddly, the confirmation of this was only identified in 1997.

The silver coins with RSR in the exergue were long thought to refer to a Carausian official, the *rationalis summae rei*, 'officer in charge of financial affairs', and which approximates to a description of Carausius' financial officer and successor Allectus. However, this is unprecedented on Roman coinage and was not repeated elsewhere (see Chapter 7).

Two bronze medallions of Carausius survive. One bears RSR in the exergue of the reverse and the other INPCDA (**86**). RSR INPCDA corresponds to the sixth and seventh lines of the Fourth Eclogue of Virgil: *Redeunt Saturnia Regna, Iam Nova Progenies Caelo Demittitur Alto*, 'The Golden Age [Saturnian Ages were a Roman colloquial equivalent] is back. Now a new generation is let down from heaven above'. This accords not only with the message of restored values and *romanitas* on all of Carausius' other coinage, but also the quality of the silver and the allusion to Virgil's Aeneid on a well-known coin of the series. The chances that the correspondence of the initial letters with the text is coincidence is most unlikely. The odds are hundreds of millions to one; moreover, it was routine practice in the Roman world to reduce slogans and titles to initial-letter form. See de la Bédoyère (1998) for more detailed discussion.

Allectus (293-6)

As Carausius' murderer and successor it is unsurprising that some continuity in coinage followed. The L and C mints remained active but all allusive, legionary, and Virgilian types disappeared. Coinage was reduced to a conventional series, dominated by the *Pax Aug(usti)* type and a new smaller bronze coin, thought to have been considered a quinarius (an archaic silver denomination once equivalent to half a silver denarius).

86 Bronze medallion of Carausius (286-93) with victory and quadriga on the reverse. The exergue legend INPCDA *corresponds to the seventh line of Virgil's fourth* Eclogue *(see text). Diameter 36mm. (Copyright © The British Museum)*

The Tetrarchy and beyond

Until *c*.325 the London mint was maintained as part of the panoply of late imperial mints, churning out locally-struck versions of standard imperial types. The days of Victory coins were gone and the coins are completely unexceptional.

Early coins in this period are attributed on style and distribution to London. The mint mark was omitted, perhaps to pass over residual evidence for the Carausian regime, but it reappeared in a revised form, normally PLN, for *P(ecunia) L(o)N(dinii)*, or perhaps *P(rima) L(o)N(dinii)*. Production was brought to an end under Constantine I in about 325 and was not resumed. No more official coinage was produced in Britain.

One series of coins, bearing the *Adventus Aug[usti]* reverse, is thought to represent three dated visits by Constantine to Britain in the years 307, 312, and 314, based on analysis of the mint-mark sequences and imperial titles (**76**).

Magnus Maximus (383-8)

With the London mint closed, official coin production in Britain ceased and was not resumed for centuries. The only exception to this is the supposed brief reopening of the London mint by Magnus Maximus between 383-8. The event is untestified in the sources though of itself this is inconclusive. None of the sources for Carausius state that he struck coins, yet not only are coins the single greatest piece of evidence for Carausius but they evidently played a pivotal role in his regime.

Some of the gold *solidi* of Maximus bear the mint-mark AVG. These are said to be the products of the mint of London on the evidence of Ammianus Marcellinus that London was named *Augusta* by or around the time of the aftermath of the 367 barbarian conspiracy (xxvii.8.7, xxviii.3.1). This may have been so but Magnus Maximus' coinage is left as the only 'verification' of the fact which goes otherwise unmentioned. It cannot have gained common currency as a name or else it would have supplanted *Londinium* in post-Roman times. Not only that but Ammianus repeats his reminder that *Augusta* was formerly known as *Londinium*, presumably for the benefit of a readership who would have had no idea where or what *Augusta* was.

It therefore becomes difficult to see why Magnus Maximus should have used the mark of a city name which was not widely known and perhaps, by his time, was even less known. No bronze coins were struck with this mark which in any case could equally have referred to *Augustodunum* (Autun). The gold coins of Maximus therefore provide no certain evidence for his use of a London mint.

11 Women in Britain

Compared to the evidence for men in Roman Britain, the record of whose activities constitutes practically the entire basis for this book, the evidence for women is confined largely to private and personal affairs. We possess a few dozen of their tombstones, which tell us their ages, occasionally the esteem with which their husbands regarded them, and some of their religious dedications but there is very little more to go on.

It is sometimes said that soldiers brought their wives with them to Britain. While this was probably true of officers, and there is no more potent source of evidence than the letters from Vindolanda between Claudia Severa and Sulpicia Lepidina (though they give us no indication of where the women came from), there is little evidence about the wives of ordinary soldiers from inscriptions. Even in the exceptional cases of a legate's wife, such as Sosia Juncina (**71**), we rarely know more than the name. In reality, very few tombstones tell us where their subjects were born. Of those which do give an origin, some refer specifically to Britain and others for a different continental origin than that of the soldiers in the associated fort. One unusual tombstone from Lincoln names two women without explaining whether they were even related (**47**).

Tombstones of women are scarcely known on the Antonine Wall (an instance is Verecunda on *RIB* 2183 from near Auchendavy but the text gives us her name and nothing else). As a frontier which was barely held for more than a generation or two, this suggests that in the short-term at least a front-line garrison was not normally accompanied by women in any quantity, regardless of where they came from. One of the very few extant descriptions of a Roman army on the march is that by Josephus (*Jewish War* III.v–vi). He makes no mention of women or other camp-followers though some modern authorities infer their presence. A reference to camp-followers in Caesar's *De Bello Africo* (ch. 75) is not specific either about nature or quantity; Dio's reference to women and children in the baggage train of Varus' army was written so long after the event it can hardly be relied on for detail (lxvi.20.2–5). Commonsense suggests women and children in some quantity will have been involved but our problem is that we have no idea to what extent they were tolerated. The specific evidence is minimal and it seems likely that the proportion of soldiers accompanied by wives to frontiers or on campaign was small.

Evidence of name might be considered legitimate evidence of a woman's origin (for example Juliona, a name of Gallic type, on *RIB* 1252). However, it is also obvious that if a woman was born in Britain to a father of, say, Pannonian origin and a British mother, she would be likely to bear a Pannonian name. This evidence is therefore ambiguous and best ignored unless the woman's origin is specifically stated. The example of Pusinna below is one such instance where the several examples of her name in north-western Gaul and the

Rhineland might suggest that she had come from there. But as that area has produced many more inscriptions than Britain, the significance of four examples is no greater than the two in Britain. She may have been brought from Gaul, she may have been born in Britain. Innocuous, all-purpose, Latin names such as Aurelia Aureliana's (*RIB* 959 from Carlisle) tell us nothing about her origins. The instance of the soldier called Nectovelius of *cohors II Thracum* at Mumrills (*RIB* 2142), but a Brigantian by tribe, shows how we cannot make assumptions about any individual's origins unless he or she specifically states it. It has long been recognized that auxiliary units were likely to recruit locally once they were established in a long-term garrison.

The consequences for social stability and integration, if wives (albeit unofficial) were imported, are interesting. Firstly, it needs to be remembered that to begin with many of the frontier areas will have had men of fighting age withdrawn for service in auxiliary units of British origin abroad. This will have left some women without husbands. Secondly, the presence of wives is unlikely to have enhanced a unit's effectiveness in the front line or on the march. While some women will undoubtedly have accompanied units the likelihood is that there were not very many. The majority will surely have consorted with women when and where they were stationed. At the risk of sounding ungallant it should be said that there are few armies in history which have experienced sustained difficulties in securing permanent female companionship in their garrisons.

The consequences for historians and archaeologists of Roman Britain is that women form a comparatively opaque part of the record. It is scarcely surprising that Regina the Catuvellaunian is so frequently cited. Her short life, and the evident passion her husband felt for her, stands as a symbol for what could never have been less than half the Romano-British population.

Childbirth was likely to compromise their chances of a long life, as has been the case until modern times, but occasional exceptions occur such as the nonagenarian Claudia Crysis who died at the age of 90 in Lincoln (see below).

British wives
Lincoln: tombstone of Volusia Faustina, *c(ivis) Lind(um)*, presumably her place of birth, and wife of Aurelius Senecio, a decurion at the colony. *RIB* 250 (**47**)

South Shields: tombstone of Regina, *liberta et coniuge*, 'freedwoman and wife', of Barates the Palmyrene (Syria). Aged 30 she was *natione Catvallauna*, 'a Catuvellaunian by tribe'. *RIB* 1065 (**87**)

Templeborough: tombstone of Verecunda Rufilia, *coniugi karissima[e]*, 'beloved wife', of Excingus. Aged 35 she was a *cives Dobunna*, 'citizen of the Dobunni'. The unit testified at the fort is *cohors IIII Gallorum* (see Chapter 2). *RIB* 621

Non-British wives or relations
Bath: tombstone of Rusonia Aventina, aged 58 and *c(ivi) Mediomatr[ic(ae)]*, 'citizen of the Mediomatrici', a tribe from the Metz region in Germany. No information about her husband survives but the stone was dedicated by her son L. Ulpius Sestius. *RIB* 163

Carvoran: tombstone of Aurelia Aia, *coniugi sanctissimae*, 'very pure wife', of Aurelius Marcus. Aged 33, she came from Salonae, in Dalmatia. Her husband's unit is not stated but *cohors II Dalmatarum* is testified at Carvoran by 300. Earlier, *cohors I Batavorum* and *cohors I Hamiorum sagittaria* are testified here (see Chapter 2). *RIB* 1828

Chesters: tombstone of Ursa, sister of Lurio *Germ(anus)*, 'the German'. The stone (now lost) also records the death of Lurio's wife Julia and his son Canio. Evidently Ursa must have been

87 *Tombstone of the freedwoman Regina, wife of Barates of Palmyra in Syria, and member of the Catuvellaunian tribe. From South Shields. Probably mid-second to early third century. Height 1.12m. RIB 1065*

German. However, the text's content and lack of any complimentary or detailed matter, makes it possible that Ursa was Lurio's sister-in-law. *RIB* 1483

London: tomb of G. Julius Alpinus Classicianus, *proc(urator) provinc(ia) Brit[anniae]*, erected by his wife Julia Pacata I(ndiana?), daughter of Indus of Gaul. See Classicianus' biography, Chapter 9. *RIB* 12

Netherby: tombstone of Titullinia Pussitta, *ci(vi)s Raeta*, 'citizen of Raetia', and aged 35 years. No husband is stated but the unit testified at the fort is *cohors I Aelia Hispanorum milliaria equitata*. *RIB* 984

York: coffin of Julia Fortunata, *domo Sardinia*, 'from a Sardinian home', and wife of Verecundius Diogenes, known from his own coffin to have served as a *sevir* in York and to have come from the Bourges area in Gallia Aquitania (*RIB* 678). *RIB* 687

Wives of unstated origin

Birrens: tombstone of Afutanius, son of Bassus, centurion with *cohors II Tungrorum*, and erected by the latter's(?) wife, Flavia Baetica. Her name makes it likely she, or her forbears, came from Baetica in Spain. The Tungrians came from the area of modern Belgium. *RIB* 2115

Hadrian's Wall (reused in mc 42): tombstone of Dagvalda of *cohors I* (or *II*) *Pannoniorum*, erected by his wife Pusinna. Her name is paralleled on *CIL* xiii.2172, 5002, 5156, and 7156A (N. Gaul and Germany), and in Britain on *RIB* 1829 (Carvoran). The mutilation and reuse of the stone in antiquity and in a location otherwise unassociated with the unit make its origin very uncertain. In any case there is no need to assume that Dagvalda was a Pannonian by birth. *RIB* 1667

Lincoln: tombstone of Claudia Crysis who died at the reported age of 90. *RIB* 263

Appendix 1: the dating of inscriptions

Throughout this book numerous inscriptions have been cited, some of which provide dates. Sometimes these dates are for single years, others are for periods of years or several decades equal to an imperial reign. No inscription provides a calendrical date. The closest the Roman world came to this concept was to number the years from the foundation of Rome in 753 BC. But it was extremely unusual for this number ever to be cited. A coin issue of Hadrian is exceptional in including the Roman numbering for the 874th year of Rome, equal to our AD 121.

Consular dates

Roman official dates were provided in two basic ways: imperial titles, and consular dates. The consulship was only open to a man of senatorial rank. A pair of consuls had originally served for a year but under the Empire the numbers increased, with most pairs serving for two months. Those who took the position on January 1st were named *consulares ordinarii*, a more prestigious rank than those who succeeded in later months of the year, known as *consulares suffecti*. This made it possible for someone to serve as consul in the first part of the year and proceed to the governorship of Britain (for example, Petronius Turpilianus, see Chapter 9). Such short consulships help dating. The joint consuls Gaius Julius Bassus and Gnaeus Afranius Dexter appear on a military diploma from Middlewich (*RIB* 2401.3). They served as consuls between 4 May and 13 July 105, supplying a narrow date range for the discharge of veterans recorded on the bronze tablet.

Consular records survive on inscriptions in Rome, though they are not infallible or complete. When an altar or building inscription provides consul names then it is usually possible to attribute the occasion to a year.

Imperial titles

An emperor might serve as a consul, have the power of a tribune, or be voted *imperator*. All these were renewable and some were held with variable frequency by different emperors. Hadrian, for instance, held the consulship only three times. The third time was 119, the third year of his reign, and the abbrevation COS III appeared thereafter on all his coins and his inscriptions. As he reigned until 138 this clearly does not give us very much help. However, he renewed his tribune power annually in December and when this is cited we can be more exact. The Wroxeter forum inscription (**34**) can be attributed to 130 or 131. Hadrian's other title, *pater patriae* ('father of the country'), conventionally abbreviated to PP, was adopted in 128 which at least allows the briefer texts to be allocated to before or after that year. Many of Antoninus Pius' inscriptions from the Antonine Wall supply none of this information, merely the PP. These can be strictly attributed only to the period 139-61.

All this information was erratically used and more problems come from incomplete or erroneous inscriptions. It is not unknown for Hadrian's *pater patriae* title to appear prematurely. A milestone from near Leicester of this reign, firmly dated to December 119 to December 120 by the statement of the fourth holding of tribune power, also carries *p(ater) p(atriae)* (*RIB* 2244). Damaged inscriptions require restoration and this will sometimes include making assumptions about the exact date when these titles were apparently once part of the text. A monumental slab from Corbridge (*RIB* 1149) from the reign of Marcus Aurelius survives in only a few fragments. It has been attributed to 163 but the surviving parts of the text only allow 161-4.

Dead reckoning

Tying Roman titles and dates to our own calendar has been done in part by dead reckoning, that is counting back from modern times, assisted by long-term continuity of the Eastern Empire until 1453. Astronomical information also helps. For example, Ammianus Marcellinus describes the appearance of a total eclipse of the sun in 360 (xx.3.1). Events like these can be computed backwards; as Ammianus helpfully also cites that this time was in the tenth consulship of Constantius II and the third of Julian (xx.1.1) it becomes easy to see how compiling all this data together provides a chronology linked to our own.

Appendix 2: imperial titles and reigns

COS = *consularis* (probably because the n was not pronounced), valid for successive years; e.g. COS III, the third consulship, would be listed on coins and inscriptions *until* the fourth consulship was held, however long that took (if ever; in Hadrian's case, never)

IMP = *Imperator*

PP = *pater patriae* (normally from the beginning of the reign and not listed year unless assumed later in the reign, e.g. Hadrian)

TRP = *tribunicia potestatis*

honorific titles = such as Parth Max or Dacicus accorded to an emperor in honour of specific campaigns

Note 1: the normal Roman convention was to present the numeral four on inscriptions or coins as IIII, not IV

Note 2: a Roman epigraphic convention was doubling, trebling or quadrupling the last consonant of an abbreviation to denote a plural. Thus AUGG, denotes two *Augusti*, useful for allocating a fragmentary inscription to one of the few periods of joint imperial rule, for example Marcus Aurelius with Lucius Verus. The convention was also applied to other lesser offices and posts. However, it was not universal. The procuratorial stamp from London at *RIB* 2443.2 provides the plural verb *dederunt* and an abbreviated subject *Proc*, which must be for *Procuratores*.

Claudius (41-54)
TRP I 41, renewed annually on 25th January
COS II 42
COS III 43
COS IIII 47
COS V 51
BRITANNICUS 46

Nero (54-68)
TRP I 54, renewed annually on 9th December
COS I 55
COS II 57
COS III 58
COS IIII 60
COS V 68

Galba (68-9); Otho (69); Vitellius (69)

Vespasian (69-79)
TRP I 69, and annually on July 1st thereafter to 79
COS II-IIII 70- 72
COS V-VIII 74-77
COS IX 79

Titus (79-81)
TRP I 71, and annually on July 1st thereafter to 81
COS I 70
COS II 72
COS III-VI 74-77
COS VII-VIII 79-80

Domitian (81-96)
TRP I 81, and annually on September 13th thereafter to 96

COS I 71
COS II-III 74-5
COS IIII-V 76-7
COS VI-VII 79-80
COS VIII-XIIII 82-8
COS XV 90
COS XVI 92
COS XVII 95
CENS(OR) 85

Nerva (96-8)
TRP I 96, renewed once on 18th September 97
COS III 97
COS IIII 98

Trajan (98-117)
TRP I in 97, altered to TRP II in 98 and then
    TRP III on September 18th 98, renewed
    annually thereafter
(COS I in 91 under Domitian)
COS II 98
COS III-IIII 100-101
COS V 103
COS VI 112
DAC(ICUS) from 102
OPTIMUS PRINCEPS from 103
PARTH(ICUS) from 115

Hadrian (117-38)
TRP I 117, renewed annually in August
COS I-III 117-19
PP from 128

Antoninus Pius (138-61)
TRP I in 138, renewed annually on 25th
    February
COS I-III 138-40
COS IIII 144
PP from 139

Marcus Aurelius (161-80)
TRP I in 147, renewed annually on 10th
    December
(COS I 140 and COS II 145 under Antoninus
    Pius)
COS III 161
ARMENIACUS from 164
PARTHICUS MAXIMUS from 166
PP from 166
GERMANICUS, SARMATICUS from 175

Lucius Verus (161-9) (jointly with Marcus
    Aurelius)
TRP I in 161, renewed annually on 10th
    December
COS II 161
COS III 167

ARMENIACUS from 163
PARTHICUS MAXIMUS from 165
PP from 166

Commodus (180-92) (with Marcus Aurelius
    from 175)
TRP I *c.*176/7, and TRP III by December 10th
    177, and annually thereafter
(COS I 177 and COS II 179 under Marcus
    Aurelius)
COS III 181
COS IIII 183
COS V 186
COS VI 190
COS VII 192
(PP from 177 under Marcus Aurelius)
PIUS from 183
BRITTANNICUS from 184

Pertinax (193); Didius Julianus (193);
    Pescennius Niger (193-4)

Septimius Severus (193-211) (with Clodius
    Albinus as Caesar, 195-7)
TRP I in 193, renewed annually on 1st January
COS II 194
COS III 202
IMP I-II 193
IMP III-IIII 194
IMP V-VII 195
IMP VIII 196
IMP VIIII-X 197
IMP XI 198
PP from 194
PARTHICUS from 195
PARTHICUS MAXIMUS from 198
BRITTANNICUS from 210

Marcus Aurelius Antoninus (Caracalla) (ruled
    jointly with Septimius Severus 198-211)
    (211-17)
N.B. see note under Marcus Aurelius
    Antoninus (Elagabalus) below)
TRP I in 198, renewed annually on 1st January
COS I 202 (under Septimius Severus)
COS II 205 (under Septimius Severus)
COS III 208 (under Septimius Severus)
COS IIII 213
BRITTANNICUS from 210
PM and PP from 211
FELIX and GERMANICUS from 213
IMP I 198
IMP II 212
IMP III 214

Geta (as Caesar 198-209, as joint Augustus 209-
    12)

TRP I 209, renewed annually on 1st January
COS I 205
COS II 208
BRITTANNICUS from 210
PP from 211

Macrinus (217-18)
COS I/TRP I 217
COS II/TRP II 218

Marcus Aurelius Antoninus (Elagabalus) (218-
22)
N.B. some coins of this reign are only
distinguishable from those of Caracalla by
portrait; some of the legends used are the
same. Inscriptions are similarly affected but
without portraits cannot sometimes be
distinguished (e.g. *RIB* 179 from Combe
Down). The military honorific title
Antoniniana probably belongs to the reign of
Caracalla but could also belong to this
reign.
TRP I/COS I 218
TRP II/COS II 219
TRP III/COS III 220
TRP IIII 221
TRP V/COS IIII 222

Severus Alexander (222-35)
TRP I 222, renewed annually on 1st January
COS I 222
COS II 226
COS III 229

Maximinus I (235-8)
TRP I 235, renewed annually on 1st January
COS 236

Gordianus I (238); Gordianus II Africanus
(238); Balbinus and Pupienus (238)

Gordian III (238-44)
TRP I 238, renewed annually *c*.31st July
COS I 239
COS II 241
PIUS, FELIX 240

Philip I (244-9) (with Philip II as Caesar 247-9)
TRP I 244, renewed annually on 1st January
COS I 245
COS II 247
COS III 248

From this time imperial titles cease to be of any
real value for dating so the following is a
summary of the subsequent reigns:

Trajan Decius (249-51)
  with Herennius Etruscus (251)
Trebonianus Gallus (251-53)
  with Hostilian (251)
  with Volusian (251-3)
Valerian I and Gallienus (253-60)
  with Saloninus (259)
Gallienus (260-8)
Claudius II (268-70)
Quintillius (270)
Aurelian (270-5)
Tacitus (275-6)
Florianus (276)
Probus (276-82)
Carus (282-3)
  with Numerian (283)
Carinus (283-5)

Gallic Empire
Postumus (259-68)
Victorinus (268-70)
Tetricus I (270-3)

Dominate and First Tetrarchy (284-305)
Diocletian (284-305)
Maximian (286-305)
Constantius I (293-305 as Caesar)
Galerius (293-305 as Caesar)

The 'British' Empire
Carausius (286-93)
Allectus (293-6)

The Second Tetrarchy (305-6)
Constantius I (305-6)
Galerius (305-11)
Severus II (305-6 as Caesar)
  (306-7 as Augustus)
Maximinus II (305-6 as Caesar)
  (306-7 as Augustus)
Constantine I (306-7 as Caesar)
Maxentius (306-12)
Licinius I (308-24)

House of Constantine (307-63)
Constantine I (307-37)
Crispus (317-26 as Caesar)
Constantine II (317-37 as Caesar)
  (337-40 as Augustus, ruling Gaul, Spain and
  Britain)

Constans (333-37 as Caesar)
   (337-50 as Augustus, ruling Italy, Africa and
     Balkans)
Constantius II (324-37 as Caesar)
   (337-61 as Augustus in the East)
Constantius Gallus 351-4 as Caesar
Julian II 335-60 as Caesar

360-3 as Augustus

House of Magnentius
Magnentius (350-3)
Decentius (351-3 as Caesar)

Jovian (363-4)

Houses of Valentinian and Theodosius

The machinations of this reign are very complicated. From 364-75 Valentinian I ruled the West, while from 364-78 his brother Valens took the East. In 367 Valentinian's son Gratian became joint Augustus with his father. From 375, on Valentinian I's death, Gratian shared his rule with his brother Valentinian II. On the death of Valens in 378 Gratian took over the East but made his general Theodosius (son of Count Theodosius who came to Britain in 367) co-emperor and gave him the East. In 383 Gratian was killed, leaving Valentinian II in sole control of the West apart from territories controlled by the usurper Magnus Maximus (383-8). The defeat of Maximus restored Valentinian II but he was killed in 392, and followed by the usurper Eugenius (392-4). Eugenius was defeated and killed in 394 leaving Thedosius in supreme control from 394-5. Since 383 he had ruled jointly with his son Arcadius, and from 393 with his other son Honorius as well. On the death of Theodosius I Arcadius took took the East until 408, while Honorius ruled the West until 423, except for those areas seized by the British usurper Constantine III (407-11).

Glossary

ala milliaria
Cavalry wing of a nominal 1000, in practice 24 *turmae* of 32 men = 768 + officers

ala quingenaria
Cavalry wing of a nominal 500, in practice 16 *turmae* of 32 men = 512 + officers

antoninianus
Modern name for a radiate silver coin first issued by Caracalla (Antoninus) and the principal Roman coin of the third century, despite a steady debasement. Thought to have been equivalent to 1.5 or 2 *denarii*

aquilifer
Bearer of the legionary standard

as
Bronze coin up to about 27mm in diameter and equivalent to one quarter of a *sestertius*

caduceus
A staff, usually associated with Mercury

centuria
Body of eighty troops, six making a legionary cohort

centurio
Centurion, senior officer commanding a century

cives Romanorum
Roman citizenship, awarded to auxiliary units prior to Caracalla's edit of universal citizenship in 212. Usually abbreviated to CR.

cohors
Generic term for six *centuriae* of troops, making 480, operating either on its own as an auxiliary unit (see the next entries), or as a sub-component of a legion. The first cohort in a legion had five double centuries (i.e. 5 x 160 = 800)

cohors equitata quingenaria
Mixed unit of infantry and cavalry of a nominal 500, in practice six *centuriae* of 80 men + four *turmae* of 32 men = 608 + officers

cohors equitata milliaria
Mixed unit of infantry and cavalry of a nominal 1000, in practice ten *centuriae* of 80 men = 800 men + eight *turmae* of 32 men = 1056 + officers

cohors peditata quingenaria
Infantry unit of a nominal 500, in practice six *centuriae* of 80 men = 480 + officers

cohors peditata milliaria
Infantry unit of a nominal 100, in practice ten *centuriae* of 80 men = 800 men

contubernium
Tent party or 'mess' of eight troops, constituting one tenth of a century

cornicularius
Military staff clerk or adjutant

cuneus
Third-century and later name for units of irregular troops

decuria
Group of ten or squadron of troops (e.g. *RIB* 1453)

decurio
Commander of a *turma*

decurio princeps
Centurion acting as commander of a *turma* (e.g. *RIB* 1991)

denarius
Silver coin about 18-20mm in diameter. The coin fell out of use by the mid-third century but an issue of similar weight and module was briefly revived by Carausius. Its name is unknown

duplicarius
Soldier receiving double pay, usually second-in-command of a *turma*. (eg. *RIB* 201)

dupondius
Brass coin similar in size to an *as* but distinguished by the metal and the use of a radiate crown. Equivalent to half a *sestertius*

emeritus
Veteran (also given as *veteranus*, e.g. *RIB* 887)

evocatus
Soldier of the Praetorian Guard who had completed 16 years' service and then retained in the military for special duties (e.g. *RIB* 1024)

exergue
zone on the reverse of a coin, beneath the image or motif, and containing abbreviations for mint-marks or slogans

familia
slave family (e.g. *RIB* 445)

gaesatorum
Spearmen, restored usually from the abbreviation G, for example *vexil(latio) G(aesatorum) R(aetorum)*, 'vexillation of Raetian spearmen'

legio
Legion, made up of ten *cohortes* of 480 men, except for the first cohort which was usually nominally double and made up of ten *centuriae*, instead of six

libertus
Freedman

mensor
Surveyor

numerus
Unit of troops, normally used for low-grade auxiliaries in the fourth century. The term seems to have been very loose and literally means a 'number'

optio
Second-in-command of a *centuria*

ordinatus
Late term for a centurion

praefectus
Officer of equestrian rank commanding auxiliary units, in certain legionary posts such as *praefectus castrorum* who had been promoted form the position of *primus pilus*

praefectus castorum
Prefect of the camp

primus pilus
Centurion of the first century of the first cohort of the legion

princeps
Centurion commanding a vexillation of troops; *RIB* 1983 shows that a *princeps* had authority over a prefect commanding an auxiliary cohort

sesquiplicarius
Soldier receiving 1.5 standard pay

sestertius
Brass coin up to about 35mm in diameter, and equivalent to one quarter of a *denarius*

signifer
Standard bearer of a *centuria*

tesserarius
Keeper of the century's password

turma
Cavalry troop of 32 men. Sixteen *turmae* constituted an *ala quingenaria*

tribunus
Commander of, usually but not always, an auxiliary milliary cohort

tribunus angusticlavii
Military tribune in a legion (five per legion), of equestrian rank and with a career as a commander of auxiliary units and other equestrian posts ahead of him

tribunus laticlavius
Senior military tribune in a legion, of senatorial rank and with a career as a legionary commander and provincial governor ahead of him

venatores
Hunters, made of troops from a unit or legion charged with obtaining food for the garrison

vexillatio
A vexillation of troops

Abbreviations

ABBREVIATIONS

() in references to inscriptions denotes letters understood, but which were omitted from the inscription

[] in references to inscriptions denotes letters destroyed or damaged, but which are assumed to have once been visible

AE = *L'Annee épigraphique* (Paris, 1888-) (N.B. some of this material is now available on the Internet from the same source as *ILS* below)

AW = Antonine Wall

CIL = *Corpus Inscriptionum Latinarum* (Berlin, 1863-) in 16 volumes (N.B. some of this material is now available on the Internet from the same source as ILS below): xiii (N. Gaul and Rhineland), xvi (diplomas, regardless of findspot)

DA = *Disiplina Augusti/Augustorum*

DN = *domini nostri/dominorum nostrorum*

HW = Hadrian's Wall

ILS = Dessau, H., 1892-1916 *Inscriptionum latinae selectae*, Berlin (three volumes) (now available on the Internet at http://gnomon.ku-eichstaett.de)

IOM = Jupiter Optimus Maximus

L & R = Lewis, N., and Reinhold, M., 1955, *Roman Civilization. Sourcebook II: The Empire*, New York

Lactor 4 = Maxfield, V., and Dobson, B., 1995, *Inscriptions of Roman Britain* London Association of Classical Teachers Original Records no. 4, London (Latin and English)

Lactor 8 = Warmington, B.H., and Miller, S.J., 1996, *Inscriptions of the Roman Empire AD 14-117*, London Association of Classical Teachers Original Records no. 8, London (English only)

mc = milecastle on Hadrian's Wall

NA = *Numen Augusti/Numina Augustorum*

NDN = *Numen domini nostri/dominorum nostrorum*

ND = *Notitia Dignitatum* (see *PNRB*, 219-21)

PNRB = Rivet, A..L.F., and Smith, C., 1979, *The Place Names of Roman Britain*, London

RIB = Collingwood and Wright, 1965 (see Bibliography)

RIB95 = Collingwood and Wright, 1995 (second edition; see Bibliography)

RIB II = Frere, S.S., and others (Eds) (see Bibliography)

RIC = Mattingly, H., and Sydenham, E.A., Sutherland, C.H.V., and Carson, R.A.G., (eds) 1923- , *The Roman Imperial Coinage*, London

RMD = Roxan, M. M., 1978 and 1985, *Roman Military Diplomas 1954-1977* University of

London Institute of Archaeology Occasional Publication no. 2, London, and *Roman Military Diplomas 1978-1984* University of London Institute of Archaeology Occasional Publication no. 9, London

SHA = *Scriptores Historiae Augustae*, available in the Loeb Classics Series, Harvard University Press, Vols I and II (also in Penguin translation, *The Lives of the Later Caesars*, trans. by A. Birley, Penguin, London, 1976)

t = turret on Hadrian's Wall

TW = installations on the Turf Wall sector of Hadrian's Wall (from the Birdoswald area west, and replaced under Hadrian or within a few decades by a stone system not always on the same alignment)

In quotations from inscriptions () indicates words or sections of words understood or deliberately abbreviated, thus *leg(atus)*. Square brackets indicate letters or words which have been lost but which can be reasonably inferred to have once been visible.

Select bibliography

Askew, G., 1980, *The Coinage of Roman Britain*, London

Beard, M., 1980, 'A British Dedication from the City of Rome', *Britannia* xi (1980), 313-14

Betts, I.M., 1995, 'Procuratorial tile stamps from London', *Britannia*, xxvi, 207-30

Birley, A., 1971, *Septimius Severus*, London

Birley, A., 1973, 'Petillius Cerealis and the Conquest of Brigantia', *Britannia* iv (1973), 179-90

Birley, A., 1979, *The People of Roman Britain*, London

Birley, E., 1953, *Roman Britain and the Roman Army*, Kendal

Birley, E., 1966, review of *RIB* in *JRS* lvi (1966), 226-31

Blagg, T.F.C. 1990, 'Architectural munifence in Britain', in *Britannia* xxi (1990), 13-31

Bogaers, J.E., 1979, 'King Cogidubnus: another reading of RIB 91', *Britannia* x (1979), 243-54

Boon, G.C. 1974, *Silchester: The Roman Town of Calleva*, Newton Abbot

Boon, G.C. 1983, 'Potters, Oculists and Eye Troubles, *Britannia* xiv (1993), 1-12

Bowman, A.K. 1994, *Life and Letters on the Roman Frontier. Vindolanda and its People*, London

Bowman, A.K. and Thomas, J.D., 1994, *The Vindolanda Writing Tablets (Tabulae Vindolandenses II)*, London

Casey, P.J., 1994, *Carausius and Allectus: the British Usurpers*, London

Collingwood, R.G. 1928, 'Inscriptions of Roman London', in *An Inventory of the Historical Monuments in London, Volume III. Roman London*, Royal Commission on Historical Monuments (England), London

Collingwood, R.G., and Wright, R.P., 1995, *The Roman Inscriptions of Britain. Volume I Inscriptions on Stone* (second edition, with *Addenda and Corrigenda* by R.S.O. Tomlin), Stroud [this is the definitive publication of all inscribed slabs, altars and so on. Wall and associated sites are represented from pp. 349-649 inclusive]. For Indexes to this work, see Goodburn and Waugh (1983) below.

Connolly, P., 1981, *Greece and Rome at War*, Macdonald, London

Cunliffe, B., 1988 (ed.), *The Temple of Sulis Minerva at Bath. Volume 2, The Finds from the Sacred Spring*, Oxford University Committee for Archaeology. Monograph no. 16

Cunliffe, B., and Davenport, P., 1985 (eds.), *The Temple of Sulis Minerva at Bath. Volume 1, The Site*, Oxford University Committee for Archaeology. Monograph no. 7

de la Bédoyère, G., 1998, 'Carausius and the Marks RSR and I.N.P.C.D.A.' in *Numismatic Chronicle* 158 (1998), 79-88

Dobson, B., and Mann, J.C. 1973, 'The Roman Army in Britain and Britons in the Roman Army', *Britannia* iv, 191-205

Donaldson, G.H., 1990, 'A Reinterpretation of *RIB* 1912 from Birdoswald', *Britannia* xxi, 207ff

Frere, S.S., 1987, *Britannia*, London

Frere, S.S., and St Joseph, J.K.S., 1983, *Roman Britain from the air*, Cambridge

Frere, S.S., Roxan, M., and Tomlin, R.S.O., (Eds) 1990, *The Roman Inscriptions of Britain. Volume II, Fascicule 1. The Military Diplomata etc (RIB 2401-2411)*, Stroud

Frere, S.S., and Tomlin, R.S.O., (Eds) 1991, *The Roman Inscriptions of Britain. Volume II, Fascicule 2. Weights, metal vessels etc (RIB 2412-2420)*, Stroud

Frere, S.S., and Tomlin, R.S.O., (Eds) 1991, *The Roman Inscriptions of Britain. Volume II, Fascicule 3. Jewellery, armour etc (RIB 2421-2441)*, Stroud

Frere, S.S., and Tomlin, R.S.O., (Eds) 1992, *The Roman Inscriptions of Britain. Volume II, Fascicule 4. Wooden barrels, tile stamps etc (RIB 2442-2480)*, Stroud

Frere, S.S., and Tomlin, R.S.O., (Eds) 1993, *The Roman Inscriptions of Britain. Volume II, Fascicule 5. Tile Stamps of the Classis Britannica; Imperial, Procuratorial and Civic Tile-stamps; Stamps of Private Tiles; Inscriptions on Relief-patterned Tiles and graffiti on Tiles (RIB 2481-2491)*, Stroud

Frere, S.S., and Tomlin, R.S.O., (Eds) 1995, *The Roman Inscriptions of Britain. Volume II, Fascicule 7. Graffiti on samian ware (Terra Sigillata) (RIB 2501)*, Stroud

Frere, S.S., and Tomlin, R.S.O., (Eds) 1995, *The Roman Inscriptions of Britain. Volume II, Fascicule 8. Graffiti on Coarse Pottery; stamps on Coarse Pottery; Addenda and Corrigenda to Fascicules 1-8 (RIB 2502-2505)*, Stroud

Goodburn, R., and Waugh, H., 1983, *The Roman Inscriptions of Britain. Volume I Inscriptions on Stone. Epigraphic Indexes*, Gloucester

Grimes, W.F., 1930, *Holt, Denbighshire: The Works Depot of the XXth Legion at Castle Lyons*, Y Cymmrodor 41, London

Hassall, M., 1978, 'Britain and the Rhine provinces: epigraphic evidence for trade', in J. du Plat Taylor and H. Cleere (eds), *Roman Shipping and Trade: Britain and the Rhine Provinces*, CBA Research Report 24

Henig, M., 1984, *Religion in Roman Britain*, Batsford, London

Ireland, R., 1983, 'Epigraphy' in in Henig, M., (ed.), *A Handbook of Roman Art and Architecture*, Phaidon, Oxford, 220-33

Ireland, S., 1986, *Roman Britain. A Sourcebook*, Croom Helm, London (a comprehensive gathering of literary, epigraphic, and numismatic evidence for Roman Britain including many items and passages connected with the Wall)

Jarrett, M.G., 1976, 'An Unnecessary War', *Britannia* vii (1976), 145-51

Johnson, A., 1983, *Roman Forts*, A & C Black, London

Keppie, L.F.J., 1971, 'Legio VIII Augusta and the Claudian Invasion', *Britannia* ii (1971), 149-55

Lewis, C.T., and Short, C.,, *A Latin Dictionary*, Oxford (various years)

Mann, J.C. 1998 (i), 'London as a Provincial Capital', *Britannia* xxix, 336-9

Mann, J.C. and Roxan, M.M., 1988, 'Discharge Certificates of the Roman Army', *Britannia* xix, 341-7

Mann, J.C. 1998 (ii), 'The Creation of Four Provinces in Britain by Diocletian', *Britannia* xxix, 339-41

Maxfield, V., and Dobson, B., 1995, *Inscriptions of Roman Britain, Lactor no.4* (third edition), London (a selection of Romano-British written records which includes Vindolanda tablets, diplomas, and stone inscriptions — available from the Lactor Publications Secretary, 5 Normington Close, Leigham Court Road, London SW16 2QS)

Mynors, R.A.B., 1964, *XII Panegyrici Latini*, Oxford

Rankov, N.B., 1987, 'M. Oclatinius Adventus in Britain', *Britannia* xviii (1987), 243-50

Richmond, I.A., 1946, 'The four coloniae of Roman Britain', *Arch. J.*, ciii, 24 (referring to Mommsen, 1877, 'Tribus imperatoriae', *Ephemeris Epigraphicae*, iii, 230ff

Robertson, A.S. 1980, 'The bridges on the Severan coins of AD 208 and 209, in W.S. Hanson and L.F.J. Keppie (eds), *Roman Frontier Studies*, Oxford, 131-40

Salway, P., 1981, *Roman Britain*, Oxford

Sear, D.R., 1970, 1981 etc, *Roman Coins and their Values*, London

Stephens, G.R., 1987, 'A Severan Vexillation at Ribchester', *Britannia* xviii (1987), 239-42

Tyers, P.A., 1996, *Roman Pottery in Britain*, London

Wacher, J., 1974, *The Towns of Roman Britain*, London

Wedlake, W.J., 1982, *The Excavation of the Shrine of Apollo at Nettleton, Wiltshire, 1956-1971*, Society of Antiquaries of London

Wheeler, R.E.M., 1932, *Report on the Excavation of the Prehistoric, Roman, and Post-Roman Site in Lydney Park, Gloucestershire*, Research Report of the Society of Antiquaries of London No. IX, London

Wright, R.P. 1985, 'Official Tile-stamps from London which cite the Province of Britain', *Britannia* xvi (1985), 193-6

see also Loeb Classical Library, *Scriptores Historiae Augustae*, volume I (Hadrian, Antoninus Pius, and Septimius Severus), trans. David Magie, Harvard

Index

It will be obvious to the reader that this book is substantially self-indexing. Therefore, only the main references to illustrations, certain individuals, army units, classifications, or sources such as Tacitus are given here. All dates are AD unless otherwise stated.